MR FOOTE'S
OTHER LEG

ALSO BY IAN KELLY

Casanova

Beau Brummell

Cooking for Kings
The Life of Antonin Carême,
the First Celebrity Chef

IAN KELLY

MR FOOTE'S OTHER LEG

PICADOR

First published 2012 by Picador
an imprint of Pan Macmillan, a division of Macmillan Publishers Limited
Pan Macmillan, 20 New Wharf Road, London N1 9RR
Basingstoke and Oxford
Associated companies throughout the world
www.panmacmillan.com

ISBN 978-0-330-51783-6

A CIP catalogue record for this book is available from
the British Library.

Typeset by SetSystems Ltd, Saffron Walden, Essex
Printed in the UK by CPI Group (UK) Ltd, Croydon CR0 4YY

Foote was a fine fellow in his way . . . irresistible . . .
and the world is really impoverished by his sinking glories:
I would have his life written with diligence
Dr Johnson

I blame Lee Hall.

It was his idea.

and Andy Sibbald.

Contents

A SHORT CURTAIN SPEECH
FROM THE AUTHOR AT
THE FOOTLIGHTS

'I have nothing against your right leg . . . the trouble is, neither have you.'

Peter Cook and Dudley Moore, *The Tarzan Sketch*

Foote had two legs to begin with. He was born with the full set and may have been buried with both when he was interred, clandestinely and at night as it turned out, in the cloisters of Westminster Abbey. Well-to-do amputees of the Georgian era were sometimes reunited with their long-lost limbs, especially embalmed by surgeons for the purpose so that they might meet their Maker with full symmetry, if not with grace. It was a similarly literalist view of the afterlife that had inspired Westminster Abbey in the eighteenth century to start reuniting in death the celebrated writers and actors of the age. They were shunted together in an area soon dubbed 'Poets' Corner', as if to add to the country's cavalcade of kings a classical pantheon of nation-builders. Or simply for a hellishly convivial afterlife.

The one-legged comedian Samuel Foote was smuggled as close to Poets' Corner as his friends dared. But his burial was a hushed and hugger-mugger affair. By 1776 Foote's name may have been one of the most celebrated in the English-speaking world, but by the time of his death in late 1777 he was more notorious than famous. He died only months after the conclusion of two of the most scandalous trials of the eighteenth century, in both of which he played major roles and in one of which he faced a charge of 'sodomitical assault'. This is why you may not have heard of him. Like Oscar Wilde a century later – another dandy-wit and epigrammatist-playwright ruined by an accusation of homosexuality – Foote's posthumous reputation was destroyed by slur and prejudice. Unlike Wilde, though, Foote had initially been supported by the establishment, even by the King. All support vanished, however, in the wake of his last, disastrous performances at the Haymarket and his sudden death. 'He sacrific'd friends and foes to a joke,' David Garrick wrote to Lady Spencer, in explanation of his absence from Foote's funeral, '& so has dy'd very little regretted even by his nearest acquaintance.'[1] More memorably, Henry Fielding had sneered that Foote died 'pissed upon with Scorn and Contempt', and Sheridan was pithier yet: 'He could never show his face again – nor did he.'

The career that ended in notoriety had in effect begun there too. Long before he wrote comedies, Foote had come to the attention of the Georgian public as a crime-writer, the chronicler of a violent murder within his own family. The crime he wrote about connects the ghoulish business of anatomizing criminals in the eighteenth century and the later interest in Foote's own anatomy, and more widely in the bodies of celebrities themselves: such that, bizarre to relate, the sources for this book include volumes still bound in human skin of one the protagonists (a sentence I feel unlikely ever to have cause to write again): the skin of a murderer who was hanged and dissected for his crimes.[2] Crime and criminal trials being the other theatrical sideshow to the birth of modern metropolitan culture, perhaps it was to be expected that Samuel Foote had been a lead player in those too.

Comedy, as they say, is all about pain.

Pro'leg/omenon. The first questions asked of authors are regularly the most pertinent.

Was 'Foote' Samuel's real name, or was this a stage-name in reference to his leg amputation? It was real. He suffered plenty of jokes about it after, as Dr Johnson put it, 'the Depeditation of Mr Foote'.

Was the *Tarzan Sketch*, performed by Peter Cook and Dudley Moore, based on the story of Samuel Foote? Probably so. For anyone who has missed this comedy classic, put down this book – temporarily – and have your life 'improved by laughter', as Foote once put it. There's always YouTube. Pete and Dud knew the works of Samuel Foote and the singular physicality at the core of many of his later stage routines. Foote cast himself a number of times in scenes in which 'two legs would be considered the minimum requirement', and the sketch, which originated at Cambridge in a 1960 undergraduate Footlights revue when Pete was studying eighteenth-century French drama, indubitably has as its ancestor Samuel Foote. Did Foote really escape through the trap-door of the Haymarket after giving his shocked audience a Wilkesian rodomontade on liberty and sexual freedom, then attempt to run away to France but die in Dover, waiting for the ferry? (A story that gave me my first laugh at Foote's expense, as told to me by a fellow actor long into his anecdotage.) No. The real story is rather better, in its way, more tragic and more political. The descent of Foote's myth, though, via the lore of old actors is one triumph of oral history over recondite fact, and is not the less telling of the style and reputation of the man for being more darn than sock.

Why should a man once famous enough to be represented by a simple icon – a foot – be forgotten now? A coiner of comedies for one-legged actors and the original celebrity-impressionist, Foote must own some of the authorship of his own obscurity. 'Few things are as fleeting as a joker's reputation,' wrote one early chronicler of Foote, 'the jest may survive, but the jester is usually forgotten'; and an impressionist's reputation falls faster than any into oblivion because it relies on the celebrity of the victims as much as the impersonator. Added to this, Foote's famous name became a whispered one in the immediate aftermath of his scandal-palled death. Neither, it should be said, are his plays very funny any more. His thirty-odd comedy 'afterpieces' relied heavily on the inwit of a celebrity-impressionist rather than writerly skills *per se* and only a few remained popular into the nineteenth century. If his ribaldry sings out still in the names of his creations – Sir Archy McSarcasm, the priapic Harry Humper or one-legged Sir Luke Limp – their lines, regrettably, now ring hollow. So relax. To trawl through the works of Samuel Foote would do him, me and you poor service: to write about comedy, as Foote allowed, is tougher even than making people laugh.

This is instead a cyclorama of mid-eighteenth-century London viewed from the unique vantage point of a one-legged master of ceremonies, a man of breathtakingly catholic experience and larrikin good humour; a tale told by an actor. The masks over the proscenium arch, however, are not so much comedy and tragedy as comedy and crime – the twin fascinators of eighteenth-century discourse and intrinsic to the story of Foote. How Samuel Foote lost his leg and thereby gained a royal licence for a theatre – one of only three such Theatres Royal in the whole history of the London stage – is one subject of his play. The supporting cast of friends – from Dr Johnson, David Garrick, Henry Fielding, Joshua Reynolds and Benjamin Franklin to John Hunter, the Duchess of Kingston and everyone from Peg Woffington to George III – lend a certain metropolitan *élan* to this panorama of Theatreland: Samuel Foote's scapegrace London on the cusp of modernity. How a man of such singular anatomy could be at the centre of one of the most sensational buggery trials in British history – a subject of hilarious conjecture at the time, wiping the American Declaration of Independence off the London papers for many months – turns out to be a story less of perplexing balance than of shocking brutality and prejudice. It is also viewed afresh here through the recently discovered and uncomfortably explicit first-hand trial records, and new evidence that, in one instance, justice may have been thwarted by greater powers. How Foote came to be on trial in Westminster Hall straight after the errant Duchess of Kingston had been arraigned in the same building in a grand state trial for bigamy is a tale of further legal prejudice and sexual intrigue. It has, of course, some resonance with the scandal that ended Oscar Wilde's career, though Foote's story turns out to be tellingly different, not least in the establishment's reaction to his trial. Yet in key regards he is indeed 'the Oscar Wilde of the eighteenth century', as he is sometimes called: with his fame, personality and tragic trajectory illuminating uncomfortable truths about his era and his posthumous allure inextricably linked to his downfall. Instead it is the question of *why* Londoners should turn their attention to scandal, celebrity and laughter through 1776, when they might have paid closer attention to events in America, that begs our attention as well as forging both backdrop and cacophonous noises-off to Foote's tragi-comedy. Appropriately enough then this is the story of the man who coined the phrase 'Tea Party' – a rallying cry at Boston harbour in 1773 – though Foote used it as an irreverent circumvention of the London censors: he sold tickets for tea, and added a scurrilous satire on the side. So now, finally, he is having the last laugh, as the unexpected godfather of an American reactionary movement, which, given his other reputation as sexual deviant and reckless satirist, would surely give him cause to smirk.

This is not, therefore, a literary biography in the usual sense, but an exploration of a myth of personality, Samuel Foote's, in an age when the idea was born and personal narratives of self-invention were first floated on the marketplace of fame as going concerns. It is a story of comedy and criminality, of rakes and revolutions, lowlifes and high art, cottaging and kings, and of the brave new world of London: the world's original anonymous metropolis. Foote used his off-stage dramas, in prescient style, to publicize himself. Consequently his centre-stage role in the first perfect media storm has some claim to be the proper prologue to modern celebrity and therefore, in a sense, to modernity. But beyond that, we who please to live and live to please, as Dr Johnson remarked, have also the simple benediction of storytelling, and Foote's is a bloody good story to tell. And it has been lost only for reasons that are indeed themselves worth telling.

Most jokes in this book are not Foote's, though many are original to the eighteenth century. Any errors or lack of taste are generally mine.

SCENES FROM
AN ACTOR'S LIFE

ACT ONE

COFFEE-HOUSE COMEDIAN

It is the faculty of laughter alone that distinguishes Man
from all other creatures

Joseph Addison, coffee-house wit[1]

LEICESTER FIELDS, LONDON, 1741. The two feet that emerge
from the sedan chair, expensively shod in buckled shoes, hit the
gravel and sea-coal ash of the square, most likely closely followed
by a cane. These feet, and the short legs above them, are those of
a young man who does not need to be carried the half-mile from
the Fleet prison – via Temple Bar and across the pebbles of Covent
Garden piazza, up Long Acre towards Panton Street – though
perhaps his costly buckled shoes do.

Dandily attired in lace and pea-green silk, the young law
student, newly released from his second spell in gaol, was pointed
at by those who noted him – the royal servants, hawkers and
artisans who frequented Leicester Fields. But this was not for
reasons of his dress. Samuel Foote, twenty-one-year-old youngest
son of a Truro lawyer and a Worcestershire heiress, was notorious
in London neither for his dress sense, eye-catching though it was,
nor his unusual lineage. Rather he was notorious, all but instantly
in March 1741, for his writings, his profiting by them and for his
debts.

Sam encouraged his fellow London law-students to introduce
him around the West End as 'the young Gentleman whose uncle

has been hanged for the murder of his brother', a presentation
that, it was said, 'had great success and caused much amusement'.[2]
Crime pays, in terms of urban notoriety. It pays especially well if a
crime links troubling themes in revolutionary times, offering a story
such as Foote's newly published account of his uncle's murder.
The crimes he wrote about in his bestselling *Genuine Account* (two
editions in March and April 1741) describe the first circle of his
notoriety. They were crimes of vicious animosity between brothers
– Sam's uncles – and across declensions of class: a story of an
interminable law case involving altered codicils, entails upon estates
and abusive marriages. It was a story about land, sex, class,
murder, dissections and insanity, and it was set against a naval
backdrop, aboard a hulking man-o'-war at sea. Little wonder, then,
that young Sam Foote's account, as nephew and heir to murderer
and murderee, outsold the sheet-music for the newly composed
'Rule, Britannia'.[3] Foote's story was similarly rousing and sea-
salted, and addressed equally contemporary anxieties of what
constituted Britishness, manliness, honour and identity. It also paid
just well enough to keep him, erratically, out of debtors' prison
through his very early twenties. Just.

The twin nexi of Foote's London, a city on the cusp of
modernity that he came to know in the early 1740s when he, too,
was just on the edge of adulthood, were the Fleet prison on what
is now Farringdon Street, and Leicester Fields, later Square, where
he took lodgings when and if he could afford them. The story of
his crime bestseller, which rescued him from debt, and of his two
abodes set the scene for the opening of his bizarre and unique
career, which straddled notoriety and celebrity, showbusiness and
crime, respectable fashionability and life beyond the Pale. It could
only have happened in London.

§

Foote had first used his lodgings in Panton Street, just off Leicester
Fields, when he was an Oxford undergraduate, but he had them
full-time from 1741 onwards and lived there when he was not in

prison, which he was, twice, over the course of that year. One of the most vibrant areas of mid-eighteenth-century London, Leicester Fields was an area in almost constant flux. The heir to the throne, Frederick, Prince of Wales, had turned Leicester House, on the north side of what would become the square, into a royal residence, but artists and writers could still afford to live in the area around it. John Gay had worked in a drapery yards to the south in New Exchange, by the Royal Mews – now Trafalgar Square – before he hit the big time with *The Beggar's Opera*, a spectacular commercial success that was still playing in London when Foote arrived. William Hogarth was working on sketches that year for what would become his *Marriage à la Mode* sequence of paintings in studios on the west side of the Fields, in sight of Foote's lodgings. Five minutes away by sedan chair was Bow Street. Here Henry Fielding was busy attacking the government in his *Grub Street Journal*, presiding later as magistrate from his own front room, arraigning, among other miscreants, the itinerant ne'er-do-well Giacomo Casanova while simultaneously working on drafts of *Shamela* and later *Tom Jones*. Bow Street was also where the actors Charles Macklin, David Garrick and Peg Woffington – the original Polly Peachum in the Dublin production of *The Beggar's Opera* – all had lodgings. It was an area for artists and writers of every school, for newcomers to London, for those who sought the oxygen of creativity and attention even in the fug of a malodorous city.

The young Cornishman was very quickly taken up by Covent Garden society. He was instantly conspicuous, soon enough notorious, and he was dazzlingly funny. Even in an age that had yet to discover minimalism in men's fashion, Foote stood out as a miniature peacock. What he lacked in physical grace – he was said to have a formless face and low-slung gait – he made up for with his ebullient presence, his many voices and his clothes. He owned, for instance, one suit in 'birds eye orange' lined with pea-green satin, one of spotted velvet, another of 'striped strawberry coloured corded silk with spangl'd buttons' and, eccentrically, a whole suit made entirely of brown beaver.[4] So attired, he soon became recognized around Covent Garden, as well one might. Descriptions of the young blade as 'one of the most distinguished wits who frequented the coffee-houses'[5] rarely fail to mention that he was also 'one of the greatest of the beaux even in those days of general overdress'. Those who first met him were almost invariably bowled over, even if, as was the case with Samuel Johnson, they had determined beforehand to disapprove because of his fast-acquired reputation as a reprobate.

> The first time I ever was in company with Foote [as Johnson recalled of this period] having no good opinion of the fellow, I was resolved not to be pleased, and it is very difficult to please a man against his will. I went on eating my dinner pretty sullenly, affecting for a long time not to mind him, but the dog was so very comical, that I was obliged to lay down my knife and fork and throw myself back in my chair and fairly laugh it out. No sir, there was no avoiding it: the fellow was irresistible.[6]

Foote was, according to Dr Johnson, a one-off. Where James Boswell, who knew Foote slightly later, was always equivocal, in awe of Foote's wit but shocked by his insouciant amorality, Johnson merely observed that he was funny: 'Foote has the greatest range for his wit,' the doctor remarked simply, 'he never lets truth stand between him and jest, though he is sometimes mighty coarse.'[7] Later he claimed, 'He has no principles and is governed neither by good manners nor discretion and very little by affection. But for a broad laugh,' and here the doctor would smile at recollection of it, 'I must confess the scoundrel has no fellow.'[8]

A great capital is a constellation of friendships as well as ideas, and London, as Foote discovered it, afforded an extraordinary array of both, all within easy access of his occasional Leicester Fields home. For a witty and attention-seeking young man, one of mixed fortune and fissured fame, as he would prove to be, it was easy to establish himself in a city that seemed as open to new people as it was to new ideas, a city stretched, challenged and enlivened by waves of ambitious new immigrants. The cast list of those who came, and prospered, and knew Foote is still recognizable in part. They enter the stage haphazardly over Foote's first months and years as a young man about town, sometimes walking centre-stage to greet him, sometimes merely walking past the stage-cloth, brief early cameos that may or may not lead to further life in Foote's drama.

His Panton Street lodgings were between an alley where Jonathan Swift had once cowered from gangs of ruffians and the studios of portraitist Thomas Hudson and his new apprentice, Joshua Reynolds. West Country boys both, new to London and to adult life, Reynolds and Foote would become firm friends. Foote was also soon spending time with the half-French jeweller based in Covent Garden, Lambert Lacam; he died young and was buried with a large enamel of his wife painted by another of Foote's drinking partners of these years, the Irish miniaturist Nathaniel Hone.[9] James Boswell would later come from Scotland to lodge in Downing Square – now Street – at that time an unprepossessing backwater of Whitehall and a cul-de-sac. His introduction to Foote came via Garrick and Johnson, Lichfield men both, and the Ulsterman Charles Macklin, who met Foote at Tom's coffee-house on Russell Street. Benjamin Franklin took lodgings on his return from America in Craven Street and met up with Boswell and later Foote every other Thursday at Davies's bookstore, below Tom's, to 'enjoy literary conversation'.[10] Boswell's fellow Scots, the Hunter brothers, John and William, had anatomy practices in Leicester Fields and became known to Foote through Reynolds. The Hunters soon moved their business – a practice combining theatre, freak-show and medical demonstration – to Great Windmill Street and a building that serves dankly still as the Lyric Theatre's dressing rooms. Some came to London to make their fortunes, some arrived with them, but for those with means, and a taste for novelty and argument, Leicester Fields and Covent Garden provided a scene of expectation and wonder, a blurring of class

delineations and upbringing in a fervent search for the new. 'Wine
and punch on the table,' Boswell describes the convivial scene of
Foote's London, 'some of us smoking pipes . . . [and] a side-board
with Welsh rabbits [*sic*] and apple puffs, porter and beer; our
reckoning about eighteen pence a head,' such that Johnson could
make the reasonable assertion, of the same occasion, that 'when
a man is tired of London, he is tired of life, for there is in
London all that Life can afford'. Or so it seemed to its many
new inhabitants in the mid-eighteenth century and certainly to the
young Cornishman Sam Foote.

When two enterprising contemporaries took it upon themselves
to walk all the way around London, keeping countryside in view at
all times, it took them seven hours.[11] The largest city in the world,
and indisputably its richest, was still small enough to be dominated
by personalities who became known by sight and voice, not
through media. Most Londoners knew exactly what members of
the royal family looked like, as well as famous actresses and
politicians or physically striking men like Dr Johnson or John
Wilkes or, soon enough, Samuel Foote, pointed out on the street
as the infamous author of the *Genuine Account*. People saw their
'personalities' on the street and in person – it was one of the
principal pleasures of London, an open, homosocial and surprisingly pedestrian city. They saw them not as we do, in frames and
in oils, but in all their human and voluble peculiarity. They saw
them often through the smirched glass of sedan chairs – three
hundred of which were available to hire daily from the chair-ranks
at St James's Palace – but just as likely walking in the parks, at
church or, of course, at the theatre. The age that gave us, via Dr
Johnson, the word 'clubbable' was perforce an age when London
felt small enough to be just that: a club – and one not just for men
but for the larger-than-life female personalities of the day: actresses
like Kitty Clive and Peg Woffington, singers like Susannah Cibber,
courtesans like Kitty Fisher, all of whom sat for Reynolds and all
of whom would become friends or close enemies of Foote. The
famous and infamous of London rubbed shoulders closely and

frequently, even more so than might be the case for those same coteries today.

So, it was apt that London should give the world its first 'celebrity-impressionist' – a man who initially made his name, those first few years in London, through a singular skill honed at his parents' table in Truro and his school in Worcester: a simple but devastatingly accurate talent for mimicry. Sam Foote was first known about town for his gifts as a coffee-house comedian, unabashed and unashamed to be introduced as the nephew of 'the uncle who has been hanged'[12] and able to 'take off' the great names and famous voices of a famously voluble age. His skill was said to be second to none. He watched people, then reproduced their mannerisms and voices instantly. It was said he could fool a tapster after hearing one order of drinks from a new acquaintance. Such a skill has probably always been prized. It found a new audience, and a new possibility as a career of sorts, in a city that was self-referential, and to some extent self-parodying; a city suddenly obsessed with personality and fame. His fearlessness was soon legendary, too, as he lampooned and caricatured people to their faces. Nearly all the meaning, and certainly most of the hilarity of this, is lost to us. But the moment is signal, historically, in the story of London. Samuel Foote was soon celebrated around the West End not just as the overdressed author of a crime bestseller, but as the funniest and wittiest man in town, and the most gifted imitator of the famous – in the first city and age when such a thing might be possible. A minor claim to fame, maybe, except that it spoke, too, of the first modern metropolis, its signal and prescient interest in 'personality' and the importance of satire in understanding the British. Foote, debt-ridden law student and briefly gaolbird, first came to the notice of Georgian Londoners by impersonating the London famous in West End coffee-houses.

§

Just five minutes east of his Panton Street lodgings, around the piazza of Covent Garden, the young Cornishman soon discovered the most fashionable of London's celebrated coffee-houses. The once grandiose piazza homes of aristocrats had been converted, variously, into taverns, brothels, bagnios and shops, and there were rooms to rent up once-grand staircases for the purposes that often befall a neighbourhood heading rapidly downhill. An image of Samuel setting foot in Covent Garden is provided by his later friend and biographer, William Cooke:

> In this early part of his life he was what the world called a *fine gentleman*: and in his morning rambles from the [Leicester] fields towards Covent Garden he exhibited a full dress suit, bag wig . . . sword, muff, rings, &c . . . He was fond of *dress* to the last; but his taste in this was not so correct: he was seldom wholly uniform; and took snuff in such quantities, as often rendered him a very slovenly beau. He lived much in taverns, and at public places, in this early part of his life.[13]

Covent Garden was where Foote saw his first professional actors. Rehearsals at the two Theatres Royal were signalled daily by a drum, beaten around the piazza to round up the two companies from their digs or coffee-drinking. He could gawp at the great names of the day as they traipsed over the pebbled market square past fruit and flower stalls, doffing hats or curtsying, as appropriate, to the crowds, interrupted from whatever distractions of the piazza they had been enjoying till their knell called them to work.

Young Foote had only to walk across the piazza from west to east, past this actorly roll-call, to reach the coffee-houses: Bedford's, Button's, Tom's and Will's were all on Russell Street, the thoroughfare from the piazza to Drury Lane that is, in a sense, the heart of Theatreland. In 1741 the coffee-houses, even Lloyd's and Child's in the City, were still open to anyone who could buy coffee, talk well and read deeply. They were not yet private clubs. William Cooke later wrote that Sam was seen 'pro forma'[14] at the Temple and the Inns of Court at this time and even acquired 'handsome chambers' there. But there is no record of him as a lawyer. He spent his days and nights instead in Covent Garden's more easterly coffee-houses, for it was here that new, more artistic and literary reputations were being made. And it is here, consequently, that he first enters the record of London wits.

Of the three great coffee-houses of Russell Street, Tom's had Foote's custom at first. It was a seat of the new English radicalism, but also of literary aspiration. Like Will's, where Dryden wrote, Tom's was a first-floor suite of rooms above a print- and bookshop. The entrance was at 17 Russell Street. The original Tom – Thomas West – had thrown himself from the upper window 'in a delirium'[15] nineteen years earlier, but the name had stuck, along with the association of fervid partying, disputation and radicalism. The bookseller that traded downstairs, Lewis's, published Alexander Pope, which was convenient, as Pope wrote and drank his coffee in Tom's above. Mainly, however, Tom's came alive at night. One foreign writer observed: 'The best company generally go to Tom's and Will's coffee-houses, where there is the best conversation til midnight. Here you will see [aristocrats] sitting familiarly and talking with freedom . . . and a stranger tastes with pleasure the universal liberty . . . of the English.'

At Tom's, as at all the major coffee-houses, there were also newspapers, 'not only all the foreign prints but the English ones . . . besides papers of morality and party dispute'.[16] Eventually Tom's had to be subdivided into a rambunctious café – alive with debate and argument and laughter – and a quieter room for readers and for perusal of a growing lending library of books and periodicals. This latter had a subscription book, which was used well into the nineteenth century and provides some insight into the bookishness of Foote's coffee-addict chums. Arthur Murphy, another lawyer-cum-theatrical, signed next to Foote in the subscription book for newspapers, as did David Garrick and Samuel Johnson. There were bankers and even scions of dukedoms signing too; the rake-hell Earl Percy, friend of Casanova, along with George Colman, the dramatist, the book-loving Polish ambassador and Thomas Paine.[17] A young aristocrat called Francis 'Frank' Delaval signed there too, borrowing play scripts. This fast-living and loud-laughing Northumbrian would become one of Foote's closest friends.

It was a convivial meeting place. One extant bar tab from this period covers a generous round of '46 dishes of chocolate and coffee' to a total of £1 3s. to which the sweet-toothed literati had added an order of '34 jelleys [*sic*] and biscuits at 2s. 3d. extra'. It is unclear who paid. There was a large snuff box, which Dryden had owned, in the middle of the upper room. A pinch of communal snuff was the reward for a tale well told, an argument won or a quip well stropped. This 'snuff of glory' soon became the regular prize of Sam Foote. It was the only free item. Beyond one's first cup of coffee – served gratis with the penny entry fee – everything at Tom's cost.

But it was the Bedford that soon became Foote's favoured coffee-house. It was the pre-eminent establishment in a city that boasted at the time at least five hundred coffee-houses[18] but, as Henry Fielding quipped, the Bedford was best known to 'those Gentlemen to whom Beds are unknown'.[19] Frequenters of this 'emporia of wit'[20] included William Hogarth – it seems he and Foote met there – the actors Macklin and Murphy, and writers and poets, like William Collins, Alexander Pope and Thomas Sheridan, when he was not in Dublin. Even the diarist Horace Walpole, not usually a man for crowds, was often there. Thomas Arne, Drury Lane's resident composer, met Foote in Bedford's too, dressed always in velvet, even in the dog-days of 1741's sticky summer. Newly famous for 'Rule, Britannia', Arne was fighting in the courts that summer for his copyrights in a landmark case, convincing other authors, Foote soon included, that they had been sold short in publishing deals. The fervid, sociable atmosphere of the coffee-houses became the essential fuel for Samuel Foote's talents and his fame.

The Bedford, increasingly, was where Foote was to be found every day, ignoring the law studies that supposedly had brought him to London in the first place, and spending money he could ill afford. It was on the piazza itself, on the corner of Russell Street, entered from the eastern side of the market through the arcades. If Lloyd's, Jonathan's, Child's, Dolly's Chop House and the Grecian spawned banks and insurance houses, newspapers and a Royal Society respectively, the Bedford, the Grecian, Tom's and Button's would also found London institutions. They were art salons, discussion shops of the Enlightenment. They were also the cradle of early book and comedy clubs, and, in the course of Foote's story, the site of the first British drama school.

The Bedford served food late into the night for the post-theatre crowd. As such it has some claim to infamy as the first critics' circle, the favoured haunt of professional theatre reviewers. One paper noted that the Bedford was 'every day and night crowded with wits ... jokes and *bons mots* are echoed from box to box'[21] [the wooden seats]; 'every branch of literature is examined, every performance of the theatre weighed'.[22] It was said actors and playwrights at Drury Lane and Covent Garden could ascertain the success or failure of their ventures within five minutes of entering the Bedford's wainscoted rooms after the curtain had fallen on opening night. Only a Broadway opening and first-night party, these days, offers such alacrity of damnation. These men of letters and of the theatre (there *were* ladies too, but they were not respectable) could use the Bedford as their postal address. There were rooms to rent by hour or day. One carrel, or booth, was especially reserved for competitive punning, another for debate on natural sciences, a third exclusively for actors. As Foote arrived in London in 1741 the 'eminent natural philosopher' J. T. Desaguliers had moved from a carrel into an upstairs room to give lectures.[23] The atmosphere, therefore, hung as thick with intellectual ambition as with tobacco smoke, and the wooden panelling did little to lessen the din of the raucous noise of the over-articulate. By late evening, the Bedford became the spill-on bar from the Green Rooms of both Theatres Royal, and this favoured haunt of the actors and actresses of Covent Garden and Drury Lane rang to the sound of singing as well as laughter: the first airings of Thomas Arne's 'A-Hunting We Will Go', if not, for form's sake, his new

National Anthem, were heard there. And, intriguing to relate, the wainscoting featured 'window soil-boxes' lined with lead: they may have been window boxes in the usual sense but seem also to have been placed high above the piazza for gentlemen to relieve themselves, rather than offending the crowd below in the manner more usual to the age – a 'London shower', as it was termed. Foote's first view, therefore, of the Fielding brothers, Davy Garrick, Thomas Sheridan or, less likely, Horace Walpole – the 'finest wits and men of letters' of the age – may well have revealed them, from the perspective of the piazza, availing themselves of the Bedford's unusual facilities while whistling Dr Arne's new 'Rule, Britannia'.

The *London Spy* described the style of Foote's new Bedford world:

> like a swarm of rats in a ruinous cheese-store . . . some were scribbling, others talking; some were drinking coffee, some smoking, and some arguing; the whole place stank of tobacco like the cabin of a barge . . . long clay pipes, a little fire on the hearth, and over it a huge coffee-pot . . . and . . . a parliamentary ordinance against drinking and the use of bad language. The walls were decorated with gilt frames much as a smithy is decorated with horseshoes. In the frames were rarities; phials of a yellowish elixir, favourite pills and hair-tonics, packets of snuff, tooth-powder made of coffee-grounds, caramels and cough lozenges . . . had not my friend told me that he had brought me to a coffee-house, I would have regarded the place as cabinet of curiosities or as [a fair ground].[24]

On to this peculiar coffee-spattered stage stepped young Foote. He made it an art form to enter a room well. One Dr Barrowby happened to be there the very first time 'Sammy' Foote came in. He spoke of Foote always afterwards as a 'young man of extraordinary talents', and seems to have been one of those many who wanted to believe that behind Foote's carapace of reckless wit and dandy disdain hid a warmth to be discerned by the elect. As another wrote, Foote was 'a man who . . . possesses a *real fund of feeling*.[25] Dr Barrowby's account of Foote's début at the Bedford, however, is more of mask than man. Foote, already a far more dandified character than his Truro mother might have imagined, thus made his first Bedford entrance up the stairs from the piazza:

> He came into the room, dressed out in a frock suit of green and silver lace with bag-wig, sword, bouquet, and ruffles, and immediately joined the critical circle of the upper end of the room. He soon boldly entered into the conversation, and by the brilliancy of his wit, the justness of his remarks, and the unembarrassed freedom of his manners, attracted the general notice. The buzz of the room went round:
>
> *'Who is he? Whence comes he?!'*
>
> etc which nobody could answer; until, a carriage stopping at the door to take him to the assembly of a lady of fashion, and they learned from the servants that his name was Foote, that he was a young Gentleman of Family and of Fortune.[26]

The style is recognizable from his later stage entrances. The servants, it seems, were all primed to speak their parts and the carriage was hired to go nowhere.

The comedic young law student who entertained the coffee-house crowd soon left a trail of anecdotes in his wake. Some were recorded eventually by his exegete, Cooke, and published as his *Bons Mots*. Others were chronicled by diarists and letter-writers. Whimsy as much as wit to the modern ear, their renown sprang equally from the speed of Foote's response as from his wordplay and his impersonations. But if Foote has an early claim to be 'the Oscar Wilde of the eighteenth century', it is because, long before he wrote a play or, indeed, worked on a professional stage, he was already famous, as the funniest man in London. As instance, one late night at the Bedford one of the theatre crowd took issue with Foote on the business of personal satire:

> 'Why, what would you have?' exclaimed Foote, 'of course I take all my friends off, but I use them no worse than myself, I take *myself* off.'

'Gadso! Now that I should like to see,' said the other, whereupon Foote took up his hat, and left. The room fell about laughing, and the story spread the faster as Foote did not return.

On an actress with a dubious past who was said to have married happily by the expedient of telling her husband beforehand of all her previous lovers, Foote remarked on her bravery to his companions at the Bedford:

What candour she must have had! What honesty! . . . and what an amazing *memory*!

On another occasion, Foote had become somewhat bored by a doctor who had had a yen to publish poems that he had inflicted, extempore, upon the Bedford group. The doctor complained he hadn't had time to get to a publisher as he had 'so many irons in the fire'. Foote fired back:

Take my advice, dear Doctor, and put your poems where your irons are.[27]

His wit turned often on frank sexual knowingness. *Covent Garden Magazine* published one Foote retort from this period when the conversation at the Bedford had turned to the vibrating effect of being driven in hired carriages over the cobbled streets of London and 'a Gentleman observed that riding in a hackney coach always gave him an e . . . . . . n [erection]'. 'Egad,' said Foote, 'never let your wife know that or she will insist upon your never hiring but *keeping* a carriage.'[28]

And so, again, the Bedford rang with laughter, heard even, it was said, on the far side of the piazza, attracting further drinkers and roisterers to admire the celebrated Mr Foote.

Coffee-houses have their unique place in the history of what would later be termed the Enlightenment, and the coffee-house comic Samuel Foote has his place in this too. As Dr Johnson noted, the coffee-houses 'had a perceptible influence on 'the conversation of the time'; they 'taught the frolic and the gay to unite merriment with decency and argument ... effects which they could never wholly lose'. It was only in coffee-houses in London, as in Paris or Venice, that all classes might find a venue for sociability. To be sure the clientele was drawn from what the French called *honêtes gens* – a literate and genteel class of mainly men – but in London the potential rough edges of different classes rubbing together were smoothed, most often, with comedy. Just as the theatre played to all at once, and had done, arguably, since the days of Shakespeare, so the coffee-house came to be a forum, too, where ideas from across all society might be aired. The point of the coffee-house was conversation, just as the point of theatre was dialogue. And all voices might be heard. Special privilege, however, was given to those who made people laugh. The discussion of the ideas, news and literature of the modern city marked a new stage in the growth of civility, the dawning, over coffee and hot chocolate, messy newsprint, lewd cartoons and tobacco, of something both dangerous and exciting: public opinion.

Coffee fuelled Foote's first experience of live comedy and performance, but also his earliest foray into writing and his first taste of fame. The largest city in the world, with a population by 1740 of more than 650,000 and, according to contemporary statistician Malarchy Postlethwaite,[29] as many as one million, may also have been the world's most literate. Fourteen newspapers were published daily or tri-weekly in London and on any given day up to 20,000 papers circulated in the capital, many with serial readers in London's coffee-houses.[30] Even while Horace Walpole might rant over the 'ridiculous rage of buying biographies'[31] something about eighteenth-century London seems to have forged a companionate love of reading and gossiping about personalities in public: dramas unfolding in real time, often sexual morality tales or crime stories, to be savoured and salivated over. It is therefore reasonable to speculate that as many as a quarter of a million people had heard Samuel Foote's name or read it within days of his account of the infamous 1741 murder of his uncle, before we even tally provincial coffee-houses and the longer-term circulation of crime-pamphlets printed to survive the thumbs of many more coffee-drinkers. It was quite a launch.

For Foote, therefore, the coffee-house was his first constituency, the site of his personal fame in London, and his wider renown in print as a crime writer. This is some of what guys his story so strongly in the fug of the Georgian coffee trade while making it conversely so very much a tale of now. Coffee-houses were reading rooms, news rooms and gossip halls all at once. They were the water-cooler of Georgian sociability, deciding what was fashionable, interesting or amusing. The rich life of London's coffee-house Enlightenment – the exchange of ideas and the creation of a fervid challenging newspaper culture, uncensored by royal or government decree – has been cited as one reason our Enlightenment led to peculiarly British revolutions in science, industry, literature, in acting and sex even, a glorious if etiolated revolution through the long eighteenth century that was more political than is often allowed, but was accompanied by laughter and satire. London's coffee-houses fed directly into the political life of the city, but also notably into its comic and theatrical cultures.

It was this 'public sphere' – the new fused world of political ideas, of coffee-house revolutions – that needed a new sort of comedy, a new sort of satire. Coffee-houses became the place where public opinion was formed, but also published. In turn they rejoiced in a sort of critical, satirical comedy that feels akin to modern political satire, to stand-up even, enacted live, over coffee, by the likes of young Sam Foote. The age that gave us the most scabrous and irreverent cartoons in the history of the medium – one signifier of new freedoms – gave us also a political satirist and impersonator in Foote. Rooted in pain, like the best comedy, fearless, which was his accidental position in life, Samuel Foote rounded his gifts with an ability to pen live cartoon sketches of 'celebrities' – in the spirit of Hogarth or of Rowlandson – drawn from the new city and brought to life, and ridicule, at the Bedford.

Life as a comedic coffee-house idler should not have been wildly expensive for a gentleman with a modest allowance and great expectations of inheritance, but Foote lived constantly beyond his means, falling repeatedly into debt. Eventually, of course, it landed him in prison. It was a pattern that had been set at Oxford in the few years he spent studying there. However, he found that debt would be the making of him, for it was because of the Fleet prison that Foote first turned to writing, and to the business of marketing his family's notoriety in an arrestingly modern manner. '*Iterum, iterum, iterumque*' (again and again and again) ran the legend on his carriage door years later when he would joke about his three terms of imprisonment for debt – twice in London and once in Oxford. By the time he was customizing his livery in London, a dazzlingly successful playwright and comedian, he could afford to be jocose about debt and his youthful fecklessness. But his spells in gaol, in 1740 and 1741, were as frightening as they were intended to be – wake-up calls to a young wastrel, eventually heeded and acted upon. In Sam Foote's case, debtors' prison scared him first into matrimony, and then into his first literary endeavours as a crime-writer.

STRIP OR PAY:
OR SHYLOCK'S ARGUMENT

In Laughter consists the true Essence of Man

Samuel Foote[1]

YOUNG SAMUEL FOOTE always claimed to be an esquire, a gentleman of good family. This was true in the strictest genealogical sense. He announced himself in London as being 'descended from some of most illustrious Families in this kingdom'[2] and frequently boasted when he was verbally assaulted as a mere comic, a drunken one at that, that he was as good 'as any Lord'.[3] If pushed on the subject – which friends knew was not a good idea – he could name connections to the dukes of Rutland, the earls of Westmorland, the dukes of Lancaster, the Duchess of Exeter, who was a sister of Edward IV, and all the way back to Edward I, and even the King of Castile.[4] It was all true. The genealogy was written in stone, in part, on a family vault in Copthorne church, Worcester. But this lordly patrimony was all via his mother's line. His father, also Samuel, sometime misnamed as John, was minor gentry in the mining town of Truro. Three children of Samuel and Eleanor Foote survived into adulthood, all boys. Sam, the youngest, had been baptized on 27 January 1720 at St Mary's, Truro, with the same name as his father and as his deceased elder brother, but the register fails to note the actual date of birth.[5] It is likely to have been 10 January.[6]

The Foote family possessed country manors at Lambesso and Pencalenick, both then in the parish of St Clement's, Truro, and a townhouse on Boscawen Street opposite Lemon Street. It was built in 1682 by John Foote, young Sam's grandfather, with a large oak staircase and 'three parlours', one of the grandest houses in Truro, and most likely Sam's birthplace.[7] At this time Truro was beginning to find prosperity through the tin and copper trade that took off through the eighteenth century, but when it was referred to as 'the London of Cornwall' it was not without irony. It was said that one was more likely to find a shod horse than a shod child, and the ancient dialect of the area, Cornish, a Brythonic language related to Welsh and Breton, could be heard still in its marketplace.[8] From his father, Sam inherited a presumption of a career in the law. From his mother, as well as an elaborately escutcheoned connection to medieval aristocracy, he inherited a rich sense of entitlement: Eleanor Foote was one key litigant in what became the most infamous inheritance dispute in eighteenth-century law – a case named after her family Dineley-Goodere v. Dineley-Goodere. It rumbled on in the Court of Chancery for a generation before and after Sam's own, but it became the living drama of his first literary success and notoriety, as it led directly to the murder that launched his career.

Samuel Foote's move to London from Truro where he had been brought up, and from Oxford where he had studied, had been predicated on his family's ambition that he should be a lawyer. His father and grandfather had been in the legal profession but, more urgently, his mother had come to believe that her fortune and that of her three sons depended on their ability to fight the Foote corner in the ongoing inheritance battle in the Court of Chancery in Westminster Great Hall. By Sam's second year at Oxford, in 1738, his mother's brother, Sir John Dineley-Goodere, had given Eleanor Foote to understand his intention to disinherit their brother Captain Samuel Goodere, Sam Foote's uncle, and to pass large Worcester estates to her son John Foote, Sam's eldest brother. The second Foote son, Edward, was ordained in the expectation that he might take one of the clerical livings in the gift of the Dineley-Goodere estates, as vicar of Burghope in Herefordshire. But Edward also had the more immediate anticipation of inheriting his father's estates in and around Truro. This left Sam. Sir John had made clear that his nephew Sam Foote could expect to inherit the Gloucestershire properties – Tockington primarily – which had come to his uncle from a propitious marriage. Yet none of this was settled when Samuel Foote found himself falling into debt at Oxford and as a supposed law student in London. The next scene of his life was intended by others to feature him as the family lawyer. It was not to be. His law studies and his London life were interrupted by his imprisonment, as a result of his Oxford and London debts, and also by a rash marriage, designed to alleviate them. At exactly the same moment, the murder of Sir John by his brother Captain Goodere, which happened within days of Sam's marriage in early 1741, changed the dynamics of the inheritance litigation. More specifically, Sam's account of it, *The Genuine Account*, and the updated *Genuine Memoirs*, written with the intention of paying off his debts, hinged the plot of Sam's life in a completely unforeseen direction.

Miss Mary Hickes, spinster of the parish of St Clement's, Truro, had a small dowry. She was 'pretty enough . . . [could] relish a witticism or a pun, and was educated as young ladies then usually were', but was no love-match for Sam Foote. They courted briefly in Bath when they were both there in 1739 and 1740, but were married in Truro, at St Clement's, on 10 January 1741. Their parents did not attend. Both bride and groom appear to have been twenty-one – indeed, their wedding day may well have been Foote's twenty-first birthday. They must have known each other since infancy as they are both recorded as hailing from St Clement's. So, too, did Mary's late father, John Hickes.[9] One of the infractions that had led eventually to Foote's expulsion from Worcester College, Oxford, had been his entertaining 'a female companion quite unrecognized by the College authorities'[10] (i.e., not a sister) some time in late 1739. In some subsequent accounts of Foote's student days in Oxford this young woman was painted as a 'lady of negotiable affections', a prostitute he had met in Bath. It seems more likely that the college porter had spotted Miss Mary Hickes of Truro, being taken on a wildly unaffordable jaunt to Oxford by her flash student beau.

Sam seems to have married almost exactly upon attaining his majority. This coincidence of dates, as much as the apparent absence of all parents (Mary's mother was still alive) is unlikely to be other than a signal that he was acting without parental consent and in somewhat desperate circumstances. Mary Hickes had married a twenty-one-year-old law student with little to recommend him. He was a man of middling height and, to judge by portraits from slightly later years, of unremarkable features. He was pale and put on weight easily. He had a talent for making people laugh and a habit of overdressing, but in a long career that spanned many of the greatest Restoration comedies and the romances of Shakespeare he never once played the Lover, except to parody old-age lusting after young flesh, or to have the audience laugh at the preposterousness of the Lame Lover being in love at all.

His marriage went awry quite quickly. If it had looked expedient for both parties – she writing off his debts, he providing an escape from rural obscurity and a ride to racy London – on all counts lay disappointment. She brought with her £140 a year. Ninety pounds of this, regrettably as it turned out, came 'only after the decease of John Hicke's Widow', her mother, who obdurately lived on. We know this because Foote tried to use the dowry immediately upon his honeymoon to appease his creditors – and because in his first year of married life he found himself in prison for debt in London and attempted to use Mary's dowry as collateral.

Sam Foote's first imprisonment was the direct consequence of high living in Oxford and around Covent Garden and the continuing lack of cash in the litigious Dineley-Goodere-Foote family. His mother, too, fell foul of the courts in 1740 as she also awaited a verdict in the Court of Chancery: 'Dear Sam,' she wrote to her son from Truro, 'I am in prison for debt. Come and assist your loving mother.'

'Dear Mother,' Sam replied, in the wry style that would become his own, 'so am I; which prevents his duty being paid to his loving mother by her affectionate son.'

It was this, his first 'bankruptcy', in late 1740, and the absence from Worcester College, Oxford, that directly resulted in Foote's rustication from Oxford and also in his marriage. His semi-clandestine nuptials had been undertaken with the express intention of acquiring access to funds to pay his college debts. But wedlock kept him from debtors' prison by months only. 'Even this [first period in London] was sufficient to exhaust a fortune,' wrote William Cooke. Mary's dowry might, 'with a genteel economy', Cooke wrote, 'have given Foote the *otium com dignitate* independent of any profession. But he was and remained incapable of the ordinary restraints of life: he dashed into all the prevailing dissipations of the time; and what the extravagance of dress, living, &c. had not done, the gaming table finally accomplished.'[11]

Foote's mismanagement of money might be seen as a familial trait, but began in earnest at Oxford. He had arrived at Worcester College on 8 June 1737, 'one Samuel Foote of Worcester School,'[12] after five years of boarding at the school that bore, by coincidence, the same name as his new college. He was entered as a Foundationer Scholar, which obliged him to study hard, unlike many of his contemporaries, and put him fairly low on the strictly stratified social pecking order of Oxford life. He wore accordingly a plain black gown – £1 12s. 6d. – and a seven-shilling mortar board,[13] bought for him as he arrived and was en route to meet the most important person in his new life, his tutor Dr William Gower, Provost of Worcester. Like many before and since, Foote had set his sights on the Oxford high life. This was exemplified by the Gentleman Commoners and sons of peers, with their elaborately tasselled gowns, their love of 'frolic and juvenile debauchery'[14] and their readiness, according to *Gentleman's Magazine*, to 'be idle, spendthrift and vicious', in exact proportion to their rank and fortune.

Foote, however, was on the very modest budget afforded by his scholarship. But this did not account for the lines of credit open to students and pressed upon them. Ticking, debt and duns came soon to feature in his life, as it did in the lives of all those around him. Eighteenth-century Oxford ran on debt. Its privileged students had credit extended to them by Oxford's tailors, tradesmen, pubs and the colleges themselves. Foote is unlikely to have paid outright for his gown: the bookseller Collicot on Broad Street published advice to students not to pay upfront for, although 'a Cap and Gown you must have . . . it is the Taylor's *business* to supply you with them'.[15] It was a recipe for disaster and, in Foote's case, soon led to it.

Young and impressionable scions of wealthy families offered easy pickings to the tradesfolk of Oxford and the colleges. Parents, then as now, tended eventually to pay up. Foote was cursed by great expectations: he was rumoured to be one of the likely beneficiaries of a case in Chancery, and he did nothing to discourage the impression that great wealth and good fortune awaited him.

The Worcester College barber was the first to become aware of the looming disaster of Foote's finances. At Oxford in 1737 he had taken to wearing his hair elaborately coiffed and powdered, though this was far from the egregious expense and vanity it might have appeared to his Truro parents. The central part of the Oxford afternoon was focused on dressing for 'dinner', which was served at high table and on the trestles at around three p.m. Foote was obliged to recite grace, on rotation, with the other Worcester Scholars. An Oxford-college barber attended to 'young shavers . . . three times [a week]'[16] or less frequently in the case of a seventeen-year-old like Foote, because students had to attend college dinners with their hair fully curled and powdered with a mixture of wheat starch and chalk and 'a bit of black ribbon to make a pigtail'.[17] It was a time-consuming and expensive business. The college barber curled and set hair and 'fluxed' the wigs, putting them into the Worcester College ovens to 'curl and bake',[18] and charged the students accordingly. But the barbers were 'of the greatest use' in quite separate ways. They had evolved into valet-cum-fixers, and Foote's peruke-dressing valet both orchestrated and chronicled his first descent into debt.

As Foote became too poor to pay the regular tips for wig and hairdressing (he wore his own dark hair long and curled), his barber-valet, knowing him to be a conspicuously adept scholar, offered to pimp his essays to richer students. A barber could 'get someone else to crib work . . . for five shillings . . . get all impositions done' just as easily as knowing 'where the best horse and the prettiest girl are in Oxford'.[19] It was part of their trade. Sam's Worcester barber became his first literary agent, negotiating terms with idler students and establishing for the first time Foote's recognizably nefarious relationships with deadlines, debt and writing.

Perversely, as Foote's funds had decreased at Oxford from 1737 to 1739, his academic and social confidence had grown. The expectation of privilege that had been bred in him by his mother combined with his enviable academic gifts to play out on Oxford's stage as intellectual and social arrogance. There is a shared manner of the born aristocrat and the intellectually precocious that is routinely misnamed as eccentricity and arrogance because it takes no heed of the crowd while seeking the attention of the masses. Such was Samuel Foote's fledgling genius – a young man who thought himself an aristocrat, knew himself an intellectual and poked fun at erudition. Some laughed. Others thought him a fopdoodle. Pedantry, one contemporary observed, 'was to Foote irresistible bait', and Provost Gower became at Oxford what Foote's headmaster Dr Miles had been at Worcester School: the butt of Foote's mercilessly arrogant schoolboy humour.

On one occasion he had been summoned to the Provost's study to answer for his 'idleness' and arrived armed with a large folio dictionary. He was admonished by the Provost 'describing the figure he [Foote] might make in the world if he [studied hard] and the contempt and misery which must follow a life of inattention and ... of following the ebullitions of fancy'. At this Foote 'immediately interrupted him and after begging his pardon, with great formality would take his dictionary from under his arm, and, pretending to find the meaning of the word would say, "Very well, sir, now please go on." '[20]

'He liked Lords,' one Oxford contemporary wrote, because he believed himself to be 'one of them, though cleverer ... so he gave himself airs of treating them contemptuously and cavalierly', and Oxford emboldened a temperament that was spendthrift and risk-seeking by nature, at a time of life when most men are inconsiderate of the future. He was further described as 'a sensual man, and a libertine [with] no sense of Religion or Morality', and consequently became the life and soul of Oxford's small but hard-drinking fast set with his 'flashes of wit and humour', those 'gemstones in conversation that may give momentary pleasure', as one contemporary allowed, but afford 'no solid basis for friendship'. At the same time, the contemporary continued, Foote 'was ridiculously fond of buying snuff boxes, Rings and Baubles, which were a great expense to him – and I think his life and character would furnish matter for a good Farce with an instructive moral'[21] had things not ended so badly for him at Oxford. Exhausting the patience of Provost, college and creditors over two years, he eventually found himself unable to meet any of their demands.

Foote's Worcester bills reveal a pattern of repeated absences during his final year at Oxford.[22] Because the college finally expelled him on the ground of his having spent 'many ... nights lying out' it is possible that, by his third year at Oxford, he was already plotting a route out of debt and penury, familiar from the plots of several of his later plays, by recourse to marriage. That the college archives, rather explicit in some cases about crimes such as 'frequenting the company of [women] of ill-fame',[23] make no specific mention of his misdemeanours, apart from deliberate absence after a warning, suggests that the college had against him a combination of long-standing grievances and a desire to rid themselves of a troublesome debtor. On 28 January 1741 Provost Gower formally records that 'Samuel Foote, after a course of many irregularities and lying out of college upon the 30th December was [warned by the college] but lay out of College again on the 16th January and went the next day out of town without leave for which reason a citation was ordered to be put up [at the college entrance] in the following form:[24]

> Whereas Samuel Foote, Scholar of Worcester College, by a long course of ill-behaviour has rendered himself obnoxious to frequent censures of the society publick and private, and having whilst he was under censure for lying out of College insolently and presumptuously withdrawn himself and refused to answer to several heinous crimes objected to him . . . his scholarship is declared void, and he is hereby deprived of all benefit and advantage of his said scholarship.

It is signed by three college authorities.[25]

His last bill in the college battels or buttery accounts was not paid until late March.[26] He did not graduate or take his final examinations.

In later life Foote referred to himself as an Oxford man, as if he were properly an alumnus, and he was right to do so. Thomas De Quincey, another Worcester man, made the same claim on a similar basis. Quite what young Mr Foote's 'obnoxious' and 'heinous' crimes were we cannot know. They refer in part to a prank Foote boasted of involving cows he had persuaded to pull the college alarums at night by attaching hay to the bellropes.[27] And there was also the arrival 'from Bath of a young lady, two footmen and a hired coach'[28] – scandalous issues for a Foundationer who was meant to set a scholarly example and who also owed the college money. It may have been that Foote was 'reckless, impudent, careless of his own interests', as later written, in the timeless tradition of feckless students, notably of the over-privileged stamp. The college may or may not have been aware that he had run away to Bath, then Cornwall, and hastily married.[29] It seems entirely possible that what the college authorities objected to was his 'lying out' of college in the arms of his supposedly wealthy young bride, while still not paying his debts to them. His 'graduation' was not as intended by his parents, but rather a graduation from the bailiffs in Oxford to debtors' prison in London, via a brief attempt to evade both by eloping with a rich bride. It was all the stuff of his later dramas. Youngsters gulling the pompous and elderly. Confused dates and identities. Alarums at night. Elopements. Life, as they say, does not always imitate art but, rather, bad comedy.

§

Sam Foote was first arraigned in Oxford for debts of a 'mere' £30. By early 1741, however, it was clear he owed at least £900 – perhaps £90,000 in today's money. When Mrs Eleanor Foote and her son Sam wrote to each other from 'prison' late in 1740 or in early 1741, they were not imprisoned in the modern sense but rather were restricted to the close confines of the bailiff's 'sponging' house, in Truro and Oxford respectively. It was the first stop en route to debtors' prison. The bailiff's house in Oxford was a regular haunt of prodigal students, like Foote. The equivalent in Truro was a major embarrassment to the chatelaine of Pencalenick House. But they were far from alone in their misery: twenty thousand debtors were in prison by 1759, which *Gentleman's Magazine* estimated as three per cent of the London population.

Imprisonment for debt was one of the hazards of eighteenth-century life. Until the overturn of the law in 1759, anyone denounced for debt by a creditor and 'taken in execution' or arrested for debt by a bailiff could be kept *in salva et stricta custodia*, that is, confined, 'until the satisfaction of the debt'.[30] Such a situation was a particular hazard for families such as the Foote's, known to have great expectations but little ready cash. Any creditor could swear an affidavit before a court claiming that he or she was owed money. A sum as small as two pounds could deprive a person of their liberty. There was a further incentive for a creditor to get in early if it was suspected that there were various debts: only the *first* denouncer had rights to full repayment. The court next issued a writ. This was called a *capias ad satisfaciendum*, known as a 'ca.sa', or 'casa'.

The apparently illogical concept of imprisoning people and thus depriving them of their ability to work off their debts had a different meaning in Foote's era, in legal and financial terms. Imprisonment – which was in the Crown's prerogative – was meant to coerce the debtor to discharge his commitments. It supposed that he or she could call on familial networks of financial aid. It also supposed that wealth was rarely related to work, but to entitlements of one sort or another, which was very much the case with Foote's family.

Debtors offered up their freedom in lieu of debts, and it could be restored to them only after the financial satisfaction of creditors – or after the whimsical clemency of the Crown in Parliament through Acts of Insolvency. There was no restriction on the time one might be imprisoned for debt. One contemporary of Foote's suffered nine years at the Fleet for a sum originally amounting to ninety shillings.[31] The action was against the debtor's body, not his goods or estate, which, oddly, had greater protection under law. From time to time, as the century progressed and ideas flourished that prioritized personal freedom over the rights of property, Acts of Parliament cleared out the debtors' prisons, providing little comfort to creditors but appeasing the masses. Those who knew the Fleet and argued for reform claimed that only 'sheer ignorance or unmixed malignity' could inspire anyone to 'seek redress for their losses [in such manner] . . . Who, that knows the real states of these prisons, would confine a man here to correct him?'[32] 'If the creditor can get nothing else,' as another contemporary argued, 'the law gives him the satisfaction, not to be grudged . . . of revenge . . . and he has a right to it.' That, in any event, and as said at the time, 'was Shylock's argument'.[33]

The *Genuine Account* and later *Memoirs* were credited on publi-

cation to one 'Samuel Foote of Worcester College, Oxford'. A
more accurate though less impressive address would have been
'The Fleet Prison, London'. Samuel Foote became a child of debt
and of debtors' prison. It was both inspiration and instigation to
his writing, but also one of the undertows to the tide of his later
creativity. Debt placed him very near to the furthest edges of
respectability but thereby gave him an audience – his fellow
inmates at the Fleet – broader than any he would experience again
until he was on stage.

§

Foote entered the Fleet in late January 1741, faced down by an
alarming cadre of creditors. His youth and conspicuous over-
spending, as well as the strength of his expectations, had made him
a rather easy target. Alexander Wood of Brownlow Street, St
Giles-in-the-Fields, Soho, had advanced him £500 during his last
year in Oxford, having been assured of his notional riches, followed
by a further £400 a little later.[34] It had not taken Foote long to get
through these sums, and he became obliged to 'render himself into
the Custody of the Marshall of the Fleet Prison', John Eyles, at the
behest, first, of Wood. The other names signing for his detention
were Charles Pearce and Abraham Heath, but, as was often the
case, more creditors soon realized that they would do well to put
their case against him. One, according to the Guildhall Debtors'
Records, was the Dowager Viscountess Castlecomer, a sister of the
Duke of Newcastle.

While writing essays for lordly students and briefly wooing
Mary Hickes in Bath, Foote had been able to borrow money from
an illustrious cross-section of Oxford and Bath society. Evidently
he was a very plausible young man. He was obliged to declare his
interest in the Gloucestershire portion of the Dineley-Goodere
estates at 'about a thousand pounds per annum . . . as he had
heard and believes . . . [plus] a remote chance of other properties
worth . . . about fifteen hundred pounds per annum in Worcestershire and . . . a figure about hundred pounds per annum in

Herefordshire, that is at Burghope'.[35] Cruellest of all, but maybe typical of the litigious family, the next tranche of creditors who added their names to the list for payment before *habeas corpus* might be restored to the prisoner by the Crown was Eleanor Foote, Sam's mother. She attested 'against all concerned in any way with the will of Sir John Dineley' but specifically 'Samuel Foote the Younger'.[36] The Dineley-Goodere inheritance was not to be mortgaged, Eleanor insisted, by her youngest son to the disadvantage of her elder sons or, more importantly, herself and her own creditors. Sam, it seemed, would have to work his own passage to freedom, or rest in the Fleet until the inheritance might be assured.

Foote entered the prison by voluntary consent, having been proceeded against by these creditors on the writ *habeas corpus ad satisfaciendum*. Presenting oneself at the Fleet was a dark little drama designed to intimidate and humiliate. 'On arriving,' one debtor wrote, 'we found ourselves opposite . . . a high wall with revolving spikes at the top. This wall, being unbroken by windows or other openings, had a gloomy, forbidding appearance, and the more so, perhaps from the very circumstance of our being conscious that beyond them was . . . solitude and . . . a mighty sepulchre of buried griefs.'[37] As a new prisoner, Foote was escorted from the main gate in this high wall on Fleet Market, Farringdon Street, and taken onto the steps by the Painted Ground, an open area, to be exhibited. This was an intended humiliation, but also served to allow the prison staff to get to know his face. There were few locked gates or doors at the Fleet – some prisoners lived outside the main prison, but all had to observe a curfew and the constant monitoring by the warden's staff. Peregrine Pickle, the eponymous debtor in Tobias Smollett's 1751 novel, 'was obliged to expose himself a full half hour' when he, like Foote, first arrived at the Fleet. 'The eyes of the all the turnkeys and doorkeepers' were upon him, along with those of the several hundred other inmates, all taking 'an accurate survey of his person, that they might know him again at first sight'. Foote was next offered the choice between the two sides of the prison – one more expensive than the other. He

chose the more expensive: a room two flights up overlooking the
racquets yard.

It is clear from the account of Dr Nash, Foote's Worcester
schoolmaster, who visited him at the behest of his father, that he
had arranged to have one of the 102 private or 'Master's' rooms.
Next he was obliged to pay 'garnish' to his fellow prisoners: a
fee towards the food and wine of one shilling and sixpence
a week.[38] Those who hadn't the money to pay were expected to
contribute with the clothes off their backs. A well-known ditty of
the period contains this stanza:

> Welcome, Welcome, brother debtor
> To the poor but merry place
> Where no bailiff, dun or setter
> Dare to show their frightful face
> But, kind sir, as you're a stranger
> Down your garnish you must lay
> Or your coat will be in danger
> You must either strip or pay.[39]

His new world was scarring and life-altering, as it was designed
to be. But it was not as dreadful, perhaps, as the Marshalsea
appeared to Dickens a generation later. For many Londoners
the Fleet was a fact of life of which many had direct familial
experience, an institution described as only 'a *little* on the debit side
of living'.[40] The Fleet prisoners who had access to the area around
Ludgate Circus were a regular sight for Londoners as they tra-
versed back and forth along the Strand from the West End via
Temple Bar into the City. Indeed, it was said the dip into the old
valley of the Fleet river was marked also by the dank prospect of
debt that lay between the City and the pleasure grounds to the
west: a fact of life as of geography; a reminder to all Londoners of
what flows beneath.

It was not, of course, a pleasant place to live. The Fleet was a
dilapidated old building, flung up in the years after the 1666 fire.
It was set in a high, walled triangle of sloping land, a kitchen block

at one end, a privy block at the other. Foote's cell had a 'bedstead, feather mattress, two blankets, a quilt, grate, two tables and shovel and tongs'.[41] The records of the prison suggest there were nearly five hundred inmates when Foote was there, though it is unclear how many lived within the prison walls as opposed to within the crowded local alleys known as the 'Rules and Liberties of the Fleet', a sort of open-prison overspill. Judging by the clearer figures for the coming decades, at least three hundred would have been interned nightly, like Foote, behind the high walls of the Fleet.[42] The din, it was said, could be deafening. Foote was left to await whatever profits he might make from his writings in the most unsympathetic environment for an author, while his debts were only compounded by the need to borrow more for the basic requirements of the prison: food, cell-rent and 'garnish'. Shylock's argument all but obliged him to strip himself of his respectability by publishing, but it paid him dividends in intriguing ways as a novice writer.

The prison directly informed Foote's writing style, as well as his hunger to profit by his work. All life and all classes were there. Foote had as company in the reading–dining room, known as Bartholomew's Fair, ten knights, one earl, a German baron, a Spanish marquis and a Prussian dwarf, 'the Chevalier Dessesau, well known in London Society', all fallen on hard times.[43] The prisoners were mainly men, but some widows and businesswomen – often madams – ended up there too. Teresa Cornelys, Casanova's lover and Soho hostess, ended her days there, as did one of the proprietresses of the hummums, or steam baths, a near neighbour in Foote's later life. The navy detained captains accused of 'neglect or cowardice' at the prison, smugglers, like James Brown of Galway, and even *bona fide* 'pirates',[44] Gabriel Tompkin and Bob Blackman, who had secured their release by turning King's evidence on others. Nor was his audience in 'Bartholemews Fair' entirely fellow debtors. 'Butchers and others from [Smithfield] market' were 'admitted [to the Fleet] as at a public-house' because the company there was so mixed, and so amusing. The Fleet prison

therefore gave Foote more than just the time and incentive to
write: it gave him his first broad-ranging audience but also provided him with the perfect research fellowship – a high table of
lowlifes, all of Georgian society briefly on its uppers. He later joked
that the Inns of Court had been reconfigured in his personal
narrative as the 'court he was in'.

If the Fleet represented a loss of freedom and respectability for
Foote it was also a continuation of his collegiate lifestyle and
experience and, like college, provided him with a wide education
and a useful one. He had easy and immediate access to the likely
readership of his sensational crime report, and its members were a
useful resource for what he would write: experts on naval matters,
crime, courts, inheritance and, of course, debt. And if there was
one key element of Foote's later success it was the broadness of his
attack – democratic or blunderbuss, depending on your point of
view – that allowed him to amuse the footmen in the gallery along
with the aristocrats and politicians in the boxes. It was an audience
he first entertained and wrote for in prison, almost certainly
reading aloud passages of the *Genuine Account* exactly as he would
read aloud previewed excerpts from his plays.

The Fleet also put him within hacking distance of Fleet Street,
its print shops and publishers. Within the 'Rules of the Fleet',
where he was allowed to walk, an area that extended down Fleet
Lane up Old Bailey and back along Ludgate Hill, past Cock Lane
and Dolphin Court, was Mr Goreham's. Young Mr Foote became
a regular presence there, settling on terms with Mr Goreham, once
he had made the momentous decision to throw family discretion
to the wind, and profit by writing about his uncles. As the differing
versions of the manuscript progressed, in accordance with the trials
and hangings, the Last Words and Confessions, Mr Goreham grew
more and more confident that young Mr Foote of the Fleet would
soon secure both their fortunes and his own freedom.

The circumstances that led Sam Foote to write about the
murder of his uncle Sir John by his uncle Captain Samuel are
therefore simple enough. He was arraigned for debt first in Oxford

and then in London. He had run up insurmountable borrowings over nearly three years as a spendthrift student. He had married, rashly and without sufficient regard to the financial details, seemingly in a bid to outflank his creditors, but his bride, poor in every sense, could not rescue him from the Fleet. Foote rescued himself with the power of his quill, and without regard to respectability, while, typically, grandiloquently claiming for himself the social and moral high ground. 'There was a vein of eccentricity, coupled with a lack of feeling' in Sam Foote, William Cooke wrote, 'a certain coolness and indifference that approached effrontery.'[45] But his publishing coup can be more sympathetically explained by expediency. Little else was open to Foote to spring the plot of the first act of his life, once the legal profession, marriage and inheritance had failed – temporarily – as devices. He made rather practical use of John Gay's dictum in *The Beggar's Opera* that many a bad marriage has been saved by a good hanging: making money out of the latter to evade entrapment in the former.

As for his young wife, her retreat into the wings, as so often with Foote's stage *ingénues*, was rapid and unexplained. Her first and only marital home was the Fleet when he was first there. She did her uxorious best for some few weeks, living in the prison in a manner that would have been shocking to any young bride but was particularly so to a Cornish gentlewoman whose fiancé had boasted of a far easier future. Soon enough her funds ran out and she returned to Cornwall. Though she did not die until 1763, it seems they never lived again as man and wife.[46] Dr Nash, who visited Foote, put a different slant on things. He had found Foote bullish about the Fleet – 'Is this not better than gout or fever or smallpox . . . this . . . mere temporary confinement' – but then noticed someone in the corner of the room. 'My foot,' punned Samuel, before going over to the bed and revealing his 'poor shrinking lady'.[47] Perhaps she was ashamed of their situation. There is one notably ugly anecdote that she visited him once and reappeared badly bruised. The story, as told by Foote, was that she had suffered a fall from a carriage, a not uncommon hazard of the eighteenth-century road, to judge by the theatre plots that rely on such. With all the insouciant cruelty of youth and cleverness, Foote made a joke at the expense of his young wife's injuries, describing her face as 'a map where you can see the Blue Mountains, the Black Forest' and, touching his forehead in telling the story, 'the Scilly Isles'.[48] From a man later arraigned for sexual assault, this ranks in retrospect even lower as a jest.

Those who have asserted Foote was homosexual naturally read the brevity and dysfunctionality of his youthful marriage in the light of their understanding. It may be that he was sexually disinterested in Mary, and women generally, though he later claimed two 'natural' children. Cooke wrote that Foote and Mary's 'tempers not agreeing, a perfect harmony did not long subsist between them' and, more pointedly perhaps, it was also said that Foote 'made her his wife but never treated her as such'.[49] It could as easily have been the sort of early mismatch that blighted the lives of many contemporaries, one that Foote, later a peripatetic member of the theatre community, was better able to escape. It was not, of course, an ideal or happy start to married life, and Foote was immediately in thrall to another drama altogether, the murder that would make his name. Foote's bride followed him only as far as a Fleet prison room up a 'dirty two-pair-of-stairs back room' and thereafter disappeared from his life. Foote later joked to his rakish friend Frank Delaval that such were his laundry requirements at the Fleet he had been forced to marry 'his washerwoman'.[50] It was a cheap joke at her expense, as well, perhaps, as at his own: he was by then a famously fastidious dandy.

The withering of love is more rarely the stuff of stage or page than the beginning of romance. There may have been many reasons that Mary and Sam Foote decided so quickly that they were unsuited to each other. Certainly Mary found herself competing for the time and affection of a young husband perhaps with tendencies he was only beginning to acknowledge but also with a mistress who would turn out to have enduring allure. The murder of Foote's uncle took place on the first day of their honeymoon.

Almost immediately, it would seem, Foote considered writing about it and his arrival within the Fleet spurred him to action. His dedication to the business of being an author may well have been a contributory factor in the fast demise of his marriage. It did, however, prove a much more dramatic opener to the first act of his life, trumping jejune romance with blood-soaked violence.

His crime story is the back-story, as it were, to his fame and notoriety, but it is also the story of his family. It remains, in his telling of it, a thrilling tale of internecine jealousy, fraternal bitterness and the vengeful machinations of eighteenth-century law and, like the story of Foote himself, it beggars belief. But it is all, so far as we may trust the sources of the period, Foote included, true. Samuel Foote's 1741 *Genuine Account of the Murder of Sir John Dineley Goodere by Captain Samuel Goodere*, and updated *Genuine Memoirs*, became the original crime bestseller a mere year after *The Trial of the Notorious Richard Turpin*[51] had proved a mass readership for true-life crime narratives and dashing anti-heroes. A writer should write about what he knows, and Foote's first literary success, though in a relatively new genre, was a story he knew well and was uniquely placed to tell. It sealed his interest in law and presaged his lifelong relationship with show-trials. But it also set the tone for his later career: beyond respectability but floated on the open marketplace of celebrity notoriety. More than this, the story is also the choral underscore of Foote's subsequent drama; an off-stage murmuring, ever present, haunting and melancholic, about ruination, crime and our peculiar fascination with the bodies of the famous and the dead.

THE FATAL TREE

'There is no more agreeable study than the lives of those
who suffer under the hands of the executioner'

*The Life, Travels, Expoits, . . . and Robberies,
of C. Speckman, alias Browne,* 1763[1]

ON THE NIGHT OF 18 JANUARY 1741, when Sam Foote first took
his young bride to bed in Lambesso House in Cornwall, another
coupling, equally infelicitous though for different reasons, was
taking place aboard a naval ship at anchor a hundred and sixty
miles north up the Bristol Channel. Margaret-Anne Jones should
not have been aboard HMS *Ruby*. She was not registered as part
of the ship's community and there were no other women on the
fifty-gun man-o'-war moored at the mouth of the river Avon.[2] But
Edward Jones, the *Ruby*'s cooper-carpenter, had planned a night
with his wife on board ship. Whatever happened between Sam
and Mary Foote that night at Lambesso, we do not know. What
Foote informs us about instead, in detail and in sensationally
published form, was what kept the Joneses up aboard the *Ruby*.

Jones's usual sleeping place was his allotted 'fourteen inches in
which to hang a hammock' near the mizzen mast. Fourteen inches
was hardly space enough for what he and Maggie-Anne had in
mind, so instead they spent that night together, attempting to make
love, despite various interruptions, in the 'slop-room' between the
galley and purser's cabin. They pressed into service there, Mrs

Jones explained, the flock bed that was set by the cabin partition. When she made to leave her husband on the morning of Monday, 19 January 1741, she checked, as was the habit of the crew and interlopers in such circumstances, the whereabouts of the *Ruby*'s captain. This was understood as routine. Wives were tolerated in port, so long as they were discreet.

Maggie-Anne had every reason to assume the captain, Foote's fifty-three-year-old uncle, would be sleeping off a hangover in the cabin hard by. Heavy drinking was endemic on board, and it had been a raucous night, more notably so as she and Jones had been disturbed by loud noises and arguments from the purser's and captain's cabins all through the evening, by cries of 'Madman!' and worse, and by the apparently drunken arrivals off the yawl that ferried crew back and forth to Bristol till as late as three a.m. They had chosen to ignore the brouhaha for reasons of their own, but she knew the captain was in the purser's cabin as she had heard him there. She pulled back the little scuttle-pane spy-hole into the purser's room, a sliding panel of wood only half an inch thick,[3] used by the crew at mealtimes, expecting to see Foote's uncle asleep. But what she saw was not as she had hoped. She saw a corpse.

In and around the dead man's mouth and nose, and on the floor that she and Jones had scrubbed with a holystone only the day before, there was a large quantity of congealing blood – so much that some had dripped into the deck below. Around the contorted neck and face of the corpse there was some sort of rope or rigging, three-quarter-inch deck-rope, as it turned out, about ten foot long.[4] One end of the rope was tied in a noose, which had cut into the man's neck. The other end was held tight in his greying hand, but he was indubitably dead. His bloodshot eyes stared at the plank ceiling. One lifeless leg was arched behind him in a position 'against nature'. And in his mouth Maggie-Anne Jones could see what she took to be a handkerchief, stiff with his blood. The small room, she said, was thick with the brackish smell of long-unwashed men and tallow, the hard fat harvested by the ship's butcher from animal kidneys and used for lighting.⁵ The men in the purser's cabin had clearly been up all night. The captain was also there. He was pacing back and forth in a distressed manner and brandishing a sword. Mrs Jones ran for her husband.

A death on a ship at anchor was not necessarily the concern of the local authorities. On the high seas or on board one of the Royal Navy's ships at anchor, a reported death was in the jurisdiction of the High Court of the Admiralty, to be investigated by naval authorities as coroner and judge. Usually details would be taken by the captain, and reported back to the Admiralty after a court martial on board. One immediate problem for Edward Jones, therefore, was that the captain appeared not to be reporting the death, and to be behaving in a suspicious manner. Moreover, the *Ruby* was at anchor and half crewed within earshot of Portishead battery in the 'King's Road', which, though open water in the Bristol Channel, was used for mooring ships to ease congestion in Bristol docks. Consequently it was deemed part of the 'City and Freedom of Bristol'. Bristol in turn had its own special privileges as Europe's primary westerly port: it was a self-governing county in its own right with special jurisdiction over its waters. Jones suspected, correctly as it turned out, that the dead man would be the concern of Bristol's water bailiff. This, he reasoned, would be the quandary facing his captain, and freezing him into his otherwise suspicious inaction. Things were further complicated, Samuel Foote wrote, for Edward and Maggie-Anne. They both knew they should not have been having sex, conjugal or otherwise, in the slop-room of His Majesty's warship, and that they had ignored shouts and alarums the night before as much to preserve their own compromised privacy as their captain's. So, Edward delayed before he acted. First, he verified what his wife had witnessed through the scuttle-pane. He, too, could clearly see the dead man, but by this time, about nine fifteen in the morning, the captain was himself slumped against the door to the cabin, blocking entry and partly blocking the view. Jones went to the first lieutenant. Mr Berry

refused to believe that the captain could be harbouring a dead
man and acting so strangely, until he, too, had the evidence of
his own eyes via the sliding panel. Berry consulted with James
Dudgeon, the surgeon's mate, and Marsh, a midshipman and the
most senior crew member. They all agreed to a stratagem devised
by Edward Jones to gain entry to the captain's quarters. Jones
went down to the lazaretto, deep in the bowels of the timber-built
ship, where stricken seamen were quarantined and where the crew
were allowed to stow trunks of valuables. Here, Edward hurriedly
emptied his own trunk, and hid his belongings in a hammock
nearby. He then went to the captain's door to report a theft on
board. Giving evidence later in open court, as reported by the
captain's nephew, Sam Foote, Edward explained what was said
and done.

First he had knocked on the door.

'Who is there?' shouted Captain Goodere.

'Tis I, the cooper,' replied Jones, 'and please your honour, I
was robbed and my chest was broke open and I want your honour
to do me Justice.'

'Upon which,' Jones later testified, 'Captain Goodere opened
the door and told me that I should have Justice.' Then the cooper
and the first lieutenant did something quite outside navy rules.
With their actions justified, they reasoned, as British citizens and
seamen at anchor in Bristol, they seized and arrested their own
captain. Once Lieutenant Berry had seen inside the bloodied cabin,
he was instantly suspicious that the captain was complicit in a
crime. Berry was intent on reporting everything to the Admiralty,
which meant communicating with London, a four-day round trip
via Bath, and keeping Captain Goodere under arrest on board
until jurisdiction was ascertained. Fortunately, for Berry and
Jones, the powers of justice of the city, port and county of Bristol
were already racing to the scene.

Heading as fast as tide and wind allowed, the Bristol water
bailiff, Thomas Chamberlayne, was forging downriver with a
hastily arranged detail of twelve men. He carried with him also an

THE FATAL TREE   45

order from the Bristol magistrates to search HMS *Ruby*. He and his crew were lashed with heavy westerly rains. One bargeman nevertheless carried aloft the insignia of the bailiff's office, a silver-plated oar, used only when the barge was about official business. Bailiff Chamberlayne, from a prominent mercantile family in Bristol, strongly suspected he would be dealing with a violent dispute between two aristocratic brothers. At worst, he suspected a fracas over money or a case amounting to forcible restraint of one deemed feeble-minded. He had been forewarned by a Bristol lawyer that one brother was likely to be forcing another to alter important codicils in a will. He had not expected to find himself investigating a murder.

§

Unconventionally, Captain Goodere was under arrest of the ship's cooper and his own first lieutenant when the water bailiff came aboard. A sturdy gentleman-officer in command of the *Ruby* only since the previous November, Goodere remained calm, according to his nephew, in the face of his apparently mutinous crew and his own arrest. After greeting the water bailiff, he forcibly articulated the first of many assertions that no crime had been committed. The body, he said, was that of his elder brother, the baronet Sir John Dineley-Goodere, a known epileptic, madman and depressive. This much, Foote was not ashamed to allow, was true. The situation was not as it appeared. The captain had had the 'horror and surprize [*sic*]', he would later testify, of witnessing his own brother's self-strangulation during an epileptic fit. The ship's surgeon's mate had been consulted about Sir John's 'lunacy'. Others testified that the baronet was called a 'madman' publicly, had been restrained by his family before,[6] and had been bundled aboard the *Ruby* 'for his own safety' while raving like a lunatic and 'fitting' all the long row from Bristol to the naval moorings at King's Road. The true story, Foote soon declared in print and personal protest, was even more bizarre than that.

Bristol's water bailiff had been alerted the day before that there

might be trouble brewing between the Dineley-Goodere brothers
– indeed, the dockside in Bristol and the tight-packed taverns and
businesses around the cathedral and College Green were alive that
rain-lashed Sunday to rumours that something altogether more
intriguing than the usual haggling over sugar, tobacco and sherry
prices was afoot. In a city used to the rough practices of naval
press-gangs, nothing had been seen quite like the kidnap of Sir
John Dineley-Goodere in broad daylight within the precincts of
the cathedral. Sam Trevett, a midshipman drinking on the Rope
Walk by the river, had seen a group of men manhandling a
'gentleman in a long dark cloak'. A small girl had been alarmed
by a tall stranger crying out to her that he was about to be
murdered. A man at Hotwells, where the river turns towards the
Avon gorge and the open sea, had heard a man shouting, 'Kidnap!'
and a Mrs Darby, who lived by the lime kilns near the hot wells
and knew Sir John Dineley by sight, saw him being pushed along
towards the quayside by the Kings Head public house, seemingly,
she said, against his will. But within minutes, the Avon being at
three-quarter flood and the man-o'-war yawl oared by eight men,
the shouting was subsiding, out of earshot and concern of most
Bristolians.

As the winter light finally began to fade, around five o'clock,
and hail set in from the west, the yawl rounded under Hotwells
cliffs and into the Avon gorge, luring boats then as now west from
Bristol with the emotive promise of the open sea and America
beyond – and Sir John, beyond sight or hearing of Bristol, pleaded
'like a man possessed, like a lunatic' without hope of anyone
hearing.

Those who had witnessed the brief despatch did not with ease
resume their business. The dockside and College Green were
crowded with drinkers, and word spread fast that something oddly
troubling had occurred. It took some while for anyone to act,
despite, or indeed because of, the fact that both brothers were
well known in Bristol. The question that exercised Bristolians was
whether the kidnap, at the hands of 'ship ruffians' of the *Ruby* –

witnessed by so many – was in truth the kidnap of an innocent or
the restraint of a lunatic by his embarrassed noble family. The
question had been apparent to those along the dockside, and for
them it was an important question, one with elusive answers. In
the balance hung issues not just for the bystanders and the Dineley-
Goodere brothers but also for a city and century that traded on
trust and on the *appearance* of wealth and status. It was a question
that allowed some men to be press-ganged into naval servitude,
with the compliance of the local community, and others, the
well-connected and well-to-do, to escape. It was a question also
of distinguishing the delusional or mentally enfeebled from truly
'distressed gentlefolk' – of establishing the difference between the
restraint of a madman and a mugging. And it was a question, too,
of the rank and unassailability of a naval captain in a port like
Bristol. Captain Goodere had been able to kidnap his brother in
'full face of the sun' because he was a man of the sea while the
baronet was a mere man of Bath. But soon troubling rumours
grew into the need for action.

In such a question of identity, and when faced with the
recognizable urban dilemma of when and how to step into a
violent dispute between people who seem to know each other, one
Bristol man decided to act for reasons of his own. Drinking a pint
of ale at the Kings Head by the river that Sunday afternoon,
William Dupree had been disturbed by a young woman at the
window alerting all the men inside to 'a great outcry' as sailors
'forced a Gentleman along' and up the gangplank to a waiting
man-o'-war yawl. Specifically, the 'tall man in a dark cloak'
shouted to Dupree and the other drinkers to find 'the lawyer Jarrit
Smith' and tell them that 'Sir John Dineley-Goodere' was being
'abducted'. William Dupree ran for Smith – he knew the notary
as 'a man of pith, an able advocate',[7] and also knew his house,
the second in the alleyway that cut between College Green and
the quayside. Smith was at dinner, he was told, in nearby Queen's
Square. Dupree managed to solicit help from a passing uniformed
soldier and together they located the man in a carriage with his

wife on the way home from their meal. By now it was past eight o'clock. Dupree reported to Smith the words shouted by the tall stranger in the dark cloak: that he was 'one Sir John Dineley-Goodere' and he was being abducted. Jarrit Smith, like others embroiled in the long-standing and bitter litigation between the brothers, feared he knew why.

At the bottom of Bristol's Park Street, which linked the old city of Bristol with the new development of Georgian Clifton, lay College Green and the outbuildings of the cathedral. This lower end of Park Street, around the old abbey church of St Augustine, was within stumbling distance of Bristol's docks and quaysides and was the centre of a little warren of small houses occupied by 'bookbinders, watchmakers, French staymakers',[8] soapboilers and taverns. Some of the inns survive. One, long gone, was the White Hart – a relatively upmarket tavern for the area and also a chophouse. Sam Foote knew it well: it was a staging post between his Truro home, his school and college. It had rooms to rent for pleasure or business. It was run by the redoubtable Mrs Morris Hobbs.

On the Tuesday prior to the kidnap of Sir John, a meal had been served in the inn, with both Dineley-Goodere brothers in attendance; it was hosted by one of the many lawyers in the employ of the infamously litigious family, the notary Jarrit Smith.[9] He lived two houses along from St Augustine's and drank often at the White Hart – sometimes claret, more often, according to Mrs Hobbs's barmaid's testimony, 'Bristol milk', or sherry. The baronet often spent the winter taking the Bath spa waters in an attempt both unsuccessful and expensive to alleviate the symptoms of a neurological disorder. His younger brother, the ship's captain, had asked Smith for a meeting with Sir John via an intermediary called Chamberlayne, another lawyer and a cousin of Bristol's water bailiff. The brothers – the baronet visiting from his water cure in Bath and the ship's captain rowed in from Portishead by his Irish sailors – met at the White Hart. They had shaken hands, Smith and other later witnesses recalled, and talked pleasantly enough.

They had all eaten turtle soup, Sir John being gouty as well as irascible and turtles being a much-trusted cure in Georgian England for both conditions. They had made toasts to love and friendship, and then, according to Smith, the brothers had parted on the doorstep of the White Hart amiably enough, 'exchanging kisses – the fashion then'.[10] Later, when events were painted with hues of biblical violence, this embrace was described as 'A Judas Kiss': a signal to the captain's sailors of the exact identity of his elder brother, as the crew were found to have been watching. Sir John then returned to Bath, agreeing to be in Bristol the next week to conclude the family business. Smith, though he had kept his counsel, claimed later he had remained suspicious of the captain's motives in seeking a second meeting with his elder brother after so many years of acrimony.

The singular architectural feature of the White Hart – demolished in the wake of ensuing scandal – was its portico. There was a balcony room set above the entrance, commanding views of College Green, of the little alleyway between the pub and Jarrit Smith's courtyard, and the horse lane at the bottom of Park Street that passed by the cathedral. The portico room became something of shrine for the ghoulish, subsequently, for it was in this room that Captain Goodere had stationed his men to view his brother and the Judas kiss.

His sailors were joined there by other men from a privateer at dock in Bristol, the *Vernon*. These hardened seamen, most of them Irish, came to know the White Hart publicans quite well. The men – up to ten of them, and rarely less than five by the bar tab quoted in court – were stationed there by the captain on the Monday, the Tuesday, the Saturday and again on the Sunday afternoon as their 'rondy', or rendezvous – a term from press-ganging parties of the period. Mrs Hobbs had noted this to Mrs Jarrit Smith in some gossipy exchange on College Green during the week. Pints of ale, hot flip – a sort of toddy – bread and local Cheddar cheese set the captain back 'four shillings and one penny halfpenny'.[11] He fed and watered the men well, which in itself alerted gossips to an ulterior motive than naval largesse. On the day of the abduction, he ordered tea for his men 'at which the Landlord was greatly surprized, as tis an uncommon drink for Jack Tars'.[12] Captain Goodere was keeping his men sober.

Around four o'clock on the Sunday of the abduction, 18 January, the room had fallen silent at the signal of an Irishman, Matt Mahony. He pointed to the window, and at this the men had filed out of the room and onto the horse path below. Captain Goodere and his brother, Sir John, had been spotted at the threshold of Jarrit Smith's house. Smith was not there. Once again, Captain Goodere went to kiss his brother, and at this signal, the men ran towards him.

Sir John screamed for help but the sailors were armed and one or two had drawn cutlasses to keep passers-by at bay. No one was about to interfere. The sailors dragged Sir John to the back alley behind the houses of the horse path and from there towards the river and quay known as Seabanks. He was bundled into the *Ruby*'s yawl, with his brother sitting impassively at the stern.

It was this daylight abduction that was witnessed by William Dupree and the many others who failed to intervene. But once Dupree had gone to Jarrit Smith, whose motivations and loyalties remain shrouded, Smith was obliged to report a possible malfeasance to the water bailiff, who in turn, eventually, was obliged to act. Perhaps it was Smith's complicity in the situation, and his close ties to the family that led to the water bailiff's delay. Perhaps it was true that the notary had deliberately absented himself from his house on a night he had reason to believe the captain would abduct the baronet. Perhaps, too, he was loath to interfere in an affair between two aristocratic brothers, one a sea-captain in charge of several dozen Bristol men, when he himself was a mere appointee. For reasons that may conversely have been as simple as the inclement weather, it took Chamberlayne until the next morning to arrange a detail of soldiers to row him downriver to Portishead. This delay, from the Sunday night into the Monday, would turn out to be fatal. Swifter action might have saved the baronet's life and would also have clarified whether Captain Goodere's intent was indeed, as his defence argued, 'merely restraint'. The Crown never bothered to argue whether kidnap had been the captain's intention on the Sunday afternoon for, between Jarrit Smith's alerting of the water bailiff and the bailiff's arrival on *Ruby* the following morning, the baronet breathed his last. The Crown contended this was very far from an 'accident' or 'suicide': rather, he had been murdered. 'Murder most foul, as in the best it is; [and] this most foul, strange and unnatural,'[13] the prosecution lawyers thundered, in a style that freely blended Old Testament and Shakespeare, a style relished by their amanuensis Samuel Foote. It was, they contended, a fratricide: the cold-blooded murder, 'with malice aforethought', of Sir John by his younger brother.

§

The story behind the brothers' bitter feud reached up into the branches of the many-boughed family tree of Samuel Foote. This made him an expert witness in the case: the one person able to make sense of the brothers' animosity. The story involved several large estates, two entails upon those estates, a bitter attempted divorce and at least one likely will-forgery with the hand of a corpse. As is the way with feuds, the argument stretched back in time and beyond the call of rationality. In Foote's account, it seemed then as now to bear insufficient motive for murderous intent. Money, blood and title, however, make for volatile ingredients and if the violent outcome was out of step with family tradition, the litigation and courtroom drama certainly were not. By 1740 the extended Dineley-Goodere-Foote family was several generations deep into Chancery, King's Bench and Court of Common Pleas proceedings, involving codicils, wills, claims and counterclaims that would deny the heirs, Samuel Foote included, proper justice until well into the nineteenth century. The Chancery suits had begun properly in 1714 and were still in dispute in 1809.[14] The last of the Dineley-Goodere baronets, Foote's younger cousin, would die in poverty as the 'pauper knight' of Windsor Castle, desperately advertising for a bride who might rescue him financially for the prize of being his lady.

If the case sounds familiar, it is because from such cases sprang the plots of countless half-remembered dramas of stage, page and real courtrooms in the eighteenth and nineteenth centuries, but more specifically because it inspired Charles Dickens to create the fictional battle of Jarndyce v. Jarndyce in *Bleak House*. This complex inheritance case, a fictional paradigm of such complexity that Dickens's main characters lived their fictive lives in bleak ignorance of the case's arguments, became a scandal in its own right. As a result of Dickens's knowledge of the Dineley-Goodere case, through the writings of Samuel Foote, the readers of *Bleak House* were finally moved to reform the legal labyrinth. A century before, a Byzantine and unreformed judiciary had brought ruin and disaster to Foote's family.

The key issues at stake were this. The two main estates of the Dineley-Goodere inheritance had, from 1706, one 'fee tail male', which only sons could inherit, one 'fee tail female', which only daughters could inherit, and one 'fee tail special', which had a further condition of inheritance: it restricted succession to 'heirs of the body' willing to carry the name Dineley. It was a classic, if elaborate, entailed estate, which meant that different branches of the family could find themselves land-rich but cash-poor, or unable to raise mortgages on potentially valuable assets because they were entailed – promised after death – to others. Some of the most valuable of the Dineley-Goodere estates had come into the family through Samuel Foote's grandmother.

Eighteenth-century marriage terms stipulated a surviving heir as full security on a wife's fortune: the dowry monies that passed by law to her husband upon their marriage. Until such a birth her 'marriage portion', though controlled by her husband, could revert to her family on her death. As the entails on the estate demanded male and female heirs, Foote's maternal grandfather had, assiduously enough, fathered eight children by his bride before she was twenty-four. Only five survived beyond childhood, and three into adulthood: one daughter and two of the younger sons. The daughter, named Eleanor after her mother, married a Cornish lawyer from Truro, one Mr Foote. Her portion of the entails female was secure, bar the issue of codicils signed by her father and grandfather, one of which, she later claimed, was signed in the dead hand of her eldest brother, before he was put into his coffin.[15] The two Dineley-Goodere brothers who survived into adulthood, Eleanor Foote's siblings, John and Samuel, had not been expected to inherit and had accordingly been sent to sea as boys in 1705 and 1708 respectively. Sir John, as he became, had been brought up among merchant seamen: it was said he was incapable of holding a knife and fork in adult life and had never been taught properly to read. He exhibited signs in childhood of what would later be described as something akin to epilepsy but may have been schizophrenia. He also appears to have been on the autism spectrum. He collected and arranged buttons. He spoke to himself. Quite separately, he had 'fits', was unsocial and unsociable, 'rough and uncouth'.[16] When it was later said of Samuel Foote that 'there was a pretty smart touch of insanity in his Family',[17] the comment might have alluded largely to his murdered schizophrenic uncle, but was also appropriate to his murderous other uncle and, for that matter, his fervidly eccentric mother. One argument put forward in court was that Sir John should have been disinherited on the grounds of insanity.

The 'insane' Sir John had entered into a violently abusive marriage with one Mary Lawford, who presented him upon their marriage with an estate and mansion at Stapleton in Somerset, another at Tockington in Gloucestershire and an annuity, it was said, of £20,000 a year.[18] She fled the marital home within a year of the marriage, with tales of having been chained up in the attic, a case 'that made a great Noise both in Town and in the Country, among all Degrees of People'.[19] She was supported in her actions against her husband by Captain Goodere. Accused of trying to murder her husband, which was untrue, and also of a torrid affair

with his neighbour, which was true, she ended up in the Marshalsea prison, financially supported by her brother-in-law for impure
motives: he wished to keep her alive and unhappily married to his
brother in order to bolster his own likelihood of inheritance. So
far, so happy families. The father of the warring siblings, meanwhile, turned against all of them, in particular against his charmless
eldest heir.

Sam Foote was at Oxford when word reached him that his
grandfather, old Sir John Edward Dineley-Goodere, had died,
'aged upwards of ninety',[20] after many years of illness, and several
years of mental instability. There was immediately a quarrel
between the surviving brothers and sister about the estates. The
terms were not at all what any of them seem to have expected.
Samuel Foote described what happened thus:

> As soon as [my grandfather's] breath was out of his body,
> Captain Goodere attacked his brother, and told him to
> depart [Burghope House] for . . . the Estate were his. Upon
> this, Sir John shewed him Sir Edward Goodere's will, which
> gave the Herefordshire Estates to Sir John for his life, and
> after him to the Captain and his Heirs Male . . . the Captain
> replied that the Will was of no consequence, because his
> deed was prior to the will, upon this Sir John desired to see
> the [deed], which the Captain refused and swore that if his
> brother did not turn out immediately he had six bulldogs at
> the door and upon this also six sturdy fellows were intro-
> duced . . . Sir John slipped upstairs where he laid hold of a
> Blunderbuss, but could meet with no powder or shot . . . yet
> by threatening to use it . . . he made the Captain sound a
> retreat.[21]

And all this while the ninety-year-old's body was, according to
another report, naked, still warm and undressed in his bedchamber. It should not be supposed, however, that the will the new Sir
John *did* recognize actually pleased him. The antipathy between
father and son had grown so great that 'Sir John found himself

in the terms of the will barely Tenant for Life [on any of the properties] ... and upon inspection found the debts [on the Estates] amounted to above £5000.' His fury with his father over the terms of the will resulted in a parsimony in the funeral arrangements that upset Eleanor so greatly when she came up from Cornwall for the funeral, with Sam, her youngest son, meeting her from Oxford, that she instinctively sided against her eldest brother: 'Neither shroud nor coffin was good as a gentleman would bury his servant in,' she said, 'and the whole County exclaimed loudly against Sir John's shameful usage of [our] father.'[22]

After the funeral, the new Sir John threw his brother and sister off the estate.

All this was to become the foreplay of Foote's titillating account of the scandalous family crime of 1741. Rarely can quite so much dirty linen have been aired about one family at one time.

As a result of this fraternal feud and after decades of litigation over wills, possibly forged wills, and latterly a wrecked marriage, Sir John went out of his way to remove Captain Goodere and his heirs from his will and the entail of all the estates. Everything, bar £600 that could not be alienated from Captain Goodere's line, was to be left, in the now likely event of the baronet and his lady dying without issue, to the little sons of Eleanor Dineley-Goodere, the young Foote boys Edward, John and Samuel, named after their ill-starred uncles. Two last possibilities remained for the captain to secure an inheritance for himself and his children: to have his brother change again the terms of the will, or have him declared insane towards a reversal of a previous will or wills in the Dineley-Goodere estate.

Such were the undercurrents of the supposedly friendly and fraternal meetings between the Dineley-Goodere brothers at Jarrit Smith's in Bristol. Such were the stories of discord and litigation told to Samuel Foote at a Truro hearthside in his childhood: of law and litigation, violent marriages and forged codicils. They resurfaced as the introduction to his crime-bestseller when the feud turned murderous. And such was the unexpected opportunity offered to him in early 1741, when his world was turned upside-down by his Oxford expulsion, hasty marriage and imprisonment for debt in the Fleet: to solve it all by profiting from the murder.

§

Captain Goodere spoke nothing of this to the water bailiff as they rowed back upriver to Bristol. Foote claimed his uncle maintained that Sir John, a man 'much disordered in the brain', had managed to strangle himself. This was immediately doubted because of the damning evidence: blood and the handkerchief in the baronet's mouth. But the captain stuck to his story, remained composed, all 'Chearfulness and Unconcern' and even insisted on being addressed as 'Sir Samuel' now that his brother was dead.[23] His nerves were only betrayed by his calling for wine for all the crew as they rowed upriver to Bristol. Chamberlayne declined the request. The corpse stayed aboard the *Ruby*. The water bailiff insisted on the purser's cabin door being sealed with wood and nails by Jones the carpenter until the coroner could arrive from Bristol. Lieutenant Berry argued ineffectively that the body would be in the jurisdiction and keeping of the Admiralty, even if the crime was not, but he was informed by Chamberlayne that he was wrong.[24]

An initial inquest was held aboard ship that afternoon. The coroner concluded that Sir John had met an 'unlawful death' – though this, of course, would not preclude a verdict of suicide, which remained, perversely, a capital crime. The captain was taken to Bristol's Council House, or in one account to the parlour of the Lord Mayor and Justice of the Peace, Henry Coombes, and thence to Bristol's Newgate prison. The water bailiff put out warrants for the arrest of two Irish sailors, Matt Mahony and Charles White, and others who had fled *Ruby* to make their way to Bristol during the night. Mahony was found in lodgings on Christmas Steps and White was arrested on a boat in the docks. Mahony had a 'great

Quantity of money about him' whereas White, who had had notice that he was being hunted, did not. His lodgings were searched, and his landlady confessed that money and a silver watch had been 'thrown into the Necessary House'. In the privy, the water bailiff's men found Captain Goodere's watch, his purse and more money. All were taken as proof that the men had either robbed the baronet or more likely been paid by the captain, having abducted or killed him. Mahony and White were taken to Newgate, along with sailors Charles Bryant, Edward McDaniel and William Hammond.

With accusations mounting around him, Goodere remained composed. 'I am surprised, Gentlemen, that you should take me into custody for this matter,' he announced haughtily, to the Mayor of Bristol, on being officially arraigned in the town hall, 'since I am quite ignorant of it [and] am as innocent as any of you . . . The worst you can do is commit me,' he continued, 'but it is a very great hardship on an innocent man.'

Rumours ran fast around Bristol that Mahony and White had confessed to the murder – and the assumption was instantaneous, given the sums of money involved, that they had been put up to it by Goodere. An apothecary, Mr Ford, came forward to present evidence that Mahony, whom he had been treating expensively and on credit for syphilis, had told him he 'was to have a share of 200 pounds' for 'the Discharge' from his captain. This may well have been true. Captain Goodere's defence, such as it was, instantly shifted from the weak position that his 'lunatic' brother had strangled himself to the equally weak one that the men in his command had misunderstood the situation and killed the baronet without his complicity or authority.

By Tuesday, all Bristol was in thrall to the case, taking sides with the abused gentleman, the wronged aristocratic captain or the ruffian sailors. What was considered most damning to the captain, and appears in many early reports, was that the fob watch found in the privy near Christmas Steps, assumed as payment to White, had, in place of the twelve hours, letters spelling 'D.I.N.E.L.E.Y.' and 'D.E.A.T.H'.

§

Sam Foote took his young bride straight to London, where her fortune was meant to appease his creditors. Had the newlyweds heard about the murder in time, perhaps they would have travelled via Bristol, but they did not. News took two days to reach the family in Truro, though less time to London, and may have overtaken Sam and Mary somewhere around Newbury. He heard of the murder precisely as he entered the Fleet. The timing proved fateful. As well as a mast on which to hoist a literary reputation, it offered him a means of securing his liberty. Sam Foote already had an ear for language and an eye for profit, and had been studying rhetoric at Oxford. Perhaps also he had a useful grasp on the genre of trial reporting. More than that, he was a lawyer, *soi-disant*, nephew to the accused captain and to the murdered or suicidal baronet. He was also one heir to the embattled estate. Though it struck many even at the time as in desperately poor taste and 'in dubious character',[25] he seems to have had few qualms about airing bloodied family laundry in public for profit. He began immediately to contact pamphlet publishers, Goreham's of Fleet Street, London, and Collet's of Castle Street, Bristol,[26] with a view to making some business arrangement.

Pamphlets had begun appearing about the case within a few days of the murder. *Gentleman's Magazine*[27] published a partial account in its *Historical Chronicle for January* and the first full pamphlet account was out by early February, titled luridly *The Bristol Fratricide*. It sold in London, Bath and Bristol at 'all Booksellers and Pamphleteers of Quality'[28] for an affordable sixpence, hitting 'all tastes and degrees of men, from those of the Quality to those of very Rabble'[29], as Foote had it, quoting Pope on *The Beggar's Opera*. By mid-February it was on sale in Dublin. But none of the other pamphleteers – there were eventually eight versions – could hope to attract the same attention as the 'true account' produced by the 'Young Gentleman of Worcester College, Oxford' who could claim unique insider knowledge of the case and its bizarre background. Foote's accounts were necessarily privileged within the domain of the various 'True Accounts', however vitiated by readers' suspicions of a certain self-interest, but for the prurient the family connection and the pall of madness only added to his allure as author. His publishers took out classified advertisements in nine different newspapers, ranging from the *Common Sense or Englishman's Journal* to the *London Post*, from the *Westminster Gazette* to the *Country Journal for Craftsmen*,[30] alerting readers that Samuel Foote would publish a comprehensive account and exposé. He set to work.

When it came to crime writing, there was an established market and a rapidly growing one. Since at least the earliest criminal biography in Shakespeare's day, an account of *One John Roper who broke the Heart of his Mother and Strangled His Father ... Desiring All Young Men to Take Warning by Him*, through *The Most Horrid and Barbarous Murder by Eliza Smith of her Child* (1711) to Daniel Defoe's own *General History of [True] Murders* (1724),[31] the general style of successful crime pamphlets was of moral indignation and repentance before death. These pamphlets – usually between four and twelve pages by the mid-eighteenth century – were the primary means by which trials were promulgated, newspapers often carrying only partial details, such as records of arrests and hangings. Just a year before the Dineley-Goodere case, however, a vital new twist had come in crime literature with the success of *The True Account of the Trial of the Notorious Highwayman* and *The Genuine History of the Life of Richard Turpin*. Tellingly, Foote chose to emulate both titles in his works. In Dick Turpin, publishers had found a new sort of hero, and a new readership dazzled by the 'celebrity' and the celebrated trial – a readership who identified with the criminal while abhorring the crime, and who were taken on an imaginative journey into the adventure and potential glamour of both crime and criminal trials through dialogue. The pamphlets about Turpin then Foote's work on his uncles' case were the founding documents

of a new sort of crime literature, which used the reported word
and the deploying of evidence to build a narrative and dazzle a
reading public with the vicarious thrill of violence. The success of
reports of Turpin's trial (heavily embroidered as the years went by
– Turpin was in truth a butcher) were not lost on Foote, or on his
publishers. It seemed that in Captain Goodere the public might
get another Turpin, whose crimes and escapes had been 'the
common discourse of the whole nation'.[32] Issues of class and
national identity, of manliness and gentlemanliness, were personified in these anti-heroes, and Goodere – renegade captain or put-
upon younger son, heartless war-profiteer or dandy pirate – looked
set to be the talk of all the coffee-houses of the land. At least, that
was Foote's plan.

The fame of the Dineley-Goodere case spread quickly. The
London Evening Post covered the story on 24 January, at some length;
the *Daily Gazetteer* and the *Daily Post* followed on the twenty-sixth
and twenty-seventh.[33] On 28 January, the *London and Country Journal*
repeated all the particulars of the case, but railed also against the
'bloody minded Papists', White and Mahony having been revealed
as Irishmen, who had, they claimed, masterminded the abduction.
One thing that marked out the Bristol case was that so much was
published and conjectured *before* the trial. By early February the
'cutting of the Entail of his Great Estate' was already discovered
by the *Universal Spectator* as the motive for the antagonism between
the brothers, and 'Samuel Foot [*sic*]'[34] first enters public record,
erroneously, as the 'sole' intended heir of the Dineley-Goodere
fortune. By the time a date was set for the trial, in early March,
several papers felt the place and moment deserved mention for
their readers. This presaged yet more coverage, likely to sell more
newspapers and, in turn, more of Foote's pamphlets.

§

It took till March 1741 to set a date for the trial. Mahony and
White were kept together in Bristol's Newgate gaol. Goodere was
in a separate cell, where he was attended frequently by a physician,

Dr Middleton, for a 'malignant fever of the head'.[35] On the morning of Tuesday, 17 March, they were all brought before the Right Worshipful Henry Coombes and the Worshipful Michael Foster, the former a judge as well as Mayor of Bristol, the latter the 'Recorder', or judge for the case, at the courtroom of the Guildhall in Broad Street. A jury was sworn in. Tickets had been sold in advance for the public galleries of the medieval hall, where Shakespeare's men had once played, and it was said the door had been damaged by the crush of people 'as it had of old'. Though counsel for Goodere attempted to delay the trial to the next assizes, on the grounds of the captain's ill-health, an adjournment was denied. Charles White was to be tried separately. His 'malice aforethought' was disproved: he had been woken by Mahony aboard ship and had not been part of the abduction party in Bristol. The two remaining men, Mahony and Goodere, were read the indictment against them which explicitly named Mahony as the murderer and Captain Goodere as being 'present, aiding, abetting and comforting'. However, given the further felony and 'Assault upon the King's Peace of Fratricide', the indictment named Captain Goodere as the instigator of the crime. Goodere pleaded not guilty of murder. So did Mahony.

§

A murder trial in the 1740s would have looked, superficially, not unlike a modern one. There was a wigged judge and a jury in a jury box. The *dramatis personae* included gowned lawyers, court attendants, turnkeys, witnesses called by the Crown and personally by the defendants, and there was a separate public gallery. Bristol Guildhall needed little alteration from its quotidian function as council chamber for the assizes held there. The scene as a whole was described as 'a giant Punch and Judy show'[36] though others likened it to the amphitheatre of a Greek tragedy. One key difference from today, however, was that the adversarial system was in its infancy, and murder trials, along with treason and felony trials, proceeded without any defence counsel. The defendant could speak for him- or herself, and lawyers might, on his or her behalf, interrupt on points of law, but cross-examination of the prosecution case was considered *lèse majesté*, and accused persons could not subpoena witnesses or have witnesses sworn in by oath. This was as true of the murder trial that made Foote's name as it was of the later trials that ended his career. The Crown was considered unassailable.

The tide was turning, though, throughout the eighteenth century and during Foote's long association with the law. 'It is hard,' wrote one contemporary judge, 'that a man should have counsel to defend himself for a two-penny trespass . . . but if he . . . commit murder where life, estate, honour and all are concerned, he shall have neither counsel nor his witnesses examined upon oath.'[37] There was, consequently, a certain sympathy in the court for the predicament of the captain and his press-ganged men as the odds seemed so stacked against them, and some believed them innocent. Murder trials, meanwhile, were also trials of stamina. They had to be concluded in one day. No breaks were allowed for judge, jury, lawyers or defendants. 'The case might go by candlelight and into the early hours of a second morning, til even the spectators,' it was said, 'wedged together in the close court, with a pestilential atmosphere, loaded with the germs of gaol fever, were well nigh exhausted; til the judge [sometimes] confessed himself too faint to sum up; til the unfortunate prisoner, bewildered, surprised by unexpected evidence . . . could only stammer out a vague assertion of innocence.'[38] It was a blood sport, or a Dionysian Greek tragedy, but the more perfectly structured, as a result, for the printed page.

The jury were sworn in at six thirty a.m., as the day was expected to be so long.[39] They were not 'peers' of the defendants. They were landowners, able to prove freehold worth over £10 – or, more exactly, their freehold worth obliged them to jury service. The atmosphere hung thick with the fug of tobacco, the odours of bodies, powdered and larded hair and thurible incense, wafted ineffectually but ritualistically around the courtroom to guard against prison fever. Sir Michael Foster, the court recorder, stood to make the opening remarks. He gave a detailed description of the charges against the 'Captain and the mariners' to the effect that they had 'feloniously, voluntarily and of malice and aforethought [sic] ... choked and strangled Sir John Dineley, baronet, with rope', adding, as if to underline the class infraction, 'a rope to the value of *just one penny*'.[40]

Next Mr Vernon, counsel for the prosecution, made a lengthy preamble on the need for the Crown to defend the morality against 'wicked intent', and then began the narrative of the murder with the meeting on the Sunday at Jarrit Smith's house. Merely alluding to the 'family differences' between the brothers, Mr Vernon painted a swift sketch of Goodere as a duplicitously 'affectionate' brother, whose only intention at Smith's had been to identify his brother to his men in order to effect his abduction. 'We shall prove,' Vernon continued, 'by witnesses how the deceased cried out, "Murder," several times ... we shall likewise prove, Gentlemen of the jury, that after they had thus violently got him into the boat, the deceased said to the prisoner Goodere – "Brother I know you have a design to murder me." ' Vernon went on to pre-empt what he supposed would be the defence case, that Goodere had been abducting his brother in order to have him committed as a madman. He said witnesses would be called who would prove that Goodere's 'premeditated scheme' of murder was only cloaked in the excuse of restraining his brother. He ended with a dramatic flourish, claiming that the prosecution would prove that Goodere had stood by as Mahony and White strangled his brother, who nevertheless had breath enough to cry out stagily, 'Murder, murder, for Christ's sake, brother, don't kill me, but save my life.'

The court was duly impressed. At this point, the judge felt compelled to draw the jury's attention away from the dramatic potential of the story towards the business of the charge and burdens of proof. The requirement was proof beyond reasonable doubt of a murder with malice aforethought. Lengthily, and quoting statutes as far back as Henry VIII's day, the judge explained the degrees of murder and the implication of the conspiracy to abduct. 'If you are satisfied from the evidence that the forcibly carrying away of Sir John Dineley was an illegal act, you will then consider that every person who was concerned in that act were principal in the murder and you will find them guilty accedingly [*sic*].'[41]

Jarrit Smith was called as first witness. He described briefly the 'cordial' meeting between the brothers on the Sunday previous to the abduction, but also his immediate fears when he had heard from William Dupree that the brothers had met again near his house, and that Sir John had been bundled away and onto *Ruby*. 'It came into my head,' he claimed, 'that the captain had taken him on board to [make him] concede to his terms, and perhaps might destroy him when they came upon the high seas . . . knowing that his ship was to sail the first fair wind.'[42] If this were the case, however, it was consequently puzzling that Smith had not gone straight to the authorities. He made some sense of the suspicious circumstance that he was out at dinner in Queen's Square when Sir John had come visiting, which had alerted some to the possibility that he had colluded in the abduction. Smith, of course, was entirely aware of the brothers' animosity, and just conceivably had advised Goodere on the necessary measures to overturn the entails by means of committing Sir John to an asylum. But Smith explained to the jury that the main point of contention between the brothers with which he was engaged was a potential mortgage on the Worcestershire estate, which required the signature of both the life-tenant, Sir John, and also the heir, Captain Goodere, in co-operation.

Here, Goodere interrupted the witness, as was his right under contemporary court procedure. He asked Smith if he knew Sir John was a baronet. This bemused the court, and the judge in the end disallowed the line of interrogation, but it seems possible Goodere was hoping to expose Smith's complicity in the affair as a lawyer who knew the intricacies of the linked Dineley-Goodere entails, title and monies. However, the court and the public were much more interested in the lurid details of the death itself.

Morris Hobbs, the landlord of the White Hart, was next into the witness box. He and Vernon between them set the scene of the week leading up to the abduction. His crucial evidence was that Goodere had left Mahony and others there on the last Sunday with an instruction to notify him when they saw 'the man in the black hat', whom he had identified with a kiss the week before. When they saw him enter Jarrit Smith's house, they were to contact him 'at the Scotch Arms in Marsh Street'. From this it became evident that either Goodere had invited his brother to Jarrit's, or that Jarrit himself was complicit in the invitation, and therefore potentially an accomplice before the fact. This was especially undermining to the prosecution case: while Vernon was the prosecuting counsel, it turned out that the Crown had as its solicitor in the case none other than Notary Jarrit Smith. Goodere's objection to this clash of interests was disallowed by the recorder.

Sailors from the *Ruby* and drinkers on the Bristol quayside were called as witnesses to the abduction. Sam Trevett (the midshipman) of the Rope Walk public house swore he was told by Goodere that he'd have his 'brains knocked out'[43] if he interfered. Mrs News and Mrs Darby said the man had cried out, 'Murder!' several times, had his clothes 'rucked up to his armpits' and had even solicited the aid of a 'little girl' to run to her parents for help. And Thomas Charnbury, aboard the *Levant* in Bristol docks, swore that he had seen Goodere as part of the noisy party restraining the 'seeming madman', but assumed he was a 'gentleman and officer' as he was carrying a sword and cane and wearing 'a coat with yellow buttons'.[44] Charnbury's account was the fullest of the abduction itself: the mayhem by the dockside, the attempt to push Sir John into a darker alley behind the horse path and then briefly across the edge of College Green. He said that Sir John had fought and shouted all the way, even as far as the warehouse by the glass-works just near the Rope Walk, before he was carried bodily 'down to lime kilns as far as the lower part of the walls, opposite the King's Head, where they put him aboard a boat'.[45]

At the conclusion of the morning of the trial, Foote wrote, it was looking about as damning as it could that Sir John had been roughly and cruelly abducted, in 'full face of the Sun', and that many had heard him cry out, 'Murder!' By the time he was under the shadow of the Avon gorge, the baronet was apparently convinced his brother was going to kill him. Several of the sailor witnesses quoted a chilling exchange between the pair. Sir John had coolly observed, as they rounded into the gorge, that 'If you are resolved to kill me, that you would do it here and not give yourself the trouble of taking me to your ship.'[46] The yawl rowed on downriver as the weather and the light grew darker, and no further Bristol witnesses beyond Hotwells had anything to say about the fate of Sir John.

The silent complicity of the people of Bristol was one dramatic undertow to the trial. Had it not been for William Dupree, no one might have reported the abduction. Eighteenth-century British cities were policed by consent, and theoretically anyone who heard the cry 'Murder' or 'Stop, thief' – known as a 'hue and cry' – was obliged by law to intervene.[47] Why no one did in the Bristol case was taken, in London, as a sign of the city's degeneracy, but might as easily have been the result of years of press-ganging, and the apparent status of one of the abductors, Captain Goodere. But it was certainly some element of communal guilt that forced the story into the public imagination in the first place, for it was, initially, a completely public crime. The people of Bristol were cast by Foote as Greek chorus, silent yet complicit, in his dramatic retelling of the murder. What had begun as a daylight abduction then travelled off-stage, *ob-scena*, into the darkening skies of Avonmouth and the less familiar but more thrilling setting of a man-o'-war at anchor.

§

It was dark by the time the yawl reached the *Ruby* moored at King's Road in the Bristol Channel. Her boatswain was called as witness to describe what happened next. He was twice asked to speak louder for the court, and his voice broke when he described the discomfort of 'seeing so worthy and gallant a commander' as

Foote's uncle 'appear in the manner as my captain doth'. 'This,' Foote claimed, 'occasioned a great talking in the court.' A number of crew who were called as witnesses were intensely loyal to the captain, whether or not they had heard the noises during the night or were charged either in the abduction or the murder. A picture began to emerge, both in court and on the pages of Foote's account, of a captain much admired by his shipmates, and possibly innocent. It was a dramatic ruse, or a shading towards the truth. Little by little, through the middle part of the trial, the sympathies of the court looked as though they might swing towards the captain. 'I went to the quarterdeck in order to receive the captain,' said one, 'which was my duty . . . the captain ordered some hands into the yawl to help his brother on board, accordingly the boatswain pip'd and order all-hands upon deck, and some of the briskest hands stept into the pinnace and in a manner hoist [Sir John] into the ship; when he cried out . . . the captain told me not to mind his noise, because he was mad, and that he had brought him aboard on purpose to prevent his making himself away [committing suicide].'[48] The sailors of *Ruby* made a compelling case that Sir John appeared mad – and they had no reason to doubt their captain's assurance that he was so.

Goodere put witness after witness on the stand to build the case that his brother was a 'lunatic and disordered in his senses', and that he was in the process of finding an asylum for him. At first, this looked conceivable. A Mrs Gethins, who rented out a locked garret in the outskirts of Bristol, 'though not', she swore, 'a madhouse', said that she had been approached by Goodere in early January about her attic space. She recalled being told about the 'mad' brother but could not remember if she had been introduced also to Mahony as the intended 'nurse'. Bridget King, who had been in service with Sir John in London, Tockington and Bath, said she believed the baronet was 'raving mad'.[49] Mary Stafford, who had been in service with Sir John as housekeeper at Tockington, described him as a 'madman by his actions' and said she 'was afraid of my life to live with him'.[50] And finally Robert

Cock was called, who had known Sir John at Charlton and swore he had 'seen him do several Acts of Lunacy as madman'. He was taken to be the more compelling witness by the court, by virtue of his sex but also, as presented by Goodere, as he was 'An Officer'.[51]

'What kind of officer?' countered Vernon, for the prosecution.

'A salt officer,' came the reply, at which the court laughed. Nevertheless, the testimony of the sailors and of staff from two of the Dineley-Gooderes' properties seemed to give a rounded image of the late baronet as dangerously mentally ill.

But if Sir John had been mad, Goodere had insufficient evidence to prove it and Sam Foote's understandable bias was to downplay the 'touch of insanity' in his family. Sir John was well known in Bath, and no witnesses were called from there. More damning than that, no case had ever been presented beforehand in all the wrangling of the Dineley-Goodere family that the heir and entailed life tenant, Sir John, was anything other than sane. But doubt was sown nevertheless that the baronet might just have been capable of the bizarre self-strangulation, and this, at the start of the trial, was a mainspring of Goodere's defence. Moreover, it seemed that his defence was building towards a position that he had been involved in a deliberate plot to incarcerate his brother. In this scenario, the murder or manslaughter might be presented as an accident: the unintended result of a volatile mix of alcohol, violent men, misunderstood instructions and a self-destructive prisoner.

The courtroom, Henry Coombes and all, might perhaps have been swayed in the captain's favour, if not towards Mahony and White, had it not been for two unexpected confessions and the next witnesses to take the oath: Edward and Maggie-Anne Jones. Some time between 19 January, when they had decided to turn a blind eye and deaf ears to the struggles in the cabin next to them, and 26 March, in front of 'the Court, their Consciences and their King', the Joneses had decided to tell a fuller version of the truth. Their perspective had been limited by the scuttle-pane that separated them from the purser's cabin that night, and the partial tallow light when they did dare to look. But it turned out they knew – or had suspected – a great deal more than they had first confessed.

Edward Jones said he had been ordered on 15 January, the Thursday, to clean the purser's cabin, but also to secure all the doors near the galley with new-fitted bolts. Probably that was why he thought he and Maggie-Anne would have privacy in the slop-room next door. When Sir John was brought on board, the captain shouted, 'Cooper, get a light!' and he was aware of Sir John being taken to the purser's room. He heard the captain say, 'Not to mind what he says.'[52] Next the captain offered Mahony rum. As he was fixing the bolts on the purser's cabin door, the cooper was asked by the distressed gentleman if he could speak to an officer.

'Do you understand,' the gentleman said, 'what my Brother is going to do with me? He is going to murder me tonight.' The words hung in the court's thick air with suitable import. Jones said he chose to ignore this plea. 'I went to bed,' his evidence continued, 'about eight o'clock. Some time about eleven of the clock at Night I heard the gentleman knocking and he said he wanted to ease himself ... and Mahony comes down with a bucket ... [After Mahony had gone] I heard the gentleman praying to God, saying he knew he was going to be murdered ... but I took no notice of it because I thought him to be a crazy man ... About two in the morning my wife waked me. She said, 'Don't you hear the noise that is made by the Gentleman? I fear they are killing him.' I then heard him kick and cry out; 'Here is twenty guineas, take it, don't murder me,' and gave several kecks [sic] with his throat like a dying man and then he was still. I got up in my bed on my knees and I saw a [tallow] light glimmering in at the crack [the scuttle-pane] and saw the same man, Mahony, with the candle in his hand. Charles White was there ... I saw [a third] person's hand on the throat of the gentleman and heard the [third] person say: ''Tis done, and well done.'

The court was ordered to silence. Sir Michael Foster asked Jones if he could identify the man who had spoken, and whose hand had checked Sir John's throat for life. He answered: 'I cannot say . . . but it didn't seem like the hand of a common sailor. It was white.'

Jones was asked if he could say, having seen the hands of the men all held up in court to swear their oaths at committal, whose hand it was. Jones ventured only that it was not the hand of 'either common sailor' and was asked to stand down from the witness box, with all eyes in the court on the captain, who sat impassively with his hands in his lap.

Maggie-Anne Jones was next in the witness box and changed the story that she had first put out. She said she had known Sir John was confined in the purser's cabin, and had been told he was a 'madman brought there to save him from gaol'. She had known about his likely death long before she reported the dead body the next morning. She had heard him being killed. She was certain and explicit that the voices she had heard through the half-inch partition belonged to Charles White, 'whom I have known for two years', and Matthew Mahony. She heard them strangle Sir John, and then discuss what they should rob from his pockets. So scared was she that she had sent her husband to look through the scuttle-pane. An image formed in the court's mind of a young couple, illicitly 'bungling', as quasi-illicit sex was termed, and at risk of discovery in the slop-room bed that exonerated and explained Maggie Anne's reticence in her initial statements. The snatches of conversation she now reported were vibrantly more dramatic than anything she had initially said: 'Mahony step this way' (this in the captain's voice) and then something whispered that she reported as 'Go call up White; it must be done at once.' Then, 'They are about it,' followed by a piercing shriek . . . a cry of supplication, and 'Ah this rope.'

Through all of this, Maggie-Anne had the impression that the captain was standing guard at the door, rather than participating in the murder, but she was paralysed with fear – fear of discovery and fear of what the men might do to her and husband when they realized there were close witnesses. But when the captain did enter the room, after the ominous silence of the struggling baronet and the snatches of conversation about looting the body, he did not at first believe, she said, that his brother was dead. He went to kneel on his chest and feel for his heartbeat. He could sense one, but then understood that it was his own heart thumping – Maggie-Anne said she believed she could feel it herself.

The next nail in the coffin of the defence case was Charles White. On trial separately, he was called as a witness in the trial against Goodere and Mahony. He chose to confess. Charles White had been a member of the *Ruby*'s polyglot crew for more than two years – since before Goodere's captaincy. He came from Drogheda in Ireland, but had fought for the British Crown for more than a decade. He was the biggest man on board, 'a stout and lusty fellow',[53] and a heavy drinker. He believed himself to be aged about thirty-six, but wasn't sure. He was asleep in his hammock on the night of Sunday, 18 January, he confessed, but was disturbed first by noise – not uncommon for a ship at anchor in King's Road – and then by Matthew Mahony shaking him awake. There was noise coming from the purser's cabin and Mahony told White they were commanded to go there to talk to the captain. White had no need to dress to attend his captain, as he slept, like all the sailors on *Ruby*, in the salt-starched clothes he wore by day. He went 'to make water' overboard 'and whilst I was doing it [Mahony] asked me to go with him . . . and he led me to where the captain was'.[54] The captain had a question for White, which he had already put to Mahony: 'Can you kill a Spaniard?'

White answered that he never had. The captain then asked if he would be able to kill a man – specifically the man he indicated inside the cabin, his brother, Sir John Dineley-Goodere. White may have been picked by Mahony and Goodere because of his size, or that he was known to have money worries and to be a drinker – they downed half a bottle of rum together while Sir John railed against them from inside the cabin. Perhaps he was simply suggestible and morally supine. He made no explanation in his confession of why he obeyed Mahony, without a direct order from the captain, went into the purser's cabin and aided the other man in strangling the baronet with the cravat he was wearing and, when that tore, with a length of cheap rigging rope. The quantity of blood in the cabin was explained simply enough. They had so tightly garrotted Sir John that they could not undo the rope, and tried, in vain, to release the noose with a penknife, cutting him badly in the process. They were paid with 'five guineas and six and thirty pieces of gold', but when the captain realized that Mahony had looted the baronet's watch, he exchanged it with his own. This was the watch found in the privy near Christmas Steps. In possession of 'about thirty pounds between them', the two Irishmen had set off on the yawl for Bristol, instructed by Goodere to keep out of sight for three weeks.

The jury were asked to consider their verdict. They were unanimous in their opinion that Mahony and Goodere were guilty as charged.

The next day White, too, was found guilty despite vociferous recommendations on his character from half the ship's company, including Edward Jones, who had heard him strangle Sir John. On the lesser charge of being accessories to the dockside kidnapping, Charles Bryant, Edward McDaniel and Will Hammond, all sailors on board the *Ruby*, were found guilty and sentenced to a year each in prison and a forty-shilling fine; they were bound over for a year beyond that 'to give Security for good behaviour'.[55] The men from the *Vernon* were set free.

Over the next few days the fame of the case spread so rapidly that when, a week later, Goodere, Mahony and White were taken to court for sentence, the crush of spectators wishing to enter the Guildhall looked set to cause a riot. With them for sentencing was a young woman called Jane Williams, who had been found guilty of 'smothering her bastard child', a case that had excited a different sort of opprobrium. Sir Michael Foster, with wig and black cloth on his head, the eyes of a packed Guildhall upon him, read out the sentence: 'You, Samuel Goodere, Matthew Mahony, Charles White and Jane Williams, go from hence to the prison whence you came and from there to the place of execution where you shall severally be hanged by the neck til you shall be dead.'[56] All four walked back from the Guildhall to Bristol's Newgate prison – Goodere in a scarlet cloak proudly denoting his supposed title as baronet. The streets fell silent and the condemned doffed their hats 'making Obeisance to the Gentry and others'.[57]

In his Fleet prison room, Foote heard of the sentence and recognized it instantly as the surety of financial success for what he was writing.

In Bristol Newgate, a blacksmith awaited White in his cell to measure him for the iron cage in which his body would be left to rot somewhere on the river as a warning to sailors. In Captain Goodere's cell, meanwhile, a coffin had been placed. Its brass plate read: 'Samuel Goodere, aged 53 years, who departed this life April 15 1741.'

It was 28 March.

§

The period between sentence and execution afforded Foote time to polish his prose and put it into circulation. It afforded the Bristol authorities time to prepare for what seemed likely to be a major 'hanging fair'. And it afforded also a turning point in the story of popular writing, and in the evolving story of Foote himself. Such had been the winds of change in publishing and in the new world of crime writing, with Foote at its vanguard, and such were the tides of opinion that swayed men for and against the captain, the press-ganged men and the litigious baronet, the city knew it had more than a usual hanging to contend with. For the captain's nephew had found himself at the centre of a minor literary storm, and the hanging itself was to be the end point of a wildly popular narrative that was followed by more than just the thousands who had read about it. As the Bristol authorities prepared St Michael's Hill for the expected crowds and as Foote's first pamphlet began to fly off the presses, he was, in his turn, afforded a brief moment to reflect on what he had wrought.

His works were published as *The Genuine Trial of Samuel Goodere* and *The Genuine Memoirs of Sir John Dinely [sic] Goodere, Bart, who was murdered by the Contrivance of his Own Brother on Board the Ruby Man of War in King's Road Bristol, Jan 19, 1740 ... By S. Foote of Worcester College, Oxford, etc., and nephew to the late Sir John D. Goodere.* They were published in March and April of 1741 respectively, and were simulated first-hand witness accounts by a family member of an eighteenth-century murder trial. Why were they so wildly popular? What was it about the case, and Foote's writings on it, that a century later it had still sufficient echo in the nation's folk memory for Dickens to allude to it in *Bleak House?*

Foote's two works are in some respects typical of the early genre of crime pamphleteering, but it was a perfect moment to publish them, as well as a unique crime. Britain was in the grip of what it perceived to be a crime-wave. Whether or not this was so, the dramatization of murder in pamphlets is now seen as one part of the dawning of modern media. Violence made occasion for voyeuristic pleasure, and created criminal celebrities. Their stories were told within the structure of legal interrogation and in the format of witness statements; in other words, in dialogue. Trials became the excuse for publishing miniature human dramas, less about detection or even about remorse than about personal narrative, often the voice of an underclass, and about the comforting structures of the law. There is a necessary cross-over between trial record and playwriting so perhaps it was to be expected that Foote should have turned his quill, with such alacrity and precocious skill, to structuring this dialogue-heavy legal drama. To this, Foote added his own insights into the complex motivations behind the murder.

Some news stories catch fire in the imagination of the public by expressing current anxieties or by illustrating emerging truths better than any fictional work. Such a case was the Goodere murder. In terms of timing and content, it had it all. It sailed off the presses just as the price of published material fell, and crime found a ready audience, largely of young men, who could afford sixpence for a brief experience of *Schadenfreude* and horror. *Last*

Words – the speeches made by men, and less often women, at the gallows – had been being published throughout the early eighteenth century, and to this had been added a new trade in printing and selling the ballads that were sung, always to the same tunes, at hanging fairs; the musical-oral histories of crime. Foote's story, however, operated slightly differently. The Bristol case had more to offer. Its back-story touched on themes that had wider appeal and interest than a mere crime of passion or highway robbery. The drama unfolded across country estates, lawyers' offices, dockland pubs and a press-ganged man-o'-war. It played to the gallery as well as the front boxes, with its barmaids and barristers, baronetcies and bankruptcies. It unfolded, too, with a keen sense of time, 'a sense of suspense in readers as they watch the world's history unfold'.[58] And before Foote's familial account of the Dineley-Goodere murder, there had been very few examples of crime pamphlets following an aristocratic narrative, and none written by a family member.

The new printing technologies meant that crime reports were linked now to the inhabited time of the readers. The action in Foote's Dineley-Goodere story unfolded in a recognizable but troubling present – press-ganged Bristol, a mutinous man-o'-war, a modern law court – and it sold before, during and after the actual execution. Foote conflated the crime report and the trial (the evidence and the story) and published yet more once the hanging provided the final narrative closure. The speed and cheapness of the printing process, along with the rapid progress of the story, created a literary first: a crime suspense-piece, printed as the drama was still unfolding, at the moment, indeed, of the final dénouement in who would inherit, and written by a protagonist: the heir.

That modern magazines and newspapers were born out of Georgian London's publishing boom is a commonplace. What is less often stated is that crime biography was the first great modern *biographical* genre, and Foote's work sits precisely where crime biography began closely to inform the novel. Crime reports, gallows writing, ballads and *Genuine Speeches* served the Georgian appetite for the prurient, the sensational and the tragic. But they were more than scandal sheets, and seem to have inveigled the sensibilities of their readers in very modern ways. Crime pamphlets articulated a sense of living at one with their protagonists in a shared present tense, and a more dramatic one at that. They forged a connection with unfinished and often evolving realities in a manner paralleled in the modern world in the discourse created by 'reality' stars or the perceived 'soap opera' of celebrities' lives. The crime pamphlet has not survived as a staple of English literature, or even coffee-house entertainment. But in three key ways Foote's work and its genre set important precedents. Crime pamphlets, and his is perhaps the best, are one parent of the modern novel, which also invited readers on empathetic journeys towards experiences they had little intention of emulating. Second, in publicizing the neither great nor good, crime pamphlets begat one element of modern celebrity culture that endures, namely the cult of 'reality' stars and glamorized criminals. Crime pamphlets are also, quite simply, the origin of the modern courtroom drama.

Foote added to this emerging genre a personal angle, a gift for capturing dialogue, and an instinct that celebrity might be coinage in more than one theatre. Not only did this work as a tool of marketing – whose account could be fuller, even if tendentious? – it also served to identify readers with the captain who, for all his violent sinning, was nevertheless regarded by some as the heroic and put-upon younger brother fighting the prerogatives of privilege. And the readership of Foote's first work seem also to have identified with the malefactors White and Mahony, who grappled with iniquities they all understood, for Foote's story was effectively and dramatically leavened with that essential yeast of classic English crime-writing: class.

Foote's two pamphlets therefore hold their place in the narrative of British social history, English literature and crime-writing. They are almost unique examples of a family member writing about a famous murder case and providing familial detail pertinent to motivation. In terms of the immediate background to the birth of the novel, criminal biographies like Foote's gave rise to the element of novel writing that obliged the reader into an empathetic present tense with the protagonists. More than this, the Dineley-Goodere case was also showbusiness. In the history of our culture, on the cusp of modernity, it sits intriguingly as the curtain-raiser on Samuel Foote's life and writings. It is also a key example of the crime bestseller that renders 'celebrity' out of infamy. And uniquely, although dastardly Captain Samuel, the Cain to his brother's Abel, was the star of the courtroom drama, someone else profited much more from the case's notoriety: the captain's ambitious young nephew and namesake.

§

In his cell during the two weeks before his execution, Goodere was visited by 'Lady' Goodere, his second wife, Elizabeth.[59] She chose never to use the title even in widowhood, though she is given the courtesy in several of the pamphlets. They took the sacrament of Eucharist together in Goodere's cell from the Reverend Mr Penrose, a curate. He, too, would go into print on the subject, in the manner of the 'Newgate Ordinaries', publishing indiscreetly his recollections of the captain's last confession.[60] Goodere's twin sons Edward[61] and John, and daughter Eleanor, all in their early teens, seem to have been kept away. On the morning of the fifteenth, having endured a fortnight's contemplation of his impending death as well as numerous sermons from visiting clergy, Captain Goodere was prepared for his execution.

Bristol was used to public hangings, but not often of fratricidal gentry. The case had become famous throughout the country, but notably in Bath, London and Bristol, and many had read all the details by the time the men came to be hanged. The hanging fair drew 'the greatest crowd as ever was known in Bristol', by some estimates at least ten thousand people. They were drawn by the prospect of spectacle, ritual and an older form of cure than was on offer even from Bath's waters. Hangings had all the appeal of eighteenth-century theatre, without the ticket price or posturing. They also had something of the old magic. Many believed there to be a 'healing virtue to a hanging fair' that spoke not just of retribution and the enactment of justice, but also of ancient faiths and superstitions. Those like Mahony, White, Goodere and Jane Williams, about to enter the afterlife, were given written messages to pass on, as if they were interceding saints. Childless women believed they could be rendered fecund by attending the execution. When a man about to be hanged had about him the whiff of glamour – handsome highwaymen like Gilbert Langley[62] or Dick Turpin, or the dashing sea-captain Goodere – there was a large female presence. Flowers were strewn, ballads composed, and there was a brisk trade in the 'sixpenny dreadful' accounts of the murder and trial by Foote. In particular, the crowds wished to hear the last words granted to felons at the gallows; traditionally, pleas for God's mercy and forgiveness. Crowds gathered not just as voyeurs: they were audience and participants in a ritual that dated back centuries.

Anyone who 'bore his fate with indifference or bravado', as Goodere did, was applauded. Some threw oranges and apples, though not maliciously. Piemen and sellers of 'gingerbread nuts and other things bawled about', while 'songs were sung and ballads sold at the corners of the street . . . carts were placed . . . to sit or stand [on] to see the culprits pass.'[63]

In Bristol, in 1741, the drama was literally heightened by the venue. The vertiginous St Michael's Hill, 'enough to kill both men and horses',[64] rises two hundred feet over a quarter of a mile, with views across the city and towards Clifton. In the 1740s it was paved with sea pebbles and beset by 'beau-catchers': ruts and puddles into which white-stockinged legs could disappear, a particular hazard for the crowds that thickened to a dangerous crush with the arrival of those who had been following the cortège and the influx from Bath. It took the condemned nearly an hour to reach the hill from Bristol's Newgate prison. A woman broke through the throng and flashed open her cloak towards them, showing inside a wizened 'marasmus-looking child, trembling with fear', whom she thrust at them to bless and for the captain to touch the goitre at the child's neck. Jane Williams screamed. The mother was forced back.

At the top of the hill the hearse, or lurch, as it was known, stopped, and Goodere, Mahony, White and Williams were helped out, with their coffins. Rather than being 'left in the lurch', they were delivered to their expected fate: the clasps in their manacles were hammered out. When they turned round, they could see the gallows.

It was said that when he came to the 'Fatal Tree' – the gallows at the top of St Michael's Hill – Goodere had only one concern. Several pamphlets claimed he turned to Mahony and White and 'embraced them very tenderly, and said he was sorry to think that he was the means of bringing them to an untimely End'.[65] Their hands were then retied behind their backs with rope and each in turn was asked if he or she wished to address the crowd. Only White consented 'and desir'd em to take Warning by him, not to be drawn into a snare, through the *Intrigue of a Captain*' before blithely slinging the noose 'over his-self'.[66]

A rope was slung next around Goodere's neck, which drew the rapt attention of the crowd for its echo of the murder. He was then placed above his trap-door. He had a 'cap' put over his head, and the noose tightened. The hangman positioned first Jane Williams, then each of the other two men over trap-doors built into the platform under the Fatal Tree, and then the under-sheriff, the elaborately christened Ody Hare, had the task of knocking out the bolts that held the platforms in place.

The crowd fell silent. This hammering was the signal of imminent death. It was expected that Williams and Goodere would take longer to die. They were lighter. Thick-set men's necks were often broken by the fall. But the crowd was thwarted in its view of Goodere's death throes. When he 'drop'd his handkerchief, which was the Signal' for the trap-door bolt to be knocked free, 'he was turn'd off', or turned away from, the crowd by the hangman. This was a gruesome courtesy for a gentleman, one not afforded to his accomplices and Miss Williams. They died in full view of the crowd, their bodies twitching and arching on their ropes, for a few moments in Williams's case, for several minutes in the others'.

The turning-off gave some privacy in death to a gentleman like Goodere. But the real and macabre point of the 'turning' was not lost on the Bristol crowd or on Foote, writing about his uncle's death, or on his readers. The throng at St Michael's Hill were alive to a gruesome urban myth that hanged men who died of asphyxiation became aroused in their death throes and even achieved orgasm as they died. It was to do with blood flow, and some modern medics believe it did happen. An embalmed relic of this priapic death-rattle is preserved in a London collection to this day, labelled 'the erect penis of an eighteenth-century hanged murderer'.[67] There seems little evidence of its authenticity. Truth and evidence being irrelevant to faith, the Tyburn and St Michael's crowds believed in this ghoulish tumescence – or the small potential of it – and even thought the ground beneath the gallows, 'where mandrakes grew', had special powers to restore sexual potency. Some of the crowd of hawkers, hustlers and health-seekers who had come from Bath and Bristol were alive to the old magic of the Goodere hanging fair and the crowd surged silently around, moved by myth or atavism.

Further horrors awaited Goodere, Mahony and White even beyond the voyeurism of the gallows. When the crowd surged forward again, Ody Hare and the executioner allowed mothers to brush their children against the hanged men's and woman's hands, a traditional cure for wens, scrofula and cancers, accepted by Bristol doctors well into the Victorian age.[68] Their bodies were left hanging for more than an hour beyond their last perceived movement. In small part, this was to confirm death; in large part it was to appease the appetite of the crowd for the spectacle and the cures. Then Ody Hare lowered the bodies into the coffins placed below, and they were brought back to Bristol's Newgate prison to be observed overnight 'and prevent any art that might be used to bring them to Life'.[69] Once they were confirmed dead beyond the term of half a day, Mahony's and Williams's bodies were taken away. Hers was returned to her family. His was conveyed to 'the Swatch' at Dumball, a small island in Avonmouth near King's Road, where it was tarred and left to rot in an iron gibbet-cage, 'making a savoury dish for ravenous gulls.'[70]

Goodere and White suffered a fate considered even more horrific. Their corpses were conveyed to the Bristol anatomists. A building then known as the Infirmary, once an alehouse and the foundation building of the Bristol Royal Infirmary, stood not far away between St Michael's and the docks. Here their corpses were accepted by three prominent local surgeons for the benefit of their students and the 'discerning public'.[71] Dissection was a punishment reserved for murderers. It was the last and ultimate sanction of the law, a post-mortem retribution designed to combine the horror of evisceration with the added impediment to bodily resurrection. At the same time, however, the increase in death sentences of this period was of enormous benefit to medical knowledge; as a result of the unlikely marriage of science, retribution and superstition, the body parts of famous murderers came onto the market and survive to this day. One Bristol surgeon even collected such anatomical specimens in a manner that frankly suggests more of an interest in the ghoulish and Gothic than in 'science'. Dr Richard Smith later bound small poetical treatises on the crimes of his anatomy subjects in the tanned skins of the criminals.[72] Body parts of Georgian murderers – and likely of Charles White – remained until recently in the anatomical collection of the Bristol Royal Infirmary, and volumes consulted for this work are still bound in the tanned skin of murderers, White included, a practice known as anthropodermic bibliopegy.[73] Goodere, being a gentleman, had only his heart exhibited to medical students – Smith claimed it was black – before his body was sewn up 'in manner surgeon-like'[74] and returned to his family. It lies still in the family crypt near

Burghope, Herefordshire, 'amongst his Ancestors',[75] added Samuel
Foote, touchingly enough, as they were his ancestors too.

§

As a result of the murder, portions of the inheritance, including
the £600 yearly entail on the Worcester estate, came to Foote and
his brothers immediately on the death of Captain Goodere in 1741.
The baronetcy fell to Goodere's ten-year-old son, the elder twin,
another John.[76] The other twin, Edward, died insane in 1761.[77]
The cousins, John and Sam, the penniless half-mad Windsor
baronet and his occasionally wealthy and constantly newsworthy
kinsman, seem never to have met.[78]

But the inheritance to Foote was more than just financial. It
was an inheritance of notoriety, with the taint of madness, only
exacerbated by his literary record of the case. The Goodere affair
achieved unprecedented attention largely because it was a crime
upon one member of the gentry by another for the purposes of
achieving title, status and money. But it was also assumed to be a
crime of a 'greater degree of horror' because it was between two
brothers – 'English Gentlemen' at that. 'The very thought is so
shocking,' spat one of the first sixpenny dreadfuls on the subject,
'that Nature itself is hardly able to support it.'[79] That a further
family member should choose to profit by the notoriety of the case,
in an age when gentlemen routinely wrote under pseudonyms and
ladies could not be seen to profit by writing at all, was taken almost
as a sign of madness in itself. It indicated to some Foote's 'lack of
dignity and good taste, that reckless use of a subject of popular
appeal',[80] a prescient quality in modern popular culture that came
to characterize his life and works.

It was a signal moment in his life because it was his first taste
of fame. It was a signal moment in the history of what it is to be
famous for other reasons. Celebrity can be dated in effect to
the moment that private life became a commodity. It happened
in Foote's era and in London – and it certainly happened to
Foote. Foote sold himself. He was, from the start of his career,

that rare thing: a highly educated and well-connected young man, but, because of the crime story he sold, utterly beyond the bounds of respectability. Which is quite a useful position, of course, for a satirist.

On 7 September 1741 Samuel Foote was finally discharged from the Fleet prison at the quarter sessions and his estate, such as it was, vested in the Clerk of the Peace. Although he had earned from his accounts of the murder it was, ironically, not the publishing money that specifically secured his release, but one of the perennial debt amnesties or Insolvency Acts provided by the Crown. *The Genuine Memoirs* had secured a brief release, but he appears to have been back in prison for some of the summer of 1741. When he was freed from his third and last incarceration in September, an advertisement appeared in the *London Gazette* informing his remaining creditors that a meeting would be held at the Angel Inn on Saturday, 6 October, at five o'clock to settle all his debts. This was the traditional site for such arrangements, behind St Clement's in the City, whose bells had once rung out, according to 'Oranges and Lemons', as the knell to settle debts. Foote's, of course, amounted to rather more than the nursery rhyme arrears of five farthings. On 17 October Alexander Wood, 'Gentleman, of St Giles in the Fields', Henry Bolney, perukemaker, of Covent Garden, and one Joe Faickney were appointed trustees and his debts were paid.[81] Foote was free again, but for ever changed. He had done more than spring his own plot and release by writing. He had positively jumped on the opportunity presented by the scandalous murder to write and profit. He had embraced the likelihood of notoriety. He had embraced, too, a new audience, one that would stick with him. It was an audience of naval renegades, Irish smugglers and debt-raddled molls, as well as *soigné* aristocrats and theatrical aficionados. It would follow him in coffee-houses and in print, and soon enough would applaud him on stage.

Foote's fame as a coffee-house wit and debt-house gaolbird was hardly the stuff to make a solid metropolitan reputation, still less a

living. And his notoriety, as a consequence of his two accounts of
the murder, not to mention any profits by them, could not last
long. During his first year living in London, between the Fleet and
Panton Street, and masquerading as a student for the Bar, Foote
hit upon a better use of his talents, or answered a calling that
may have been apparent to him as to others beforehand. At
the Bedford, he was constantly in the company of actors, writers
and commedia stars, as well as the usual clientele of pimps and
prostitutes, actresses and their admirers. He was introduced there
to a theatre impresario called Henry Giffard. Over the course of
late 1741 and 1742 it became clear to many at the Bedford – and
in particular Henry Giffard – that Sam Foote, a media star already
for his crime bestsellers, had his eye on the stage.

OTHELLO, THE COMEDY

'Mr Foote's talents are so much out of the common road, that I cannot settle what his excellence is . . . and will therefore leave every reader to rate his merit'

'The Scale of Comedians' in the *Theatrical Review*[1]

IF YOU HAD STEPPED OVER THE THRESHOLD into the Bedford coffee-house late one evening in the spring of 1742, a sight and sound would have commanded your attention, along with the mixed aromas of over-brewed coffee, smoke and damp worsted. Above the concatenation of voices, the shouts of drink orders and catches from the latest songs, could be discerned, perhaps, the Irish accents of the many stars of the Theatre Royal, Dublin, then dominating the London stage, and also, doubtless, the over-enunciation of the many lawyers-turned-actors who frequented the tavern. But in one corner, above all of this, and commanding instead by a simpler presence, a twenty-three-year-old from Lichfield was proselytizing in the name of Shakespeare for an actors' shrine in Westminster Abbey. His name was David Garrick.

Foote was far from alone in launching himself upon London as a refugee from family expectations and a career in law. Nor was he alone among the drinkers at the Bedford in edging ever further from the law and nearer the professional stage. Henry Fielding, with whom Foote would do battle on and off stage and in the press, had also intended to be a lawyer. He was a few years ahead

of Foote at Middle Temple, and drank at the Bedford. They met
there in late 1741. David Garrick, along with his older friend
Samuel Johnson, had also come to London with the stated aim of
entering the law. Or so he had told his family. Foote was only a
few years younger and a few years behind him in truanting from
the Inns of Court so, of course, they had a great deal in common.
Like Foote, Garrick was a provincial younger son intent on making
his mark in the metropolis. He and Foote soon fell under the spell
of the London theatre.

The Garrick family had a wine firm that sold to the Grecian
and to Tom's, but their main client was the Bedford,[2] and
consequently Garrick drank there too. It is traditionally thought
that Garrick and Foote were introduced there by the teenage
Joshua Reynolds, although a rival claim has it that they met at
Tom's coffee-house, with its more literary bent, and where indeed
they both signed the subscription book. But neither Garrick nor
Foote would have needed an introduction as such because both
would have been aware of the other. Garrick was making his first
moves towards a professional stage career, and had already had
one of his plays, *Lethe*, performed at Drury Lane, while Foote had
parlayed his notoriety as author, nephew and heir in the infamous
Dineley murder case into conspicuous quasi-celebrity around Covent Garden as possibly the piazza's most overdressed and wittiest
young blade.

To fund his supposed intent on the law, Garrick worked half-
heartedly at the family business as partner to his brother Peter.
'I must desire you to send me up [money] as soon as possible,'
he wrote to his family in Lichfield at this time, 'for cash is rather
low.'[3] Funds were low in part because the Bedford – 'ye best
[tavern] in London', according to Garrick – had not paid him.
The London end of the business was faltering, largely, it must be
judged, because David Garrick spent so much time on, or talking
about, the stage. Foote later quipped that such was Garrick's dis-
interest in the family wine business at the time that he had 'but
three quarters of vinegar in his cellar' to sell.

The years 1741 and 1742, which led Foote away from the law, saw Garrick, too, make the break from desultory wine trader and supposed law student to professional actor. Yet Garrick still had time to be the central exponent in an initiative to erect a monument in Westminster Abbey to William Shakespeare. He espoused his cause, garrulously and nightly, at the Bedford, and it is therefore most likely that the first image Foote had of him was the one that comes down to us today through the works of Zoffany and Hogarth, which Foote later parodied, an image of An Actor Being Shakespearean.

One effect of the controversial 1737 Theatre Licensing Act, which obliged new works to be submitted to the Lord Chamberlain for censorship, had been a rash of productions of long-dead writers' works, so championing Shakespeare was a semi-political act. The Westminster memorial was a keystone in Garrick's and others' ambitions to have the acting profession made more respectable by turning the actor-playwright of Stratford into an icon of British culture. In this they succeeded. More pertinently and personally, it was also a launching strategy, a self-publicizing audition for a vertiginously ambitious performer: Garrick quoted Shakespeare as part of his fundraising effort at the Bedford, in the presence of James Quin, Charles Macklin and Thomas Arne, all three leading lights of Drury Lane and Covent Garden.

Like Foote, Garrick did not appear physically well equipped for the stage. Both men were quite short and stocky, and neither had voices that combined the limpidity and strength then so admired on the professional stage. Initially they spoke with accents that would not have been lauded by metropolitan critics. Foote, moreover, was said to move oddly and fidget constantly, 'plucking his beard',[4] and he had a marked verbal tic – 'hey-hey-what' – that some claimed marred his acting, although it punctuated his best punchlines. He became stouter as the years went by – a letter of Garrick's refers to Foote's sweet tooth and rounded belly – but from the outset he had the sort of soft-featured face that can never be lit or made-up to look handsome: a flat, asymmetrical nose, eyes set too wide, a large mouth, thick and wide-set eyebrows, 'a large inexpressive apology for a face',[5] as one cruel critic had it. And yet. Even at the time, it was written that portraits and prints could not do justice to a face and figure that sparkled only in movement. At the time it was said he had 'witty eyes'. Some disputed whether he was the finest ever mimic or impressionist – Dick Estcourt was said to be more accurate. Garrick, too, was gifted at accents, and his crown was never to be forfeit as the finer *actor*. But Foote's satirical monologues at the Bedford, virtuosic in mimicking other personalities' styles of delivery, were also of that school of stagecraft that is at the same time *comment* and self-analysis. He commented on what he was doing as he was doing it. His later roles were always, also, Foote.

Garrick, it should be allowed, was a much handsomer man. He had large, expressive eyes, a glinting smile and a litheness of body and mind that had been evident since his childhood. And, in contrast to Foote, he was a pleaser and an appeaser. Where Foote was fearless in his witticisms, which Garrick noted 'seemed to please everybody by sparing nobody',[6] Garrick's instinct was to win over his audience with charm. Even so, he soon admitted that he found his new young Cornish friend at the Bedford 'the most entertaining companion he had ever known'.[7] As Dr Johnson remarked to Boswell, after spending an evening with Garrick and Foote together, 'Garrick's gaiety of conversation has elegance; Foote makes you laugh more' – it was the salient distinction. Also, Foote appeared always to strive to be funny, which to some gave him 'the air of a buffoon paid for entertaining the company'.[8] Garrick would later aver that Foote was easily disloyal to a friend for the sake of a joke, which can only have spoken of pain or pique that Foote frequently made comic mileage out of the actor and his perceived artistic earnestness. How much of this tension surfaced in the first weeks and months of their acquaintance cannot be judged. But because they had so much in common, in terms of background and aspiration, they circled ever closer in the same orbits through the winter of 1741–2: at the Bedford, Tom's,

Giffard's Theatre at Goodman's Fields, out east by the Tower of London, and at 6 Bow Street, Charles Macklin's house, where Garrick would later lodge. In turn, Garrick introduced Foote to his friend from Lichfield, Samuel Johnson, and later still to the beguiling Peg Woffington.

Dr Johnson and David Garrick, aged thirty-three and twenty-five respectively in 1741 when first Foote knew them, had set out three years before to try their fortunes in the capital. Both men had been forearmed with introductory letters for landlords. 'Davy Garrick is as ingenious and promising a young man as ever I knew in my life,' read one, while Samuel Johnson was more tersely recommended – 'He is scholar and poet.' Garrick was the Lichfield charmer, not the eccentric hulking Johnson. In later years among the salons of London's theatrical élite, Garrick would squirm, it was said, when Johnson reminded the company that when they had arrived in town, he, Johnson, had had only twopence half-penny and 'thou, Davy . . . three halfpence'.[9]

Garrick's rise to prominence as an actor remains unparalleled, and Foote's arrival in London and early friendship with him coincided precisely with Garrick's emergence from promising new-comer to major star. Rarely has a young actor before or since stepped onto the London stage seemingly fully rounded and utterly informed as to his craft. At the beginning of 1741, barely anyone beyond the panelled interior of the Bedford or the close Huguenot circles of the Garricks would have heard of 'young Davy'. By the beginning of 1742 he was being described as a 'theatrical [Isaac] Newton',[10] a young man changing for ever the physics of acting. But it was not quite as it seemed. If his bounding ambition was fully formed when Foote met him, his technique was not. His launch was planned and orchestrated by some of the major figures of the contemporary London stage through the course of 1741, and Foote took close notice of how this 'début' was handled, as he began to plot – and have plotted for him – something similar for himself. One important footnote therefore in the story of Sam Foote is that his early career throws new light on the legendary début of David Garrick. More than that, their linked stories highlight an emerging truth about the early constructs of celebrity. Theatrical lore is always less dramatic in the colder account of the *business* that is show, and it turns out Garrick and Foote were stage-managed towards stardom in a cynically modern manner. Accordingly, the furore around Garrick's début – Alexander Pope wrote that the new star had 'no equal as an actor', and prophesied rashly that 'he never will' – can be explained partly by the preparation that he and Foote were gaining from an unlikely source: the Irish actor, playwright and voice-coach called Charles Macklin. Macklin, in turn, was in business with the fifty-year-old theatre impresario Henry Giffard, of Lincoln's Inn and Goodman's Fields theatres, whose story is mired in the muddied political waters of the era's stage censorship and the unexpected role played by the new theatre-licensing law in the careers of David Garrick, Samuel Foote and the long-dead William Shakespeare.

Charles Macklin was another drinker at the Bedford. Despite recent triumphs at Drury Lane in roles as diverse as Malvolio, Shylock, and Fondlewife in Congreve's *The Old Bachelor*, he was violently antipathetic to the regime at the theatre and had fallen foul of its management. He was one of the coterie at Bedford's who argued loudly and nightly over matters literary and theatrical, lubricated by wines provided by Garrick & Co., in the carrel that was reserved for actors. Macklin soon saw in the crime-writer Foote what he had already spotted in Garrick: a potential new star of the London stage. He introduced him to Henry Giffard. 'Being just then disengaged from Drury Lane', as it was tactfully written (he had been temporarily sacked), '[Macklin] adopted a plan of supporting himself'[11] by acting as coach and, in effect, agent to assorted 'young gentlemen'. They included Garrick and Foote. His first great triumph as drama coach was undoubtedly Garrick, but Foote's initial career as a classical actor was modelled on the success that Macklin and Giffard achieved with the 'lad from Lichfield' through late 1741.

Charles Macklin is the godfather of modern naturalistic acting.

He lectured also in elocution and what might now be termed presentational skills. But his role as tutor in voice, movement and naturalism to Garrick and thence to Foote was foisted upon him to a large degree by troubles in his personal life. Drury Lane's management had struggled for some years with the violent temperament of their ageing Irish lead. In 1736 he had been arraigned for murder and tried at the Old Bailey after an altercation backstage with a fellow actor, Thomas Hallam, about his wig. Hallam, of whom it was said his ambition 'o'erleaped his talent', was killed 'accidentally', Macklin claimed, after Macklin 'poked him in the eye with his cane'. The cane entered Hallam's brain. It's an easy mistake. Unfortunately for them both, the row took place in the original 'Green Room', the actors' common room at the Theatre Royal, Drury Lane, in the middle of the Robert Fabian comedy *Trick for Trick*. Things get tense in farce, especially with props and during quick changes. There were many witnesses, including the author Colley Cibber, whose newly published autobiography was, according to Cibber, the only other sensational distraction in the room that therefore prevented clear witness to what had happened. Be that as it may, several actresses were sufficiently distracted from the green-room reading material to have fainted, no one ran for a doctor, and by the time one came, Hallam was dying. To add to the farcical nature of the scene, the prevailing remedy for eye injuries at the time was urine: several of the actors were importuned to provide some for the blinded man, but in their panic none could. The hero of the hour was 'young Mr Arne' – a nephew of the composer – who was at least dressed with convenience for the business: his role in *Trick for Trick* obliged him to dress as a woman in knickerless petticoats.[12] Poor Hallam, unloved by the critics, uncast in roles for which his vaulting ambition had so ill-prepared him, pissed on by a stripling transvestite in his last mortal moments, made his final dramatic exit at Drury Lane, and died from a haemorrhage behind the eye.

Macklin necessarily conducted his own defence at the subsequent murder trial and made a rather good job of it. He was let off on a charge of accidental manslaughter and an ineffectual sentence of 'branding with a cold iron'. Hallam's ghost remains one of the more enduring fixtures of Drury Lane's Green Room, bumping into furniture, and Macklin's tomb in the actors' church in Covent Garden sports a Greek thespian's mask pierced through the eye, which may or may not be some form of stone-carved contrition, but has a strangely farcical air nonetheless. It was at this tragicomic point in Macklin's career, it would seem, that he looked to voice-coaching and acting-tuition to pay his way.

This man who played puppet-master behind the scenes of Foote's and Garrick's début had been born Cathal MacLochlainn in Ulster, later Anglicizing his name to Charles Macklin. Apparently possessed of a dazzling wit, he is cited repeatedly, along with Alexander Pope, in *Joe Miller's Jests*[13] – a compendium of West End *bons mots* – as the funniest Irishman in London when the title had stiff competition. Sir Pertinax Macsycophant, a high point in stage foppery, was his most famous creation, but he was also a noted Macbeth and also Mosca in Ben Jonson's *Volpone*. And his Shylock has gone down in theatrical history. He chose to play the role sympathetically, as a real Jew. He returned to the original text, eschewed the comedic noses and buffoonery that had accompanied the part in the early eighteenth century, studied accordingly even down to the real costume of the Venetian ghetto, and inspired his friend Alexander Pope to exclaim from his stage-side box that 'this the Jew/That Shakespeare drew'.[14] The role received the approbation of everyone from Horace Walpole and the theatre-loving Princess of Wales to the old King George II who said he was unable to sleep having seen 'dat Ivishman'[15] and recommended the performance to parliamentarians. Though his research was revelatory, as was the daring use of modern costume allusions to the British legal system, it was his quiet and determined naturalism that drew gasps. This was new and daringly radical. 'The awful, solemn silence' of the audience, 'as if a pin might have been heard if dropt upon the stage', was followed after the initial shock by a recognition that this was affectingly 'real'. 'A thunder of applause' greeted his first exit, which grew 'by louder and louder plaudits and acclamations'[16] of a stunned Drury Lane into a full ovation. It was a sea-change in expected acting style. Never again was Lord Lansdowne's *Jew of Venice* played in place of the original Shakespeare text, and never again was Shylock played for laughs. More pertinently, Macklin's success ushered in a new generation of actors – Garrick as lead tragedian, Foote as first comic – who sought psychological truth and natural delivery, even in comedy.

Macklin's lessons took place at the Bedford during the day, in the rooms upstairs. Soon enough he was teaching pupils at his home in Bow Street. Foote took his classes there too. His drama school contemporaries included Domenico Angelo, the Covent Garden fencing master, who had a yen to become a *bona fide* actor, one Dr John Hill, a local apothecary, and young Jemmy Worsdale, colour-grinder to the portraitist Godfrey Kneller.[17] Their previous professions denote a clear fact: lessons cost money and were not for the faint-hearted or uncommitted. The students worked on Shakespeare, Congreve and Vanbrugh but the telling concern was for character work and the speaking of lines 'as if in real time and real life' as preparation for the stage. 'At this time when he was excluded from the theatre,' one former student wrote, 'Macklin supported himself by our company, whom he taught to play, and some of whom afterwards made no inconsiderable figure. It was his manner to check all the cant and cadence ... he [asked] nothing more than what is *natural*.'[18]

John Hill later provided the clearest voice on this first ever British drama academy. One of Foote's fellow performers at the Haymarket, Hill later wrote *On Stage Recitation* and *The Actor* along with at least seventy other works, largely concerned with stagecraft. He trailed another notoriety altogether, not unlike Foote, in that he had made a reputation and a small fortune selling quack medicines of his own devising. This 'company of persons', he said, was 'almost wholly unacquainted with the business of [acting]' but they undertook to take instruction from Macklin 'in the science of acting' in the natural manner. This was defined in counterposition to the former 'kind of singing' delivery, 'the gestures forced . . . beyond all that was ever in nature'. The new Macklin naturalism eschewed 'the elevation of voice' calculated 'to excite admiration'[19] in favour of training Foote and his colleagues to 'speak the passage as [one] would in common life'.[20] It was a simple idea, but revolutionary.

To some, like James Quin, the head of the Drury Lane company, it was anathema. Quin, whose 'utterance [was] like the chanting of vespers . . . his actions that of heaving ballast in the hold of the ship',[21] was at war with Macklin's new naturalism from the start and wanted nothing to do with his pupils. Canute-like, he resisted the tide of naturalism and stuck to his old ways: orotund, stentorian, monotonous and self-important.

'[We] spoke so little in the hoity-toity tone of tragedy of that day,' wrote one student, that it was suggested by Quin that Macklin have his pupils study rather the homiletic style of Drury Lane and 'go to grass for another year or two to acquire more gravitas'. Macklin's was in part the Dublin style, it was in part simply his own, but it matched some of the radicalism of the age: an interest in the inner life, character and personality. It was also a manner that found its moment in stage development as much as the development of urban culture. Seemingly, audiences calmed as theatre audibility improved, as theatre finances afforded slightly better lighting and actors found consequently that they didn't have to shout so much. At the same time, though, there was also a realization that 'celebrity' spun gold beyond mere box-office, that it was part of a changed relationship across the footlights. In wanting to sense a connection with a real person on stage, audiences begged or imagined knowledge not of performance but of performer. 'Naturalism', and a delivery that was nearer to the speaker's habitual timbre, was part of the sales patter of a newly commodified celebrity culture.

Acting styles go in fashions down the ages, generations from time to time believing they have found a newer, fresher, truer 'truth', and those attempting the Macklin style, which became infamous and then parodied, found themselves ridiculed for their earnest new truthfulness. Foote and his student contemporaries were seen at their exercises ad-libbing on stage, and Macklin encouraged them to pause a great deal for emphasis, or draw their audiences into a thought by lowering their voices and even appearing to mumble. He was said to teach three pauses in his repertoire: a short pause, a long pause and what he termed 'a grand pause'. One ill-informed prompter had once interrupted a 'grand pause', as taught by the Maestro, by giving Macklin his next line. The prompter did this not once but three times, as Macklin continued to pause. Macklin went to the prompt side of the stage – to the right as the audience looks at it – and knocked the man off his stool before returning centre stage and addressing his student audience. 'This fellow,' he explained, 'interrupted me in my *grand* pause.'

By the spring of 1741 it was clear that *primus inter pares* of Macklin's students was not Foote but Garrick. He was to be the first off the starting block of this rare and rich assortment of London characters who aspired to the new style of acting that, Macklin proposed, would change the manner of English stagecraft. The lessons in the rooms above the Bedford and at Bow Street were followed by small London try-outs. Garrick had several such 'auditions' before his much vaunted 'début', as did Foote: outings in front of invited audiences, which make a mockery of the publicized claim in the cases of both Garrick and Foote, that when the London public first *paid* to see them they were 'Gentlemen never before seen upon the Stage'.

On 19 October 1741 David Garrick 'launched' himself in Colley Cibber's version of *Richard III*. In the audience at Goodman's Fields, in Whitechapel, was young Sam Foote, watching his fellow student and the audience attentively. The young in particular were thunderstruck by seeing on stage that which they recognized as reality: 'Heavens, what a transition,' wrote one Westminster schoolboy with a front row seat to see young Garrick, 'it seemed as if a whole century has been stept over in . . . a single scene; a new order at once brought forth, bright and luminous and clearly destined to dispel . . . the illusions of imposing declamations.'[22] Garrick's performance was greeted with 'the most extraordinary and great' acclaim, said the *Daily Post*, ever accorded a London début, and a family friend of the Garricks wrote back to Lichfield to proclaim that 'not one in the House was not in raptures'. What the young actor seems to have surprised his audience with was merely simplicity of characterization, lack of bombast or, as was written at the time, 'the just modulation of the words, and . . . genuine workings of *nature*'.[23] Foote aspired to do the same, and to link to this naturalism his performative satire and impressionist mimesis, to 'be' recognizable characters on stage. Word spread quickly about the 'gentleman never before seen upon the stage', and another contemporary wrote that 'the public went in crowds to see [this] young performer, who came forth at once a complete master of his art. From the polite ends of Westminster the most elegant company flocked to Goodman's Fields, insomuch that from Temple Bar the whole way was covered with a string of carriages.' By mid-November, Garrick was writing back to his brother, giddy with excitement, that even 'Mr Pitt . . . ye greatest orator in the House of Commons said I was ye best actor ye English stage has produced.'[24] Flush with sudden success and the acclaim of an astonished London, Garrick proclaimed his independence from the law and the wine business for ever. 'Last night,' he wrote, 'I played Richard the Third, to the surprise of Everybody, and as I shall [now] make very near £300 per annum by it, and as it really is what I *doat* upon, I am resolved to pursue it.'[25] Samuel Foote, younger, less certain perhaps of his talent as a tragedian, watched all this from the wings. The close-up view of a friend's elevation to fame and fortune held, no doubt, that mixed pleasure for him of seeing a near contemporary's massive public and early success. It's a challenge to self-belief as to equanimity. Foote determined to have his début stage-managed by Macklin and Giffard in exact imitation, but for him there was to be no such roaring approbation of the crowd and literary London. Rather, he would be greeted by laughter.

Why Samuel Foote, a well-known London figure in the early 1740s and a notoriously successful author, or the well-liked Garrick should be launched onto the stage in an elaborate subterfuge advertising amateurism as if it were a virtue when they were both training for the stage and well-known Bedford performers thickens the plot of their mid-century play. Foote, like Garrick, had arrived in London just as the theatrical economy – and licensing laws – shifted. Henry Giffard, who sponsored Garrick's début at Goodman's Fields and then Foote's at the Little Theatre on the Haymarket, had more cause than many to be intensely aware that Macklin's drama students were notionally amateurs who performed Shakespeare. It made for a marketing triumph. It also allowed him to evade the law.

§

When Garrick and Foote launched themselves upon the London stage, the literal and the figurative, they found themselves at turning points for both. For the generation since royal patents had been granted by Charles II to Thomas Killigrew and Sir William Davenant, the successive holders of the two patents – for Drury Lane and Covent Garden – had kept an effective duopoly over London theatre. Within yards of each other on the eastern fringes of Covent Garden, but ideally placed between Westminster, the City and the major Thames bridges, the Theatres Royal supported a series of different buildings and companies through the Restoration and into the early eighteenth century. Things began to strain during the 1720s. The growing West End audience supported other theatres too – Vanbrugh's King's Theatre, known as His Majesty's, and the Little Theatre, both on the Haymarket, and another theatre at Lincoln's Inn Fields. But they were either sites of operatic production, or seasonal, or subject to the caprices of government to shut them down. The only securely profitable and legitimate theatres for the spoken word were the two Theatres Royal. Nevertheless, as London grew, one more patent-less theatre had opened at Goodman's Fields, Whitechapel, in the late 1720s. The field in question was a tenter field, for tanning hides, and the whole area was on the final fringes of London – another few streets took Londoners into open countryside.[26] If the theatre smelt of tanning and used tenterhooks for its curtains, it was nonetheless at the centre of theatrical innovation and political satire. Because of an increasingly competitive market and the political turmoil that culminated in the Jacobite rebellion, these patent-less theatres – Goodman's Fields in Whitechapel and the Little Theatre – experimented in ever more daring satirical drama. This led to perceived and actual attacks on government, and even the royal family.

In 1728 John Gay's *Beggar's Opera* at the Little Theatre had pushed things still further. It had been an explosive success – Londoners found themselves accurately represented in all their venal fallibility, and their government ministers lampooned in semi-disguised caricature. The theatre, which had until then been mounting short runs of topical plays, found itself the focus of intense political paranoia. Henry Fielding daringly followed Gay's work with his *Welsh Opera*, or *Grub Street Opera*, which frankly mocked the royal family and Walpole, the prime minister. It was the final straw. The government began to see sedition in theatre everywhere – in comedy houses and non-patented theatres in particular. In April 1737 two provisions were inserted into a Bill on vagrancy that would have a long-standing effect on British theatre – and on actors.

First, anyone who performed a play for money without a royal patent or special licence from the Lord Chamberlain would be deemed a 'Rogue and a Vagabond' and suffer the consequences – potential imprisonment. Second, a 'true copy' of *anything* new due to be spoken or sung on stage by an actor had to be submitted to the Lord Chamberlain – as Master of the Revels of the Royal Household – prior to performance. Any company failing to comply could be fined fifty pounds, but also, ominously, 'silenced'. All of the London theatres, bar the royal ones, were put out of business, or into the business of burlesque and opera. In effect, therefore, from 1737 not only were there only two theatres in London where securely profitable drama could be produced, there was also strict censorship of what went on in the theatre, with an eagle eye on contemporary comedy. Just four years before Foote's arrival in London, the West End was put in a stranglehold that persisted to some extent until the 1960s. The 1737 Act had immediate effect on the career and writings of Foote, as it would, too, on those of Henry Fielding, John Gay, Oliver Goldsmith and the Sheridans. One short-term effect, however, was a sudden boost to the moribund career of William Shakespeare, whose plays were not subject to licence and rereading by the Lord Chamberlain's office. Another was an encouragement towards creative advertising on the part of theatre managers, like Henry Giffard. Where some turned to burlesque and music, to burying comedies in evenings of concert music, to commedia stars who prat-fell in improvised Italian, Giffard circumvented the Lord Chamberlain, for a while, by advertising his plays as performed by apparent novices in private amateur dramatics, usually essaying one of the works of Shakespeare. Such was the background against which Foote's début was set.

Although it was roundly criticized as one of the most vicious acts of state censorship, the 1737 Act had some unintentionally positive effects. For one thing, it is cited as a parent to the novel for it forced writers such as Henry Fielding to abandon the stage for the page. It also forced political satire off the main stage and into other, potentially more subversive, genres: the graphic arts, and live comedy at events where tickets were bought for an 'evening of music' or a 'dish of chocolate', with a sideshow. These occasions formed the basis of Foote's early career. At first, however, in the early 1740s, the Licensing Act led to the famed débuts of David Garrick and Samuel Foote, in the works of William Shakespeare, billed disingenuously as novices. It wasn't true. For this, too, then, Walpole's government deserves some thanks.

Henry Giffard might not have been overtly political, but his Whitechapel theatre soon became so through Giffard's singular skill in dancing around the 1737 Licensing Act. One blatant advertisement advised 'A Concert of ... Musick in 2 Parts' that would feature 'between these Parts ... *gratis* a Comedy'.[27] In other words, by not charging directly for the comedy, Giffard and his company at Goodman's Fields could claim they were a music venue and say what they liked. Or so they hoped. They evaded the spirit if not the letter of the law for many months. Giffard next struck upon using Macklin's company of student actors, whom he advertised at Goodman's Fields as being 'in training for the stage'. 'No money will be taken at the doors,' explains one advertisement, 'nor any person admitted, but by printed tickets which will be delivered by Mr Macklin at his house in Bow Street, Covent Garden.'[28]

The concept, born of expediency, turned out to have *X-Factor* appeal. These 'students' were to be launched on the stage of public life and their talents and personalities dissected in the immediately recognizable manner of modern celebrity culture: Everyman turned star. Giffard's theatres – he briefly also ran the theatre at Lincoln's Inn Fields – consequently became private subscription theatres, encouraging the artistically adventurous to slum it in less than fashionable parts of town, in another instantly recognizable manner of modern arts promotion. 'Did I tell you about [Giffard's]?' gushed Thomas Gray, the poet. 'The town are gone mad after [it] ... there are a dozen *dukes* of a night at *Goodman's Fields*!'

So it was that Samuel Foote, infamous young crime writer and noted coffee-house wit, came to be advertised as 'the Young Gentleman' who would be making his début 'for [his own] diversion'[29] and opposite his acting coach Macklin. What is shocking is what they chose to perform. Macklin was to play Iago, and Samuel Foote, still in his early twenties, was to make his London theatre début daringly blacked up as Othello.

Foote had been in training for a year or more with Macklin, and it is likely he had been 'tried out' in amateur productions in the tradition established by Macklin with Garrick. Nevertheless, Othello was not likely casting. The imposing Moor, a man of war and of raging sexual jealousy, was to be played by a small, pale, twenty-something Cornishman, tending to overweight, of indeterminate sexuality but known around the coffee-houses of Covent Garden for his 'hey-hey-what' punchlined gags and his noted penchant for lace. Perhaps Macklin thought it was a useful challenge for his *protégé*. Perhaps he hoped to shine as Iago. Perhaps he and Giffard were particularly alive to the blood sport of live performance and the salivation of a live audience for pained celebrity, performing outside its comfort zone. It was announced in exactly the same style that had heralded Garrick's début, though this time the venue was more daringly the Little Theatre on the Haymarket. Giffard and Macklin suspected they could draw a West End crowd with the notorious Mr Foote. It was billed as

A Concert, and After it Othello

Othello to be Played by a Gentleman Never Before Seen Upon the Stage ... The character of Othello ... will be new dressed after the custom of his country ... No money will be taken at the doors, nor any person admitted but by printed tickets, which will be delivered by Mr Macklin.[30]

The evening saw also the début of Foote's fellow student John Hill, the apothecary, as Ludovico.

'How a man so exclusively comic as Foote, should [even] *think* of a tragic part as his debut!'[31] was beyond his friend William Cooke. He suggested that maybe Foote had felt he could be both 'lover and hero ... the general pursuits of young minds', merely out of 'the rashness and arrogance of youth'. But there were worries from the outset. Macklin delayed the opening and put out that this was due to the 'violent indisposition' of some cast members. He later wrote that Foote had neither 'the figure, voice, nor manners'[32] that would convince as the Moor – but he must have had some mad faith that Foote could do it, or he would not have risked his reputation as drama coach and co-star. Word got out that all was not as it should be. The Little Theatre sold out.

The doors were opened at four o'clock on 18 February 1744 and footmen were 'desired to come at half an hour after three to keep places'.[33] The play started eventually, once the crowd had calmed down, at six. By the end of the second act, Macklin pronounced to Foote that the evening was 'little better than a failure'. They battled on through the final acts – it was an adumbrated version of the text – but Foote's performance 'was found to be too imperfect [even] for private patronage'. 'He was,' Macklin declared cruelly, 'miserably defective.'[34] It could have been worse. John Hill, as Ludovico, was so scarred by the experience and the booing of the packed house that he returned to his apothecary business and didn't set foot on the stage again for several years. He persisted instead in writing, prompting Garrick into uncharacteristically catty poesy:

> For physic and farces
> His equal there scarce is
> His farces are physic
> His physic a farce is.[35]

Foote, meanwhile, had discovered something for himself. 'Though the generality of the audience received [Foote] with . . . indulgence,' wrote one critic, 'many of the first distinction cheered him from personal and family [sympathy].'[36] Utterly miscast in a role and play of grand complexity, he had made, at points, the audience laugh – and had found an easy complicity with them, based, perhaps, on their half-imagined intimacy with his dramatic back-story or some more complex relationship. People warmed to Foote on stage. Even in boot-blacking and wig, even with Macklin upstaging him as Iago, people watched Foote, and smiled. One publisher advertised a compendium of acting advice to be 'speedily published' for 'the Gentleman who lately acted the part of Othello'.[37] There were insufficient subscriptions and it was never published. What soon becomes apparent in the newspapers of the period is that Foote's début, cited sometimes as a debacle or as 'Othello, the comedy', was far from a disaster – it merely put him off tragedy. A month later the production 'with the Gentleman who lately performed at the Haymarket'[38] was still in repertoire, not only at the Little Theatre but even for benefit nights at Drury Lane. If forced to recognize that tragedy was not his metier, Foote nevertheless scored a partial success with Othello: a commercial and sort of Pyrrhic comic victory. He was persuaded consequently to try his hand at something nearer his own mien: Lord Foppington in Vanbrugh's *The Relapse*. It was set to open on 9 April 1744. Nonetheless he was advertised as the Mr Foote 'who lately acted Othello',[39] which can only express some positive reaction on the part of the London public to his interpretation – however comic – of the Moor of Venice.

Garrick is silent on the issue. Their almost contemporaneous 'launches' saw him catapulted into the first ranks of the then theatre establishment as a major Shakespearean actor who had also the common touch with comedy. Within a year he had played leads in *The Recruiting Officer*, *The Lying Valet*, *The Old Bachelor*, and then given his first King Lear. A year after that he was negotiating with Charles Fleetwood, the proprietor of Drury Lane, to take over rehearsals there with Charles Macklin, and by 1747 he had made enough of a name for himself, and enough money, to take over the patent. He ran the theatre for most of the rest of his life.

Foote's Foppington on the other hand was only a minor success. He opened at the Little Theatre with Macklin as Loveless. Cooke says that reactions were mixed. Though Foote had a following as a coffee-house comic, he was not universally admired, at first, as a comic actor and his stage confidence was lacking. Cooke wrote that 'neither his figure nor his manners could represent, in dress, *hauteur*, and *nonchalance*, the high-bred and formal coxcomb of fashion, Lord Foppington'.[40] Yet Cooke admitted that 'as there is extant no *critique* on his performance of this character, it can be only spoken of from conjecture', and as he was invited to repeat it on 13 April at Drury Lane, his interpretation of the most egregious coxcomb in English comedy clearly met with some approval.

Macklin, meanwhile, was unperturbed. He accounted his work with his academy a great success. Emboldened to quit acting completely and set up an Academy of Oratory – or what he termed 'a coffee-house for actors and authors' – he was soon fundraising for backers. He took a twenty-one-year lease from the Duke of Bedford for chambers on the Covent Garden piazza, 'a Magnificent Coffee Room', which he advertised as a 'School of Oratory'.[41] The décor alone cost him £1,200, which goes some way to express both his confidence and the profits he must have made with the Giffard, Foote and Garrick seasons in the Haymarket and Goodman's Fields. In his magnificent chamber he presided with great formality, as his teacher-practitioner role slowly elided into that of academic and maestro. 'This institution,' he would advertise, 'is upon the plan of the ancient Greek, Roman and Modern French and Italian Societies of liberal investigation.' In other words, acting and oratory were to be elevated to the temple of formal rhetoric, debating and discussion and in so doing Macklin founded the original British drama-school.

Foote continued with his studies under Macklin, but his natural impishness nudged him towards dissent. Macklin unwisely lectured on much more than stage technique and Shakespeare – subjects he knew well. Soon he was lecturing with all the ebullience of an Ulsterman on such broad themes as Protestantism (arguments for), bear-baiting (arguments against) and the 'ingenious nation of the Pygmies [*sic*]' with what political bias is unknown. Eventually Foote couldn't resist making some remark under his breath. Macklin, in the recognizable manner of heckled teachers, shouted sarcastically, 'So pray, young gentleman, do you know what I was going to say?'

'No, sir,' came Foote's reply. 'Do you?'[42]

The critical failure of *Othello*, wrote Cooke, 'induced Foote to listen to the advice of his friends, to think of comedy as more suitable to his talents and natural feelings'. He followed Lord Foppington with Pierre in *Venice Preserv'd* at the Little Theatre, which then transferred, albeit briefly, to Drury Lane. Pierre is, if anything, a political rather than a comic role, and his performance was greeted with muted praise. It was apparent to Macklin, as it must have been to Foote, that his second great *protégé* was not setting London alight quite as Garrick had done, and Macklin, as manager if not friend, struggled to know what to do next with the unusual talent and celebrity of Mr Foote.

'If they won't have me in tragedy and I am not fit for comedy,' Foote wailed to Macklin and Garrick, 'what the deuce *am* I fit for?'[43] He answered his own question by beginning to write material for himself: 'I must find,' he said, 'some other department for which I *am* fit.' This took him full circle back to the stage he had found at the Bedford, as mimic, impressionist and what would now be called 'stand-up' – 'a path', as was written at the time, 'untrodden by any of his dramatic predecessors'.[44] The London theatre in the mid-eighteenth century, with its evolving acting style and new relationships with audiences and censors, amounted to a shifting empire in need of reckless colonialists, young Turks like Foote seeking new audiences and novel means of communicating and mirthmaking. The stage that Foote came to know and love, this brave new world that had such acting in it, was evidently dangerously and excitingly in the throes of a performative revolution, that was, compared to the safeties and industry prejudices of today, and for want of a better analogy, rock 'n' roll.

THE TEA PARTY MAN

Mr Foote's Friends are desired to drink a Dish of Tea
with him, at half an hour after six in the evening.

Advertisement for Foote's first 'Tea Party'[1]

IN THE WINTER SEASON after his début with Macklin, Foote
secured work both at Drury Lane and Covent Garden. He was
credited as the prologue speaker and billed tellingly as 'the same
performer as in the Bedford Coffee-house',[2] as if he were primarily
a celebrated comic. Soon this particular skill and his unique
marketability took him onto the main stage of the Theatre Royal,
Drury Lane, at Garrick's invitation. He was asked to join the
company there, and this brought him the role that would change
his fortunes and his career – Bayes the playwright in George
Villiers's *The Rehearsal*. This play, a parody of plays and playwrights,
is now better known in the version re-penned by Sheridan as *The
Critic* – a reworking suggested by Foote. His usefulness to Garrick
at Drury Lane, however, was not primarily as actor or indeed as
literary adviser but rather as a speaker of prologues and epilogues.
To do so, to stand centre stage at Drury Lane, where he had
recently played *Othello* to such unexpected comic effect, was to
stand at the epicentre of the Georgian theatre world, for the
prologue speaker, dressed as himself, was ringmaster and mediator
in a very different theatrical world from our own.

Foote can hardly have been unmoved by the spectacle of Drury

Lane. He would have been standing at the centre of a stage with a slight rake, forty-five feet wide and twenty-eight feet deep. Fifteen feet of the stage projected forward as an apron, three boxes deep, 'fully as deep as the space reserved for scenery'.[3] The rest, ill-lit, lay behind the proscenium arch. To either side of him were the proscenium doors for the actors' entrances and exits. Balconies above them were used for stage business when required but might also be occupied by fashionable members of the audience. On some nights, more seats might be constructed on the stage itself. In front of Foote were the footlights: oil lamps or candles standing in front of tin reflectors. Beyond them were spiked railings, and the audience.

In Foote's London, around twelve thousand people a week went to the theatre. It was an experience greatly different from theatre-going today, but much more commonplace for the population of London then than now. In the eighteenth century the theatre was the primary evening entertainment for the 'middling sort' and above. Even so, a great number of Londoners attended the theatre who might be classed as of the lower orders – first among them the footmen, who kept seats for their masters and mistresses, and who very often had the bizarre experience of seeing only the first or last halves of plays or operas. The theatre 'held a [looking] glass to Londoners'.[4] Though there were concerts and pleasure gardens and evening venues for music and dancing – Oxford Street's Pantheon and the pleasure-gardens of Vauxhall, Marylebone and Ranelagh – it was the theatre where London was best on view to itself. Foote's friend Arthur Murphy declared that there were four Estates in London: 'King, Lords, Commons and . . . playhouse'.[5] It obliged an entertainer like Foote, or for that matter a grand tragedian like James Quin, to communicate to all levels of society at once if they wished to hold their audience, the full cross-section of London society that Foote had first encountered at the Fleet but here conveniently splayed before him in stratified tiers. From the footmen and tailors in the upper galleries to the quality in the pit, from the ladies in the front boxes to the ladies in the 'green boxes', who retreated into the shadows for reasons of their own, from the serving classes to the upper classes to the royal box itself, a theatre audience could have wide tastes.

In this regard, although theatres of this architectural stamp survive as working theatres to this day, the world of Foote's stage work was nearer to that of Shakespeare's than to the rhythms of a modern theatre community. The generally restrained and respectful attitude of a modern theatre audience would shock Foote and his contemporaries. An eighteenth-century theatre crowd regarded itself as the master to paid servants – the actors – who were there to gratify every whim and desire, while being, simultaneously, admired and lusted after. It was a position not dissimilar to that enjoyed by courtesans. The companies at the two Theatres Royal were referred to as 'His Majesties Servants' in advertisements not unlike those for the working girls in Crown Passage, known as 'Their Royal Highnesses Serving Girls'.[6] However, the response of an audience to non-compliance on the part of an actor or production, again not unlike the implicit threat that hung over whores, could move swiftly from the robust to the riotously violent.

Nowadays there is a transitional moment in the theatre, signalled by the dimming of lights and the commonplace announcement that interruptions from the world of electronic communications will not be appreciated. This is the moment when the outside world is left behind. The theatre begins to function as a black box into which the focused imaginations of a playwright, designer, actors and a director will ply the minds of an audience. Darkness falls on an audience in the modern theatre and they become as one – not a crowd but an audience, not of their own worlds primarily but entering someone else's. There was no such moment in Foote's theatre, and no such sense of darkened uniformity. The narrative was given from the stage to an audience but the story was created by all. Theatre was not marked as 'other' from the rest of life, any more than it was delivered as one uniform experience to its audience – it was, in Casanova's resonant phrase, a mutual complicity of imagination and demanded that complicity of all.

For all these reasons, as well as the likely presence of noble and even royal patrons, there had developed a tradition, especially since the Restoration, of prologues and epilogues. They bookended a play, but also they mediated between stage and audience, and tended to beg an audience's indulgence in the most obsequious manner, while acknowledging the shared space in which the narrative would unfold. These orations – many supplied by the great writers of the day, from Fielding and Johnson to Garrick and Foote – were almost invariably in rhyming couplets, and always delivered at the cusp of the pit, in front of the curtain when there was one, centre-stage. The topical allusions that litter these works have defined their obscurity since, but they provided richly rewarding moments for actors, especially those willing to step even partly out of character, and they were the rich seam that Samuel Foote mined.

The figures most likely to be mimicked and ridiculed within prologues were not politicians or those in the newspapers but audience members and often, too, the actors waiting fretfully in the wings. These were the 'personalities' most familiar to a London audience, so Foote began to work on his impersonations of the leading actors of the day – the sonorous James Quin, the new *wunderkind* Garrick, Kitty Clive, with her tremulous hand gestures and ever-increasing girth, Macklin and his pauses. It cannot have made him many friends. Yet it was a novel use of Macklin's School of Oratory lessons. Foote knew the style that was waning and the one that was waxing, and the London audience was quick to respond to the ridiculing of cant and the mocking of actorly pretence.

Prologues and epilogues have their classical antecedents of course. Yet in Georgian London they evolved into an implied joke about the imaginative complicity of the theatre – even more than might have been the case when they solicited the indulgence of ancient gods – a way to link performer and audience in the shared ludicrousness of their joint endeavour. Foote was a performer but also a member of the audience, commenting upon the action and the actors, the forms of the drama and the news of the day. If he made the classical prologue into a current-affairs joke-fest – much of its humour now lost but its purpose presciently modern – he also allowed the audience into the inner circle of imagination by flattering them that they were as clever and sophisticated as the make-believe being played upon them. In some discourse, of course, this is called post-modernism.

Henry Fielding saw and admired what Foote was doing because it was in a tradition he had defined. His *Tom Thumb* had been a vehicle for ridiculing acting styles, while in his *Pasquin* and *The Historical Register* he had parodied and mimicked politicians. This sort of thing, post-1737, would have brought down upon Foote the wrath of the Lord Chamberlain, but the burlesquing of actors, or personalities, was beyond the bounds of the Licensing Act so long as they were not directly named. Something of Foote's essential warmth must have allowed him to be taken to the heart of an audience. Even while delivering fellow actors' reputations to destruction, his 'rollicking heartiness', his 'roguish eyes, perpetual good humour, and a certain slyness of manner'[7] won over his crowd as he nailed the mannerisms of others in prologues.

It was thus a natural progression from prologue master to the character of Bayes in the 1672 play *The Rehearsal.* Its strong new relevance after the 1737 Licensing Act was that *The Rehearsal* is a parody *about* theatre and theatrical politics. The play that had so infuriated Dryden in the 1670s, with its close parody of the high-flown rhetoric of *his* period, found an audience afresh in the 1740s when it was less the *writing* than the *acting* of a waning generation that came in for ridicule.

Bayes, a young playwright, is trying to mount his new play, a maritime epic, and lectures his truculent cast in the heroic import-ance of his work and the sacerdotal function of the actor. Bayes is traditionally used as a vehicle for parodying other actors and antiquated styles of writing. The text was changed for Foote to play to his strengths in satirizing 'well known actors in their easily recognized speeches'.[8] Bayes is a large part, requiring wit, warmth and a sort of insane self-belief. For Foote it presented the ideal challenge. He based his portrayal on Macklin. It is a leading role for a comic who is also a writer or improviser, careers for which Foote was already famous. But it also put him in the mediating position between the worlds of the audience and the stage – of the play, but not of it – the centre-stage position of the prologue speaker indeed that had become his favoured locale. William Cooke recalled how well suited he appeared, and how at home in the part:

> He had the authority of his predecessors for adding what new superstructure he pleased to the original building; and in this respect his strong sense, and the rapidity of his imagination, gave him great advantages. The flying follies of the day, the debates in Parliament, the absurdities of playwrights, politi-cians, and players all came under the lash of his wit and humour: he seized on everything, and everybody, that could furnish merriment for the evening; and all seemed pleased and delighted with the agreeable mélange. Foote's Bayes excited the smile of approbation [and] the irresistible laugh which carried all before it.[9]

The critic Robert Hitchcock noted that when Foote played the role, and ever after, he 'brought crowded houses and was well received'.[10]

It was Bayes that secured Foote a place at the high table, as it were, of Covent Garden and Drury Lane acting society. He went on to play Lord Foppington again in Vanbrugh's *The Relapse*, this time with Peg Woffington as Berinthia and Mrs Clive as Miss Hoyden. He played Sir Harry Wildair in Farquhar's *Constant Couple* opposite Peg Woffington as Lady Lurewell. The season went on to include his first performance of Sir Novelty Fashion in Colley Cibber's *Love's Last Shift*, as well as the title role in *Sir Courtly Nice* by John Crowne, and Dick in Vanbrugh's *The Confederacy*. All this before Foote ended his first Drury Lane season in 1745, again playing Bayes in *The Rehearsal*,[11] a performance lauded by *Gentleman's Magazine* as 'past compare' – which must have raised an eyebrow backstage, as Garrick had played the role a season or two earlier. In other words, in the course of his five months as new company member at Drury Lane, his first proper season as a professional actor, Foote learned over four thousand lines of dialogue, played five major comic leads, rehearsing during the days and playing at night, and secured thereby, as Garrick said, 'the adoration of London'.

We begin to get some impression finally of the 'impressionist' Sam Foote as a performer. One contemporary noted his 'palpable simplicity of nature' when he was taking on the character of another:

> . . . in his person, voice, and manner, but more particularly in his face . . . he seemed to confirm us in the opinion that he was not an actor, but the real person he represented, nay, he at times supported this delusion in a manner so peculiarly his own, that in those ludicrous distresses which low comedy occasionally affords, he seemed to feel so piteous a pusillanimity that after the bursts of laughter were over, we considered within ourselves, whether we should not pity him in turn.[12]

Foote had something of the tearful clown about him, only aided by his reputation as the nephew in the infamous murder scandal. But he also had a comic's understanding that sometimes an audience is inspired by the mediation a performer can enact between multiple meanings and audience. He was in on the joke. 'To sum up all,' as one contemporary wrote, 'as an actor he was bold, original and warm and his talents lay rather in the exhibition of caricature than character and in this peculiar line he was superior to every competitor.'[13]

The life of an actor is very little taken up with those few hours fretting on the stage, and the actual business of being in acting, then as now, sees a great deal more graft behind the scenes than in front. Drury Lane was redecorated shortly before Foote was first invited to appear there. Since 1674 its thousand-strong capacity audience had been able to read over the gilded proscenium *Totus mundus agit histrionem* – All the world's a stage – the motto that was said to have hung above Shakespeare's playhouse. It was painted over during the 1740s with something a tad more Augustan: *Vivitur ingenio* – Live or die by wit. Actors in Georgian London had good cause to keep their wits about them for their careers lived or died by superhuman feats of fast-thinking. Theatre was played for high stakes to a dangerous crowd, and the actors had as support a very different structure beneath and around them than exists in the working theatre today. Foote's days, back and forth to Panton Street, began to be mapped out by the haphazard regimes of the two patent houses.

Rehearsals were erratic at best. Foote rarely saw a whole script, he had his words written out, with cues attached, usually in the hand of the last person who had played the role or the prompter, in the manner that had persisted since Shakespeare's time or earlier. 'Rehearsal' seems to have meant 'individual rehearsal' or 'study' as it was sometimes known – in other words, private time to memorize lines and rehearse on one's own, often in the room hired out at the Bedford. Foote talked about his parts as 'lengths'. The actor John Brownsmith even printed a catalogue of several hundred roles in different plays of the period, 'with the Number of Lengths noted that Part Contains'. Thereby managers might divvy up the roles so as not to overburden actors with too much rote learning, and actors could instantly look up how much 'study' a role would take. Foote's primary skill, developed in his early twenties as a working actor and prologue speaker, had to be in memorizing, out of context and without stage directions, vast gobbets of dialogue from the text-heavy dramas of the day. Consequent to this, it was Samuel Foote who invented the nonsense word 'panjandrum' in relation to the primary skill of actors of the age. He wrote a verse piece, a word-heavy 'rodomontade', as a challenge to a fellow actor believing, wrongly as it turned out, that a great panjandrum of unrelated ideas would prove impossible to memorize. Macklin had said an actor ought to be able to take one look at a piece of text and commit it to memory. Foote lost his bet, though the word remains in the lexicon. His test, should you care to try it, was to memorize this in one reading:

> So she went into the garden to cut a cabbage leaf to make an apple pie and at the same time a great she-bear coming up the street pops its head into the shop: 'What! no soap?' so he died and she very imprudently married the barber and there were present the Picaninies and the Joblilies and the garcelies and the grand Panjandrum himself with the little round button at the top and they all fell to playing the game of catch as catch can till the gunpowder ran out at the heels of their boots.

Good luck.

Sometimes used as an example of apparent schizophrenic echolalia – disjointed dialogue – it did not quite stump Macklin, for whom it seems to have been written as some sort of prank to ease the tension coming up to opening night.

In rehearsal, and even in performance, the prompters ruled the stage; they were the only people with the entire text. The prompter copied and distributed the parts, and was therefore the major casting assistant; he arranged the daily schedule of stage use, as there was nowhere else to rehearse; and most vitally he supervised line run-throughs, which alerted him to who knew their roles and who didn't. Thomas Dibdin, Foote's prompter at Drury Lane, writes of being 'on stage, with one play book after another in my benumbed fingers',[14] trying to sort out a whole season of plays, and knowing that he would end up playing any role that was unlearned. So vital was Dibdin to the running of the theatre that he barely ever left the building; neither did his deputy, Mr Cross, who consequently has recorded the death of his only child in the margin of the prompt copy of a play Foote was in because he was unable to leave work for the funeral.[15]

Once the roles were allocated by the theatre manager, and the cast given whatever term was necessary to study their lines and attend the brief rehearsals timetabled by the prompter, the play was considered ready for its public. The main advantage of the lack of rehearsal was that an unloved play could be instantly replaced: it was never clear which plays would run for how long. The managements consequently advertised at the last minute in the *Daily Post and Advertiser*, which published the main London theatre listings and was consequently where everyone turned to find out what was going on in Georgian London. With its ebullient recording of gossip, news and show business, the *Daily Post* could be found in every coffee-house in multiple copies for fear one edition might not make it through an entire day of fingering and coffee spills.

Advertised, cast, learned and ill-rehearsed, the company put its work before the public. The theatre evening began at six, and could run sometimes till midnight, with no particular expectation that everyone would stay for every item. People arrived as early as three p.m. Footmen and sedan chairmen, till later in the century, were allowed free access to the upper galleries for afterpieces or beyond the fourth act on the principle that they might recommend programmes to their patrons. The theatre hubbub grew through the afternoon, but windows stayed open for the last of the daylight. Candles were lit only as the final attendees arrived: candles being the main expense – and danger – to eighteenth-century theatres. One of the reasons that the front boxes were favoured by the 'quality' over the pit, or stalls, was the likelihood that one would be dripped on by chandelier wax or disrupted by the constant comings and goings of the candle-snuffers if one sat in the main body of the auditorium. Then, just before the curtain rose, the footlights were lit by the snuffers and the musicians struck up. But the noise and kerfuffle continued. Chandeliers rose and fell through the performance, snuffers used etiolated bamboo cues to extinguish guttering candles and relight others. It was quite a palaver. 'This theatre is all very fine,' observed one country servant to Henry Fielding the first time he saw Drury Lane, 'but the play is as *nothing* to the ingenuity in snuffing!'[16]

First nights for new plays and new actors were particularly stressful. As George Colman the Elder articulated, they were often 'little better than a Publick Rehearsal',[17] potentially hilarious, dangerously free-form, every man and woman for themselves. No wonder actors fell back on stock mannerisms and stagecraft – and put themselves at the mercy of the prompter. Play prefaces and prologues are littered with plangent begs from playwrights and from actors.[18] Prompters hurled directions from the downstage corner, not just during rehearsals but in performance. Actors stepped forward and recited lines they had learned in private. Authors sat nervously in side boxes, in one case with 'three flasks of burgundy to support his spirits'.[19] Performers and playwrights literally begged the indulgence of their audiences in prologues and epilogues written for the purpose, and if they were not met with such indulgence, as Foote came to recognize as prologue speaker, they could be pelted with orange peel or worse. Both Drury Lane and Covent Garden had 'strong iron spikes'[20] running across the stage front. They were there to guard the actors against personal attack. It was a shared space, but a dangerous one. Riots were common. One of Foote's key roles was as a mollifying ringmaster, soothing with a joke, for his theatre straddled the opposing forces of the Augustan age: it was violent yet formal, exuberant and restrained, and on the faultline was the prologue speaker, at the iron-spiked cusp of the stage.

It was not such a leap then from this self-referential, meta-theatrical world of the prologue and from his success as Bayes to the next phase of Foote's strange ascendancy over the London stage: *Diversions of the Morning* – or what later became known as *Mr Foote's Dish of Tea*. The prologues and epilogues Foote wrote and performed to appeal to his riotous crowd often included mimicry. These became known as 'diversions' because they were often the most memorable aspect of an evening at the theatre –

doubtless to the dismay of the cast of the play. Moving between prologue-speaking commitments with the companies at Covent Garden, Drury Lane and the summer seasons at the Little Theatre on the Haymarket, Foote developed enough material to write a 'diversion' that might stand in its own right. 'It was neither play nor monologue [but] an original device,' wrote one contemporary; an entertainment spawned out of the formal business of the curtain speech and the confidence borne of taking centre stage as Bayes.

By 1746 Foote was sufficiently established as a comic draw to advertise a première of his own work, a new piece 'for performances during the morning' – the first ever matinées that became, in early 1747, the cultist new diversion for those leisured enough not to work. To evade censorship or the ire of the patent-holders, Foote used a device learned from Giffard, with a slightly new twist. He advertised his new venture not as performance at all but as an 'encounter' with Mr Foote at which dishes of chocolate – later tea – would be served. There was no text, he argued, so there was no need to submit anything to the Lord Chamberlain.

The doors of the Little Theatre opened for *Diversions of the Morning* at eleven a.m. on Wednesday, 22 April 1747.[21] The 'matinée-play' owed something to *The Rehearsal*, and later it was said that Richard Sheridan modelled *The Critic*, or portions of it, on Foote's sketch. Although later versions were published, there is no complete record of Foote's first *Diversions*. It seems that it was not a play so much as a parody *about* plays and bad acting. These were subjects upon which Foote's audience was happy to see him deploy himself. According to the advertisements, the 'principal character*s*' would be played by Mr Foote.

Diversions of a Morning consisted of 'the introduction of several characters [from] real life, then well known, whose manner of conversation and expression [Foote] very ludicrously hit off . . . by imitation not only of their tones of voice, but even of their very persons'. It was a one-man epic – a solo show involving a vast cast of characters and, eventually, the introduction of 'real' characters as themselves or versions of themselves. To begin with, Foote had as co-stars 'pasteboard figures'[22] with whom he interacted and gave voices. In later versions he would simply play all the characters, and later still other actors were involved, appearing as themselves, the subjects that had been parodied in the first place. These characters included 'a very famous occulist at that time at the height of vogue and popularity' and 'a theatrical director [manager]', as well as 'the most principal performers on the English stage'.[23] Chief among these impersonations was his quondam tutor Macklin and his own bosses at Drury Lane, James Quin and David Garrick.

In one celebrated sketch, Foote became a young actor being taught to play Othello. Puzzle was the name of the acting coach, closely modelled on Macklin, and the novice Othello, clearly Foote, attempting the new naturalism, was named Bounce.

> PUZZLE: . . . bring it from the bottom . . . with a grind – as
>   r . . . rr.
> BOUNCE: *Torr-rture me . . . Never pray more, abandon all remorse* –
> PUZZLE: Now out with your arm, and shew your chest –
>   There's a figure!
> BOUNCE: *On Horror's head.*
> PUZZLE: Now out with your voice.
> BOUNCE: *Horrors accumulate!*
> PUZZLE: Now tender.
> BOUNCE: *Do deeds make heav'n weep.*
> PUZZLE: Now terror.
> BOUNCE: *All earth amaz'd – for no thing canst thou to damna—*
> PUZZLE: Grind. Na-na-nation—
> BOUNCE: *Na, na, na, tion* add greater than that?[24]

The audiences adored it. *Diversions* was 'met with every degree of success', and immediately word spread that there was something 'quite novel on the stage' at the Haymarket: 'a young man, independent of any auxiliary [than] that of the fertility of his own . . . performance',[25] switching roles and impersonations with 'Protean dexterity'.[26] It was, simply put, stand-up and was a stand-out success.

Having established his ability to satirize his fellow performers and fellow London celebrities in the course of his prologues and epilogues, and having successfully mocked his own status as celebrated writer and aspiring classical actor as Bayes in *The Rehearsal*, Foote found audiences would attend a whole event based around his peculiar genius. It was not quite the Garrick-style launch he, Macklin and Giffard had envisaged a few years earlier, but it was, as it turned out, a firm foundation on which to build a career. Immediately *Diversions* was re-advertised not as a matinée but as a diversion or interlude in an evening of music, again evading the Lord Chamberlain. In a nod to his origins as a coffee-house comedian, Foote even advertised that the epilogue would take place in the Bedford, a joke in itself. The *General Advertiser* ran this notice:

> At the [Little] Theatre in the Haymarket this Day will be performed a Concert of Musick. With which will be given Gratis a New Entertainment called The Diversions of the Morning. The Principal Parts to be performed by Mr Foote . . . To which will be added [as Afterpiece] a Farce taken from The Old Bachelor called The Credulous Husband . . . With an Epilogue to be spoken [at] The Bedford Coffee House. Tickets to be had at Mr Waller's, Bookseller in Fleet Street. To begin at Seven o'clock.[27]

Major figures of the Drury Lane company soon joined in the fun – big names in the arts given the *Saturday Night Live* treatment, as it were, during interludes. James Quin came on as a nightwatchman, deploying his famously sepulchral voice, Peg Woffington, reigning West End vamp, came on as an orange-seller in the guise of Nell Gwynne: 'Have a bill of the play! Glass of lemonade?' And eventually a second act was added to *Diversions of the Morning* known as *Tragedy à la Mode*: a satire on tragic acting. If performers were unwilling or unable to make fun of their own celebrated styles, Foote would take them off himself. Garrick was one such. In the role of Lothario in *The Fair Penitent*, during the winter of 1746,

he had taken so long to die that it was said some people had left
the theatre: Foote's 'my heart is dy-dy-dy-dy-dying'[28] in imitation
of this friend brought 'unbounded applause'.[29] Garrick forced a
reluctant smile.

Foote began to make money, and the fun spilled into his
evenings back at Panton Street. Arthur Murphy jotted this recollection of dinner with the man who was conquering, through satirizing, London theatrical society:

> Foote gives a dinner – large company – characters come one
> by one – sketches them as they come – each enters, he glad
> to see each – At dinner, his wit, affectation, pride, his expence,
> his plate, his jokes, his stories: all laugh; all go – one by one –
> all abused – one by one – his toadsters stay; – he praises
> himself; – in a passion against all the world.'[30]

It is hardly unalloyed in its depiction of a comic in his first
flush of success. Foote's glory was based on the pain of others and
his table became the site of ridicule and one-upmanship. No one
wanted to be the first to leave an evening at Panton Street because
as soon as one had left, one assuredly became the next subject of
satire.

Diversions was quickly successful enough to be complained
about. It was a flagrant attack on the spirit of the Licensing Act, it
'alarmed the treasuries of the theatres royal',[31] and according to
another source, it was also proving too controversial with fellow
actors. 'The Civil Magistrates of Westminster were called upon to
interfere', seemingly by the powers at one or other of the Theatres
Royal such that 'a posse of constables' was deployed to break up
one of Foote's performances: 'The audience was dismissed . . . and
the laughing Aristophanes [Foote] suffered many days of anxiety.'[32]
Foote was not to be outdone: however. He issued a card, with a
change of title and of emphasis.

> Mr Foote's compliments to his friends and the public, and
> hopes for the honour of their **Drinking Tea** with him, at the

Little Theatre in the Haymarket, every morning at playhouse prices.[33]

The joke of the calling-card advertisement 'proceeded to a title' such that Mr Foote's *Tea Parties* ran for a further forty performances at the Little Theatre and later had an even longer run at Covent Garden.[34] Nor, again, was he restricted to his new invention of a matinée. Tea could be served later than chocolate: 'At the Request of Several Persons who are desirous of spending an hour with Mr Foote,' ran one advertisement, 'but find the time inconvenient, instead of Chocolate in the Morning, Mr Foote's Friends are desired to drink a Dish of Tea with him, at Half an Hour after Six in the Evening.' *Diversions* therefore became subsumed in the title of '*Tea*' or '*Tea Parties*', which in turn became a catch-all title and idea for a Samuel Foote satirical performance: a Tea Party. 'He [first came to prominence] with a piece called *Diversion of the Morning*,' wrote one contemporary in explanation, 'afterwards altered to *Mr Foote Will Give Tea* or *Mr Foote's Tea Party*.'[35] And so Foote became the Tea Party Man. There was no need even for the evasion of matinées – his piece could run before or instead of the main play. 'Mr FOOTE will give TEA,' ran one subsequent advertisement, on 6 June 1747, 'the thirty-fifth day' of a solid run of the hit comedy spectacle 'having prevailed at the desire of several Persons of Quality, on the performers to postpone their journey [to Dublin]'.

Mr Foote's Tea Party has, of course, its unexpected place in the history of eighteenth-century political satire, revolt, and even modern American elections: the Boston Harbour Tea Party of 1773, which saw imported tea flung overboard in protest at a luxury-goods tax, was referred to as a 'party' rather than a rout or riot in reference to Foote's satirical skits. A Tea Party was a witty circumvention of the establishment, an act of defiance, revolt even, attached to a genteel British ritual and drink. More immediately, the 'Tea Party' phrase quite simply had marketing genius about it. There was no 'text' to be submitted, as there was no play, and the whole relied on the person and personality of Foote. It had about it, too, the style of subversion. 'If any dirt was thrown at him,' wrote one friend, 'he could wash it off with his Tea.'[36] It bemused some, of course, who 'expected a real dish of tea, with all its paraphernalia', but they were soon won round by Foote's perform-ance and by the sort of material that could be seen nowhere else in London.

The Tea Party phrase plausibly headed across the Atlantic at this period, courtesy of Foote's occasional dinner companion, Benjamin Franklin. Franklin appears at length in Foote's *Memoirs*, as written by their mutual admirer, William Cooke, who rightly pointed out that 'this celebrated philosopher' Dr Franklin, and the comedian Foote were 'very different in general temper and habits'. Franklin's rationale for being in London as both publisher and writer was to explore all that the capital had to offer, in particular its emerging literary style, to which end, for instance, he committed to memory *Spectator* essays, then tried to reproduce the Addison style of essay writing. He similarly found himself drawn to the Tea Party Man's 'junto and his wit . . . as a seasoning to deeper thoughts and graver studies'.[37] They had in common a love of metropolitan life, once sharing a joke that those who were tired of London should 're-tire to the country', and Foote was seemingly at dinner on the celebrated occasion that Franklin admonished the son of their host with the famous put-down that 'Any boy who is *good at excuses* is generally *good for nothing else.*'[38] Cooke recalled a number of conversations between Foote and Franklin at dinner that ranged from the American Stamp Act to the wisdom of Native Americans. To some extent Franklin's project of emulating London style can be seen in his anecdote, in imitation of Foote, on the business of Westminster's relations with the 'Council of Pennsylva-nia'. News had reached London of the burning of the Stamp Act papers – a preliminary skirmish in what Franklin and others dubbed a Tea Party and that later became a rallying cry towards revolution. London at first attempted mollification, writing to the colonial council 'that if Americans would engage to pay for the

damage done in the destruction of the stamped paper, then
Parliament would repeal the Stamp Act'. Franklin laughed at this
to Foote and told him it was like the story of the Frenchman with
a red-hot poker who offers to stick it 'only one foot into' an
Englishman's arse, then offers 'six inches' instead and at last gives
in but asks for the expenses incurred in heating the poker.[39] The
anecdote, with accompanying gestures, is not the usual image of
America's Founding Father; some of Foote's style had, as intended,
rubbed off.

The success of *Diversions of the Morning*, advertised as *Mr Foote
Gives Tea* or simply as *The Tea Party*, through 1747 inspired Foote to
write more in the same vein but, of course, there was only so much
humour to be wrung from the vanity of actors and the preposterousness of performance. He turned next to another metropolitan
vanity: art-collecting and auctions. His *An Auction of Pictures* opened
on 18 April 1748 at the Little Theatre and was another overnight
sensation. Again, he cleverly evaded the attentions of the Lord
Chamberlain's office and even the jealousy of other theatre managements by advertising his piece not as a play but as an auction.
It was unclear to some quite what was going on, but the unconventional talent of Mr Foote was appealing to more and more. There
had been a mania for auctions and art-collecting during the
economic boom years of Georgian London: Sotheby's was founded
in 1744,[40] Christie's a little later. The advertisements were deliberately misleading:

> Tomorrow at his Auction Room late the Little Theatre at the
> Haymarket, Mr Foote will exhibit for the Satisfaction of
> the Curious a choice Collection of Pictures, All warranted
> Originals and Entirely New.
>   Several new Lots will be exhibited for the public, with
> SOME ORIGINALS by a NEW MASTER.[41]

This satire was neither 'Tea Party' nor 'Diversion' but an 'Auction'
in structure. Foote had found a new arena for satire – high art and
auctioneering – one that allowed him to explore new territory as

well as old but also a highly mutable and sophisticated new comedic structure. Art mattered to Foote, which may be why he found it an important issue for satire, and he would return to the theme in later works, notably in *Taste*, another satire on the art trade, designed to 'ridicule the . . . persons of fashion and fortune . . . and the absurdity of paying immense prices for a parcel of . . . busts'.[42] *An Auction of Pictures* and *Taste* allowed him also this dazzlingly simple but perfectly timed framing device, literal and figurative. He had giant gilded frames on stage into which he could step in order to bring to life a portrait, ridicule the celebrated sitter and artist before returning to the compère role, often as the celebrated auctioneer Mr Cock.[43] It took his meta-theatricality into new areas, visually and comically, but was also topical stuff. It was a moment in time when the idea of personality in art and comedy came to fascinate the London public, and the new style of portraiture, with its emphasis on real character and its obsession with celebrity, had at its epicentre Foote and his friend, neighbour and fellow West Countryman Joshua Reynolds. *An Auction of Pictures*, with its simple framing device used again in *Taste*, ran as part of the repertoire almost every season through the rest of the 1740s, easily adaptable for current news and personalities, the very stuff of the Age of Surfaces and instantly recognizable to its original audience as the key reference in the gallery scene in Sheridan's later *School for Scandal*.

With Foote's increasing success came a greater ease with which to indulge in the artistic tastes he also ridiculed. He bought art and artefacts, books and sculpture. He commissioned work and had collections of drama and historic texts bound for a growing library, one that would eventually squeeze him out of Panton Street. But also, such was his fame, his fastidiousness and his love of fine clothes, that in 1747 Sam Foote bought himself his own sedan chair, which sat in the hallway of his lodgings, like a gondola in a Venetian palazzo, and provided him with his only degree of privacy around the bustling West End in his increasingly public life. The impersonator of celebrities was becoming himself a highly celebrated and recognizable figure in his own right.

§

A pattern emerges as Foote's fame increased through the 1740s. Each summer he performed afterpieces at the Little Theatre; often these would transfer to one of the patent houses in the winter, and even attain the level of main show, some being submitted properly to the Lord Chamberlain. The text was not often the issue, so much as the personal parody of the famous, many of whom were known to Foote. His ability to satirize characters, personalities and, indeed, styles long lost to us brought him fame. It also brought him into collision with one of the other great political satirists of the day, Henry Fielding, and consequently into a new arena of theatrical life.

Henry Fielding had been a quietened voice after the 1737 Licensing Act but nevertheless a local force to be reckoned with. It is some signifier of Fielding's extraordinary energy but also his broad-ranging taste and abilities that in the late 1740s he hit upon the idea of satirical puppet show. It was to have great impact on the career of Sam Foote in the immediate and longer term and, by coincidence, was staged on Panton Street near where Foote lived. Fielding announced his latest literary-satirical venture in the *General Advertiser* on 7 March 1748: 'A Puppet Show after the Ancient Manner, in which the true Humour of that most diverting Entertainment will be restored.'

'We are glad to hear of this,' wrote Fielding, puffing his own advertisement in the *Jacobite's Journal* on 12 March, and with a swipe at Foote, 'as the true Humour of the Stage is almost lost.'[44] His plan, in brief, was to mount as a commercial West End venture a permanent Punch and Judy as the centre of a coffee-and-satire club. It was a blatant ruse to evade censorship. The house he rented on Panton Street, he 'fitted up in the most elegant manner', with a coffee room 'suitable even for ladies, and boxes, as at a theatre'.

In the largest room there was a puppet stage for Mr Punch. Punch and Judy, then known more often as 'Punch and Joan', was, of course, a staple of open spaces like Covent Garden, and also at Tyburn for hanging fairs; indeed, the dénouement in the eighteenth century of the tale of domestic abuse was the hanging of Punch that turned, *deus ex machina*, into the hanging of the hangman. Children loved it. It was not quite what was expected of 'the Great Mogul', Henry Fielding, as his theatrical comeback. Nevertheless, the first performance of this novel satirical puppet show – a company of puppets representing politicians – on 26 March 1748 was crowded with 'a great many persons of the politest taste, who express'd the highest satisfaction at the Performance'.[45]

It was, of course, a direct copy of what Foote had been doing in his Tea Parties or for that matter what Macklin had done with his acting academy. If audiences were not charged for the perform-ance of a play by professional actors, the scruples and scribblers of the Lord Chamberlain's office might be evaded. Fielding, as the lead player against the whole problem of censorship in the first place, could hardly have thought he would get away with it for long. He inveigled his wife, Mary, into catering for the occasion in Panton Street in order to emulate Foote's success with his *Tea Parties* in a house only yards from the Haymarket and on the same street where Foote happened to live. With the *nom de cuisine* of 'Madame de la NASH', Mrs Fielding opened 'her large BREAKFASTING ROOM' with her husband and published this diverting invitation:

> for the Nobility and Gentry . . . for the price of a cup of tea, coffee, or chocolate, and the very best of jellies, customers [will be entertained Gratis] with that Excellent and Old English Entertainment called a PUPPET SHEW . . . with the Comical Humours of PUNCH and his wife JOAN, With all the Original Jokes, F-rts, Songs, Battles, Kickings &c.

It was to run from 28 March to 2 June. 'Breakfast' – served to the percussive beat of the original 'slap-stick' with which Punch's jokes were punctuated – was to be served twice a day at prices of three shillings for the boxes, two shillings for the 'pit' – presumably the middle of the room at a lower level, and a shilling for the 'gallery' above the boxes.

The puppet show was a success, though not for long. It brought Fielding the wrath of Theophilus Cibber, actor-manager of Covent Garden, who put on his own puppet epilogue to each show that was on that season at the Theatre Royal, as competition and retort on stage and featuring a life-size marionette Punch making fun of Fielding. Foote, meanwhile, was greatly agitated by the puppet business. Political satire, and evading the censors, was his *métier*, and Fielding, round the corner on Panton Street, was trespassing in stylistic as well as territorial terms. Fielding had already ridiculed Foote's satires in print, as well as his impressions of celebrities, which made it all the richer that he should emulate the style with the rather cruder business of caricature puppets. Foote's imperson-ations, through 1747, of Garrick, Quin, and even Peg Woffington, as well as the 'Orator' Henley, Christopher Cock, the auctioneer, and Sir Thomas DeVeil, the Bow Street justice, had all been criticized, in print, by Fielding. As early as 6 February 1748 Fielding had railed against impersonation satire in the *Jacobite's Journal*, criticizing Foote's audiences for 'suffering private Charac-ters to be ridiculed by Mimickry and Buffoonery ... All such mimickry,' his editorial continued, 'is indecent, immoral and even illegal.'[46] Which was not without its irony, coming from Fielding, satirical thorn in the side of the Walpole government and now proprietor of a satirical 'puppet-shew'. His defence, such as it was, was to ridicule the ridiculer, by having one of his star puppets dubbed Puppet-Fut – 'Grocer and Mimick': a failed actor who impersonates, badly, others.

'Puppet-Fut' was the wooden star of Fielding's new satire, *Fair Rosamond*, advertised for April 1748. The themes are familiar enough from *Tom Jones*, the novel being print-set that very spring. Card games, assemblies, the wearing of madly wide hooped skirts or tartan waistcoats, the badge of Jacobite sympathizers, the pre-tences of literary and theatrical critics, the mania for whist – it was all immediately reminiscent of the days before 1737 when one could get away with laughing at high society and politics in the theatre, with real actors. A new butt for Fielding's humour, however, was the business of mimicry itself, a tautological position that enraged Foote. Only because Fielding had been once or twice mimicked on stage himself – he was not famous enough a personage or recognizable enough in speech pattern to have much comic stock – did he see fit to criticize Foote as an impressionist. The war between Panton Street and the Haymarket escalated. Foote did not appreciate Puppet-Fut, and the actorly slur contained in his being made of wood. He retaliated. He advertised that the Little Theatre would put on, in direct competition to *Fair Rosamond*, 'An *Auction . . . a choice collection of pictures all warranted originals, and Entirely New.*' Inside these 'frames', as before, Foote took off various figures, but mainly ridiculed Fielding. A writer in the journal *Old England* described the central scene in which Foote nominates the portrait of Fielding for an official hanging in the hall of the 'Hospital of Scoundrels . . . his picture to be hung up in Hall, drawn from Mr Foote's original, all in Black . . . and the Flap of his shirt hanging out, just as was exhibited on stage'. Foote's caricature of Fielding – dishevelled, his wig askew, his barrister's robes besmirched with snuff and tobacco juice – was drawn from life, but was designed to hurt. It also acknowledged that Fielding, in picking Foote as an adversary, was entering the realm of 'celebrity' himself, precisely the arena of personal attack and personality-driven satire that he had set out to disdain.

The ball was back in Fielding's court. On 21 April 1748 he, too, advertised a hanging, but not of a picture of Samuel Foote, rather of Puppet-Fut itself. To *Fair Rosamond* was to be added a new ending, 'the Comical Execution of Mr Puppet-Fut, Esq., Grocer and Mimick, With a New Scene representing Tyburn'. On the one hand this was a reference to the traditional eighteenth-century climax of *Punch & Joan* – the hanging of the hangman, and thus a somewhat tidy Tyburn allusion, the satirist hanged on the gibbet of his own joke. But given Foote's original fame, as the author of the *Genuine Memoirs* – the story of a family murder and gruesome hanging – it had also its tasteless, not to say tactless, element; an element of gloves-off satirical combat. Furious and offended, Foote, this time, wrote back in print in the *Daily Advertiser*:

> Whereas there is a dirty fellow in shabby black Cloathes and a Quid of Tobacco in his Jaws that runs up and down calling himself Henry Folding [*sic*] begging Money and complaining about one Fut, a Grocer, from whom he said he had lately received a severe Drubbing; this is to inform the Public that the said dirty fellow is an Imposter [and not the fine author Mr Fielding] this imposter . . . was yesterday morning seen . . . in Panton Street, officiated to a Puppet-Show, and in the Afternoon with his Wife and Two Children hawking Dying Speeches about the Streets.[47]

It was all great publicity and rather good for business, both at the Haymarket and at Panton Street. Fielding, however, was not about to be drawn into a season-to-season rivalry and tried to draw a line under it all, again in print rather than on stage. In the *Jacobite's Journal* on the 30 April, he arraigned Puppet-Fut in a show-trial that, again, had echoes of the trials in Foote's own family. The puppet is found guilty of the 'very High Crime' of bringing 'Real Facts and Persons upon the Stage' as contrasted with the true business of satire, which is not personal animus but the exposing of hypocrisy. Or so Henry Fielding, puppet-wrangler to the stars, claimed. He sentenced Foote accordingly:

> I shall proceed therefore to pronounce the judgement of the Court: which is that you, *Samuel Fut be p--sed upon, with Scorn and Contempt*, as low Buffoon; and I do, with the utmost *Scorn and Contempt, p-ss upon you accordingly*. The prisoner was then removed from the bar, kicking and pulling a chew of tobacco from his mouth, while the p-ss ran plentifully down his Face.[48]

It hardly shows this Titan of English letters in his finest light or at his most Augustan. Some satirists, of course, turn apostate when they find themselves the butt of satire in person. There was one final sally in the public sport of Fielding v. Foote, and it took place more appropriately on stage. On 9 May 1748 Fielding offered a final performance of Puppet-Fut in a burlesque of his own composition titled *The Covent Garden Tragedy*. Contrary to his written position that all personal satire was mere buffoonery when compared to the elevated business of political satire, the piece featured a company of puppets modelled on well-known Covent Garden personalities. The actresses of the company were advertised as Mrs Puppet Duggleass, a wooden cartoon of 'Mother' Jenny Douglas, madam of the piazza's most successful brothel, along with 'Mrs Puppet Fllips [*sic*]' and Mrs Puppet Morrey, caricatures of a briefly famous adulteress and high-class courtesan respectively, 'Con' Philips and Fanny Murray. The villain of the piece was to be played by Mr Puppet-Fut in his last performance, literally kicked off the stage in the finale by the master of Panton Street, Mr Punch. The curtain came down on one of the strangest spats in stage history on 14 May 1748.[49] Foote later remarked, apropos his wooden leg, that he had already had half a career as a marionette.

He then revived *An Auction of Pictures*, and added *The Credulous Husband*, adapted from Congreve, as an afterpiece to *A Dish of Tea* at the Little Theatre on the Haymarket, which ran intermittently from 22 April 1747 to 6 June 1748. Then, in late 1748, *Tea* or *The Tea Party* was transferred to Covent Garden and Foote was in the company as Fondlewife again in *The Old Bachelor* by Congreve, Sir Novelty Nice in *Love's Last Shift*, which he had first played at Drury Lane in December 1745. The play was produced as an afterpiece to *The Tea Party* on 2 February 1748 but ran for just a couple of nights. Finally, he appeared again as Bayes, in *The Rehearsal*, for two nights in November. But when Foote returned to the Haymarket for a thirty-six-night run there of *An Auction of Pictures* in 1748, it played as a main show, not an afterpiece. It did so again the following season. Foote's ascendancy as the West End's premier comic had been fleet and fast. He lacked only a name as a comic writer of plays but that, too, was about to change.

ACT TWO

AN ENGLISHMAN ABROAD

'There is no position in life so full of incessant temptation'

Peg Woffington, on being an actor

FOOTE LEFT LONDON IN 1748, first for Dublin and then for Paris. Though he was back in London briefly in April 1749, and in 1751, he did not base himself there for several years. His friend William Cooke gives the impression that Foote's virtual disappearance from public life, at the height of hard-won fame, was a result of an inheritance, via his mother, of some of the Dineley-Goodere monies attached to the Burghope estate. In part this was true. Yet at the same time Cooke hints at 'the idle stories circulated relative to Foote'[1] and 'all the splendour of dissipation which was so congenial to [Foote's] temper'.[2] 'There was much talk and speculation',[3] according to another record, that Foote had been forced to quit town. One rumour had him hanged in Bordeaux for further crimes of dissipation. Another was insistent that he had 'run away', and Garrick acknowledged in a footlights prologue that 'after such Disgrace/No Gentleman would dare to show his Face'.[4]

The 'speculation' and 'disgrace' are defined more closely by those who have read Foote's story in the light of his subsequent trial and accusations against him of homosexuality. It seems plausible that his disappearance from the London stage, at the height of his new-found fame, can be explained by an earlier scandal than the ones that finally ruined him. And, if so, given his near three-year absence, almost certainly the London scandal related to homosexuality. Years later when he was attacked in the press as a sodomite, his previous absence in France became a subject of conjecture. 'Is it, or is it not true,' fumed one paragraph in the *Public Ledger*, 'that when you were first [in France] your friends found it necessary to PREVAIL on you [to go]? . . . who knows what the *Beau-Monde* of Paris may be entertained with the secret history of your intrigues? . . . Have you not been intimately well acquainted [there] with the Prince d'Elboeuf [a flamboyant self-proclaimed homosexual]?'[5] It was all hearsay, but it hinged upon Foote's time in Paris and the supposed necessity of his quitting the London stage, which he had first done in 1748. Charles Macklin, his drama coach, assumed Foote to have had homosexual experiences, and Mrs Thrale, beloved of Samuel Johnson and latterly very much part of Foote's circle, notes in a private manuscript that Foote was indeed 'sodomitical' and risked all his life 'a hideous detection'.[6]

Foote was too circumspect to say directly, and may not have been so easily defined. 'Many my passions are,' Foote stated daringly, live on stage, 'though one my View: They all concentre in pleasing *you*.'[7] In living to please and pleasing to live, Foote somewhere overstepped the mark and faced the rancour of his protectors and the opprobrium of the law. It is not entirely clear how.

Celebrity and success in the arts create a tension in individuals, performers perhaps more than most, a fissure between external acclaim and, very often, an inner lack of security. Like the blades of shears, if one side is the roar of the crowd the other is doubt about its objective taste. This, combined with the anxiety based on experience that it can all turn sour overnight, has classically meant that the extension of one blade encourages a similar but opposing extension of the other. Especially with comics. There is no security, necessarily, in pleasing the crowd. The risks are greater in comedy, even before one considers the bear-pit cruelties of the Georgian stage. The supposed fearlessness of Foote and his need to push away friends with the lash of his wit might have signalled a deeper anxiety, a feeling of self-loathing rooted in his strained relationship with his parents and the manifold dysfunctional issues in his family. Where many celebrities since have knitted across this tension with addictions to chemical highs that are also destructive, others, of course, seek out older but no less thrilling paths of self-destruction. The highs, and the danger, are familiar to anyone who loves the stage. It is little more than a surmise with Foote, but the man who set one of the earliest paradigms of what it is to be dazzlingly famous and then destroyed seems likely to have set early patterns, too, in more quotidian self-harm and dangerous living. Which is not to say there was anything inherently unhealthy or dangerous in homosexual practice in eighteenth-century London. The prejudice of doctors at the time was that a '[heterosexual] gallant' was more likely to catch the clap at one of the established 'nunneries' of Covent Garden than, were that his taste, at the molly-houses of the Minories. But it was dangerous to anyone's career to flaunt homosexual activity in an age that was ambivalent about it. And Foote seems so to have done.

A description of Foote at this period is worth quoting at length as it gives clear insights into the style and substance of the man in his prime, but also to the potential for disaster that was, tragically, some cost of his fame:

> His company generally consisted then of men of rank and fashion, some literary characters, and a selection from the stage. Everybody was talked to, and attended, in turn; everybody was drawn into his best subject of conversation; and often the man of modesty . . . was supported by the well-timed and polite interference of the host. In short, he set everyone at ease with himself, the better to enable him to please and be pleased. In these exercises of hospitality he knew his own station perfectly well, and supported it with great propriety. He carved well and expeditiously; and his table was covered . . . with everything suitable to a man of taste and fashion: two

or three courses, a handsome dessert, French wines, &c. He added to these his best treat, his own conversation: not only in the brilliancy of his wit, but also on the more solid topics of taste and literature. It was often astonishing to those who . . . had only given him credit for mere humour, to see with what versatility he could turn from the broadest mirth to subjects of history & politics. His more familiar days were passed with a few friends, and one or two needy actors or authors, who constantly hung upon him, and to whom he was kind in his purse, his table, and advice.

Yet as 'no man is a hero to his valet-de-chambre' so these intimates were witnesses to great occasional dejection of spirits. He would suddenly fall from the height of mirth to the lowest note; then burst into a flood of tears, exclaiming that 'his follies . . . would bring him to a workhouse!' But these seemed to be mere momentary fits of despondence: at the first object of ridicule which presented itself, he instantly seized it; and with a spring of fancy, that seemed to rebound in proportion as it had been compressed, he again blazed out in all his meridian brightness.'[8]

What Foote's sudden flashes of self-hatred and dejection betrayed might well have been within the usual compass of professional pleasers and comedians – the tears of the clown. They might, though, have betrayed a more troubled psyche, and a more troubled relationship between private man and public star.

Much earlier than his final demise, the groundwork had been laid in the London public's mind that the bizarre persona of Mr Foote was a sexually ambivalent one. The ease with which the slur of sexual deviance was levelled at him later in his career, and the lack of explanation for his various absences from the stage, add credibility to the theory that Foote was obliged to quit London in 1748–9. It made no sense financially or artistically for him to stay so long away from the theatre capital of the English-speaking world. Some historians[9] have been greatly troubled by the possibility of Foote's moral or sexual free-spiritedness, as if this somehow undermines his reputation as a man of letters and an important voice in comedy. Conversely it turns out he is far from the 'gay' martyr that others have painted him. The balance of evidence of the late 1740s tends towards a picture of Foote that was at best scapegrace and at worst, in the legal parlance of the times, vicious. The evidence for this vice is, however, patchy. For what it is worth, it must be stated that Foote cannot have been exclusively homosexual, even had such a term existed. This is evidenced not so much by his brief early marriage but by the existence of two putatively 'natural' sons – who might or might not in truth have been his but were beneficiaries in his will – one of whom, sadly, predeceased him. However, the later attacks upon Foote, in the press and in person, the unexpectedly compelling evidence of one of his servants, only recently discovered in all its persuasive detail, necessitate a step back from the main player to the scenic background of Foote's sexual London.

§

The law was simple: sodomy was illegal and, indeed, in some instances, was a capital offence. But then equally deviant would be considered *coitus interruptus* and masturbation. Sodomy was just one of a series of offences, deemed 'unnatural' through being non-procreative, that were noted as having brought down the wrath of God in the Old Testament against earlier troubled conurbations, usually in times of war. The history of attack against supposed sexual deviance in eighteenth-century London, as against actors and actresses as mis-representative of their sexes, parallels the waxing and waning fortunes of the nation at war. The law could be applied or not applied and prejudices ran with the times. 'Sodomy', meanwhile, was a term for many acts – sex with animals, as boasted of by friends of John Wilkes, and oral sex, as practised by various of the votaries of Venus, detailed in *Harris's List of Covent Garden Ladies*. Specific cases and charges would not and could not be reported directly in the coffee-house press. There was no clear published record of what Foote, for instance, was eventually charged with. Rumour spread by word of mouth. However, the issue that was dangerous for Foote as for others was what the law really had in its sights: sex between men and the intention to have, or actual practice of, anal homosexual sex, which, by a statute of 1533, was a hanging offence. It continued as such until 1861.

There was as a result the potential for much confusion, and an unclear understanding within the semi-tolerated molly-houses – some brothels, many just 'gay-friendly' establishments – of what constituted flouting of the law. Eye-poppingly, full penetration *and* emission had to be clearly witnessed, which was nigh on impossible, so records of trials tend to involve couples who had been denounced, and infamous entrapments as at Mother Clap's Molly House in 1726. Much more common than a trial leading directly to a capital charge was one that relied on the perceived persona of the accused as a 'sodomite', involving a charge instead of sexual assault. This would eventually be Foote's undoing in his 1776 trial. What troubled people about Foote was his ambiguity, his reckless otherness.

Foote lived dangerously all his life. His comedy relied on it, and his nature seemed to relish it. It was and remains part of what it sometimes means to be a celebrity – to play out the tension between paranoia and adulation by deliberately risking 'outing' in one form or another. The man who stated that his 'passions are many' in the same prologue sentence in which he offered to 'kiss the rod whene'er you [the audience] point the fault',[10] a man who had one of his greatest stage triumphs playing a brothel madam, and another simulating a sexual encounter between men,[11] was a comedian who traded on a public persona that was on a scale from sexually daring to downright provocative. To do so in an era that was notably troubled by the notion of the actor as representative of masculinity, and which also traded for the first time in the private lives of the celebrated, was dangerous in itself. It was eventually the scenic background of that which would destroy Foote, irrespective of his guilt or innocence. More specifically, it is the clearer plot hinge to Foote's flight from town in 1748: a fugitive from prejudice, rather than a man bored with London, in love with French classical theatre or the dubious charms of Dublin's Smock Alley.

§

Church attendance declined rapidly in the latter half of the eighteenth century, and especially in London. Despite the Wesleyan movement, parodied by Foote among others, and the new religious 'Enthusiasts', who sought a reinvigorated Church, there was no widespread religious revivalism as there had been in the century before or would be in the century after. Georgian Londoners were discovering a new worldliness. The factors that influenced this apparent modernity of thought and action are complex. The Enlightenment was antipathetic to organized religion, of course – the superstitions so derided by the French *philosophes* – and there was much emphasis on personal freedom and freedom of conscience. In this Londoners were closely bound to the American revolutionaries and to French anti-clericalism, though they would not have voiced a connection, and were at the centre of what has recently been described as the First Sexual Revolution,[12] one with its epicentre in Foote's London.

Londoners moved among scientists and industrialists and, perhaps as vitally, among antiquarians and their findings. Where science was positing a godless universe, antiquarians and classicists found a whole world of classical thought on sex that chimed readily with the age. The excavations at Pompeii and Herculaneum only confirmed what many classical antiquarians had been more or less privately preaching: the ancient world had held vastly more tolerant attitudes to sex, to the sex trade, to corporeality, towards sex outside marriage and to sex between men.

When it came to whoring, Europe's capital cities were undoubtedly London, Venice and Paris. Of the three, it was London that had the most widespread and, indeed, commercially successful and conspicuous sex trade. Where the arches of the

Piazza San Marco and the Palais Royal respectively semi-shad-
owed a well-established and successfully corralled sex trade, in
London it was everywhere. 'As soon as the street lamps are lighted,'
noted one slack-jawed foreign visitor, 'they begin to swarm with
street girls, who, well got-up and well dressed, display their attrac-
tions. Certain it is that no place in the world can be compared
with London for wantonness . . . the number of evening and night
prowlers is so unbelievable.'[13] Daniel Defoe decried the same laxity
in the City from the puritan freshfields of Stoke Newington: 'Go
all over the world and you'll see no such impudence as in the
streets of London.'[14] Another foreigner who bothered to note what
Londoners might well have taken for granted observed that 'the
corruption of morals is very great [and] even shows itself in broad
daylight [when] lords and other rich people go in daylight to
houses of debauchery without attempting to make a secret of it'.
It was this, perhaps, that was most striking and most shocking
to foreigners. Everyone knew that young men went to Venice to
enjoy the courtesans as much as the carnival. In London, sex was
on display easily and openly. 'A stranger might think,' wrote one
Londoner, 'that such practices, instead of being prohibited, have
the sanction of the legislature, and that the whole town was one
general stew.'[15] It was easy, in the West End in particular, to begin
to believe that anything goes. Nowhere more so than at the theatre.

The atmosphere in London for those of broad-ranging sexual
taste was not utterly unsympathetic. It was a debauched town,
according to the moralists of the age, but at the same time there
was a distinct ambivalence towards openness and towards what
would now be termed homosexuals. The word itself, coined more
than a century later by a German-Hungarian named Hans Benk-
ert, was barely used in English until the dawn of the twentieth
century. Georgian Londoners talked of Greek love, of Uranians, of
Satodists, inverts and persons of 'contrary sexual instinct' – some
even used the term 'methodists' as a slur against the new religious
Enthusiasts. Yet it has been estimated there were up to thirty
thousand adult male homosexuals in London by the end of the

century, and molly-houses had existed since at least the Restoration. To these the London authorities turned a blind eye, until it suited them not to.

Cruising areas abounded around Foote's West End. To the south of Panton Street, just past his friend Delaval's and James Boswell's lodgings on Downing Square, was the graveyard of St Margaret's, Westminster, whose walls and buttresses served as urinals and as a cottaging venue. There was also Smithfield Market at night, Lincoln's Inn Fields itself, just by the theatre of the same name and featuring what was known as a 'bog-house' for cruising. There was another by the Savoy. There was Covent Garden, once emptied of market traders, where al-fresco sex between the colonnades was a summertime commonplace, and Moorfields, near the molly-houses of Holborn. Sodomite Walk – which, according to Old Bailey trial proceedings, was located (in case you were looking) 'on Upper Moorfield by the side of the wall that joins the watch house and part of the Upper field' – only added to an area from St Paul's to the Barbican to Cheapside that provided sufficient cover and crannies for extra-mural sex to satisfy all tastes, both sexes and even in British weather. If information, anecdotal as it is, has survived along with the legal record of those caught out, it is reasonable to suppose that during some decades of the eighteenth century there was fairly easy tolerance of 'crimes' that had no clear victims. 'Can I not do with my body as I will?' one man is reported as having shouted, when caught with a companion under the portico of the actors' church in Covent Garden.

Then there were the parks – Hyde Park, Kensington Gardens and Birdcage Walk but notably the areas of Green Park and St James's Park, alluringly close to the barracks of the household regiments and their biddable guardsmen. These were frequent scenes of arrest during those periods when the public became gripped by an occasional fit of moral indignation – as organized by the new Society for the Reformation of Manners, which funded prosecutions. Such areas were also the site of the widespread trade in blackmail, where guardsmen threatened to expose or accuse other men of 'sodomitical acts' whether or not they had taken place. Might it be, like the actor Isaac Bickerstaffe or the aristo-cratic sons of the Earl of Denbigh, that a scandal with a guardsman forced Foote to flee London? We cannot know.

With Foote it has proved impossible to elicit clear details of what went on in 1748–9. He was living increasingly in the public domain – a man who had courted controversy and publicity. He was an actor in an era that became troubled by the supposed deviance and in some cases effeminacy of its dramatic heroes. He was accused of being homosexual no more frequently than many other actors of the era – Garrick included – until the 1770s when the attacks on him became more consistent and concerted. But he flaunted an aura of sexual ambiguity all his life. And then, just before his sudden departure from London in 1748, he chose to flaunt himself more conspicuously still: in the company of the controversial transvestite figure of Christopher Smart.

Kit Smart knew Foote through John Delaval – Smart and Delaval had been at Cambridge together – and by the late 1740s Smart was back and forth to London from Pembroke College, *liber absentiae*, beginning to forge the contacts in Grub Street that would later make his name. One of his literary personae, in prose and in live performance, was 'Mrs Midnight', a midwife. He played her, on request, in drag. Mrs Midnight began her life in a transvestite revue, and at some stage in the late 1740s Samuel Foote joined in, also in drag. 'Mr Foote and others invented an entertainment called Mother Midnight,' explained a foe of theirs at the time, 'in which several Geniuses exhibited *surprizing performances*.'[16] They toured London taverns in the 1740s, seemingly late at night, and their act, in modern parlance a 'drag-act', began to feature Sam Foote as Mrs Midnight's niece 'Miss Dorothy Midnight'.[17] Smart and Foote wore expensive dresses that betrayed an interest beyond theatrical profitability. One outfit cost thirteen pounds. This, it must be noted, is within a long comic tradition that stretches back before Shakespeare and forward to modern British pantomime or the cross-dressing of contemporary comic Eddie Izzard, and in no sense can be taken as more of an indicator of sexual preference than of, well, Britishness. Foote had always had an interest in clothes. Smart, on the other hand, later lived semi-openly as a transvestite.[18] However, it seems not to have been their frocks that raised eyebrows but their venues: their 'show' seems to have been performed at molly-houses. As a result of their collaboration, Smart and Foote were understandably tarnished with some innuendo that they were a homosexual couple, and more credibility is given to the possibility that they were – or were considered to be – by the pseudonym 'Mr Toe', accorded to Foote in a benefit performance for Christopher Smart when he was ill.[19] A subsequent invective against Smart and Foote occasioned by the benefit puns repeatedly and lewdly on 'the length of [Sam's] foot', then directly accuses them both of 'buggery', and of 'being part of a coterie of sodomitical'[20] cross-dressing aristocrats. Perhaps it was no more than dangerous comedy. At the time, it was viewed by some as evidence that Foote was transgressive in more ways than the satirical.

Whatever Smart's orientation, he was repeatedly harangued as a 'molly'. Whatever Foote's orientation, he was risking censure and opprobrium by dressing as a woman, no matter the content of his piece with Smart. *Mother Midnight's Oratory*, as this lost revue by Smart and Foote was titled, was highly provocative for a man of the theatre who was recognized and well connected. It might have been the project that tipped Foote just beyond the bounds of acceptability.[21]

In *Nocturnal Revels*, a semi-pornographic guide to the fun to be had in London's West End and collection of anecdotes about the sex-lives of those unable to sue, there are two chapters dedicated largely to Foote. It was not published until 1779, by which time one might write what one wanted about Foote, but refers to a period earlier in the century. In *Revels*, Foote is portrayed as an habitué of Covent Garden brothels and bagnios, but tellingly in the homosocial company of other literary 'geniuses', George Selwyn and Chase Price. In the course of forty pages detailing a debauched evening that features Foote, Selwyn and Price at

Charlotte Hayes's famous 'nunnery' near the piazza, Foote emerges as an ironical non-combatant in the rakes' adventures. He takes no interest in the girls, other than in their madam's assertion that 'a girl might lose her virginity five hundred times' in her establishment for 'a maidenhead was as easily made as a pudding'.[22] The fact that one partner in this brothel-creeping was George Selwyn flags up other possibilities. Selwyn, famous for one of the longest parliamentary careers never to feature a single speech or utterance, was also a cross-dressing bisexual, dabbler in necrophilia and member of the Hellfire Club.[23] His sexual fascination with executions and murderers may have drawn him to Foote in the first place. Chase Price, meanwhile, *one of the most celebrated and ribald wits of his time*', according to one, and the '*Falstaff of the ... age*'[24] according to another, also functioned as a contact between supporters of sexual revolutionary John Wilkes in London and their exiled hero.[25] Foote's depiction as what Boswell described as one of these 'Geniuses of the Town' also places him squarely with the gallants and sexual reprobates of the era, but where *Nocturnal Revels* seeks to titillate with all and any anecdotes on the heterosexual shenanigans of its various heroes, Foote and his pals are noted only as voyeurs. In a quite separate anecdote, but at a similar venue, Foote is recorded as being accosted by Lord Carmarthen, who pointed out to him that 'Mr Foote, your handkerchief is hanging out of your pocket' – a signifier of sexual availability in some London parks and brothels. 'Upon which,' an observer wrote, 'Foote, looking suspiciously round, hurriedly thrust the handkerchief back into his pocket and wittily retorted, "Thank you, my Lord, you clearly know the company [here] better than I do." '[26] The evidence is circumstantial, and open to various interpretations. For historian Laurence Senelick, Foote was 'debilitated' by 'homosexual anxiety'; for Netta Murray Goldsmith he was 'the pitiable victim' of anti-'gay' prejudice; for Kristina Straub he is a 'sexual suspect' whose 'case illustrates the full potential of the actor's vulnerability to homophobia'.[27] For Matthew Kinservik, as with Goldsmith, we are left with the sage point of view that 'It is impossible [for us] to say whether he was heterosexual, homosexual or bisexual', just as it was 'equally impossible for the general public' in Georgian London.[28] Which didn't, however, stop them speculating.

§

Foote's easy rapport with women, actresses in particular, may be read as evidence in either direction on the subject of his sexuality; it was nonetheless a subject of record and remark. His London roundelay had been noticeably masculine since the return to Truro of young Mrs Foote, but as he established himself in the professional theatre, he worked increasingly with women. They were not of that rank of respectable society that Eleanor Foote might have wished for her youngest son, but they were undoubtedly some of the most enticing characters of mid-eighteenth-century London. Peg Woffington had become David Garrick's mistress within a year of the young actor's first launch on the London stage, and exactly as he became acquainted with Foote. She and Foote seemingly met at the Bedford. A Dublin-raised actress, exactly Foote's age, Peg's naturalistic style matched the new fashion and she and the soprano Kitty Clive, along with the wives of Henry Giffard and Charles Macklin, were the reigning queens of the West End. Peg was a celebrity in her own right, by dint of her aquiline beauty and gift for low comedy, but was a seasoned pro in comparison to Foote or Garrick. She had débuted in Dublin in *The Beggar's Opera*, playing Polly Peachum when she was only eleven in a company of child actors called the Lilliputians, and had filled out the breeches role of Sir Harry Wildair in *The Constant Couple* to huge acclaim in 1739 when she first came to London. She became renowned for playing breeches roles – principal boys – or women who, for the purposes of a play's plot, impersonated men. Thomas Davies described her as 'the most beautiful woman that ever adorned the theatre' but her appeal was frankly sexual, and quite a lot about her legs. Over the early years of his career, Foote would appear with her in *The Relapse*, in Colley Cibber's *Love's Last*

Shift, as Dick Amlet in another of Vanbrugh's plays, *The Confederacy*, and as the Younger Loveless opposite her Scornful Lady, in the play of the same name.

When Foote and Garrick were students together under Macklin, Peg was asked to tutor Garrick in the comedy role of Sir Harry Wildair. It was not unusual for actors to 'pass on' roles in this manner or even to teach them in part to students – teaching stage business and potential comedic moments to a new generation and a new star. This particular tuition exercise was only worthy of remark in that it was imparted by a young comedy actress to an up-and-coming actor now more famous as a Shakespearean tragedian. Macklin thought Garrick could do comedy, too, and he was proved right. Peg soon moved in with Garrick, or he with her, at Macklin's house in Bow Street.

Garrick was not Peg's first lover, or indeed possibly her only one at the time. She was unashamedly promiscuous, which Foote teased her about, and trod the boards in an era when to be an actress implied often a duality of careers. Horace Walpole, in a letter to Horace Mann in Italy, passed on a tale then doing the rounds in London that seems to have originated with Foote: 'One night the Earl of Darnley [an admirer of Peg's] told her that she had pleased him so well [in her breeches role on stage] that he should play Five Acts that night as well as she had. She offered to bet him ten guineas that he could not – but he did – and then asked *her* to pay *him*. "No M'Lord," said she in her Dublin lilt and with a wink; "double or quit!" '29

It is uncertain who first rented rooms from Charles Macklin at 6 Bow Street, Peg or Garrick, but in any event, soon enough they were sharing a bed. It was an unconventional domestic arrangement, occasionally misrepresented as a school for actors or indeed as a *ménage à trois* in the full sense, but Woffington and Macklin were never sexually involved and it was only ever Macklin who lectured; his lessons with Foote took place there. Nevertheless, the domestic and professional set-up that Foote experienced in visiting their digs was arrestingly modern. Garrick and Peg split the

Samuel Foote (1720–1777) in his comedy *The Mayor of Garrett*. This Zoffany portrait hung in Foote's house adjacent to his theatre, the Haymarket.

Foote's London was spilling westwards from the old limits of the C[ity]
but centred on Covent Garden (centre left) a[nd]

nd was bounded for him by Westminster and London bridges

s Panton Street and Haymarket homes.

Foote's Irish-born leading lady Peg Woffington was one of the many Dublin stars who were equally at home on the London stage. The miniature she is holding is traditionally taken to be Garrick, her lover when Foote first knew her.

David Garrick as Richard III by Hogarth. Foote, known also as 'the Hogarth of the stage', was a constant satirical thorn in the side of his friend and contemporary, Garrick.

Seaton Delaval near Newcastle, the family seat of the Delavals. Seaton Delaval was the site of wild parties, amateur theatricals and the sort of elaborate practical jokes that later led to Foote's riding accident.

The elder Delaval children: Frank, John, Ned and Rhoda.

Frank Delaval, 'consummate puppy and unprincipled jackanape' according to Lord Chesterfield, and Foote's boon companion in bad behaviour.

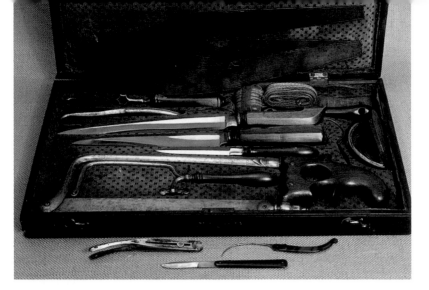

Foote's era, known as the Heroic age of Surgery, led to an increasing number surviving amputation.

The tourniquet as used by Bromfeild.

Foote's prosthesis made by Thomas Addison, surgical instrument and puppet maker. It may have been the world's first fully articulated artificial leg.

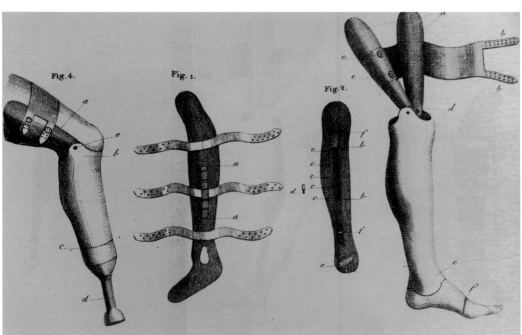

THE RESURRECTION
or an Internal View of the Museum in W—d—m—ll Street, on the last Day

Foote's surgeon friends the Hunter brothers collected anatomical specimens and performed semi-public dissections.

The Lame Lover, written during Foote's convalescence, and the only image of Foote suggesting it was his left leg that was amputated.

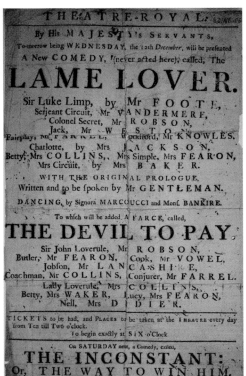

'Mrs Cole', Foote's transvestite role in *The Minor*, was his most enduring comic creation. The play and the part remained popular well into the nineteenth century and Mrs Cole is one certain godmother to the modern panto dame.

household bills – she paid one month, he paid the next. They were both working actors, though soon his salary was vastly outstripping hers – nearly £1,000 a season by 1743 against her regular £160 benefit nights and occasional £50 gratuities from Drury Lane's management for clothes. She and Garrick went their separate ways after about two years.

Kitty Clive, another Irishwoman, also appeared frequently with Foote on stage and she became his main comic foil in his sketches and plays, especially if singing was called for. 'There is no beholding this excellent actress,' wrote one critic, 'without laughing at every turn of her countenance,'[30]and she and Foote discovered an easy rapport in low comedy that led to their creating together the Cadwalladers in Foote's play *The Author*, a coupling Horace Walpole claimed gave Clive the best role of her long life. Her London career had been launched, like Foote's, in 1741, in Thomas Arne's *King Alfred*, in which she had sung 'Rule, Britannia'. Kitty was a noted soprano but it was her comic acting that was most admired, along with her dark-haired beauty and a winning attentiveness to her men, on and off stage. Dr Johnson once said she was his favourite dinner companion because 'Clive, Sir, *always* understands what you say.' She turned to Foote for advice in attempting to parlay her singing and comedy career towards classical acting, but he was not alone in diplomatically advising her to stick to what she was good at. 'Mrs Clive [is] the best Actress in her *Walk*, that I, or perhaps any Man living, has seen,' Foote wrote, in his *The Roman and English Comedy Compared*, 'peculiarly happy in hitting the Humours of Characters in *Low Life* . . . the awkward Forwardness of a Country Girl [or] the ridiculous affected Airs of a Lady's Woman, or the pert Behaviour of an intriguing Chambermaid.'[31]

However, his praise was tempered: one reason Foote thought Kitty ill suited to grand tragic and romantic roles was her stoutness. She battled with her weight most of her life and consequently also with the tight strictures of Georgian corsetry, once resorting to ad-libbing a request for a maid to pick up a love letter on stage as she was unable to bend down. But in the comedy stakes she was the one true competitor to Woffington. Unsurprisingly, perhaps, she and Peg Woffington became rivals on and off stage, as witnessed by Foote. One night when Peg was again in a breeches role she rashly boasted to Mrs Clive that the response of the rapturous Drury Lane crowd proved that 'half the audience' believed her truly to be a man. Kitty retorted, 'And half the audience *knows the contrary*.'[32]

Foote found an easy affinity with actresses that he had not experienced with other women, as partners in comedy and as complicit colleagues in petticoats; after all, a number of his most successful comic creations were female impersonations. But there was more to it than that. Eighteenth-century actresses, like comics, and like notorious authors in Foote's mould, straddled two hemispheres. They toiled in the reality of a business and profession, but also within that other world constructed for them by the gaze and fascination of others; their careers, self-worth and sanity were pitched between these sometimes opposing realms. Although they earned as performers, and in some cases were highly respected for their artistry, comic verve or textual sensitivity, actresses were also on view to a paying public and worked in a profession that had long elided the roles of actress and courtesan. They were, like Foote, beyond respectability. Aristocratic patronage confused matters further. This could be innocent: some wealthy men subscribed regularly to a particular actress's benefit nights. It could be sexually loaded, as was the case for the actress Lavinia Fenton, mistress to the Duke of Bedford and mother of his children. At one extreme were the many actresses who had worked before, during or after their stage careers as Covent Garden prostitutes. At the other was the later Duchess of Bedford. Which is all by way of background to a semi-lost text of the Foote canon, based on his experiences as voyeur and seeming non-combatant in the realm of Georgian actresses, the Green Room.

Foote's ribald play or, rather, skit *The Green Room Squabble* played homage to the broad and dazzling spectrum of actresses in Georgian London with whom he was friends, and to the stage on which these women performed in both senses, as actresses and as courtesans. The world that Foote and his actress friends shared, the Green Room, was where contracts of every sort were negotiated, and where Foote and the rest of the company performed on the alternative stage of their rackety careers. It was also, of course, where men courted actresses, something Foote appears never to have done. Though gentlemen, in the loosest sense, might pay for access to an actress's dressing room, it was the Green Room that served as withdrawing room after the show for actresses, actors and their admirers. Lord Dapper, in Fielding's *Historical Register* of 1736, declines to criticize a play on the principle that he was 'half the play in the green room talking to the actresses', and Dr Johnson famously remarked to David Garrick that though he loved the theatre he feared for his moral well-being in the Green Room 'because the white bosoms of the actresses' who presented themselves there aroused his 'amorous propensities'.[33] One of the most famous Green Room incidents of the Georgian stage was both witnessed and parodied by Foote. It also exemplifies the drama of the locale, and Foote's voyeuristic gaze in the company of his fellow-pleasers: actresses.

Much gossip had swirled around Peg's poor opinion of the actress George Anne Bellamy in the early years of the 1740s when Foote knew them both. George Anne Bellamy, yet another Irish woman on the London stage and discovered by Peg in Dublin, was as famous for her sexual liaisons as her acting. She and Peg were cast together in Lee's *Rival Queens*. George Anne had made a London début as Juliet, but had become better recognized as a fashion-plate after a series of aristocratic protectors bought her clothes, which she wore both off stage and on. These were given or acquired in return for what favours we cannot know. It was not necessarily an indication of indiscretion: some gowns were even handed down from royal ladies in the spirit of patronage. George Anne let it be known that she favoured French gowns and she wore a new one in the Green Room before the opening of *The Rival Queens*, to the consternation of Peg. It was an eye-catching ensemble in yolk-yellow and purple. Peg was wearing straw-yellow, a gown given to her by the Princess of Wales, but so demure in comparison that 'it dwindled to dirt-white under the candle-[light]s'.[34]

'Madam!' Peg was quoted by Foote, among others, as declaring in the Green Room at the first interval. 'I desire you will never more upon any account wear those clothes in the piece we perform tonight.'

George Anne acquiesced, but appeared instead in another gift from the same admirer, 'yet more splendid' and yet more upstaging. She found herself being chased off the Drury Lane stage at the point of Peg's stage dagger and 'the Green Room resounded with . . . thinly veiled allusions to certain diplomats and cabinet ministers who followed in the respective ladies trains'.[35] The two leading ladies of Drury Lane had to be physically removed from the building and never worked together again. Foote parodied all of this in his *Green Room Squabbles* and no one in London needed any further clues that the incident depicted in the skit was that which had become infamous via the gossips of the West End, Foote included. Peg failed to see the joke.

It was a precarious position to be an actress, and few stories ended as well as Lavinia Fenton's with a ducal coronet and equipage. Some actresses went into print, like George Anne Bellamy; others found patrons who would support their retirement, as was the case with Kitty Clive and the besotted Horace Walpole. Peg collapsed and nearly died on stage aged only thirty-seven. Two more found employment in the household staff of Foote, which goes some way to pointing out the likely brevity of an actress's working life, and the protective spirit of Foote towards actresses in his wealthy middle age. As a young man, however, there is no record that he had any affairs, or that he forged with any actress the sort of protector-and-muse relationship that was common among his colleagues, writers, actors and managers. His professional relationship with comediennes, Clive and Woffington especially, was long-standing and mutually profitable, and his admiration for women on the stage is incarnate in the many rounded and sympathetic roles he wrote for them. Even so, there is probably further likelihood, evidenced in his apparent distance from physical intimacy with any woman during his twenties and thirties, even within the louche environment of the Georgian stage, that women were not primarily his taste. It is only surmise to acknowledge also that those who project feminine sexuality for whatever professional purposes – and this would often include actresses then as now – often seem to forge close rapports and long-term friendships with men who offer a non-sexual complicity . . . and useful advice on clothes.

§

Gay or straight, fugitive from prejudice or restive adventurer, Foote left London in 1748, packing up his permanent London home, and headed west towards Dublin. It was a journey he had made before, but only for brief months in the past. This time he would be away from the London stage for several years, in Dublin and then Paris. It may be that he left without a clear plan of action, and was warned while in Dublin that lying low for longer might be opportune. He might also have been facing up to the *ennui* that plagues those who have enjoyed very early success and celebrity in the performing arts. Despite Dr Johnson's avowal, Foote may have tired of London. The city and those Londoners who had been turning a blind eye to his dangerous behaviour certainly seemed to have tired of him.

§

At noon on 17 March 1748 Foote began his first foray into the theatrical world of Dublin as a stand-up. It was a matinée – again, a theatrical first in Ireland – of his *Diversions of the Morning* or *A Dish of Chocolate*, which had been marketed in London as *Tea*. Foote had come to Dublin in 1744, with Garrick and Peg Woffington when they were first in love, and he performed there again in 1757 and 1760.[36] Yet his 1748 season was his most adventurous, and most comically daring.

He travelled via Bath and Bristol, then took the sea crossing along the Avon past the scene of his uncle's murder, which had brought him fame, fortune and infamy. It was a route with which he became familiar. Dublin and London at this period were twin theatre capitals, their thespian communities intricately linked, and like so many of the Irish men and women who worked the London theatres, Foote found further fame in Dublin. Henry Woodward of Covent Garden, for instance, was in Dublin that season of 1748, along with George Anne Bellamy, the 'tolerable actress', who had been Woodward's lover in London. Thomas Sheridan, father of Richard Brinsley, ran Dublin's Theatre Royal, referred to simply by its address, 'Smock Alley'. He had just played Hamlet, but similarly was back and forth to London along with Irish stars, like Peg Woffington, Charles Macklin and Spranger Barry. If Dublin was the junior sibling in this familial relationship, by virtue of smaller population, smaller audiences and smaller opportunities for actors, it was nonetheless a vital part of the theatrical economy of the English-speaking world and the seedbed of a disproportionate amount of writing and performing talent.

The Smock Alley company Foote later joined would eventually première many of the most famous works of George Farquhar, Oliver Goldsmith and Richard Brinsley Sheridan that have survived as part of the canon of classic 'English' comedies. And it was on this stage that Garrick had first played Hamlet as a try-out before London. It has been estimated that up to 25 per cent of London actors had played Dublin at some point in their careers, and many were originally Irish. Similarly, at any given time, nearly 10 per cent of those on stage in Dublin might be accounted London names, of varied provenance.

Accompanying Foote as he sailed west towards Ireland was an eighteen-year-old actor called Tate Wilkinson, who has left us an unabashed account of his professional and personal infatuation with the comedy star Foote on the road, and especially in Dublin. 'If ever one person possessed the talents of pleasing more than another,' Tate wrote, 'Mr Foote was certainly the man,'[37] and Tate's career followed later in the shadow of Foote's as mimic, comedian and writer. Accompanying him also on the Dublin trip, bizarre to relate, were various of Foote's marionettes, commissioned from Mr Addison of Hanover Street, Long Acre, and soon to be tested in front of an Irish audience. Foote travelled always with his collection of books and a London-made portmanteau. It comprised a concealed lifting lid revealing a mirror, which in turn hid a 'silver soap box, brush case . . . five bottles with tops, strop and razors' from the prying attentions of highwaymen. Further compartments revealed 'a neat chas'd oaty colour'd gold toothpick case' and a 'powder knife',[38] with which Foote could shave off chalk, kohl and paint powder to mix with lard for theatrical makeup. This, and his famous wardrobe of brightly coloured silks, allowed him to present himself in Dublin, and at its famed Smock Alley theatre, in the style by which he was recognized.

Foote's name preceded him. London papers were widely read in Dublin, and many of the theatre community had seen or worked with him already. Aged twenty-eight in 1748, Foote had already spent a quarter of his life constantly in the company of Dubliners. His affection for Ireland and the Irish remained undiminished all his life – it was simply part of what it was to be on the stage. 'They possessed more native wit,' he used to say, 'than any other peoples,'[39] and the Celtic spirit, broadly speaking, suited Foote's own: the music, the oral literary tradition and the drinking. Asked years later if he had seen Cork on his Hibernian travels, Foote replied, 'No, Sir, though I have seen a great many *drawings* of it.'[40] He was also widely quoted as quipping that 'Before visiting Dublin I never knew what English beggars did with their cast-offs.'[41] The slur appears to have been in riposte to Thomas Sheridan's teasing him about his dandy over-dress when he first saw him on the banks of the Liffey outfitted in orange and green silk, rather than a true reflection of any disrespect to the Dublin audience. Then again, even Sheridan once said that Smock Alley crowds could look rough.

The company at Dublin's Theatre Royal is thought to have numbered about twenty-five (handbills tended not to list dancers, musicians and apprentice actors), which represented a core body about half the size of Drury Lane or Covent Garden. Henry Giffard and his wife, Mrs Lydall, introduced Foote to many of the Smock Alley actors. One reason the London and Dublin actors all knew each other was that Dublin employment was a temporary haven for a London performer who had fallen foul of a West End management, or who wanted to profit from a role that had already proved a commercial hit in London, and vice versa. This was the case, for example, for Theophilus Cibber in 1743 and David Garrick in 1745. Some roles were 'owned' by one star whose name did not travel so were played by another elsewhere. Susannah Cibber, as an instance, triumphed as Polly in *The Beggar's Opera* in Dublin only once Peg Woffington had based herself in London, whereas in London the role was 'owned' by Kitty Clive. Samuel Foote's London impressionist satires might therefore have looked unlikely to triumph in Dublin, had it not been for this linked community of celebrities, Foote's own literary notoriety and his ability to reinvent his parodies as Dublin satires, compounded with the whiff of whatever London scandal had obliged his peregrinations in the first place.

Foote advertised to the nobility and gentry of Dublin a performance known as 'Tea' or 'Chocolate in the London manner'. Everyone in theatre circles in Dublin had heard about his *Tea Party*, as *Diversions of a Morning* was more widely known, but it was a risky venture. Described as 'an exhibition which consisted of mimicry, wherein he imitated or took off the voice and manner of most of the performers in England', it is unclear quite what the Dublin audience was meant to make of it. 'I never could find out,' one bemused Dubliner opined, 'what analogy there was between Tea and the talent for mimicry,'[42] which rather missed the point, and was perhaps the least of Foote's marketing problems. Until he could reacquaint himself with the newest players on the Dublin stage and the idiosyncrasies of Dublin's politicians and celebrities, many of the jokes of *Tea* would be lost on his audience. A Dublin paper, *The Reformer*, advertised rashly on the day Foote opened that he would supplant the reigning king of Dublin's Theatre Royal at Smock Alley, Thomas Sheridan, 'by exhibiting Entertainments still more monstrous and incoherent' than Mr Sheridan It was an audacious boast. Foote had landed in the middle of a theatrical turf war, and was not as well set up to triumph as he had imagined.

'There is,' as Macklin wrote, 'geography in humour,' and it was, as it remains, a challenge and a joy to an actor to respond to the differing ways jokes work – or don't work – as they travel. Foote had played Dublin before, admittedly in plays rather than in plays about plays and players, and set about concentrating his 1748 act on the personalities that he knew from London but whose fame was as great or greater in Ireland: Woffington, Clive, Barry, Macklin and even the dramatist Oliver Goldsmith. These were at least Dublin celebrities, their mannerisms and voices recognizable to the Irish audience, but an imported London impressionist mocking the great names of Irish theatre was taken, by some, as a sort of insult. Foote moved on to locals as and when he met them or became aware of their fame.

Dublin in 1748 was Europe's sixth largest city, after London, Paris, Constantinople, Moscow and Rome. London was vastly larger than any by population, and Dublin, by contrast, was compact. It measured, by one survey of 1747,[43] only nine and three-quarter miles around. Many of the buildings that make central Dublin still an elegant neo-classical capital were being built in the years just preceding Foote's years there – Trinity Library, the Parliament House, the Lying-in-Hospital – and the new grid perspectives of smart houses[44] and regular spacious streets all date from this period. At least a quarter of it had been built in the previous twenty years. Between 1724 and 1764 Dublin was 'built afresh',[45] or so it was said by contemporaries.

The area where the theatres flourished, however, was old Dublin, nearer the quayside and the castle. The Theatre Royal, Smock Alley, had been rebuilt in 1733 on a cramped site near the bustle of the river Liffey – by common consent 'the most convenient situation in the Entertainment of the Town'.[46] It was intimate, elegantly designed and acoustically pleasing, with the novel additions of slips or lattices high above the front boxes that allowed low-price ticket holders to be close to the stage. Its royal status attested to the relationship with London and, of course, Dublin's position as the second of the three royal capitals, then, of the British Isles. The side boxes opened directly onto the street towards 'a spacious thoroughfare for coaches'.[47] Rich and poor alike approved of the theatre. For a while there was an 'alternative' Theatre Royal, grandly decorated but unloved by actors and audience, on Aungier Street near the castle, but in 1743 Thomas Sheridan, theatre manager, and sometime orator and actor, united the Smock Alley and Aungier Street companies under one patent. Almost as a mirror to London, then, Dublin had a duopoly of Theatres Royal, challenged by occasional newcomers and comedy houses. There was a sort of Haymarket comedy house in the form of the small theatre first on Capel Street and, later, on Crow Street. The Crow Street theatre was housed in what had been, in effect, a music hall and played to the lower end of the market. Capel Street, on the other hand, took £150 on a good night at the box office, which was as much as Smock Alley. The theatres were licensed by the Lord Mayor on behalf of the Crown.

It was to the 'little playhouse' on Capel Street that Foote went to perform in 1748, in competition with Smock Alley. It opened onto a small alley between 136 and 137 Capel Street and was squeezed dangerously into a little strip of land fifty by a hundred feet. Candle-lit, cramped and wood-lined, the theatre required 'certificates of the best Master Builders'[48] to calm audience fears that it was a firetrap. Nevertheless, because it was born as an alternative venue when the two Theatres Royal merged, Capel Street had a rebellious aura from the start. 'Like an aggrieved

People in the State of Rebellion,' wrote one, 'this hasty building was erected in the great Cause of Liberty!'[49] Foote had landed on a perfect venue for his subversive style of comedy.

Capel Street had recently been home to a company of over-sized puppets, 'artificial comedians', as they were advertised,[50] similar to that which Foote had used to comic effect already in London. As with Foote's puppet work in London, the marionettes were a satirical take on the 'celebrities of the age', deliberately advertised, in competition to Smock Alley, as if they were star names, and in a style in direct parody of Thomas Sheridan's verbose playbills for the Theatre Royal. So when Foote opened at Capel Street in March 1748 he brought a London satirical form to a house that was well suited to essaying alternative-comedy styles of theatre. Dubliners flocked to see him, and his first clear success was with a satirical puppet show, to the immediate chagrin of Thomas Sheridan.

The speed and intensity, however, of the counter-attack from Sheridan and from the *Dublin Journal,* edited by George Faulkner, demonstrate Foote's impact. The *Journal* dubbed him a 'dancing Punch' and a national insult for, seemingly, attacking the Irish patriot Charles Lucas. In retort, Foote made George Faulkner, who had only one leg, the subject of a series of 'one leg too few' gibes and sketches. The *Reformer*, meanwhile, another Dublin coffee-house sheet, sided with Foote against Sheridan and Smock Alley, supporting the little Capel Street satire of Dublin characters despite its English star. The press spat became known as the Dublin Chocolate War. To some small extent, the production and paper one supported signalled also an affiliation with one or other side of the Dublin gentry – those in favour of home rule and those aligned with London politics. Ironically, the Londoner, Foote, found himself as lead comedian in 'a company . . . zealous for their Country's [Ireland's] Honour'.[51]

'The attention of the [Dublin] publick,' runs one anonymous Irish letter in the British Library manuscripts collection, 'has been taken up lately by the two rival theatres, the old one in Smock

Alley and the new one under the direction of Mr Foot [*sic*] in
Capel Street, but the last is in the greatest esteem at present, Mr
Foote having played ... to as crowded Audiences as ever were
known.'[52] The *Reformer* insisted that Foote was 'supplanting' the
manager of Dublin's Theatre Royal and risking the profitability of
the patent houses, but the Smock Alley company simply put their
own London star, Woodward, into a hastily convened afterpiece
called *A Dish of His* Own *Chocolate* and ran head to head against
Foote, to the evident delight of George Anne Bellamy, Woodward's
co-star and lover. Foote was, she wrote, driven from Ireland
'precipitately'.[53] This was not quite the case, but even so, Woodward's *Chocolate* (and *Coffee* and *Tea*, as it was variously advertised)
became so popular that other actors paid him ten guineas a night
to add it as an afterpiece to their own benefit performances.[54]

For as long as he was there, Foote relished the opportunity to
rework *Tea* for the Dublin audience. As in London, part of the fun
was not quite knowing who would appear as themselves, and who
would be impersonated by Foote. One unlikely subject of his satire
was the Anglo-Irish bluestocking Letitia Pilkington, sometime
friend of Jonathan Swift and newly arrived back in Dublin after
many years in London. Her only play, *The Turkish Court* or *The
London Prentice*, was mounted at Capel Street during Foote's time
there, and he seems to have contemplated taking a role in it.
A manuscript scrap filed under his name in the Dublin archives
records that Mrs Pilkington 'lived very unhappily with her husband
and separated when he discovered a gentleman in her bedchamber
... after this affair she ... raised a considerable subscription on
her memoirs', which is in part true, and exactly what she was
about in 1748. 'This unhappy female,' the anonymous manuscript
continues less accurately, 'died in great penury having had recourse
to the bottle.'[55] What became of her planned benefit night in
collaboration with Foote is unknown.

Little by little, Sam found his footing in Dublin with his semi-
improvised satires, adding more local colour and dropping London
references if they failed to register. Word spread back to London

that the scapegrace Foote had found a new home in Dublin. By Christmas 1748, Garrick, at dinner with Dr Johnson, heard that Foote had been horsewhipped by an outraged Dublin apothecary who had seen himself depicted on stage. He expressed wonder that anyone should show so much resentment. Surely, he opined, Foote had 'a sort of licence for such liberty [in London and] nobody ever thought it worth his while to quarrel with him'.

Johnson quipped back, 'I am glad to see that Foote is rising in the world.'[56]

Foote might have been avoiding London but, like any West End actor coming to Dublin, he was also there for the money. Dublin allowed an author-actor like Foote to benefit not only from roles that had been seen already in London but also from Irish editions of the printed text. A playwright in London would contractually receive the box-office profits from the third, sixth and ninth performance of their plays. In Dublin the same applied, with an additional profit from benefit nights, in Foote's case as both writer *and* actor. Special lighting was usually a feature of such evenings – beeswax candles rather than tallow, oil-lamp footlights, special seating to allow for more hooped dresses in the pit, the creation of boxed areas within the pit in which meals were served, extra musical pieces, specially written prologues, epilogues and, in Foote's case, one-off impersonations of benefactors who were expected to be in the auditorium. It drummed up support and publicity for the published text, as well as personally profiting the playwright. It was also, like any gala, a night of extra buzz and bustle, the ideal moment to try out new business on stage. Profits could be considerable and certainly were for Foote in Dublin. One Foote benefit with an epilogue commissioned from Jonathan Swift was considered disappointing in raising a mere £73 profit – by the 1740s they usually netted at least £190, and, when directed towards charitable ends, had been known to release more than 140 debtors from a single night's takings.[57]

The Dublin-based actors were understandably equivocal about all this. A London star like Foote setting up camp for a season in

Dublin creamed off potential benefit takings, especially with his unique appeal as impersonator of those attending. The scramble then for audience numbers and benefit-night profits, the Chocolate Wars, was not the only skirmish to enliven Foote's time in Dublin. He also found, as an author, that he was pitched into the uncomfortable business of the rival Dublin and London publishing cultures, which was one reason he fell out with and parodied Faulkner in the first place. George Faulkner, a 'fat little man with a large well powdered wig and brown clothes', in Thomas Sheridan's memorable sketch of him, was well known around Dublin. Foote first clashed with him after his impersonation of him in *Tea*, but found in him eventually the inspiration for not one but two stage characters and two plays, as well as a combatant in a publishing war over rights. Regrettably for the one-legged Faulkner, his business was that of printing pirated London plays, novels and scientific works.

Faulkner was 'super-eminent in the kingdom of Ireland, and the printer of the *Dublin Journal*',[58] having founded his reputation on his publishing relationship with Jonathan Swift and his newspaper, which espoused Swift's politics and his literary style in weekly 'Paragraphs' penned by Faulkner. He lived in central Dublin, quite near Smock Alley. He was also in the forefront of the business of publishing Irish editions without respect to the original London copyright agreements. He had, one Dubliner wrote, 'a solemn intrepidity of egotism and a daring contempt of absurdity', but was frequently 'the butt and buffoon of [all Dublin]'.[59] He was, in other words, sufficiently akin to Foote in personality and recklessness that they were perhaps fated to come to blows. Unblessed in love and life, Faulkner had been injured by a falling shop sign, and in 1730 had had to have his leg amputated as a result of a gangrenous infection. Samuel Foote would later regret his stage impersonation of the afflicted gentleman as all too prescient of his own later misfortune, but in Dublin they clashed over the rights to Foote's published works.

Copyright was a new concept in British law and at the time only a few decades old. A book imported from London could be expensive for Irish readers, both due to the transportation and an importation tax, which persisted between Great Britain and Ireland despite their being subject under one crown. Irish printing costs were much lower than London's so Irish booksellers could produce copies at a much lower cost than the authentic London editions. They might, or might not, address the business of the London copyright, or be faithful to the original. Foote's works exist, for instance, in the collection of Trinity College Library, in both London and Dublin editions – the latter conspicuously better bound and, where it can be ascertained, sold initially at lower cost. It seems Foote did not profit from the Dublin editions. Samuel Richardson, conversely, had a copyright arrangement with Faulkner for his novel *Clarissa*, but was pirated by others. London playwrights, like Foote, were particularly vulnerable in Dublin, as demand for their play texts would be instantaneous if the show proved a hit, favouring the fast production of pirated Dublin editions that earned them no money. At the same time, unlike London-based authors, actor-playwrights on the Dublin stage were far more likely to notice the illicit trade, and repine their lost earnings. Foote decided to take on Faulkner, as easy butt of a stage routine, first as a one-legged marionette, then as by Foote himself, then in epistolary contest over the business of royalty payments.

Foote was not the first or only author so to do. Samuel Richardson freely distributed *An Address to the Public* to protest against his treatment by Faulkner and other Irish printers. Faulkner found himself open to ridicule, by Foote and Richardson, for trying to maintain his relationship with the Dublin government and literary friends like Swift while simultaneously profiting from literary piracy when it suited him. He was blackballed, as a result, when he applied to a London based literary-scientific society, but his prominence rose over the years due to his secondary career as a public speaker. This, together with his pronounced lisp and noted limp, made him an easy and an alluring target for Foote on stage.

Foote's character Peter Paragraph first appeared in his play *The Orators*, seemingly written in Dublin, and later, too, in a companion piece *The Trial of Samuel Foote for a Libel against Peter Paragraph*, which was never published but appears in Tate Wilkinson's papers[60] as one of Foote's great Dublin successes. Paragraph is a one-legged publisher, with a lisp.

The main satirical targets of Foote's *The Orators* – his greatest Dublin hit, which exists in various forms – were Faulkner and Thomas Sheridan. Sheridan was increasingly devoting his impressive energies less to actor-managing and instead towards elocution; 'the present fashionable taste for oratory', as *Lloyd's Evening Post* declared, being the bane of mid-eighteenth-century Dublin life. Sheridan instructed on classical rhetoric and voice production. Perhaps it was no surprise that Dublin actors were at the forefront of the new interest in the spoken arts. Macklin charged for lessons in London, and politicians were adjured by the King to watch his oratory and learn. Sheridan claimed 'a right Elocution . . . could cure all the ills of venality in public as well as private life'. One reviewer remarked that 'One might imagine that he considers elocution as the consummation of all earthly perfection and that even the virtues of the heart depend on the utterance of the tongue and the gesticulation of the body.'[61] Foote, adept at rhetoric himself, loved nothing more than to mock orators – and those who taught elocution.

Foote advertised *The Orators* in typical style, not as a play but as a *Course of Comic Lectures on English Oratory*, in imitation of Sheridan's lectures and Faulkner's books on the subject. To confuse and amuse further, of the various roles he played, there was one in drag, Lady Pentweazle, a character that harked back to his time with Christopher Smart and the transvestite oratory of Mother Midnight and her niece.

Act II of *The Orators* is a trial, at which Peter Paragraph appears, 'avid of his chance to talk about himself, his paper, his aristocratic friends, his charm with the ladies'.[62] It was all easily recognizable as Faulkner, even down to his voluble assertions that he was a ladies' man, despite his lost limb, which, indeed, he sometimes boasted had been lost as he escaped from a jealous husband.[63] Faulkner's friend Lord Chesterfield suggested the printer bring an immediate action against Foote: 'Would it be amiss,' he wrote, 'that you should . . . either by way of stricture or contempt or by bringing an action against him . . . show some spirit upon this occasion?'[64] Faulkner took the bait, and the implied warning, too, that a challenge to Foote in the courts was tempered by the admission that the impersonation must be true to life. Foote was charged and bailed with security of £400 from his grateful Dublin audience. An injunction nevertheless was laid against the play being performed, which, reckless as ever, Foote immediately disobeyed and 'not only most daringly performed *The Orators* several times since [at Smock Alley] but wrote and spoke a poetical address'[65] in which he made the attack upon Faulkner even clearer, 'with greater wit than discretion', according to the *Dublin Advertiser*.

'From the obvious sentiments of the court, and this additional contempt thereto', it was assumed that Foote would be 'sentenced either to the pillory or to a public whipping'. Neither of these was forthcoming, though Foote ended up having to forgo his bail as well as paying damages to Faulkner, thus eventually obliterating the bulk of his 1748–9 profits. As Lord Chesterfield had intimated, whatever the courts awarded Faulkner, the play was likely to prove successful, and therefore damaging, and the trial only served to publicize it. Smock Alley, when Foote went to perform it there (Sheridan was no longer manager), prepared itself for 'anarchy and uproar' – exactly what a Dublin audience really looked for at the theatre. The resultant comedy, based on the audience's knowledge of the personality, trials and talents of Samuel Foote, is one of the clearest examples of Foote's manipulation of his 'criminal' celebrity and the theatre. This became a moment of comedic gold that was long remembered by contemporaries:

> When Peter Paragraph was called upon to give evidence [in Act II of *The Orators*, as played by Foote] no Peter appeared – he was called again, but the second had no more effect than the first. It was then thought that George Faulkner's threats

had intimidated Foote from performing, and the audience (according as they were [sympathetic] to either party) were ready to break out into murmurs or triumph, just as a third summons brought Foote before them – there was such a striking resemblance in the person, and so laughable an extravagance of the manners of Faulkner that before the opposers could settle themselves for an opposition, he got sufficient time to apologize to the court for his absence by assuring them that he had been detained at his lawyer's, in giving instructions to bring an action against a rascally fellow called Foote who, by a vile imitation of his voice and figure had brought him on the Dublin stage.[66]

It brought the house down. It must indeed have been a very compelling imitation of Faulkner, as some remained entirely convinced that they had not seen Foote but Faulkner himself on stage. This is evidenced by the story of Faulkner's attempt to incite a theatre riot. Having failed in the courts to win more than ineffectual injunctions and some money, Faulkner sought instead to ruin the play and his cameo in it by having it hissed off stage by a paid mob. He hired a 'hunger of Dublin ragamuffins', whom he supplied with a meal and a 'shilling apiece and the promise of more tomorrow', if they hissed Foote off the stage of Smock Alley. One might imagine Faulkner's confusion and chagrin therefore to find that the play was greeted on this next outing at the Theatre Royal with even more applause than before, and roundly praised by the critics. The next day the young Dubliners appeared at Faulkner's – he had a house near the new Irish Parliament – and were bemused to be refused payment:

'Plase yer honour [their young leader explained], we did all we could, for the actor-man had heard of us, and did not come on at all, at all. And so we had nobody to hiss. But when we saw yer honour's own dear self come on, we did clap, indeed we did, and showed you all the respect and honour in our power. And so yer honour won't forget us because yer honour's enemy was afraid to come and left yer honor to yer own dear self.'[67]

Perhaps Faulkner should have paid for seats with a better view.

Neither could Foote leave it there. Such was the furore surrounding the play, the trial and the character of Peter Paragraph that he decided to add another act, played sometimes as an afterpiece on its own and titled with nonchalant self-reference, *The Trial of Samuel Foote Esq., for a libel on Peter Paragraph*. The play takes place in the Four Courts in Dublin – the Irish equivalent of the Court of King's Bench in London – where Foote has been arraigned for libel and slanderous impersonation against Faulkner. In the piece Foote played both the lawyer, Demur, and afterwards (slipping off the barrister's gown and wig) appeared as himself, Sam Foote, in the dock. It played, once again, upon his notoriety as a former lawyer turned crime writer and actor. It allowed, him, once again, to forage the middle ground between imagined drama and the audience's appreciation of reality. He also impersonated Faulkner and the real judge.[68] It ended, perforce, with Foote's acquittal, whereupon he asks the judge if he may read out 'a few couplets' that he has 'thrown together'. He then read out verses entitled *Mr Foote's Address to the Public*, in imitation of or homage to Samuel Richardson's attack on Faulkner.

As a comic and literary coup it could hardly have gone better for him in Dublin. He triumphed over the well-connected Faulkner, despite falling foul of the law. He turned one small joke and impersonation into two theatrical sensations, building upon the added notoriety of being taken to court and losing. And he ended it all with a comic ditty that appeared to stand him shoulder to shoulder with the author of *Clarissa* as a clarion for free speech and authorial rights. The Trinity College archives contain a hand-scribbled note from one who witnessed it all, but written with the benefit of some years' hindsight.

Faulkner prosecuted Mr Foote the actor for exhibiting his character on the public stage [and] the matter was tried [and] after a long hearing a verdict with damages was given in favour of Mr Faulkner ... Mr Faulkner was lame in one leg occasioned by a fall from the outside of his house near parliament when it was [a] building [site] this lameness was one of the peculiarities imitated by Foote, of whom, when he afterwards lost his leg by an accident, Faulkner used to say it was 'A Judgement on him by Providence'.[69]

For many in Dublin, Samuel Foote was remembered always for his impersonation and his gulling of his one-legged publisher. Faulkner, of course, had some of the last laughs, as he continued to publish – copyright-free and to huge profits – the works of Samuel Foote, with, after his amputation, a small graphic image of a severed foot penned by the young Thomas Rowlandson.[70]

It was in Dublin also that Foote decided to introduce Tate Wilkinson to the world, and where a relationship that informs a good deal of source material on Foote originated. Wilkinson later wrote extensive memoirs, notably about his management of the northern circuit of English theatre. But his career began with Foote, and in Dublin. Wilkinson, part Welsh, part Northumbrian, adored Foote and, some have speculated, was his lover. His later *Memoirs* and *The Wandering Patentee* are unabashed in their admiration for Sam, professionally and personally. In Dublin, Wilkinson writes, 'Foote was my chief food.'[71] His very early career in London had been launched in imitation of Foote, as 'A Gentleman never seen before' in a minor role in Garrick's *Lethe* at Drury Lane, but it was soon apparent that his real skill lay in impersonation and mimicry. It was said he could imitate Garrick's voice and also Foote's sufficiently to fool the companies at all three subsequent Theatres Royal. By the time he travelled to Dublin with Foote, he was already being criticized as 'a mere mimic's mimic',[72] an acolyte of Foote rather than a proper actor, and there was certainly jealousy and discontent within the Drury Lane company at the young actor's close relationship to Dublin's latest star.

Garrick referred to him and Foote together, with what precise meaning is unclear, as 'The Exotics'.[73] When they had arrived in Dublin together, Wilkinson had fallen ill with some unspecified fever and Foote had nursed him back to health. The form of Foote's offer to Wilkinson to join him on his westward journey was typical of his occasional insinuations against Garrick. He told young Wilkinson that Garrick would only cast him as 'the hobby-horse in *The Rehearsal*' but that he, Foote, could 'fix him' with 'genteel terms' with Mr Tom Sheridan in Dublin.[74] Foote was true to his word once Wilkinson had returned to health in Dublin, and his later memoirs are a testament to what it was to bask – albeit briefly – in the high regard of both Foote and the Dublin public. He acted with Foote in *Diversions of the Morning*, but made the capital error, 'elated with the applause of the audience', of imitating Foote himself, in front of Foote, on stage before a Dublin audience. 'He hit him off so successfully,' one critic wrote, 'that many voices from the Pit cried out "Foote outdone!"' Foote himself moved from the stage to one of the side boxes for Wilkinson's next set, and acknowledged the applause of the audience and their enjoyment of seeing the mimic mimicked. Backstage afterwards, however, he remonstrated with Wilkinson for having overstepped the mark of a junior company member, and someone Foote had tried to help, with 'all the irritation,' Tate wrote, 'of offended genius'.[75]

Nevertheless, the Dublin public had warmed to Tate Wilkinson and he was offered by Sheridan the extraordinary accolade of giving his first King Lear – he was in his early twenties – and his Zamti, in *The Orphan of China*. Rashly he accepted Sheridan's offer that he play these as benefit evenings within days of Foote's own at Crow Street. 'Mr Foote,' he later recalled, 'with his *Tragedy à la Mode* [the afterpiece] . . . was not well supported . . . the house did not amount to above one hundred pounds,' whereas Tate's own benefit night four days later, despite heavy snow in Dublin, 'overflowed from every part . . . and made 172 pounds'. Foote was not pleased. Wilkinson followed up this slight to his mentor's reputation and pocket by scoring a huge hit in James Townley's *High Life Below Stairs*, being asked to give a command performance to the Duke and Duchess of Bedford, and by the end of the season, Foote was treating him as a 'perfect stranger' when they met strolling in the nearby Trinity College Gardens.[76] It was soon enough forgiven and forgotten, but it surely was 'a striking instance', wrote Wilkinson, of how touchy Foote could be about competition, and in particular the success of friends, which 'galled, mortified and enraged'[77] him. Eventually, once Foote left town, Wilkinson would take over the Foote leads in *Diversions* or *A Dish of Tea*.

Foote was and remained a Dublin star. He made repeated trips back over the Irish Sea, both via Bristol and the more northerly route that became faster through the eighteenth century, up to Parkgate on the river Dee and across the Irish Sea past Anglesey. In Dublin he came to be received not only as a 'very eminent dramatic writer', according to William Cooke, 'but as a man of wit and pleasantry; and as such he was noticed by the Lord Lieutenant and the principal nobility and gentry of the capital, at whose tables he was a constant guest. He always respected the people of Ireland, and spoke of their good humour and hospitality with a kind of congenial delight.'[78] He understood Irish humour well enough even to risk on stage at Smock Alley 'Before visiting Dublin I never knew what English beggars did with their cast-offs',[79] which by repute brought the house down. More pertinently, Dublin's literary and theatrical interconnectedness with London helped forge careers as diverse as those of Goldsmith, Thomas and Richard Brinsley Sheridan, John O'Keeffe and later Dion Boucicault and even Oscar Wilde. Foote's experience therefore as sometime star of the Dublin stage puts him in line with one important truism about English stage comedy: it is very often Irish.

His Dublin seasons, from the 1740s to the 1760s, did not merely replicate and reiterate for profit his London successes. He also embedded himself in two important Dublin debates – the rivalry between the Smock Alley Theatre Royal and the Capel Street and Crow Street pretenders (which would, eventually, form the crucible of a national theatre of Ireland and a truly independent theatrical

economy), and the publishing scandal of George Faulkner's copyright infringement. In so doing, he high-wired once again between
show-trial and show-biz, using the one to help sell the other, and
emerged victorious in both the courts of justice and public opinion.
Lord Chesterfield remarked that the publisher Faulkner, who
might have made Foote his 'Foot-stool', had instead only made
himself look foolish for, after all was said and done, 'Socrates had
never prosecuted Aristophanes as Faulkner had Foote, merely 'for
having attempted to ridicule him'.[80]

§

There is very little extant correspondence of Foote with any of his
friends or family for the period he was back and forth between
Dublin and France – through 1749 and possibly as late as 1752.
Tate Wilkinson claimed that Foote 'was not seen [in London] from
the spring of 1748 til at Drury Lane in October and November
of 1753', though this was untrue. For one thing, he was back in
London in April 1749 for the première of what was, in truth, his
first proper play. *The Knights*, premièred eventually on 3 April 1749
but written earlier, was perhaps the best regarded of his proper
plays and is often cited therefore as Foote's first *bona fide* piece of
theatre writing – Goldsmith and Sheridan were later admirers.
The play was, however, in its way also stand-up in that it relied
on the impressionist skills of Foote, and on a blurring of distinction
between him as actor, impressionist and celebrity. But there were
at least full roles for other actors. Foote was billed as taking the
role of one of the eponymous knights, 'Sir Penurious Trifle', but
also as one 'Mr Hartop', who is obliged to impersonate Penurious
within the usual confusion structures of eighteenth-century comedy. We hear about Penurious from others and from Hartop, but
wait in vain for his actual entrance. He is one of the largest off-
stage characters in English drama in that, Godot-like, he never
makes his vaunted appearance but is known only via Hartop's
impersonation. The delineation between 'Foote [as] himself, [as]
Sir Penurious [performed by Hartop] and Hartop' was, according

to one critic, the primary joy of the performance, playing as it did with Foote's skills as impersonator and his background in 'one-man epics'. Audiences loved to watch him switch characters, and then return to himself, as he had done to great effect in *An Auction of Pictures*, an audience being rarely more flattered than when it feels itself in on the joke with the performer. The joke was further informed by the enigma surrounding Foote's personality, disappearance and his sudden reappearance in London, performing, as he was, not quite as himself at all, or in the lead character he had written, but as another character impersonating the lead.

The two eponymous heroes of *The Knights* and also Hartop were based on characters Foote knew – or so he boasted, 'neither vamped from antiquated plays nor pilfered from French farces, not the baseless beings of a poet's brains'.[81] But he refused to explain who they were, allowing London audiences to play a guessing-game that, in turn, worked its usual magic at the box office. *The Knights* involved in addition an extended parody of Italian opera, something achieved to more lasting effect in *The Beggar's Opera* of 1728, but Foote's was equally admired. It featured, eccentrically, a duet of castrato cats, which became a high point of the evening, and crowds once again flocked east to Goodman's Fields for the spectacle when the play moved there. The show-stopping duet was performed by Mr Shuter, a comic actor and singer, and a Mr Harris, who became known as 'Cat Harris'[82] for his singular skill – hitherto unprofitable to him – in feline impersonation. On one occasion Harris went missing and was discovered and retrieved from the Minories, haunt of rougher trade around the Tower of London, drunk and no longer in possession of his breeches. His whereabouts had been ascertained by an understandably flustered prompter – no one else could perform the cat duet – by the expedient of caterwauling around the Minories until Harris, drunkenly, responded. He was persuaded to go on – inebriated – though presumably reunited with his breeches. For Foote, *The Knights* represented a brief comeback only, an attempt perhaps to assert his renewed interest in being more writer than performer, and soon enough he quit England once again.

§

The West End buzzed to rumours through late 1749 that Foote had fled for ever, and had even died of a 'fever resulting from dissipation' – in other words of some sexually transmitted disease – or had been killed in a duel. Another story circulated that he had been apprehended for an unspecified crime and hanged in Bordeaux.[83] Doggerel written on the subject entertained theatre audience during prologues:

> How's that – cries feeble Grub – Foote come again?
> I thought that fool has done his devil's dance.
> Was he not hanged, some months ago, in France?

Where he was, what he was doing and why remain unclear. By late 1749 he had taken lodgings on the rue Colombier, met up there with his friend from Downing Square, Frank Delaval, and his former student friend from Macklin's classcs, Domenico Angelo, the fencing master, and together they soon introduced themselves to Parisian theatrical society. The tall blond Northumberland aristocrat, the short Cornish impressionist and the Anglo-Italian chancer: they must have made a striking entrance.

Foote had various scams in action with Frank Delaval, financial and other, which must remain off-stage rumours for now. However, his ability to support himself in some style in Paris by the early 1750s suggests that Cooke was right to add as one factor relating to Foote's absence from London the monies afforded to him by his inheritance. He had some financial support also, it would seem, from Frank Delaval, and from Dublin. His funds would go even further in France where the eighteenth-century pound was notably strong after the 1748 treaty of Aix-la-Chapelle. The British ceded Louisbourg, Nova Scotia, back to the French, planting one seed of the American Revolution; the French accepted the Hanoverian succession; Handel wrote his Firework music; and Samuel Foote found he could rent a room in Paris for the cost of a London sedan ride. Even so, elements of life in mid-century Paris must have been a struggle for a man with no long-term means of support, which lends further credibility to the idea that Foote was obliged to lie low abroad.

One important new friend for the three was Pierre Louis Préville. He was the juvenile lead at the Comédie-Française. Angelo recalled being invited to dine with Foote at the rue Colombier and meeting Préville there, introduced by his real name of Pierre Louis Dubus. Newly burst onto the scene in mid-eighteenth-century Paris, Préville was talked of as the French Garrick, an actor who had appeared 'meteor like', as *Gentleman's Magazine* had it. One of five orphaned boys from the aptly named rue des Mauvais Garçons, Préville had run away at an early age to be an actor and risen by 1749 to be the lead player of the Comédie-Française. He would later create the role of Figaro in Beaumarchais's *The Barber of Seville*. Small, dark and wiry, he impressed with his devotion to naturalism and to the sort of research and preparation that sounds more Method than mannered – but was familiar to Foote from his lessons with Macklin. Centuries before Stanislavski, stories went round Paris that Préville stayed 'in character' in the wings, to the extent of being deemed drunk and incapable by one literalist theatre manager when he was about to make an entrance playing a drunk. He also had a facility akin to Foote's in dazzling with mercurial shifts of character and impersonation. He played six different roles in Boursault's *Mercure Galant* closely followed by one of the leads in Molière's *Amphitryon* at Court. Louis XV, having seen these, announced simply, 'M. Preville *must* be of my Comédie-Française.'[84]

Quite how Foote came into such close contact with Préville is a subject of interesting conjecture, as Préville chose to project a stage energy that was described often as sexually ambivalent. The Café Procope was one likely meeting point: Paris's equivalent to the Bedford, it was where Voltaire could be seen nightly, 'apparently absorbed in the contents of the Gazette, with a small roll of bread and a milk posset',[85] trying to eavesdrop on his critics. Foote entertained his new young friend at the rue Colombier with imitations of stars of the West End and Dublin stage, but took the trouble to tell Angelo not to report back to London that he had done so or 'I'll have you broke on the wheel.'[86] An adept linguist, Foote quickly polished his school-boy French into something quite passable even in the intimidatingly voluble foyers of the Comédie-Française at the rue des Fossés St Germain, at the Comédie-Italienne and at Court. Eventually he would even publish in French.

It was through Préville that Foote found himself invited into the wit-loving coterie around Madame de Pompadour – *maîtresse en titre* to Louis XV. Part of the royal mistress's hold over the King was her ability to alleviate his periodic depressions with small informal dinners cast with amusing companions. Either at Versailles, Fontainebleau or her property at Bellevue – it has proved impossible to verify the story – Foote was invited to one of La Pompadour's *'petits soupers'*. Louis XV himself sat laughing at her side at Foote's mimicry of Versailles courtiers – it was all quite a long way from Truro.[87]

As a result of this royal favour, Foote was exposed to a great deal of theatre while in France. As Voltaire wrote to fellow dramatist and critic Jean-François Marmontel in 1748, Pompadour provided a 'school for all of us', in terms of the theatre access she allowed her acolytes,[88] the 'free admission' given to favoured writers like Foote that formed, perhaps, the most artistically profitable aspect of life in the lee of the King's mistress. Foote consequently saw premières of tragedies by Crébillon, Marmontel and Voltaire, as well as the first productions of Lachaussée's *L'École de la jeunesse*, Voltaire's unsuccessful comedy *Nanine* and Jean-Jacques Rousseau's *L'Amant de lui-même*.[89] But the bulk of Foote's theatregoing in Paris and at Court reflected the King's and La Pompadour's taste for theatre of the previous reign: the comedies of Molière. These were performed at Court, but also were constantly in repertoire at the old Comédie-Française, still at that period housed in the former tennis-court of Henri IV, haunted, it was said, by the ghosts of Marivaux, Racine, Molière and the grand tragediennes who had once trodden its raked boards. All this furnished Foote eventually with plenty of material to parody and emulate, but also the basis of a major later work in his publishing career: a collection of French comedies he translated into English.

Foote became convinced that of all the French dramatists he was exposed to it was Molière who would work best in the London theatre, 'most easily to be adapted', as he wrote 'to the English manners'.[90] The work he eventually published was titled *The Comic Theatre, Being a Free Translation of all the Best French Comedies*.[91] It ran to five volumes. In particular Foote noted admiringly that Molière's plays often had characters drawn straight from life, not that he can have witnessed this directly a generation after Molière wrote. All this was familiar from his own work: 'one advantage' to a comic dramatist, he stated in Paris, 'is to have characters known to the audience' such as the Duc de Montaunfière, the acknowledged model for *The Misanthrope*.[92] It was a very similar trick to Foote's own of using metropolitan personalities to amuse an audience who knew them. It was why he began to be known around Paris with a title that stuck even back in London: *L'Aristophane anglais*, the English Aristophanes.

One thing became clear to Foote as a result of his time in Paris: French comedy would supply an almost endless source of potential material for future West End plays. To the modern mind it sounds dangerously near to plagiarism but Foote opined that stealing plots was in a grand Shakespearean tradition. As Boswell overheard him advising Arthur Murphy soon after his return to London, if stuck for a plot one might always open 'a French magazine, in which you will find a very pretty oriental tale . . . translate that, and send it to your printer'.[93]

The scheme formed in Foote's mind to mark a London comeback with a tale specifically referencing his time as an Englishman abroad. Louis de Boissy's *Le Français à Londres – The*

Frenchman in London – had caught his eye for obvious reasons. The play dates from 1727, but had come back into vogue in 1750. A parody of the English from a French point of view, it was also a satire on Anglophilia, enjoying one of its occasional florescences in mid-eighteenth-century Paris, as it had in the 1720s. Foote started work on a retort, or mirror piece, about a British Grand Tourist in France, titled eventually and unimaginatively *The Englishman in Paris*. He intended, he told William Cooke, 'to expose the absurdity of sending our youth of fashion abroad to improve themselves' when in truth they availed themselves mainly of 'the vices and follies'[94] of the Continent. Foote wrote to Macklin about his new work, and a scenario was hatched that the piece would form a triple-threat marketing coup: it would provide a role for Macklin as his swansong performance, a relaunch for Foote and a vehicle also for a new London performer, Macklin's daughter Maria.

Macklin was to play the male lead, Buck, in *The Englishman in Paris*, a character based largely on Foote's experiences in Paris. Nevertheless, *The Englishman*, when it opened in London in 1753, appeared to many 'written with the express intention of giving opportunity for display of his [Macklin's] daughter's talents'.[95] This, indeed, also helped disguise the fact that it was also Foote's full reintroduction into London theatrical life.

By 1753 Macklin had spent plenty of his profits from his acting academy on the education of his talented daughter. Maria Macklin was proficient in French, Italian, singing, dancing and drawing – essential résumé points for a young gentlewoman being launched on the marriage market as much as upon the stage – and was considered, by her father at least, as 'one of the most accomplished women in England'.[96] Maria was to play the heiress, Lucinda, with Mrs Macklin as Mrs Subtle, her guardian. Foote allowed Macklin, twenty years his senior, to play young Buck while he modestly or politically spoke only the prologue. Buck, a boorish Englishman, is the dupe of Mr and Mrs Subtle's plan to have him marry their ward, Lucinda, so that they can swindle her out of her inheritance. To do this, they must turn him into a *soigné* Parisian sophisticate with the aid of tailors, dancing masters and a fake French marquis who is supposedly his rival in Lucinda's affections. It is perforce a trade-show in national stereotypes – the bluff Briton, the epicene Parisian, the thinly disguised mix of disdain and jealousy on both sides. It played rather well in an era of overt Francophilia in Britain, and at the height of the Grand Tour vogue.

It is politically interesting, though, for two reasons. First, as Foote advertised, it was 'an answer to the French farce called the *Frenchman in London*',[97] thus acknowledging his self-imposed exile in Paris, but also because in his prologue, Foote clearly stated his political independence: patronage, he avowed, was no longer for him or for the theatres in which he intended to work. His comedy would be radical, and would answer only to the adjudication of 'The Pit'.

The play was not especially well regarded but the characters were, and so Foote, all but imperceptibly, slipped back into West End life, and set about writing a sequel. Buck and Lucinda were to return in *The Englishman Returned from Paris*, which takes up the story where it had been left off. More to the point, this would mark Foote's proper return to the London stage, as a performer, after several years' physical absence. The sequel had not, however, been his idea but rather Arthur Murphy's. Murphy went on to great acclaim as a playwright and, indeed, biographer of Garrick, among others, but in the 1750s he was editing the *Gray's-Inn Journal*. Murphy suggested to Foote a sequel to *The Englishman in Paris*, even providing some ideas for the plot, and asked permission to create it. This in turn led to a professional entanglement between the two that provides the side-stage view of Foote's return to the West End. It is unclear when exactly he decided it was safe to come back, but he was installed in Pall Mall by mid-1753, because he writes it as his address in dealing with Murphy on the vexatious business of copyright on a play that was part plagiarized in the first place. Before quite answering the question of what should be done with Murphy's idea of a sequel to *The Englishman*, Foote appropriated the idea, the sketched plot, and wrote the sequel himself.

The Englishman Returned from Paris premièred at Covent Garden on 3 February 1756, advertised as 'a sequel to the *Englishman in Paris* by the Same Author'. This was intended to be equally a spoiler and a puff, for Murphy, undaunted by Foote, had gone ahead with his own version, titled confusingly, *An Englishman from Paris*. Although modern authorial scruples would favour Foote in this situation as the original creative force behind the franchise, as it were, his contemporaries were more sympathetic to Murphy, who certainly remained profoundly aggrieved at what he perceived as Foote's plagiarism of *his* idea. In the strange ways of Georgian theatre, the leads, Lucinda and Buck, were played in Foote's and Murphy's versions by the same actors, and Murphy produced a prologue for his opening 'in which he was very severe on his friend Samuel', but, as one audience member who saw both observed, 'Sam had got the money, and it disturbed him not.'[98] Murphy's version did not do well – but, then, it was the second to arrive before the public, whose interest was diluted accordingly. He published, rashly, a farce titled *A Triple Revenge* against those he felt were thwarting his ambitions for the stage: Foote, Garrick, John Rich and Theophilus Cibber. 'Dapperwit', who represents Foote, is found fingering his chin and saying, 'A new Farce – it's true a Gentleman told me of the subject first, and in confidence too . . . A Blockhead! He should know me better.'

The spat between Foote and Murphy did nothing to dent the commercial success of Foote and his French-themed plays. By February and March 1756 Foote's *The Englishman in Paris* and its sequel *The Englishman Returned from Paris*, as well as *The Knights*, were all staged at Covent Garden and ended up playing later in the year at Drury Lane. Foote was in the cast every time and at both theatres – and in some instances was appearing twice nightly, first in one of the Paris plays and then in *The Knights*.

Foote's Parisian years left him with more than a taste for French comedy and the occasional work on French literature. He was also remembered widely and well in France. He had met Denis Diderot while in Paris, between his commercial success with

the heavy-breathed *Les Bijoux indiscrets* in 1748 and the announcement of the rather more respectable project of the *Encyclopédie* in
1750; Foote later published in French and in France a translation of his own work on Diderot, *Avis au public sur Sieur Diderot*,[99]
a perplexing satire on Diderot and the sex trade and on Diderot's
supposed interest in transplanting hymens and renewing virginity.
The original English, regrettably, has not survived. Nevertheless,
Foote's name is credited as the translator and the piece exists
widely enough in French collections of the period for us to presume
it sold reasonably well, where Monsieur Foote, 'of diverting memory', as he was advertised, was evidently recalled affectionately
from his time in Paris. Decades later, Dr Johnson and Mrs Thrale
were bemused to find Foote's *Englishman in Paris* receiving its
première, in French translation, at Versailles. 'Dr Johnson was,'
wrote Boswell, 'much of a *John Bull* – a blunt true-born Englishman',[100] which may indeed have been the root of Mrs Thrale's
joke in suggesting they go and see Foote's play in French. 'No
indeed!' Dr Johnson told her. 'We will [instead] act *Henry V*
[ourselves].' Dr Johnson and Mrs Thrale were patriotically antagonistic to almost everything they encountered in France,[101] so their
preference for an evening at their lodgings enacting together the
victory at Agincourt over an evening with Parisian theatre-goers
seeing Foote's play is understandable. How regrettable, however,
that as a result we have lost Dr Johnson's thoughts on Foote's
satirical language, rendered from English into French, on the
subject of the French and English.

§

The mid-1750s proved busy and successful years for Foote, re-
establishing himself back in London with whatever pall of scandal
slowly sliding into desuetude and an ever-expanding circle of
influential and aristocratic friends willing to enjoy his talent to
amuse on and off stage. In March 1754 his father had died and
was buried in the church of St Clement's in Truro. His will left the
whole of his estate to Sam's eldest brother, John, with money set

aside for Sam and his other brother Edward to buy mourning rings for the funeral. John was the eldest son and the provisions of the will are not surprising.[102] Mr Foote had therefore lived to see his son's first theatrical successes, including his satire, in 1749, of the provincialism of Cornwall, *The Knights*. There is no record of any correspondence or comment, and it seems likely, if his father was aware of his son's metropolitan successes, he did not attend them. Foote's mother Eleanor, on the other hand, lived to eighty, dying only three years before Sam. Despite the scandal of her brothers' deaths, her son's separately suspect name and her many debts, she was a sprightly London presence from time to time, and adored her admissions to Sam's theatrical circle, however infrequent. William Cooke recalled dining with her at Gray's Inn when she was seventy-nine and describes her as 'witty, humourous and convivial', though her remarks occasionally (considering her age and sex) 'rather strayed beyond the limits of becoming mirth, [yet] she ... was confessedly the heroine of that day's party.' Cooke remembered that as they grew older mother and son came to resemble each other more and more – noted, too, by those who saw Foote in drag on stage and also knew his mother. 'Short, fat, and flabby' was one description, 'with an eye that eternally gave the signal for mirth and good humour: in short, Mrs Foote resembled Foote so much in all her movements, and so strongly identified his person and manners, that by changing habits, they might be thought to have interchanged sexes'.[103] Cooke also added sadly that Eleanor Foote, 'by a carelessness and dissipation so peculiar to this family', became increasingly mired in debt and 'in a great measure dependent on her son's bounty'. Foote, dutiful West End star and increasingly a man of stable means, if of dubious reputation, began to give her a pension of a hundred pounds a year, which lasted until her death in 1774.

METHODISM IN HIS MADNESS

'I would give a hundred guineas, if I could say "Oh!"
like Mr Whitefield.'

David Garrick[1]

BENJAMIN FRANKLIN KNEW what to expect of the preacher he
went to see off Tottenham Court Road because he had seen him
before in Philadelphia. The evangelist George Whitefield was a
phenomenon of the age. Odd-looking and cross-eyed, he had a
prodigious gift for oratory, and could throw his voice over crowds
of thousands in a manner that communicated pure emotion as well
as religious fervour. By 1760 Whitefield was probably the most
recognized of the new breed of London celebrities, by virtue of his
strange appearance certainly, but also because of the huge crowds
he drew and the emotive responses of his religious disciples. He
was also famous for his intrepid travels. He went to America seven
times, making thirteen Atlantic crossings in total in an age when
few risked more than one or two. His epic journey from New York
to Charleston was at the time the longest land journey ever
attempted by a European in America. It is estimated that throughout his life he preached more than eighteen thousand formal
sermons in his mission to spread the Great Awakening, a doctrine
of born-again Christianity, in Britain and in the American colonies.
He spoke at gallows, at race courses, in open fields and assembly
halls to crowds of tens of thousands. But his home territory was

London. His brand of evangelism was dubbed 'Enthusiasm', not without a hint of disdain – and his followers 'Enthusiasts'. Garrick remarked with professional jealousy that Mr Whitefield could reduce an audience to tears simply with the word 'Mesopotamia'. Foote, however, saw in Whitefield's rabid religiosity and eccentric celebrity the potential for some fun.

Franklin was, as he admitted, a partisan witness to Whitefield's ministry in London because he had had him as a house guest in Philadelphia, and Whitefield 'us'd . . . to pray for my conversion'.[2] Whitefield never succeeded in convincing the worldly Franklin to embrace Enthusiasm, but they nevertheless persisted in 'civil friendship, sincere on both sides', which 'lasted to . . . death'. What Franklin, and later Foote, witnessed in the chapel and fields off Tottenham Court Road that still bear Whitefield's name happened almost everywhere Whitefield preached. As one awestruck listener commented, Whitefield was 'as rousing and searching as I ever heard – he aimed directly at the hearts and consciences of his hearers', and his fire and brimstone warnings that the resurrection day was at hand brought 'the terrors of God rising fresh in his mind'.[3] People succumbed to his passionate arguments, fell under his spell or the power of his oratory and rhetoric, were moved with innocent passion – or at the behest of the Holy Spirit – and sought to be 'born again' in Christ. The faithful would be saved simply by having faith, an 'assurance' that would be manifest in 'inward and outward holiness'.[4] Or so John Wesley wrote, in a series of open letters to *Lloyd's Evening Post* in November 1760, following the hullabaloo at Samuel Foote's parody of 'Enthusiasm' on stage.

In his youth, Whitefield had been an admirer of the theatre, but he and the Wesley brothers, Charles and John, who had all met at Oxford, later set their faces against actors and the theatre – 'the devil's children grinning at you', as he described comedians. The actress George Anne Bellamy told of a Methodist crowd so fired by such rhetoric in Glasgow that they burned down her theatre, with her nearly in it, destroying her precious collection of costumes. Similar had happened elsewhere. A man of the stage like Foote had therefore a reasonable animus against Whitefield and the Methodist anti-theatre rhetoric. But Foote's growing distaste for Whitefield and the Enthusiasts was compounded through the 1750s into a clearer political antipathy towards organized religion. For one thing, it struck Foote as hypocritical that Whitefield should rage against the theatre while manipulating an audience in an obviously stagy manner. Further to this, Foote recognized in Whitefield a fellow self-publicist. He employed print systematically – which was also how he knew the printer Benjamin Franklin – sending 'advance men' to distribute handbills announcing his sermons and arrival in town. These were often posted over theatre advertisements. One thing that Foote sought to parody was a fellow celebrity. He also seems to have had a particular distaste for what he once termed the 'cant' of religion and, more than this, he thought Whitefield a hypocrite. A popular preacher was an impolitic victim, however, for Foote's satire as the comedian's hold on public opinion and sympathy was far from secure.

The Minor opened in London in June 1760. It became the most famous and controversial of Foote's plays in his lifetime and the most extravagantly praised. The Dramatic Censor declared it 'the most entertaining, original and useful drama now in possession of the stage'; James Boswell wrote that the constant laughter had 'not failed to produce a violent concussion of the sides of each and every spectator';[5] and the critic Richard Cumberland went so far as to say, 'I cannot recollect [a] scene in any play or comic passage by any author that I think comparable.' Sadly it has not stood well the test of time. In its day it had as huge advantage not only the performing talents of Sam Foote but more vitally a subject then of dangerous volatility on stage and off: Enthusiasm and 'born again' Christianity. This much might mark its universal appeal, but Foote had a more specific target for his satire in the religious notions of the Methodists and the persons of George Whitefield and John Wesley.

Foote was writing the piece all through 1759 but tried out *The Minor* first in Dublin, at the Crow Street theatre, in the winter of

1760. As was his usual practice, he puffed the piece beforehand, enacting excerpts from it on his arrival in the city, and even en route in Bath, so that everyone was well aware of the intended subject matter and the audaciousness of an author flouting a long-standing taboo: religion was not ridiculed on stage. It purported not to be a direct attack on Methodism or Whitefield by the expedient of seeming to be about the irreligious and hypocritical – not an attack on religion but on cant. Many saw it differently, not least as the role Foote played was in drag – a flaunting of convention that had brought censure upon him, first with Christopher Smart a decade earlier and again when he appeared as Lady Pentweazle.

When the curtain rose the audience was greeted with Foote as himself, in conversation with actors 'discovered' talking about the comedy they intend to put on about an 'itinerant field orator'. Because one of the actresses supposedly has refused to play in it as a prostitute, Foote declares, 'I'll do the character myself,' and while the burlesquing of religion is excused on the principle that 'ridicule is the only antidote against pernicious . . . madness',[6] Foote's drag is excused by the fictional expedient that they are in want of an actress. The play proper then begins.

The bones of the plot were familiar to the audience. Sir William Wealthy has decided to test the character of his son George – the minor of the title – whom he suspects of being a wastrel. With the impenetrable logic of eighteenth-century comedy, Sir William does this by disguising himself as a Bavarian baron. Meanwhile Sir William's brother, Sir Richard, is likewise at his wits' end with his daughter, who has refused her intended fiancé and has been turned out of her home as a result. She has happened into the house of a Covent Garden madam – Mrs Cole, the main role played by Foote in drag – a procuress who has been part-converted to Methodism by a preacher, though not so far as to affect her business in the sex trade. The preacher, Dr Squintum, was also played by Foote. George's rakish intents in Mrs Cole's house, as well as her own hypocrisy, are neatly delivered in the style of the era: 'There I had been' she declares, 'tossing in a sea of sin, without rudder, and had not the good gentleman [the Methodist preacher] piloted me into the harbour of grace I must have struck against the rocks of reprobation . . . but however, George, if your mind be set upon a young country thing, tomorrow night I believe I can furnish you one [as] I have advertised in the register office for servants under seventeen, and ten to one but I light on something that will do . . .'[7]

Squintum, of course, was the famously squint-eyed Whitefield. Mrs Cole was recognizably Jenny Douglas, the most famous of all the madams of the Covent Garden brothel, known by sight to anyone who was familiar with the piazza and to many of the men in the audience for her business empire. Lord Clive was a client, the East India Company officers were all advised to trust her establishment, John Cleland immortalized her in *Fanny Hill*, and even William Hogarth was on intimate enough terms there to have sketched in and outside the house and featured Jane Douglas and her girls in his *Industry and Idleness*, *March of the Guards to Finchley* and, later, *Enthusiasm Delineated*. In 1756, the 'Empress of the All the Bawds', as she was termed in *Covent Garden, A Satire*, was said to be able to teach 'every luring Art'[8] but by 1759 a different fame attended her name for, to the amusement and bemusement of many, and encouraged by Whitefield, she did indeed embrace Methodism.

The first shocking element, then, for the audience was not so much the depiction of the famous Methodist as Squintum but the portrayal on stage of London's most infamous madam, played by Foote in drag, converting to Methodism. Foote had known Jenny since his first arrival in London, as she had worked then out of a house opposite the Bedford on the Little Piazza on the corner of Russell Street. By 1759 she had moved to much larger premises by the Inigo Jones church, the former King's Head, with sufficient funds built up on the backs of her girls to install running water and a private bagnio, among other 'Oriental luxuries'. The converted tavern was alluded to in the comedy, its rococo interiors with purportedly two-way mirrors and its liveried servants. Jenny had

added a dining room, after a series of complaints that her customers, often falling into the arms of her girls fresh from the
theatre or the other local bagnios, were drunk and obstreperous.
She supplied condoms – something of a vogue in London, as
evidenced by Casanova – manufactured by Jacobs of the Strand
as a by-product of the Smithfield slaughterhouses, but presented in
silk bags and tied 'with ribbon round it', as ladies of the night, like
Kitty Fisher, demanded. And for those for whom her *préservatifs*
had not worked, she also had on hand, at discount, Dr Misaubin's
anti-venereal *pillule* – possibly mercury. She made, as a result, a
great deal of money. *Harris's List of Covent Garden Ladies*, in which
Mother Douglas and her girls feature, disputed her assurance that
she had always on offer country virgins, but she and her 'nunnery',
or 'cattery', were famed also for providing the most elegant,
accomplished and ladylike of working girls. They were colleagues
of Samuel Foote: elegantly mannered resting actresses, in plentiful
supply in the area. All of this was immediately recognized by the
audience of *The Minor* without a single direct lewd reference: the
pretence of gentility, and indeed the cant of religious conversion,
was all easily open to satire.

Foote was an instant sensation as Mother Douglas. It remains
perhaps his most famous role, and a much iterated image in print
form. Ungallant to mention, he and Jenny Douglas bore a super-
ficial resemblance to each other by 1760. In 1759 the once svelte
Scotswoman had been described as 'much bloated by Drink and
Debauch ... her Legs swelled out of shape ... suffering great
discomfort', and her *parvenue* overdress and makeup made her ripe
for transvestite parody. She had borne a child to either Lord
Fitzwilliam or another client, had overspent on the luxurious
entertainments on offer at her establishment, and was struggling so
much with debt that she was forced to sell at auction some of the
contents of the former King's Head. The auctioneer, her friend
and client Abraham Langford, was likewise to be a butt of Foote's
jokes and caricature in *The Minor* – another easy target in the
continuing auction mania. The allusion, however, to the auction

and the auctioneer was firmly grounded in the reality of Jenny Douglas's debts. Above and beyond any of that, the impersonation became recognizable and scandalous as it linked a rackety brothel-keeper to the world of Enthusiasm. By making a new transvestite impersonation the centre of the religion sub-plot in *The Minor*, Foote achieved a triply audacious assault upon the intentions of the 1737 Licensing Act, putting two known characters up on stage, and marrying religion and Enthusiasm to the sex trade.

On 28 June 1760 *The Minor* opened at the Little Theatre on the Haymarket, slightly reworked and remodelled since the Dublin run. The patent houses were closed for the summer, and it was a huge success. Foote advertised a 'New Comedy of Three Acts. By Authority', in other words licensed; he had no need of his old subterfuges and had secured the Lord Chamberlain's assent to both the text and performance of the play. It is to be surmised therefore that one needed a certain cynicism and a certain worldly knowledge of Covent Garden to 'get' all the in-jokes and *double-entendres*, so the Lord Chamberlain's office somehow let it pass. It ran for thirty-five nights, which would not have been possible at the patent theatres, and from 4 to 11 August it was performed every single night except Sundays, and was advertised as doing so again from 18 to 30 August, the last and thirty-fifth night of the run. Tate Wilkinson made the journey from Winchester, where he was performing, to see it and had to stand at the back of a box for lack of room. Foote was advertising, by mid-August, that as his Haymarket summer licence was expiring at the end of the month, 'and Vast numbers of people now being able to gain admittance', he was therefore 'encouraged to open the Theatre Every Night'.[9] In the mania to see Foote as Mrs Cole, there was just no point in mounting another play.

The Minor transferred to Drury Lane, and by the following winter it was considered such a smash that, uniquely, *both* Theatres Royal put it into their repertoire, with Foote moving between the great houses on alternate nights.

§

Many in the successful Haymarket company that opened *The Minor* and transferred it to Drury Lane and Covent Garden were new to Foote, and some were quite young. One, the twenty-three-year-old Thomas Weston, made a striking impression on the London audience and on Foote, though his role in *The Minor* as Dick is neither showy nor large. Colley Cibber, however, was so struck with his 'laughing levity' and 'natural countenance . . . that, had you not known him,' he wrote, 'you could not have believed him'[10] to be acting. This new wild boy of London theatre – he lived with a sixteen-year-old prostitute, 'surrounded by pig-styes and slaughterhouses'[11] off Smithfield and often had to be dragged out of taverns onto the stage – established himself as Foote's new favourite in his *Minor* company. They made an odd couple. After an apprenticeship as a cook at Hampton Court Palace, Tom Weston had briefly been a midshipman and was 'discovered' acting at Southwark Fair. *The Minor*, his first play in the West End, netted him a full £180 in a single benefit night[12] such as an established star might expect. It proved to be the beginning of a long career at Drury Lane and during summer seasons in the Haymarket, during which he was in and out of debt and scrapes. It was 'from Mr Foote,' Tom Weston later wrote, that 'I derived all my consequence in life.'[13]

The Minor was immediately published. This was not usual for Foote's plays, as he made little money on the published texts compared to the box office, and tended to retain single prompt copies for a season or more for fear of plagiarism. *The Minor*, however, was causing more interest, and many whose principles forbade them to attend the theatre nevertheless wanted to read what all the fuss was about. On the page, as one review made clear, the satire was somewhat blunt. 'The success of the [*The Minor*],' wrote the critic in the *Monthly Review*, 'arises from the author's extraordinary skill at mimicry . . . but the satire levelled at the Great Leader of the Methodists seems . . . absurd: to suppose a man of his penetration . . . being the dupe of an old bawd's hypocrisy in continuing to follow her occupation while she . . .

cants about the New Birth!' The publication of the play, however, begat a literary spat that provides rather more evidence for the impact of a Foote comedy than is the case for almost any other of his works, a minor literary storm, as it were, that raged through the summer of 1760 and was Foote's second taste of national infamy. He seems to have quite enjoyed it.

First into print was one Reverend Martin Madan with *Christian and Critical Remarks on The Minor in which the Blasphemy, Falsehood and Scurrility of the Piece is . . . exposed*, a pamphlet that took a stock line against theatre in general and Foote in particular. It was answered anonymously by an equally title-heavy piece that made up in prolixity what it lacked in subtlety. Foote decided to answer his critics himself. *A Letter from Mr Foote to the Reverend Author of the Remarks Critical and Christian on the Minor* was published as a pamphlet towards the end of the summer of 1760. He chose mainly to address concerns over impersonating real-life characters. 'You err,' he wrote, 'in your notions of the nature of . . . comedy,' and he cited Shakespeare, Molière, Dryden and Pope among other 'comic' authors who had also taken characters from real life. This led to yet another open letter from Mr Madan, which was sold outside churches and at evangelical meetings all over London as *An Exhortatory Address to the Brethren in the Faith . . . occasioned by . . . Mr Foote*. It was soon reprinted with a black-edged appendix for, on 25 October 1760, on the very day *The Minor* was meant to reopen in London after its transfer to Drury Lane, old King George II died.

The theatres were obliged to go dark for three weeks. The good reverend sought to blame Foote for 'the nation's calamity',[14] and for many of the Enthusiasts the coincidence of dates looked ominously providential. The pamphlet correspondence continued, in ever longer titles, selling at congregational meetings and coffee-houses alike, uniting for a while the theatrical and evangelical worlds in one long interlocution on the ethics of comedy. Among the more ridiculous was *An Old Woman's Answer to 'The Minor'*, in which the female author appears to believe that Mrs Cole was played by an actress, and among the most amusing was one written by James Boswell under the self-promoting pseudonym 'A Genius'. He coined one of the best of the titles that had vied with each other over the course of the summer and autumn of 1760 in etiolated silliness. Boswell persuaded Wilkie's of St Paul's to publish his at fourpence apiece: it was titled *Observations Good, Bad, Stupid or Clever, Serious or Jocular on Squire Foote's The Minor by A Genius*.

All of this could hardly go unnoticed by the authorities, and the Duke of Devonshire, as Lord Chamberlain, had correspondence with the Countess of Huntingdon, a devotee of Whitefield, and the Archbishop of Canterbury, Thomas Secker, on the uncomfortable subject. The play had been passed by the Lord Chamberlain's office before its Haymarket opening and, indeed, by the parallel authorities in Dublin, but Lady Huntingdon, among others, was alarmed at its success and transfer to Drury Lane and wanted it suppressed. On 25 October, just before news came of the King's death, Devonshire had written to Garrick to say he had seen the archbishop. Secker had wisely refused to 'point out' the offending passages of *The Minor*, for fear it would later be republished as 'corrected and prepared for the press by the Archbishop of Canterbury'. He was clearly a man who understood comedy. Lady Huntingdon meanwhile appealed directly to Garrick to disallow its continuance at Drury Lane. With charming insouciance, Garrick wrote back that 'had he been aware of the offence it was calculated to give, it should never have appeared with this concurrence',[15] then allowed it to fill his box-office coffers for several more weeks. Another pamphleteer, thought to be Abraham Portal, published an open letter to Garrick after the King's death, quoting the Book of Revelation on the destruction that would rain down upon Drury Lane if Foote's play, 'so derogatory to the honour of God', were mounted there.[16]

As the controversy and the pamphlets spun on, *The Minor* began to have a life of its own. Songs, squibs, dramatic verses and doggerel were written for Squintum, Mr Foote and the auctioneer, anonymous authors published additional scenes, and 'a Mrs Cole' for a time was used even beyond London to denote a ridiculous

'Enthusiast'. *The Minor* became that media sensation that transcends
the community for which it was written and presses upon the minds
of those who have neither seen nor read it. It became part of the
conversation about life, religion and lechery in Georgian London.
And accordingly at the theatre it continued to be a phenomenon,
attracting the sort of cult following entirely recognizable from the
modern musical theatre, devotees who called themselves 'Minors'
and booked tickets for 'a half dozen nights in succession'.[17]

The Minor was rarely out of repertoire through the rest of Foote's
life, and the enduring image of him before and after the accident
that led to the loss of his leg was of a comedian in drag. When
Fanny Burney published *Evelina* in 1778 her eponymous heroine
could allude to seeing the play as one of the perennial highlights of
a night out in London. Foote had died the year before. Its fame
outlived Foote's and even outran his performance: the role of the
cross-dressing comic bawd became and remained a favourite of
middle-aged character actors and comedians well into the nineteenth century, establishing Mrs Cole as one of the godmothers of
the pantomime dame. For some the play's resonance was pitched
around its attack on Whitefield, Enthusiasm and Wesleyan Methodism, and necessarily there were many who were strongly offended
by it. The attack seemed cheapened by the easy physical mimicry
of Whitefield's physiognomy. Others were offended by the close
alignment of the 'cant of Enthusiasm' with worldly hypocrisy and
sexual knowingness as personified by Mrs Cole. Though the *Monthly
Mirror* expressed the view that 'No true religion can suffer injury
from the ridicule of . . . mountebank[s]', another critic reasonably
pointed out that 'It is no easy matter to ridicule the pretenders to
religion without ridiculing religion itself,' and *Thespian Magazine* was
clear years later that 'Foote's Mother Cole . . . has been of great
dis-service to religion.'[18] All of which helped cement in the public
mind an image of Foote that was not only sexually ambiguous – a
comic in drag as a bawd – but also recklessly cynical and radically
anticlerical. It would not help his cause in years to come.

In the meantime, however, Foote had helped kick off a press

and pamphlet war of words about Methodism, Enthusiasm and the ethics of preaching the doctrines of the born-again that might well have bemused as much as amused him. Though he distanced himself from the debate that raged around him in the press, his friend James Boswell gives some insight into his likely true feelings: 'Poor Sam,' wrote Boswell, 'has endeavoured to ward off the blows of his furious antagonists,' but even so, Boswell let slip, Foote was of the opinion that Methodism and Whitefield presented 'a gross burlesque upon religion'.[19] Actual blasphemy would have 'silenced' Foote and his theatre by the terms of the 1737 Licensing Act. Mere parody of Methodism and Enthusiasm comically deflected laughter onto a controversial sect, and onto two eccentric individuals. Those who chose to see an attack upon religion could do so. Foote, meanwhile, had again danced audaciously around the authorities.

§

As Foote reached the end of his thirties he could survey the London theatre scene from a perspective not just of a professional controversialist but also of a member of the established order. Every year since the mid-1750s he had starred in summer seasons at the Little Theatre in the Haymarket, and from 1762 to 1776 he was manager there also, creating a new play nearly every year. He kept the loyalty of a stable core of performers each summer but also recruited a stream of fresh talent. His repertoire grew steadily and there were many new plays by other authors. Moreover, he managed his theatre with remarkably little backstage strife, despite his almost compulsive showmanship and determination to take the extrovert and controversial path. A protean quality in his personality, however, a restive habit of engaging in petty feuds, suggests that his fame came without contentment; he felt insufficiently respected by his contemporaries and undervalued perhaps because of his métier, comedy. It is not an unusual position for a professional funnyman. The summer after *The Minor* was first a hit in London, for instance, Foote attempted to repair his relationship with Arthur Murphy. They had barely spoken since the accusations that Foote had stolen

Murphy's concept of a sequel to *The Englishman in Paris*, but Foote found he was unable to engage the Little Theatre on the Haymarket for a summer season so he asked Murphy, who was then on very good terms with Garrick, to enquire in his place for a rental deal on Drury Lane. This Murphy did with full success. He and Foote between them were to provide three new plays each, as well as some afterpieces. But Foote reneged on his side of the bargain, so busy was he with the continuing success of *The Minor*, and only got round to writing one prologue. When Murphy was asked if he was put out at this, he said only, 'Of what use was it to be angry with [Sam Foote] when within five minutes he would have laughed me into a good humour.'[20]

Soon after, Foote's most famous spat with Dr Johnson took place. The two men were in and out of contact throughout the 1740s and 1750s – noted as dinner companions at the Garricks' and doubtless bumping into one another at the theatre. Foote made his intention clear, as Johnson's star rose, of satirizing the learned doctor in his new work, *The Orators*, when it moved across the Irish Sea. The main subject of the satire was to be the notorious Cock Lane Ghost, and Samuel Johnson's controversial stance that this supernatural apparition was worthy of serious investigation.

In 1762 a house between Smithfield and Dr Johnson's house in Gough Square was the site of a reported haunting. The ghost story involved three people: William Kent, a widower, Richard Parsons, a parish clerk, and Parsons's daughter Elizabeth. Following the death during childbirth of his wife, Kent became romantically involved with her sister, Frances, known latterly in the scabrous press of the time as 'scratching Fanny'. Parsons claimed that Fanny – who died soon after her sister – haunted his property in ghostly or poltergeist form, and later his daughter, too, swore she heard the unfortunately named scratchings. Regular séances were held to determine 'Scratching Fanny's' motives – which were revealed to be the exposure of Kent as a murderer.

It turned out to be a scam perpetrated by Parsons and his daughter to avoid paying a debt owed to Kent, but meanwhile the

Cock Lane Ghost became a focus of controversy between spiritualist Methodists and old-Church Anglicans. The story became celebrated enough to feature in the prints of Hogarth but also, a
century later, three works by Dickens. Samuel Johnson, meanwhile,
was dragged into the debate as both near-neighbour and respected
man of letters. Although he maintained a healthy scepticism about
the whole affair, despite the frenzied fascination of Londoners, he
also wrote about it at length in *Gentleman's Magazine* and was
consequently perceived as one of the ghost's supporters.

The poet Charles Churchill had already lampooned Johnson
on the subject in his poem 'The Ghost' and Foote intended to
have the doctor as a character in *The Orators* with Foote himself
alternating the role with another drag creation as 'Fanny Phantom'. The lumbering Johnson, with his tics and bizarre speech,
was an easy target for Foote's impersonating skills and well recognized around London, but according to Boswell, the doctor had
called Churchill a 'blockhead' for his satirical poem and seemed
alarmed to distraction by the prospect that Foote might also attack
him. Boswell wrote: 'Being at dinner at Davies's the bookseller,
from whom I had that story [about Foote] Dr Johnson [said] that
"I am told Foote means to take me off, as he calls it, and I am
determined the fellow shall not do so with impunity." '[21] He said
he intended to buy cudgels. Thomas Davies, the Scottish bookseller, reported this exchange to Foote, whose works he also sold.
Johnson sent word to Foote that 'The theatre being intended for
the reformation of vice, he would go from the boxes to the stage,
and correct him before the audience.'

Foote relented, and withdrew his suggestion that he would
parody Johnson in *The Orators*. It is a rare example of his bowing
to pressure from friends or the public, and may speak of some
particular regard for Johnson. Johnson had another theory. 'Did
[Foote] not think of exhibiting you Sir?' Boswell said to Johnson
one evening, years later, when they were discussing Foote's accident. 'Sir,' replied the doctor, 'fear restrained him; he knew I
would have broken his bones. I would have saved him the trouble

of cutting off a leg: I would not have left him a leg to cut off.'[22] But when Boswell challenged Johnson on Foote's morality in parodying friends and acquaintances, Johnson had a more considered response: 'Why Sir, when you go to see Foote ... you go to see a man who will be entertained at your house, and then bring you on the Publick stage, who will entertain you with the very purpose of bringing you on a publick stage. Sir, he does not make fools of his company; they whom he exposes are fools already, he only brings them into action.'[23]

§

Through the late 1750s and early 1760s a novel experiment in theatrical criticism arose in London: a ranking of stars or theatre celebrities in a table. In its way it was within the spirit of the Age of Reason and the era of the Encyclopedists for it chose to address the business of stage talent with the tools of rationalism and the rule of numbers. *The Critical Balance*, as it was known, or *Scale of Comedians and Tragedians*, was also, of course, a very modern exercise in talent-contesting. It is a telling document on Foote, and one of the few that attempt to contextualize his singular talent within the world of Georgian theatre. In tragedy, according to *The Critical Balance*, Garrick stood supreme with eighty-eight points in total across columns of 'genius', 'judgment', 'expression', 'action' and 'voice'. *The Scale of Comedians*, however, ranked only 'genius', 'judgment', '*vis comica*' (comic face) and 'variety', in which, for instance, Peg Woffington scored higher than she had done in tragedy, almost equal to Garrick and ahead of Mrs Cibber. Samuel Foote, meanwhile, though listed, was scored in no categories at all by the anonymous pamphleteer-critic. He is awarded instead simply an asterisk and the legend: 'This Gentleman's talents are so much out of the common road that I cannot settle what his is in each particular, and will therefore leave every reader to rate his merit according to his own feeling.'[24]

There was nothing and no one quite like Foote. To rate or rank him was impossible. To talk about him continued to be one of the great pastimes of Georgian London.

THE RAKES' PROGRESS

'The friendship – call it a league – he formed with the
Delavals, a family renowned for wild profligacy, spread
his fame through the Northern Counties.'

The Letters and Journals of Lady Mary Coke[1]

'THERE IS AN EXTRAORDINARY HOUSE on a windy hill,' wrote
Laurence Whistler, on his tour of the north of England, 'with an
unkind sea at its foot, and there came to live an equally extraordinary family, the most charming, spendthrift people, utterly without
morals, loved by the people of the countryside and damned from
birth: the gay Delavals.'[2] Whistler was at Seaton Delaval Hall,
Vanbrugh's caliginous masterpiece on the Northumberland coast.
The house and its family were subjects also of Samuel Foote,
subjects to his love and of his satire. Frank Delaval, eldest son and
heir, 'consummate puppy and unprincipled jackanape',[3] according
to Lord Chesterfield, has some claim to having been the greatest
love of Samuel Foote's life. Whether this love was platonic, sexual,
romantic or more simply a meeting of like minds, restive tempera-
ments and dangerous personalities is difficult to assess, despite the
unexpectedly intimate source material, unpublished, that has survived in a Northumbrian family archive.

Seaton Delaval has to this day the capacity to take one's breath
away, if any breath is left from the assault of the North Sea and
the steep climb from crashing waves on the coast. This granite

mausoleum of a house, described even in its eighteenth-century heyday as 'uninhabitable', is now empty, and the family, exhausted by its own exuberance, died out within a generation of Foote's time. On a winter night in 1822, however, only a few years after the death of the last male Delaval heir, news reached nearby Newcastle that the house was on fire. People came from as far away as North Shields and Tynemouth to watch a blaze of such intensity that 'the lead of the roof poured down like water'.[4] Astonishingly, a cache of papers was included in the armfuls of artefacts flung out of windows and doused with water: the Delaval papers. Twenty thousand manuscript documents survived, soot-marked and waterstained, including letters and memoranda, arcane account books, and even play scripts. Within their leaves there is also much to glean about Samuel Foote – despised by many Delavals as the man who ruined the heir to the estate, adored by others, including that heir. Now, the letters and poems, play scripts and even theatre tickets[5] that narrate an important motif in the story of Mr Foote are to be found in a municipal archive attached to a disused coal mine, once part of the estate: a very English, very literary type of love affair, one with an entire aristocratic family.

§

Frank Delaval, heir to the family fortune and seven years Foote's junior, had been part of his London orbit since the late 1740s. 'Pleasure,' William Cooke noted, 'through its infinite ramifications, was the great object of Frank's life and both he and Foote having, intermittently, fortunes – one patrimonial the other acquired, they pursued pleasure in all its source, from books ... to the lowest species of [pleasures].'[6] Knighted after an almost accidental naval triumph in which he featured at St Malo, 'Sir Frank' was heir to a large swathe of Northumbria along with Seaton Delaval Hall. The Hall was the family seat, though they had another grand property in Lincolnshire, Doddington Hall, also visited by Foote. While his younger brother, John, toiled diligently and remodelled Doddington, Frank built a reputation in London as a rake and roustabout of such heroic proportions that cartoons and plays alluded to his exploits across the gaming tables and mattresses of Augustan London. He had all that Georgian manhood might aspire to: title, wealth and property, epicene good looks and 'gentlemanly bearing', a vast sexual appetite matched by a reckless disregard for its consequences, and an unexpected yearning for metropolitan celebrity as an intellectual polymath and even as an actor. 'In modern gallantry he vied with the first fashionables in Europe,'[7] Cooke wrote, quoting an anonymous friend of both Foote and Delaval. Another friend, Richard Lovell Edgeworth, wrote that 'In six weeks [with Frank] ... the most seductive of [any of my] companions ... I saw more of what is called *the world* than I would probably have seen elsewhere in as many years. I was twenty-two.'[8] Yet Frank had also been expelled from Oxford after the death of a college porter 'in rough play' [*sic*],[9] and had turned Seaton Delaval into 'a perfect Eastern profusion of coloured lights, amid which flitted throngs abandoning themselves to extraordinary follies';[10] in 1771 his bad behaviour was immortalized in William Renwick's novel *Damon and Celia*. He used his fortune, or the prospect of it, 'alternately as a means of generosity and of dissipation,' wrote one friend. 'Active in his pleasures, he was the leading showman of his day, *whatever* the species of frivolity'.[11]

Frank boasted that he modelled himself on Hogarth's Tom Rakewell, anti-hero of *The Rake's Progress*, and expected accordingly to end his days in Bethlehem Hospital. In one key scene of his life, arranged by Foote, Frank followed precisely the plot of the rake's progress in marrying an old widow for her money. But he has some further claim to be a Rakewell or indeed a 'Casanova', whom he and Foote met and admired in 1763, in that his profound interest in the sensual and the sybaritic belied a truly questing mind, one with a broad-ranging interest in science, invention, architecture and even stagecraft. And, like Casanova and, indeed, Foote, Frank may well have been what today would be called bisexual. Some have speculated at a sexual relationship between

Frank Delaval and Samuel Foote, but they had a great deal more in common than possibly free-ranging sexuality. Men of the theatre and scapegraces both, they also shared an instinctive carelessness for propriety and a recklessness in their humour that elided closely with the sadistic. They were gentlemen of their era not only in dangerous practical jokes, but also in expressing effusive affection for one another in manners that today raise eyebrows, perhaps unnecessarily. They began their friendship, however, out of a shared love of inventions. While his other friends turned the scientific discoveries of the age to account on their estates or indeed in factories, Frank Delaval tended to put them to use in pursuit of pleasure and wonder. But then he was a very rich man. Or had expectations eventually of so being.

Delavals had been selling coal from Newcastle for generations, but things had taken off in a much bigger way with the opening of the Seaton Sluice Dock. By the 1760s 177 vessels a year were shipping coal direct from the estate's mines. Nor was Delaval coal merely floated away for profit: it was used to fuel the Delaval glass-works – the largest in the country – and to heat seawater for salt, which in turn supported the preserved-fish trade up and down the east coast of England. Salt was worth more than coal until the end of the eighteenth century. Both were equally profitable by 1750. Foote said that no man had ever made better use of salt and coal to make gold than his friend Frank; it was a truer alchemy than that of the Philosopher's Stone chased by so many of their contemporaries. Inheriting the estates, but also the expensive and half-complete Seaton Delaval, Frank found himself torn between responsibilities in the north – to architecture and his patrimony – and his natural inclinations towards the arts, sciences and theatres of London.

Frank moved to London around 1747. He set up home in Downing Square. Young Mr Delaval, the *St James's Chronicle* informs us, was immediately at the centre of 'the gaiest [*sic*] parties and most esteemed company'[12] at Ranelagh Rotunda. He also, unconventionally, enrolled as a student of elocution under Charles

Macklin in Covent Garden. So his introduction to Foote could as easily have come there as at Tom's coffee-house and bookstore where they both read and drank. Frank became a devotee of the London theatre. Not only did he move in the same crowd of critics and actress-chasers as Lord Lyttelton, John Wilkes and Horace Walpole, he also befriended the backstage crew, 'the property men, the candle snuffers, the prompters and the authors', as one friend wrote, and 'took in all the players cant together with their diet of pint pots of porter and mutton pies in the green room'.[13] He had an easy and a democratic charm, and, like his later friend the young Duke of York, seems to have preferred the warm embrace of the theatre to the supposed refinement of Court.

He and Foote found an alignment of wit and temperament, it might seem, over such pint pots and porter or after their Macklin classes and Foote became his *de facto* tutor in dramatic literature. Delaval began collecting play scripts on Foote's advice. One receipt in the Delaval papers lists Frank's play-buying requirements for just one London season: nearly thirty titles at £2 1s.7d.[14] He studied text and acting, and sought advice of those, like Foote, who were published or performing already. At the same time, he sought backstage advice on stage machinery, his twin fascination. He filled his Downing Square house with the instrumental and scientific wonders of the age: a mechanical horse, automata, magnets, flywheels and pendula, and some of the first 'steaming engines' in London. He rigged a signalling system from Epsom races to Hampstead that allowed news to reach the rooftops of Blooms-bury 'to the amazement of sporting gentlemen', and experimented with glass smelting in Downing Square to the horror of the fire-watch and his housekeeper. It was this, as much as Frank's love of theatre, that had brought him the admiration and complicity of Foote, as equally Benjamin Franklin and the scientist and painter Benjamin Wilson, all of them meeting at soirées in Downing Square, freely mixing the arts and sciences – electricity and mesmerism, steam, theatre and the Enlightenment – in the spirit of that other age of wonder. Frank Delaval went one further than

his many theatre- and science-loving aristocratic friends. He built
his own small auditorium in Downing Square for the purposes of
scientific demonstrations and amateur dramatics. Perhaps, then, it
was not surprising that he kept only half an eye on the profitability
of his estates in the north, spent rashly in the metropolis and fell
precipitously into debt.

Frank, like the rest of his large family, was tall, fair and
confidently attractive – which would prove his temporary route
out of debt. John, the next in line, was said to be handsomer, but
this was mitigated by his studious concern for the family estates
and his obdurate attachment to his married cousin. There was
then brother Edward, also a scientist, and Thomas, Robert,
George, Henry and Ralph. The girls, Rhoda, Ann and Sarah,
known as the Hussey-Delavals in respect, partly, of a maternal
family name, were all noted beauties as they each in turn came
down for London seasons. Along with the eight boys, they filled
Downing Square, but also Seaton Delaval, the 'coldest house in
England', with noise and laughter and wild experimentation of
every sort. Foote was understandably dazzled and flattered by their
attentions. They were a family seeded with the many gifts –
confidence, beauty, talent and wealth – that so often seem kernel-
led with tragedy or its potential. Certainly the family tree cleaved,
as the century wore on, to the darker aspects of their native
landscape, and the Delavals, so gregarious, so expansive and
libidinous, and so very numerous, were all gone, without issue, by
the time Seaton Delaval was finally complete. Yet for Foote, they
fascinated as only and rarely a whole family can: more alluring
en masse than as individuals, more compelling through being beautiful, rich, glamorous, and not one's own. And in the Delavals' case,
they were every bit as reckless and devil-may-care as Foote himself. Like him they were unrestrained essentially by the quotidian
concerns of parents, Church or conventional morality – and they
had money and position.

At Seaton Delaval and at Downing Square things could get
radically out of hand. The Hall, half built, lent itself to architectural

and theatrical pranks. Entire *trompe-l'oeil* walls were created in guest bedrooms, which could be removed exactly as a guest was known to be naked, at their ablutions, or *in flagrante*. One room was built such that an entire four-poster bed was 'suspended by pulleys over trap doors so that guest might be rapidly let down'[15] into a bath of cold water, which is one way to stop a party. 'Ducks and hens were put between sheets, manikins like the ghosts of ancient Delavals were set up in clothes-closets', horses were ridden down the great stairs, and the beautiful Delavals, Frank, his sisters and brothers, would cavort naked or 'mysteriously appear somewhere quite else by means of the secret underground passages' of Seaton Delaval.

An invitation to the Hall was therefore not to be taken lightly, or by the faint of heart, but was accepted gladly and often by Foote whenever his theatrical timetable allowed. Though his relationship with Frank was always the strongest, he seemed to fall in love with each family member in turn, squiring the sisters to the theatre on their visits to London, and introducing Edward, two years Frank's junior, to his scientific friends. At Seaton Delaval, as at Downing Square, Foote became, for the family, their '*arbiter deliciarum*' – a master of revels – organizing house parties and evening frolics, which, if not quite of the sinister hues of the Hellfire Club, featured by turns 'an ass-race, a puppet show, a grinning match and a shift race by the women [in their undergarments]'.[16] Larrikin stuff.

Like a series of tableaux from Hogarth's *Rake's Progress*, the romping fun of Seaton Delaval and Downing Square led, inevitably, to debt. And, like Hogarth's original, the narrative required some young *ingénues* . . . and perhaps a wealthy widow. Onto the stage, then, for this next scene in Foote's life step the Misses Elizabeth and Deodata Roach. Rather as if the genteel sisters of a Fanny Burney novel had accidentally wandered into a Covent Garden brothel, Elizabeth and Deodata, expensively educated in Paris, orphaned heiresses of the East India Company, came upon the rakes' progress of Foote and Delaval at a dangerous moment for them all. Betty and Deodata were eighteen and nineteen respectively when they became wards of court in November 1749, having been adopted by the husband of one of Frank's cousins, who then died. Seemingly they were illegitimate. They had connections, education, looks and, indeed, money, though this was attached, as was often the case, to their marrying, and was the subject of one Chancery case for their previous guardian had married one of them, illegally, to his son. But they had no 'family'. It was a mixed hand to play on the Georgian marriage tables, but they played dangerously and poorly – as Betty set her cap at the family's eldest son, Foote's boon companion, Frank.

As was the way of things in extended Georgian families, the Roach sisters came to live briefly at Seaton Delaval, and then on Albemarle Street, Piccadilly, 'two little golden fishes with the bags of diamonds and their East Indian fortunes'.[17] It was while they were at Albemarle Street that their protector, Mr Potter, a relation by marriage to the Delavals, died suddenly. The Roach sisters fell consequently under the protection of the Delaval family, whose London head, unfortunately for them, was Frank.

By Christmas 1749, Deodata had been discovered to have married secretly one Mr Tom Quane, who claimed her fortune,[18] and Betty had fled, or been abducted, from Albemarle Street and was living in Poland Street, Soho, with Frank. One rumour spread that she had persuaded Frank to marry her. Another, nearer the truth, soon eclipsed the first: that she had become his mistress. According to one writer who knew them, she 'met his libidinous affections with ardour', which could mean one of several things, and this witness, a later mistress of Frank's, added cattily that 'it was a doubtful point whether she was the seducer or the seduced'.[19] Be that as it may, Frank introduced his young mistress, supposedly in the care of his family, around what he termed 'the circle of noise and show . . . the *beau monde* . . . that theatre which affords philosophical scenes of unknown worlds: the Little Theatre in the Haymarket'.[20] In other words, he ruined her, and generally he did so in the company of Foote. Foote was not greatly taken with this new member of their party. 'She flattered well,' he remarked, 'and to flatter well requires study,' but he noted that her expensive French convent education had left her unable to comprehend his wit, and with skills that amounted to little more than an ability to speak 'French tolerably, and cut and paste together silly shapes'.[21]

Up to this point Frank's coterie had numbered Foote and Macklin, William Kelynge, a lawyer, and Jemmy Worsdale, quondam colour grinder to Sir Godfrey Kneller. After Frank had convinced Betty Roach to be his paramour in Poland Street, his friends noted his absence, and the distraction of funds it represented, and began to hatch a plot that was somewhere between a practical joke and a scam. They met together – Foote and Worsdale, Macklin and others – and plotted in the Cardigan's Head tavern in Charing Cross. Frank's money was entailed to his estates and, despite his lands and position, he was, by the late 1740s, more than £9,000 in debt. His friends at the Cardigan's Head thought it might be a wheeze to marry him to someone very rich, very antipathetic to his young mistress, and very old.

Samuel Foote had known Lady Isabella Pawlett, the widow of Lord Nassau Pawlett, for some years. She was as old as the century, prone, like Foote, to overweight, a huge fan of the theatre, a little blind and remarkably gullible. Foote was on intimate enough terms with her to visit her at Watlington Park, the estate she rented from Lord Falkland near Oxford, relatively soon after the demise of her husband and seemingly with the intent of securing her investment in the Haymarket. 'As unhealthy a situation as you could have pitched upon,' he opined, about the Christmas Common property she rented, which was so damp that 'the cloathes one pulls off at night are so wet by the next morning'. But he visited her there nonetheless, in the spirit of pan-handling for a Haymarket benefit night, but with more in mind than just the hire of a front box. He had a mind to marry Lady Isabella to his impecunious young friend: as dare or bet or scam.

'I am but a poor widow,'[22] Lady Isabella insisted to Foote,

when he importuned her for funds for the theatre, but he knew
this to be largely a lie. She was in benefit of over £100,000,
inherited largely from her late husband though in small part in her
own name as the daughter of the Earl of Thanet. It was all held
in trust by her male in-laws, unless or until she should remarry.
She was, in theatrical terms, a sponsor worth nurturing, and some
speculated that she became Foote's mistress, such was her seeming
infatuation with the comedian. But Foote was alighting upon an
altogether more financially astringent agenda. As matchmaking
goes, the idea of netting Isabella for Frank could not have reflected
worse on all the lead players and in particular the *yentl*, Mr Foote.
But as a plot it was worthy of any of his farces and, indeed, he cast
many of his friends in minor roles. The opening scene took place
at dank Watlington Park. Here, Foote told the biddable widow
that he had come across a new spiritualist and fortune-teller in
London who was the talk of all the *Bon Ton*: 'an astonishing fellow,
up two flights of stairs in a back alley . . . off Leicester Fields . . . as
black as Othello'. This medium could, Foote assured Lady Isabella,
'foretell the future'. The 'blackamoor' spiritualist had already
foretold two marriages and an elopement, Foote added, and
everything he had foretold had come to pass, 'with the greatest
felicity for all parties . . . people of the highest distinction'.[23] He left
his bait hanging, and returned to London.

Frankly, it would be unworthy of credit and credibility as a
plot, let alone a historical narrative, but there it is in the legal
accounts of the Delaval papers: the gulling of Lady Isabella Pawlett.
The lawyer Kelynge put in for his and Foote's expenses, and
seemingly provided advice also on the likely financial settlement if
Lady Isabella Pawlett became Lady Isabella Delaval.

Jemmy Worsdale blacked up as 'Othello', the fortune teller, in
a darkened room near Panton Street, Foote fed him beforehand
some details of Lady Isabella's life so he might appear clairvoyant
in the manner she expected, and poor gullible Isabella was
informed that her new husband would be found the next day,

dressed in blue braided silk and walking by the artificial lake that
then graced Green Park.

Foote's and Frank's interest in necromancy and prophecies is
very much in keeping with the age of Mesmer, and it is unclear
how much even the practitioners really believed of what they did.
But Isabella Pawlett was not the first or the last of their dupes. The
Leicester Fields address they used was described by another friend
who knew it: Lady Isabella would have entered, hooded, 'via a
long narrow dark winding passage lighted by a few dim lamps.
The conjuror [Jemmy in this instance, sometimes Foote] was
seated on an Ottoman in the middle of the room . . . dressed in
the Eastern fashion, with a turban . . . from time to time he hit a
drum from which there emanated a deep and melancholy sound.'[24]

On the occasion Lady Isabella came, according to an actress
who heard the story separately, Foote and Jemmy together disguised themselves in the Stygian gloom, consulted for Lady Isabella
'a planetary system, signs of the zodiac and fixed stars', and came
up with a description of her husband to be. 'His person', they
described as 'elegant, his face handsome, his education liberal, his
conversation sprightly',[25] then they told her where, when and how
she might meet him.

Foote instructed Frank to walk as intended by the Green Park
lake and, acting the part with *élan*, young Delaval let fall in Lady
Isabella's path a silk handkerchief at which, presumably, the
curtain was due to fall for the interval. It didn't take much more.

'Three days later',[26] Lady Isabella, rich, poor-sighted, middle-
aged and 'monstrously fat',[27] walked out of St George's, Hanover
Square, as bride to the heir of Seaton Delaval. Frank was twenty-
three. As in the tableau from Hogarth's *Rake's Progress*, whose hero
also marries an elderly widow to clear his debts, somewhere in the
background lurks the figure of his young mistress. Betty Roach was
now the mother of two small children by Frank. Foote's only
comment at the time was that 'As he had made the match, he
must likewise make his friend's apology, which was, that he bought

her by weight and paid nothing for the fashion.'[28] In an age noted for its cynicism the match had the potential to catch the imagination and beg questions. Even on the steps of St George's, it was written, the astonishing pulchritude not of the bride but of the bridegroom brought 'sighs and cheers from all the newspaper sellers, mantua makers, footmen servant maids and ladies of the Town who, with vast curiosity, had assembled there'.[29]

It was a brutally audacious plot by the gang from the Charing Cross tavern and, quite blatantly, it was financially motivated. Frank allotted Foote £12,000 for helping him rearrange his debts with Lady Isabella's £100,000, which he pocketed with all due cupidity. Regrettably for all concerned, the Pawlett family lawyers pointed out that the bulk of the money was held in trust for Isabella's only daughter, leaving the expectant young bridegroom, after he had paid off his matchmaker, with less than £11,000, or £2,000 only above his debts. In the spirit of the gaming table, Foote was said to have given back some or all of the money to Frank but out of largesse, not honour. The ill-matched pair became, quite understandably, a laughing stock.

The letters in the Delaval papers from this period are breezy and blatantly complicit between the Delaval brothers and Foote about what was going on. Letters from Frank to John often begin with the likes of 'I have just come from Mr Foote's farce, which went off with great applause,' while from Foote to the Delavals they are as likely to end with rakish allusions to the fecundity of Frank's extra-marital affair: 'I congratulate you on the fertility of [your mistress] as every additional blessing to your Family can't but give pleasure,' or later, 'The town is as empty as your aunt's head . . . but . . . to the latter you have this morning a collateral addition in the birth of a son to Miss Roach.'[30]

Frank's eldest sister, Rhoda, clever, articulate, an admirer of Foote's plays, was disquieted by the news of the alliance Foote had arranged for her brother. None of the Delavals had been invited to the wedding, and even Lady Isabella had had last-minute concerns about what she was doing. Frank's friendship with Foote had long alarmed John Delaval, but the marriage brokered by Foote, with both sides hoodwinked in their different ways, put the whole family in an embarrassing position. Frank had already ruined the reputation of Miss Roach, sometime ward of the family, and he had now married without prospect of an heir a woman widely credited in London as 'mad',[31] roundly condemned as of loose morals and without a substantial portion to her name. Rhoda began to refer to Foote in letters to her brother as 'that other person with you', and when she came upon Foote unexpectedly at Doddington wrote to the hostess, her new sister-in-law Mrs John Delaval, 'Could this not have been *prevented*?' Rhoda, after Frank's marriage to Isabella, formed an intractable belief that contact with Foote attended 'certain ruin' for them all. John wrote back to his sister: 'You seem to think by your letter we could have prevented Foote's coming here. It was impossible, as we did not know of it until he came into the room. Remonstrances had no effect. [Frank] had been here two months [but] the day after Foote arrived, they . . . set out for London together.'

The marriage of Frank and Isabella was the end of Foote's welcome at Seaton Delaval.

The only way out of such a disastrous impasse – a marriage of financial convenience that turned out to be nothing of the sort – was annulment or divorce. With the backing of his family – though tellingly not his heir presumptive John Delaval – Frank put in motion the expensive proceedings of divorce from Lady Isabella within months of their marriage. To the great delight of the press in the form of the *St James's Chronicle*, the *Gazetteer* and *Lloyd's Evening Post*, the Pawlett family countersued, with the very rare step of petitioning for damages on the grounds of a husband's adultery. It seemed there would be plenty of evidence that there had been infidelities on both sides, and Lady Isabella, 'at the height of one of their disputes' about money soon after they were married, 'had discovered the secret of the conjuror'.[32] Hell hath no fury like a woman duped. The Pawlett family lawyers believed Frank's continuing co-habitation with Betty Roach – and the existence of children – would provide sufficient grounds.

The Trial of Sir Francis Blake Delaval KB for Committing Adultery with Miss Roach, alias Mss La Roche, alias Miss Le Roche is typical of the so-called 'criminal conversation' (adultery) trial records of the period. They provided widely promulgated titillation for Georgian Londoners about the sexual practices of the upper classes, and details were picked up and reproduced in the wider press, usually with the names semi-obliterated. This 'crim-con' was atypical only in so far as it, unusually, featured the infidelity of a husband. Servants were subpoenaed for the prosecution: the coachman, groom and valet to Frank at the house he shared with Betty Roach in Soho. To the consternation of the Pawlett family, they all swore they had never seen any 'indecent familiarity' between Sir Frank and his mistress, despite the strong evidence, one might have thought, of the two children she had already borne him and confidently if unimaginatively named Francis and Frances. Frank wanted to end the marriage on his own terms. Next, and separately, Lady Isabella's name was dragged through the courts and evidence presented that she had carried on several liaisons since her marriage, in some of the seedier environs of the capital.

Foote colluded in the attempt to dissolve the marriage just as he had colluded in its conception. It remained a matter of money. Various male staff members of Haddock's bagnios in Covent Garden, as well as habitués of the Cardigan's Head in Charing Cross, were all willing, for a fee, to give evidence against Lady Isabella. They all swore that she had frequently engaged rooms at Haddock's baths – where rooms were rentable by the hour and less – with a male lover. Foote was involved in almost every stage of the unprepossessing proceedings to accuse Lady Isabella of adultery.

Here, at the trial of Lady Isabella Delaval and at the place of William Haddock's bagnios in Covent Garden, a figure from the shadows of Sam Foote's early life comes back to the stage: William

Dupree. Dupree had been one of the witnesses to the abduction of Sir John Dineley-Goodere in Bristol in 1741, and he was also, by a coincidence that has as its clear plot-machinist Samuel Foote, witness to the multiple infidelities of Lady Isabella at Haddock's. At her criminal conversation trial William Dupree made the astonishing avowal that he, Foote and Frank Delaval had all met at the Cardigan's Head tavern in Charing Cross. Here, because Frank Delaval had 'talked freely before them all of his wife's infidelities',[33] Dupree and others 'volunteered' to spy on her and her paramours. Of course, it had to have been more compromised than that: there was clearly money involved. Yet this was unlikely to trouble the court. Dupree and Foote had seemingly, and for whatever reasons, stayed in contact since the Bristol trial. What Dupree said, however, is almost as eyebrow-raising as the fact that he was in contact with Foote to say it: Frank Delaval, Dupree told him, had 'made the statement that [Lady Isabella] lay with more men than he himself'. The syntax is, of course, unclear, but this may hold some small clue as to how and why Dupree and Foote had stayed in touch, if it is read in the light of a separate understanding: the Cardigan's Head had a dubious reputation and was considered by some a molly-house.

The conclusion of this tawdry tale was that the Cardigan's Head witnesses who went to Haddock's, Messrs Dupree, Quarme, Shaw and Saunders, all swore that they rushed the private room hired by Lady Isabella and there, by the light of candles and 'a fine fire', plainly saw 'Lady Isabella Delaval and one Mr Craig naked in one and the same bed'.[34] Frank and Foote, their testimony irrelevant, presumably stayed at the pub. This ought to have been an end to things: sufficient evidence to sue Mr Craig for damages against the 'property' of Sir Frank, his wife. But there was too much money, or the potential of it, on both sides, and Isabella's lawyers had the case dismissed on the not unreasonable grounds that all the witnesses had been drunk. Her daughter, Miss Isabella Pawlett, petitioning quite separately as an infant, reclaimed from Frank the entirety of the Pawlett money, and Frank returned, yet poorer, to the arms of Betty Roach, though still a married man.

Foote might have been welcome no longer at Seaton Delaval, but his relationship with the family was far from over. In the wake of the marriage débâcle, one with financial, familial, legal and romantic implications that can have pleased no one but the lawyers, it is little short of astonishing to consider what the Delavals and Foote did next. With the last of Isabella's diminished marriage portion, her own as opposed to the Pawlett family money, Frank Delaval and Samuel Foote mounted one of the strangest theatrical productions ever to grace the West End: a production of *Othello* starring most of the warring Delaval family.

The Delavals had long been devotees of amateur dramatics. They had staged private theatricals at the auditorium at Downing Square, with family members and professionals in the cast. At Seaton Delaval, according to the family papers, things were a good deal more lavish. One invited audience of more than a hundred was served '2 swans and boarsheads, and 120lbs of ham'[35] while the family performed a Restoration comedy; another Seaton Delaval performance, presumably al fresco, was attended 'by four thousand' spectators, a number of them bemused Tyneside tenant-farmers. Nor was Frank the only devotee in the family. His financially astute and diligent younger brother John, later Lord, Delaval was also a devoted, and gifted, amateur actor.

Foote suggested to Delaval 'that as he, Frank, was fond of a stage, it would be turning his talents to some account to get up some creditable play, in which himself and friends might fill up the characters'.[36] The idea was first mooted in Paris when they were there together in the early 1750s. It is unclear if this was ever intended as a money-making venture or a loss-leader towards a prospective career but, for one night only, *Othello* was to be performed for a paying London audience, with the entire Delaval family, including the Roach sisters, as the cast. Frank would play Othello. The play was Foote's suggestion: it had been, of course, his London début too. This time, Frank would take the title role, under the direction of Charles Macklin and Foote, with John as Iago, younger brother Thomas as Cassio, and the scandalous Roach sisters, Betty and Deodata, as Emilia and Desdemona respectively. Christopher Smart was commissioned by Foote to write a prologue and epilogue, to be spoken by the sisters, which, once published, ran through three editions in three days. Foote had enormous confidence in his *protégé* and laboured also under the apprehension that his Othello would reposition Frank in the public imagination as less the playboy and more the artist: 'Whatever Dissipations the World may suppose our Days to have been consumed,' he wrote, 'many, many Hours have been consecrated to other Subjects than generally employ the Gay and the Giddy and unless I am greatly mistaken, it will soon be discovered, that joined to the acknowledged best heart in the World, Mr *Delaval* has a head capable of directing it'.[37]

According to the *London Literary Gazette* and the *Evening Post*, Frank and Foote had originally wanted to use the Little Theatre on the Haymarket for this venture, but once word got out, such was the public interest in this 'novelty'[38] and in this latest 'Gentlemen never before seen upon the Stage' that Drury Lane was booked instead. Garrick interrupted a run of Thomas Arne's *Alfred* 'especially to oblige them'. The fact was, he agreed 'without hesitation'. With a full house at Drury Lane, he could only hope to take £190 a night and averaged a mere £134. Frank, it was reported, offered him £1,500.[39] The rental figure may in truth have been nearer the market rate, for the Delaval papers seem to suggest that the *overall* costs amounted to £2,000, which was, even so, a staggering sum. By the accounts there, it seems more likely Frank spent the bulk of the money not on the rental of Drury Lane but on new settings and costumes for himself and his fellow cast members with which to dazzle his London audience.[40]

Frank's hubristic ambitions necessarily attracted the curious, and an audience might have been drawn simply in the expectation of disaster. But the family, according to Tate Wilkinson, aided Frank in 'filling the theatre with their own acquaintances', and this

'included all the nobility of the three kingdoms then in London'[41]
up to and including the royal family. The excitement was almost
palpable in London, according to the newspapers,[42] in the run-up
to the performance, and the rehearsals were talked up by Foote,
among others. William Cooke recalled that this 'drew much
attention of the town', and 'the rage was so great to see the
performance', according to Horace Walpole, that 'the House of
Commons itself was adjourned' to enable the Members to be
present. The business of government would have to be suspended
for the business of show, and Walpole was not alone in noting that
the fascination was only partly artistic. People wanted to see the
Delavals, 'people of some fashion', as Walpole described them,
essaying their skills as thespians on the premier stage of the land.
The greatest interest was reserved for Frank, 'the eldest of [them]',
Walpole pointed out, recently 'married by Foote to Lady Nassau
Pawlet [sic]',[43] the handsome and wastrel Delaval heir, parlaying
his gossip-column notoriety into a stage triumph.

The Macklin-styled marketing coup that had launched both
Garrick and Foote was repeated for an entire family in what
became known as the Delaval Othello. It was also a triumph of
celebrity over art, for there was never any real intention of any
of the family starting full-time careers as actors. They seemed to
want only to buy the one thing that money and position do not
always afford: attention. In this they proved rather successful. 'The
company', it was said, was due to be 'more brilliant than anything
ever seen in a Playhouse in this kingdom' and, indeed, on the
night itself Drury Lane was 'filled with coaches and chairs', such
that 'the greatest company of ladies and gentlemen were obliged
to wade through the dirt and filth to get to the house'. Though
initially it was only the 'pickpockets and other gentlemen of that
trade' who benefited from the crush, the audience was not to be
disappointed either. For the Delavals proved star performers.

Drury Lane furnished an even clearer view of the audience
than was the norm, seventy-two candelabra flickering over the
stage and extra illumination for the auditorium paid for by the

Delavals. Tickets had been delivered 'to as many as could conveniently fill the house, without specifying any particular part', and as a result many of the gentry had a view the like of which was usually reserved for their servants, from 'the gods', 'so that the shilling gallery was as much crowded with nobility as the boxes; diamonds shone, and ribbons were peeping out of the slips',[44] and 'the upper gallery was as brilliant with stars and garters [nobility] as the boxes and the pit below'.[45]

Backstage a sudden change of plan, or stagefright on the part of the Roach sisters, led to John Delaval stepping in to deliver Christopher Smart's prologue, as commissioned by Foote. Walking to the centre of the Drury Lane stage, and with Garrick and Foote in the audience, along with, presumably, some of the Haymarket and Drury Lane companies, he made his plea for stage amateurs:

> While mercenary Actors tread the Stage
> And hireling Scribblers lash or lull the Age
> Ours be the Talk t'instruct and entertain
> Without one thought of Glory, or of Gain.[46]

The gain was indeed minimal, but Frank and John were covered with glory, as was the lavish but naturalistic design.

Frank, though he sweated a good deal through his thick black makeup, was widely admired. 'Noble, handsome and commanding,' according to one, and said to 'give a striking resemblance of the Moorish general', which is hard to credit, given his blandly blond appeal. His brother John, playing Iago, was accounted 'perfect to a "t"' and 'a guisard born'. One critic noted that 'birth and associations of elegance' all worked in Frank's favour: he was naturally commanding, military and aristocratic, not having to *act* such qualities, and, schooled by Macklin and Foote, his delivery was deliberately naturalistic, within his own register and experience of nobility. They dressed in contemporary uniforms as the brother-officers of the play, a further element of the evening that felt uniquely charmed. 'Sir Francis played with true dignity and much pathos,' wrote one critic, 'and in his amend with Cassio, where he takes his hand, and says, "*I do believe it and ask your pardon,*" it was felt that there was the tone and manner of *true bred gentlemen,*[47] addressing one another. The Roach sisters fared less well with the audience. Both spoke with French accents, which was accounted a good deal less distracting than the jewels they also sported: 'stomachers ablaze with diamonds'.[48]

The Delaval *Othello* stands at an intriguing point in the history of Shakespearean productions. There was suitable comment in the press that this 'amateur' triumph begged questions over what constituted the business of acting, naturalism and theatre. Macklin, Foote and Garrick's insistence on star personae who could be recognized by the audience and indeed sold as such at the box office, and characterization that elided perceived personality and dramatic role, was a familiar trope from Foote's own notorious début, but used to better effect in this later *Othello*. Frank's Moor was 'noble, commanding, generous and thoughtful' because he was known, or thought to be, himself. His sexual persona, as part of a celebrated crim-con case, had its bearing, too, on his Othello, as some might have felt he had personal experience of sexual jealousy and spousal deceit, from both perspectives. Foote's 'singular talent', as Dr Johnson called it, had been to create a marketable stage persona out of a constructed notoriety, and he taught a similar lesson to the Delavals, more valuable, perhaps, than Macklin's work on verse and natural movement. John Hill, the former actor turned critic, had an answer to all this: the Delavals had succeeded, just as Foote did on stage, by force of *personality* and 'natural charm'; they would not suit all roles and productions. They 'were inspired by the sentiment to be the thing the author expected them to represent', Frank's Othello as the prime example, 'that in which he was particularly superior to every [professional actor] was simply the natural expression of the . . . *gentleman*'.[49] He was to the manor and therefore to the manner born. Beyond that, Hill assumed, he would flounder.

Perhaps he would have done, but his appetite for acting was sated by his one-night stand. Its impact played out in other ways, for the Delavals and for Foote. Those who saw Frank's Othello included the Princess of Wales, the Duke of Cumberland and the young Prince Edward, later Duke of York. The audience, like the newspapers the next day, were as taken with this as with what was going on on stage: the spectacle of high society *en masse* at the theatre, like a grand private theatrical to which fortunate members of the middling sort might have access. The young prince, however, did not forget his evening at the Delaval *Othello*, and to that extent the evening marked the beginning of a new chapter in all their lives. What Foote, meanwhile, really thought of his friends' début is hidden behind a well-recorded and likely well-rehearsed riposte he gave afterwards. Doubtless proud and pleased with his own and his friends' triumph, he held court to comment on proceedings afterwards in Drury Lane's Green Room. He was heard to remark by several that he had never felt so sorry for anyone in his life. When asked if it was his friend Frank who deserved his sympathy, Foote started. 'Why no,' he said. 'I meant *Shakespeare* of course.'[50]

§

Thirteen days after the Delaval *Othello*, the heir to the throne, Frederick, Prince of Wales, died. Some said this was the result of a knock to the head from a cricket ball, others that it was pleurisy. The Princess of Wales, aged only thirty-one, was left a pregnant widow with eight children, an uncertain future and substantial debts. Foote's immediate orbit around Leicester Fields was changed by more than just the mourning hangings at the windows of Leicester House. The death, and its effect on the younger members of the royal family, brought the Hanoverian throne rather nearer to the West End, and to the world Foote shared with Frank Delaval. For the second son of the late prince had, like Frank, a strong hankering for the stage, and less and less parental control over how much time he might spend with actors.

Prince Edward Augustus, soon created Duke of York, was second in line after his brother George. But he had been his father's favourite. Unlike his serious elder brother, Edward Augustus was outgoing, quick to laugh and, by the standards of the genetically challenged House of Hanover, handsome. Portraits show a high-coloured, pale-haired youth, with thick white-blond eyelashes that betray his Germanic ancestry. He looked, indeed, a little like Frank Delaval. Edward Augustus had spent his teenage years going to the London theatre and making fun of his tutors, learning to mimic their speech traits in an attempt to make his sententious brother giggle. It was the beginning of Edward's love of performing. He tended to make a quick impression on people, and a good one; 'simple Ned', as Boswell dubbed him with both sneer and approbation – a people's prince. Perhaps, had their father lived, a tighter rein would have been put on the second in line to the throne, as Edward became, but the death of the Prince of Wales led in time to Edward earning the privilege, along with his elder brother, of their own establishment on Leicester Fields. This was only a stone's throw from young Prince Edward's beloved Covent Garden – it was also a house owned by the Savile family, the Mexboroughs, into which Sarah Hussey-Delaval had married. While his elder brother, now titled Prince of Wales, galloped back and forth through Hyde Park to meetings with their supposed mentor, Lord Bute, Prince Edward would sneak out with an equerry for high raillery in the piazza. His hours became theatrical, his mornings sluggish, and the princely brothers, once close, drifted more apart as their teens came to an end.

Principal among the new friends cultivated by the young Duke of York were Frank Delaval and Samuel Foote. The coal heir and the playwright, both more than a decade older than the prince, should have known better than to be impressed by a puppyish royal out to nip at the heels of actresses. Foote and Delaval, however, trailed the rich aroma of celebrity and notoriety that proved so often catnip to members of the House of Hanover and they could be enormously and irreverently funny. In time, Delaval and the young duke became intimately complicit, both supporting a few years later the actress Ann Catley as shared mistress who bore them both sons. She named them Francis and Edward, for ease, one supposes, of recognition. It was an appealingly different atmosphere from the court of George II, the prince's grandfather, and that which followed, of the prince's dutiful older brother George.

The boy from Truro found himself entertaining backstage not just the heir to Seaton Delaval but the second in line to the throne. Foote organized dinners at the Bedford and at Panton Street, and increasingly prided himself on his table. 'Mr Foote possessed . . . with all [his] mingled excellencies,' wrote one dinner party guest, 'generosity, and humanity but vast ostentation annexed to them. His table was open – he loved company at that table, and if they pronounced his wine had a superior flavour, you could not have drank too much, nor could he himself have been gratified till he had produced claret of the best vintage.'[51]

At these soirées a new coterie developed that was in some regard an extension of the old days with Garrick and Macklin, but with better food and more liveried servants. 'They resorted to this constant table,' wrote one young man who entered this privileged circle, 'which was open to all men of genius and of merit, in every department of literature and science.' This new young friend of Frank, Foote and the prince, Richard Lovell Edgeworth, wrote later of being 'dazzled' by the inventors, polymaths and literati who swam in the wake of the young royal. 'I can truly assert,' he added, 'that none but those who were an *honour* to the stage, were admitted into the company.'[52] It was only the standards of the Downing Square kitchens that were complained of, never the conversation there. 'I've dined here six times since I returned from Ireland,' Foote was heard to complain, at a dinner hosted there by him and Frank for the prince, 'and each day a damned loin of pork! I suppose [Frank] means to run his loin of pork against *The Beggar's Opera!*'

At one of these dinners at Downing Square in 1765, Prince Edward mentioned his admiration of the Drury Lane *Othello* featuring Frank. This seeded an idea in Foote's mind and in the

Delavals' to remount an evening of aristocratic theatre, but featuring the prince himself in one of the leads. According to Edgeworth,
Macklin was consulted as the leading authority on preparing an
amateur for the stage and, the Downing Square auditorium considered too small for the purpose, a hall was booked on Petty
France, near the park, that would serve as a unique Theatre Royal
for one night only. Foote and Macklin together, again, seem to
have co-directed.

Although members of the Jacobean court had appeared in
masques, and French and Russian royal family members had acted
on stage, usually semi-incognito, no member of the British royal
family had trodden the boards since the Restoration and, once
word got out, many were scandalized. Nicholas Rowe's *The Fair
Penitent* was chosen as the play – one that the Delavals and very
possibly the prince had performed privately before. Long forgotten, the play boasts one character whose name echoes down to us:
Lothario, the young lover. Prince Edward was keen to play the
role. Sarah Hussey-Delaval was to play the lead *ingénue*, Lavinia.
Anne Hussey-Delaval, now Lady Stanhope, played Calista, and
Frank, of course, kept a strong role for himself and a lesser one for
his brother John, who also toiled, in effect, as producer, for he now
held the purse strings to the Delaval family finances.

Foote and Frank persuaded John to pay lavishly for the
occasion. 'No trouble or expense were spared,' wrote the *Annual
Register*, 'to render the Petty France theatre suitable to receive
royalty',[53] for which privilege, John was also to début as an author.
He penned a lengthy new epilogue to Nicholas Rowe's play, to
be spoken by the disreputable Earl of Strathmore. The original,
in John's laboured scrawl, exists still with the Delaval papers.[54] 'As
to some of the parts,' wrote Edgeworth, with faint praise, 'it was
extremely well performed,' and the duke's Lothario was 'as warm,
as hasty and as much in love as the fair Calista could possibly
wish'.[55] Afterwards, Macklin and Foote took everyone to slum it at
the King's Arms in Covent Garden, like real actors; 'plays, playwrights, enunciation, action, everything belonging to eloquence'

were discussed, with Macklin tossing his wig on the table to reinforce his points, and Domenico Angelo, the fencing master, passing comment on the duke's and Delaval's stagecraft. It was just like the old days at the Bedford.[56]

§

The Haymarket seasons grew in popularity and profitability through the late 1750s and early 1760s. By 1765 Foote could mount at least seventy sell-out nights of assorted comedies, where once a hit like *The Minor* had been considered a phenomenon with a thirty-four-evening run.[57] Nor did the Haymarket define or confine his London career. Throughout this period almost every successful Little Theatre summer hit was taken up by Drury Lane or Covent Garden, such that in the winter months Foote had the choice of West End work or profitable sojourns in Dublin. In the winter of 1758–9, for instance, he played in Garrick's company at Drury Lane, appearing in his own *Diversions of the Morning* and *The Englishman in Paris*, but also as Foppington in *The Relapse* and Fondlewife in *The Old Bachelor*. For the last time he essayed a Shakespearean role, persuading Garrick to let him take over for one night as Shylock, on 18 December 1758 for his benefit night. Kitty Clive, used by now to Macklin and Garrick's style of more naturalistic Jew, was not keen to appear opposite a comedian: '*My* Portia! To *Foote*'s Shylock!'[58] she was heard to wail as she exited the theatre. It is unrecorded who took her place, and Foote never again risked the dismay of his colleagues with a Shakespearean role.

§

His life on stage was only the most conspicuous and the most monied aspect of his social ascendancy. He was also on increasingly intimate terms with the royal household, whose patronage was essential to the success of London theatre ventures, and with high-society figures from young Edgeworth and Delaval to Horace Walpole. His social-climbing and close association with the heir to Seaton Delaval and the second in line to the throne were later seen as the essential background to his downfall, and to his accident. But Foote was also, through the late 1750s and early 1760s, steadily and consistently building a commercially solid career as theatre producer, writer and performer. In 1762 he took over the Little Theatre on the Haymarket as manager for all its summer seasons: the royal jester and rake's companion was now also a businessman. The period immediately before his accident, from January 1762 to June 1765, was the most prolific of his entire career, and saw Foote producing, writing and acting in five full-length plays and a sketch: *The Minor*, *The Orators*, *The Mayor of Garrett*, *The Lyar*, *The Patron*, and *The Commissary*. The Haymarket's grew to be the second largest theatre company in the country, and though the theatre was still called the Little Theatre – until 1766 – it became more profitable than the patent houses themselves. With its proceeds Foote invested wisely, collecting art and rare books, while also travelling, intermittently, back and forth to profitable seasons in Dublin and Edinburgh and to the country estates of prospective patrons where and when he was invited.

Yet his greatest challenge, and his greatest opportunity, was about to be dealt to him.

ON LOSING A LEG AND
GAINING A THEATRE

I have seen a man die almost immediately upon the loss
    of a testicle.
The loss of a limb above the knee is more than most
    men can bear.

       John Hunter, surgeon friend of Samuel Foote[1]

WILLIAM BROMFEILD, THE ROYAL SURGEON, rode at full gallop the last miles of the two-day journey from London to Methley Hall in Yorkshire, changing horses at Kippax and reaching Leeds by nightfall. His final ascent through the dark Calder valley signalled both the nearness of Leeds – the river ran 'inkily from the washing of shoddy'[2] – and his arrival at Methley Hall, seat of the new Earl and Countess of Mexborough. He was summoned there to perform an amputation.

Ancient and crenellated, Methley Hall squats above the Aire and Calder valleys in a manner both ostentatious and threatening. It was not a favoured residence of the Mexboroughs.[3] They spent more time in their Piccadilly town house, number 102, and occasionally at Cannons Park, 'a small hunting-box' near Newbury. But Methley's Elizabethan builders had created in Oulton stone and Armada oak a lasting monument to the rural pleasures of the English aristocracy. Like the country seat of Lady Gay

Spanker, in the comedy *London Assurance*, it was any West Ender's worst nightmare of country-house living: draughty, cold, reputedly haunted by grim Tudor forebears, and high, it was said, on the sweaty aromas of dogs, game, horses and horseplay. Foote had not wanted to go there. But his trip turned out to be the turning point of his career – his lucky break – in the most traumatic manner possible.

Foote had been invited to join the Mexboroughs at Methley early in the new year of 1766. Lady Mexborough was Sarah, formerly Hussey-Delaval, and Frank was to be there too. 'If necessity does not drive me there,' Foote had written, 'every pleasurable motive will attract me to a family to every branch of which I have so many obligations.'[4] Necessity was the murderer of pleasurable intentions, as things turned out. It was a hunting party – not usually Foote's scene. Yet his presence at Methley was a command performance for the entertainment of the Mexborough's royal house guest, the twenty-seven-year-old Duke of York. Fellow house guests included Frank, Thomas and Edward Delaval, brothers of Methley's chatelaine, who was heavily pregnant with her third child,[5] along with 'various others'[6] of the Mexboroughs' London set. The house party was due to be high-spirited in the manner of Seaton Delaval at its wildest, for she and her husband were celebrating momentous news. The Mexboroughs were about to be elevated from baron and baroness to earl and countess, for services to the Crown.[7]

It would turn out to be a momentous occasion, too, for Foote, who managed likewise to ingratiate himself with royalty at Methley but in a most unorthodox manner: through the loss of his leg after a bet.

§

The jocund gathering was dominated by single men in their twenties and thirties, most of them a decade or more younger than Foote, all of them determined to entertain the boisterous duke. It was this visit that Lady Mary Coke alludes to in her journal when she writes that the prince 'visited Frank Delaval and his sister Lady Mexborough at their country seats; and Yorkshire rang long and loudly of the orgies therein celebrated'.[8] Frank Delaval was well known to the prince, but it was the younger Delaval, Edward, who came to dominate the early part of the Methley trip. 'Ned' Delaval, the third son, was emerging as one of London's foremost wits and an intellectual of catholic interests. He frequented science lectures, not just his brother's, and studied optics and electricity – he later designed lightning conductors for St Bride's Church, Fleet Street, and St Paul's. Among Ned Delaval's minor achievements was the creation of 'the completest set of musical glasses then known in England',[9] part of the amusements on offer at Methley that February. Doubtless he used this to accompany comedic songs sung in a famous, if rough-hewn, baritone. Because by far the greatest luminary in this unusual constellation of London high society was the Delavals' celebrated friend, Mr Foote.

Then as now, a metropolitan dandy like Samuel Foote would have been somewhat out of place in a country-house hunting party in Yorkshire. Foote owned guns but had little interest in horses or in hunting. His expeditions outside London had almost invariably been to other theatre capitals – Dublin, Paris and Edinburgh. Cast in the role of jester at the court of the Duke of York, he appears to have sulked to begin with, and then decided to play joker as best he could. Foote might have felt challenged to assert his masculinity in terms better understood by his fellow house guests, or simply been bored, or decided upon a rash new joke. For whatever reason, at some point he began to boast about his horsemanship – repeatedly – to the great amusement of the duke in particular. It was a foolish and idle boast. He was quoted as having said that 'he could ride as well as most men he knew,'[10] and could even race post-chaises. It was true that he had grown up in the countryside, and rode as well as any eighteenth-century gentleman, but he was far from being a huntsman, jockey or athlete. The aristocrats – the duke, the Delaval brothers and Lord Mexborough (family motto: *Be Fast*) – decided to upbraid their celebrated guest for his boastfulness with a practical joke. A bet of some sort ensued, and money was placed, with the duke's strong encouragement, on Foote's riding. They then had their grooms mount the actor on one of the duke's fiercest stallions, a 'mettlesome steed'. 'Many gentlemen,' wrote one actor friend of Foote's, 'wear different faces on seeing an actor in London and seeing him in the country.'[11] Perhaps they enjoyed seeing Foote out of his West End comfort zone. Perhaps money was laid on how long he might stay in the saddle. Perhaps it was some sort of a race. Certainly, to judge by his later contrition, Prince Edward Augustus was intimately implicated in persuading Foote to take part in what turned out to be a radically ill-judged prank.

The prince, Lord Mexborough and the Delavals gathered in the stable yard at Methley, on the morning of Monday, 3 February 1766,[12] loudly encouraging their fellow guest onto the duke's horse. Foote mounted. At the first touch of his spur, according to later reports, the duke's horse reared so violently that Foote was flung out of the saddle and dashed straight onto the granite cobbles of Methley's yard. If anyone laughed, they did not do so for long. It was a bad fall. Foote fractured his leg in two places and raw bone broke through his boot leather, rupturing skin and muscle. This was a catastrophic injury: a compound fracture below the knee and another injury at or above it. Riders often died of such wounds unless amputation was quickly and well performed. The duke immediately sent to London for a surgeon.

§

William Bromfeild (sometimes Bromfield), of Conduit Street, London, had the title by 1766 of 'Surgeon to Her Majesty and to St George's Hospital and Member of the Court of Assistants [Surgeons]'.[13] Apprenticed first to a country surgeon, he had been lecturing and demonstrating in anatomy since his early twenties – a route very similar to that of his friends and mentors John and William Hunter, whose collection still numbers Bromfeild's anatomical specimens.[14] There were various surgeons upon whose services the Methley party might have called to minister to their injured guest, surgeons who had warrants from the Mexboroughs, Delavals or from members of the royal family. But the duke suggested Bromfeild as the ideal candidate for Foote. He was his personal surgeon and had been intimately connected with royal circles since at least 1761 when he had been sent over to Mecklenberg on the delicate business of verifying Princess Charlotte's potential fecundity and intact virginity before her engagement to the duke's elder brother, George III.[15] Bromfeild was 'one of the most eminent surgeons of the times', according to *Gentleman's Magazine*,[16] attended the Dowager Princess of Wales at her residence in Leicester Fields and within a few years of the operation on Foote was to become Master of the Company of Surgeons in London.[17] His name therefore graces the entrance to the Royal College of Surgeons to this day, as a former master – on the site, as it happens, of the Lincoln's Inn theatre where Foote had once performed. Bromfeild also had an unexpected connection to Foote and to the theatre. Uniquely for a surgeon of the period, he had co-written a comedy for Drury Lane in 1755 – he rewrote Jaspar Maine's *City Match* as *The Schemers*.[18] This was performed as a charity gala in aid of the new Lock Hospital for the Treatment of Venereal Disease – and it was this gala that had introduced Bromfeild to Foote. Fundraising for the Lock Hospital was often achieved with the co-operation of Bromfeild's patroness the Dowager Princess of Wales and the involvement of the musical and theatrical élites of Covent Garden and Drury Lane, who met at her home. (They had, it should be allowed, some vested interests in the provisions on offer at the Lock Hospital for themselves and their audiences.) Bromfeild was a doctor, a theatre-lover, a venereologist, and at the vanguard of the new theories on inoculation. But primarily the fifty-three-year-old[19] Londoner who travelled to Yorkshire for Foote was a barber-surgeon who had risen to move – and operate – at the very highest levels of society.

§

Precisely what greeted Bromfeild when he arrived at Methley Park is unknown. Foote must have been injured more than forty-eight hours earlier, such were the distances involved, and he would have been in increasing pain ever since. Bromfeild was accompanied by, or hired locally, 'two other gentlemen of the Faculty [of Medicine] who attended him'.[20] He examined Foote immediately and not just with regard to his leg wounds. He ascertained Foote was concussed and had serious head pains, presumably from a swelling of the brain. Bromfeild was considered a leading expert on concussion, having established, controversially, that bleeding and 'draining of fluid' were not necessarily the best recourse with head wounds.[21] He felt for the strength of Foote's pulse. He believed in using four fingers of one hand to do this, in the interests, he claimed, of operating only on those with a 'plethora' of blood,[22] and closely inspected the fractures. Bromfeild's notes do not survive, but Foote's was clearly a complicated, dangerous and therefore highly painful set of injuries, what would now be termed a floating knee fracture, and there was then only one known course of treatment. Injuries such as Foote's, Bromfeild wrote, 'are always dangerous and their event often fatal'.[23] He immediately informed Foote that they would have to amputate his leg.

§

Amputation. The word has a sort of childhood horror to it – then as now – a dismembering before death. The origins of the word, from the Latin '*amputare*', 'to cut off', in turn derived from '*putare*', to prune, and '*amb*', 'about', belie the genesis of its meaning, for in antiquity, as Bromfeild knew, *amputare* was not used for medical surgery. It meant the removal of a thief's hands. It has about it a sense of judicial barbarism, an atavistic nightmare, especially when contemplated in this era before anaesthetic. Only when devoid of alternatives or as extreme censure do we sever limbs, and for Bromfeild as for Foote this was the crux of the discussion: the choice was between amputation of sentient flesh, or death.

As often as not before the eighteenth century, surgeons would use the term 'dismembering' instead of 'amputation', as if the patient were already dead, or as good as. The 'dismembering saw' and 'dismembering knife' feature in medical texts well into the nineteenth century. Often death was the outcome. In the history of medicine, Bromfeild's era has been called the Heroic Age of Surgery. The heroism refers partly to the radical changes in surgical knowledge and practice made during eighteenth-century warfare. The human body paid the price of the industrial revolution's contribution to armaments: cannons, guns and blades that cut through tissue with greater efficiency than previous generations had had cause to fear. It was the resultant sepsis and gangrene that necessitated amputation. The heroism applied to the surgeons certainly, but more so to the patients. The eighteenth century radicalized the types of surgery attempted – complicated amputations even to the hip joint – and all of this before the possibility of anaesthetic. The severing of a limb remained a desperate measure, but one that more and more frequently, as the skills of surgeons increased, allowed some patients extra years of life.

Amputation became, therefore, an all too necessary part of military life and increasingly common in civilian life too. Surgeons skilled in battlefield amputations found surprising numbers of civilians brave enough to submit themselves to the knife and saw. Speed was one key skill for a surgeon. Strength, and an ability to help stem blood loss, came close seconds. Dr Guillotin developed his infamous machine in pre-revolutionary France initially as a tool for the instant removal of the limbs of those thought too feeble to sustain the harrowing extra minutes under the tools of regular surgery: women and children. Patients put astonishing faith in their surgeons, and in God. In 1740 a nine-year-old girl submitted in silence to the amputation of her right arm while holding a nosegay in her left hand, uttering words only when she heard and felt the sawing of her bone, and saying simply: 'Oh.'[24] She survived. Lord Erskine, who asked to see his amputated leg after Waterloo, joked, as Foote would, that he was better off without it. Foote's was not a battlefield injury, but it might as well have been. It was one very familiar to a surgeon like Bromfeild. Compound fractures from riding accidents dominate the annals of surgeons in the eighteenth century. Falls from greater heights tended to lead to inoperable head injuries, but horses kicked, crushed or threw their riders and there were many accidents in the crowded streets and busy roads of eighteenth-century Europe. If these injuries proved complicated, as in Foote's case, the only option was amputation.

The surgeon's primary task was to avoid gangrene. With Foote, gangrene was considered inevitable, as there was a series of fractures breaking the skin, and infections from mud, clothing and horsehair might result. One contemporary account of the same injury makes plain both the agony and the agonizing prospect: 'My horse struck at me with its heels and he brake both the bones of my left leg, some four fingers breadth above my ankle . . . and as I flew back, the broken bones flew in sunder and breaking through the flesh, stocking and boot, shewed themselves, whereby I left as much pain as it is credible a man was able to endure . . . yet I knew more was to follow.'[25]

Foote had at least one protrusion below the knee but also significant trauma at or above it. Surgeons were loath to create an above-knee stump if it was possible to amputate below, but in Foote's case his injuries obliged Bromfeild to amputate mid-thigh, with enough flesh to fashion a cushioned stump but not so near the hip joint as to further risk the likelihood that Foote would bleed to death.

The clock, meanwhile, was ticking on a fracture of this sort, and not just for the patient. Surgeons and medical students became increasingly aware, even before a proper understanding of antisepsis and surgical hygiene, that they, too, could become infected from suppurating wounds the longer an operation was delayed. Hospital authorities dutifully noted the deaths of medical students and nurses infected during surgery and post-mortem examinations, from infections spread by pins in bandages on stumps, or dressings on those awaiting operations, and those who suffered amputations themselves. The quicker it was done, the better all round.

The operation was set for the middle of the day. Bromfeild operated in daylight only, in 'the roseate hue of a rainshower of blood', as one more poetic medical student described it, with as much light as was possible. In the north of England in midwinter, this was a problem. Satisfactory coagulation of a major blood vessel could fail at any moment during the operation, leading to a desperate grappling, ligaturing and re-cauterizing to prevent the haemorrhaging of life itself. There was also the need to see tissue and bone clearly when cleaving. Light was imperative. The winter daylight at Methley was supplemented by as many candles as were practical, but for reasons of light it is almost certain that the operation took place in the house's Elizabethan Long Gallery: it had by far the best daylight. The many paintings were removed or covered – including the strikingly lifelike portrait of Frank Delaval[26] – and the floor thickly strewn with sawdust. Furniture was arranged: a long table for instruments and a sturdy chair. Late in the morning, Foote was carried in.

Bromfeild occasionally used 'anodyne drafts'[27] and 'anodyne sudorifics'[28] – dangerously inaccurate doses of opium and alcohol – to prepare some of his patients for amputation. But, as Foote was also concussed and it is on record that Bromfeild had written, 'He is either ignorant or insane . . . who recommend[s] a use of opium in a concussion of the brain,'[29] it is clear the surgeon eschewed all painkillers for his patient. Alcohol on its own was rarely administered pre-operatively except by naval surgeons – and then more to stiffen resolve than reduce pain. Although he may have suffered the minor indignities of being given an enema, 'sweating salts' and, ironically, being bled by leeches[30] prior to the operation, it is certain that Foote faced Bromfeild's scalpels and saws with no anaesthetic whatsoever.

First he was stripped. Sheets were wound around his upper body to provide a firmer hold for the assistants. Then he was strapped into a chair. The wounds on the leg were cleaned 'with warm wine, spirits of wine or salt water'[31] and the 'hair was shaved off '[32] his thigh. Behind the chair, and out of view of Foote, 'who

might be a little terrified and disheartened by them',[33] Bromfeild and his assistants laid out their instruments. They are listed in
the Hunterian collection to this day:

  1. The tourniquet
  2. Linen ligatures or tapes, 'a fingers breadth and about an
     ell and half long'
  3. 'A middling size knife or scalpel for dividing the skin'
  4. A crooked knife for dividing flesh
  5. A Caitlin or double-edged scalpel
  6. Linen bandages – some cut halfway up and plates of steel
     instead to 'elevate the flesh'
  7. 'A well tempered, sharp saw for dividing bones'
  8. 'A pair of forceps for arteries'
  9. Some crooked needles, threaded
  10. Square compresses
  11. A large quantity of scraped lint
  12. Astringent powders
  13. A bolster large enough to cover the stump or a puff-ball
      fungus, *lupi crepitus*
  14. A calf's bladder, washed
  15. Plasters cut in the shape of a Maltese cross
  16. Compresses and five ells of bandages, and lastly, 'some
      wine and other cordials to assist and relieve the patient'[34]

As well as the two medical assistants hired locally, Bromfeild
recruited more muscle power. He may have brought apprentices
from London, given the fame of the patient and status of the duke;
he may just have enlisted the aid of the young gentlemen who
were known to Foote and to the surgeon: the younger Delaval
brothers. Six or seven men were considered the minimum number
to assist at an unanaesthetized operation.

One [stood] behind the Patient, to hold the body [in the
chair] another on the other side of the affected limb, which
he . . . held fast by grasping the upper part, a third assistant
must hold the [lower leg] about to be amputated, and a fourth

[stood] on one side with the Apparatus of Instruments, to hand them as they may be wanted by the Operator, a fifth assistant must stand ready with the . . . Dressings . . . and a Sixth should be at liberty to assist the Patient and Operator.[35]

Bromfeild put on an old and bloodstained apron. He and the rest of the men had no cause or reason to wash their hands or sterilize instruments: an understanding of sepsis was still a century away. Spreading Foote's legs wide, he first applied the tourniquet. It was of the type designed by Jean-Louis Petit at the beginning of the century, commonplace on the battlefields and then the surgeons' tables of Europe by this time (though it had been developed from technology used by French cheesemakers and viticulturists). It looked, to all who dared to contemplate it, like a giant thumb-screw. The placing of the tourniquet, for the decreasing of blood flow and the securing of arteries before surgery, was dependent on the intended site of amputation. The 'deligation of the vessels' was the first task in hand and could be as hazardous and as brutal upon the patient as the amputation itself. Bromfeild considered it 'the principal part of the operation'.[36] The arteries needed to be stretched out from the limb, cut, tied and cauterized. Bromfeild relied on styptics – caustic salts and turpentine – to try to stem blood flow from smaller vessels, and for larger vessels and worrisome arteries he used heated irons and a complicated system of ligature tying. No vessels were rerouted or joined up as such – anastomosed. Rather, with primitive tourniquets, Bromfeild would have had to tie each vessel as he found it, just to minimize blood loss. Nerves and blood vessels tend to run together, so an easy error – as happened on Nelson's arm – was to tie the vessel ligature around the nerve, leading to constant neuralgic pain. Nelson was fortunate in that wound infection led to the ligature being discharged in pus, without catastrophic bleeding, which led to an instant relief of pain. Major nerve trunks also needed to be cut as high as possible so that the highly sensate nerve stump, the neuroma, could be buried as deep as possible. For eighteenth-century leg amputees who survived, the neuroma would usually take a hammering. Bromfeild had to locate the major nerve trunk of Foote's leg then stretch it manually so that it retracted proximally when cut. Modern surgeons surmise that this must have been the furthest extreme of agony for a conscious patient, like Foote. At the very last moment – as was the custom of surgeons of the period – Bromfeild asked Foote's permission and forgiveness for what he was about to do.

Bromfeild describes the beginning of the amputation simply. 'With sharp knives and extreme speed', he would flay skin and cut into thigh muscle to expose the arteries, veins and nerves. '[My assistant] and I secured the tourniquet, and then pulled back the skin and muscles,'[37] he wrote, halfway up to the groin and above the site of the bone amputation. Next he would begin the cutting and cleaving of muscle. The first cut was therefore a circular one, near the knee around the lower thigh. This was performed at great speed by a special curved blade, sometimes by a scalpel around the leg, which then cut deep into the flesh: 'a circular incision through the integuments'.[38] The assistants held fast, as patients tended to flinch most at these first cuts. Next, Bromfeild skewered deep into the thigh near the groin, turned the knife around and cut the muscles of the lower thigh downwards in the direction of the knee, towards two sides of the leg, exiting, ideally, within 'three fingers breadth'[39] of the knee. The first cut and stabbing was followed therefore by two excruciating cleavings that would form two sides of the stump, while the shaved, flayed skin of the upper leg was hoisted up to the groin. These two hefts of muscle were then pulled to the side and held by assistants with the aid of metal retractors so that Bromfeild had access to the bones in the centre of the thigh. Foote bled profusely. Only the main artery of the leg was tied. Bromfeild was perhaps less than eighty seconds into the operation. 'The bones were then denuded as high as possible,' he wrote, 'to make room for the application of the saw . . . I ordered the assistants that had care of the limb to keep the leg quite steady that the bones might be sawed exactly smooth.'[40] As Foote was bound into a chair, sitting upright, he had the opportunity at this point of the operation, and assuming he had not fainted with the horror, to watch the amputation itself.

It was vital to work at great speed but it was conversely vital not to splinter the bone, or leave the edges ragged or sharply angled such that the stump could not heal. Bromfield had learned from the classic text of the period that he must 'saw gently at the beginning, until the saw is well entered, and then go on faster with Discretion'. At this moment, the assistants put gentle pressure on the upper thigh and on the knee, and pulled slightly, 'so as to allow the saw to move freely'. 'And thus,' as Bromfeild's text advises, 'in one minute or two, the Amputation may be completed.'

Foote's shattered limb fell to one side, into the sawdust.

§

There are very few accounts of surgery in the eighteenth century from the patient's point of view. The thousands of case notes in the Hunterian collection of the Royal College of Surgeons yield plenty of case studies, but little from the sharper side of the surgeon's knife, unless the patient happened to be a medical man also. Set against this masculine reticence is one lonely voice, and it is female. The novelist and playwright Fanny Burney suffered a mastectomy in Paris many decades after she had first laughed at the antics of Samuel Foote in London. She eventually put quill to paper about what it was to be an eighteenth-century surgery patient, and her record gives some insight into the excruciating drama enacted around Foote at Methley.

> when the dreadful steel was first plunged – cutting through veins – arteries – flesh – nerves . . . I began a scream that lasted unintermittingly during the whole time of the incision – & I almost marvel that it rings not in my Ears still! so excruciating was the agony. When the wound was made, & the instrument was withdrawn, the pain seemed undiminished, for the air that suddenly rushed in . . . felt like a mass of

minute but sharp & forked poniards, that were tearing the
edges of the wound – but when again I felt the instrument –
describing a curve – cutting against the grain, if I may so say,
while the flesh resisted in a manner so forcible as to oppose &
tire the hand of the operator, who was forced to change from
the right to the left – then, indeed, I thought I must have
expired . . . The instrument this second time withdrawn, I
concluded the operation over – Oh no! presently the terrible
cutting was renewed – & worse than ever . . . Again all
description would be baffled – yet again all was not over . . .
& – Oh Heaven! . . . not for days, not for Weeks, but for
Months I could not speak of this or think of it . . . the recollection is still so painful [though] the operation, including the
dressing, lasted [only] 20 minutes![41]

Most amputees fainted. Some died of shock. Those who remained
conscious through the exquisite and rough-hewn agonies of the
operation perhaps decided not to revisit, imaginatively, a site of
pain traditionally described as indescribable. Burney's is a rare
account. Foote referred to it only, and evasively, as the subject
for comedy. But of course what happened dominated the rest of
his life in professional and physical terms. The disability became a
self-styled running joke – *Sir Luke Limp, The Lame Lover* – 'the
depeditation of Mr Foote', as Dr Johnson had it, the man only
'half as wooden as Garrick', etc. But the laughter came as much
from the shocking image that was inextricably linked with Foote
ever after: of a man who had been 'dismembered, alive'. Conversely, amputees like Foote have a changed self-image and not
always a negative one: the years after such a near-death experience,
nearer indeed then than it might feel today, may find that afterwards their allotted years have the gilding of gifted time.

With the leg amputated, the operation was far from over, and
the wound was still open and fast losing blood. Bromfeild had the
task first of securing the blood vessels in Foote's leg. The pioneering
technique, taught to him by William Hunter, was described by a
medical student:

[the surgeon] exposed an artery, then grasped it in his finger-tips and separated it from the cellular membrane, the vein and the nerve for a distance of eight inches, making use only of the slender handle of his knife. This done he passed under the artery a grooved probe, and ran along this a silver needle threaded with a thick ligature which he tied on the lower part of the artery to block it off. The pulsation [of] the blood thumped with such force against the ligature that to diminish the knocking and the danger of the thing bursting he made another ligature two inches away from the first one and tied it less tightly. Above this second one he made a third, tied even more loosely, and then a fourth [and so on] and . . . then, after pulling the threads to the outside, and separating them he [was ready to close] the wound.[42]

Eventually a mixture of lint, flour and ground bark could be used to dress Foote's wounds and to sprinkle between bandages, but after the pressure of the tourniquet was partially removed, Bromfeild and his assistants first had to check for blood flow from minor vessels – all this before the wound could be properly covered or sewn and a rough-hewn stump fashioned. Water was used, but also turpentine to get a less bloodied view of what was going on.

Infection was expected. Indeed, it was thought to be a vital part of healing – hence the phenomenon known queasily as 'laudable pus'. Wounds were usually kept partly open to allow free drainage. Bromfeild loosely sewed together the anterior quadriceps to the posterior (hamstring) muscles, and the skin was drawn over, and cut quickly, with scissors, for a partially watertight closure. It was all rough-sewn together with waxed cotton button-thread,[43] and the stump, still bleeding, was then tightly bound with absorbent bandages of linen mixed with flour. A washed calf's bladder was stretched over this first layering, along with sponge and dried puffball (it being February, fresh puffball was unavailable). This was rightly regarded as a balm and coagulant. More layers of the Maltese-cross cut bandages were applied, and tied in ever heightening layers, up to the groin and to the tourniquet.

After the cleansing and application of bandages, constant pressure was applied to the stump by Frank and other assistants to stem the flow of blood and thereby encourage coagulation. The tourniquet was kept on through the first night. It would not be removed until Bromfeild was confident that the blood vessels had been efficiently tied, coagulated, or were finding their new collateral route of blood flow round the adumbrated limb. Whether, by 1766, Bromfeild was still in the practice of leaving stray arteries and nerve endings dangling beyond the bandaging, in the French manner of the era, is unclear.

At some point, either during the horror of the amputation or through blood loss in its immediate aftermath, Foote fainted. He was taken back to his room unconscious where a mattress had been covered with extra layers of canvas and straw to soak up blood. He was attended through the night by Frank, Sarah Hussey-Delaval and sometimes the duke, with the Delaval brothers and servants taking it in turns to maintain pressure on the stump, and checking that the tightly wound Maltese bandages showed no telltale signs of haemorrhage. For a whole week, servants and house guests in rotation were delegated to keep watch on Foote and his stump, with the thigh tourniquet screw to hand, in case of sudden bleeding.

On the third or fourth day after the operation, the bandages were removed. If a patient had survived thus far, the prognosis improved rapidly. 'After the putrid limb was removed', as Bromfeild's textbook had it, the patient might well enjoy a counter-intuitive euphoria, 'as a tree refresheth after the dead bowes are pruned off'.[44] Even so, the first removal of bandages was hazardous. It was another excruciating ordeal for Foote, 'when the mouths of [blood] vessels ... supposed to be well closed and united' were exposed for the first time and the coagulated blood and bandages, the calf's bladder and puffball matter, would tear away at the sloughed flesh edges and raw, unhealed stump. But it held. It was not infected, or not so badly as to hinder Foote's recovery. No blood vessels burst. He must have been in agony. But he was alive.

§

Despite sudden heavy snows, word soon got back to London of Foote's accident and operation. Within hours of the amputation, according to friends, Foote was concerning himself with the future. 'If Providence has left you less corporal perfection than it has to the rest of mankind,' wrote John Delaval, with pompous encouragement, 'it has made you ample amends in the allotments of intellectual excellence and [ambition].'[45] Foote knew bookings for the summer season would rely on his good health and positive spirits, even if he could not be there in person or could not perform. He feared for the immediate and long-term future. His skill was in laughter and, as he wrote to Garrick almost as soon as he could hold a quill, 'Who would laugh at a cripple?'[46] Plenty, as it turned out. He wrote a few days later that 'I am better rather from what I am told than what I personally feel. I am weak from pain and get no sleep but from opiates. But however, the artery's bleeding is stopped and they flatter me in less than a fortnight I shall be upon crutches, and then with safety may be conducted to London.'[47] He did better than that. He was not on crutches, but was considered safe to move by early March, nearer to London and medical attention, to Cannons Park. Here he would recuperate for many weeks, visited on occasion by the duke, the Delavals and, after her confinement, by Lady Mexborough.

Foote soon put out that it had all been a bit of jape, and was said to be in 'extraordinary good spirits', cracking uproarious jests about himself and his limbs. He claimed that 'he had himself urged amputation'. He continued to jest at his own expense before and after the operation. 'He would not change his one leg with the Devil's two drumsticks,' it was said, 'he would now be able to play Faulkner [the one-legged Dublin publisher] *to the life*'; 'If he could not walk, he could hop' etc. And in retrospect he joked too that he had immediately decided, it all being somehow the Duke of York's fault, that 'he hoped to become a *"patientee"* [*sic*]' of a theatre licence.

How much of this is true to the reality of Methley, Cannons Park and the aftermath of the operation is unclear. The jokes about his lost leg — that he was now indeed half wooden, that Mr Foote had found an act to match his name, that he was not half the man he was made out to be in the press – smack more of Foote in his anecdotage. He had learned from an early age to set adversity to his advantage, but the horror of the operation and the very near brush with death left their mark on him. His defence was to be deprecatory about the matter, to make jokes at the expense of his infirmity before others did, and to disavow completely the imagined horror of the amputation itself. But he also turned the accident and amputation immediately to his advantage in very practical terms. He asked the duke to speak to his brother, now George III, about the Little Theatre on the Haymarket becoming a Theatre Royal.

§

David Garrick tried to visit him at Cannons Park in late March, but wrote instead from Bath of his admiration for Foote's courage and determination to return to the stage, and to fill him in on London gossip. 'I have read your letters with ye highest pleasure,' Garrick wrote on 21 March, 'and will ever keep them as incontestable proofs of your wit and philosophy.' Garrick even showed them to mutual friends. 'By God,' said one, 'Foote writes better than anybody, and I don't know which to admire most, his pleasantry or his courage.' Friends rallied round, but there was an awareness, too, that Foote's position and the future of the Haymarket company hung in the balance so long as he stayed away from town. Garrick wrote again, declaring, 'Should you be prevented from pursuing any plan for your theatre, I am wholly at your service and will labour in ye vineyard for you in any capacity, till you are able to it, so much better, for yourself.'[48] Foote tetchily rejected the offer:

Nothing can be more generous and obliging, nor, I am sure, at the same time would be more beneficial for me, than your offers of assistance for my hovel in the Haymarket; but the rage for me at present is a very distant object, for, notwithstanding all the flattery of appearances [of being able to move to Cannons Park] I look upon my hold in life to depend upon a very slender tenure; and besides, admitting the best that can happen, [I am] a mutilated man, a miserable instance of . . . frailty of human nature, a proper object to excite those emotions which can only be produced from vacant minds, discharged of every melancholy or pensive taints.[49]

Garrick was not the first either to point out that Frank Delaval and the prince were talked of a great deal as a result of the accident, though largely with the sympathy afforded to practical-jokers when japes go disastrously wrong. '[Frank]'s tenderness and humanity to you my dear friend,' wrote Garrick, 'has endeared him to everybody.' He closed by attaching a little ditty doing the rounds in London and Bath, which ended with these encouraging words:

> What though the Wit a Limb has lost
> You soon will find it to your cost;
> He has not lost his head.[50]

1766, which started so badly for Foote, turned into a rather good year for the theatre, and for him. Garrick and George Colman the Elder premièred *The Clandestine Marriage* at Drury Lane, while a new theatre opened on Kings Street, Bristol, and, for that matter, on South Street, Philadelphia – both of which survive as working Georgian theatres to this day. And on 25 June 1776, at St James's Palace, the attorney general put before George III this document for his signature:

> Our Will and Pleasure are that you Samuel Foote, Esq., . . .
> do . . . gather together . . . a Company of Comedians to Act
> [at the Haymarket] between the Fifteenth Day of May and
> Fifteenth Day of September in Every Year . . . And that the

said Samuel Foote [shall charge] such sums as have been
accustomarily given and taken in regards of the great expense
of Scenes, Musick, and New Decorations.[51]

It was, as intended, a licence to print money – a licence to turn
the Little Theatre in the Haymarket into a Theatre Royal, if
only for the summer months. As such, it was some consolation
for the result of the Duke of York's disastrous bet. Foote was
quite open about it all in private. The duke had 'expressed a
desire of securing me from . . . poverty', he wrote to John Delaval,
after the accident, and his princely 'singular humanity and generosity' had inspired Foote to make an unblushing request for the
licence. 'I took the liberty to mention to His Royal Highness
that a patent from the Crown for the House in the Haymarket
during my lifetime would protect me from want, and that I had
hitherto been permitted to exhibit there at only the time that no
other playhouse would open.'[52] Prince Edward, attending the
King and Queen, on 25 February 1766 at St James's Palace,
made his request to his brother.[53] A new Theatre Royal in the
Haymarket would entail upon Foote for his natural life a patent
house west of Covent Garden nearer the increasingly fashionable
Piccadilly. Nothing quite like it had been seen since Restoration
times in terms of bestowing theatre privilege upon a sort of
royal favourite. The King signed and sent out letters to Foote, to
the Lord Privy Seal, the Duke of Newcastle, and to the Lord
Chamberlain, the Duke of Portland. The Little Theatre on the
Haymarket was henceforward to be known as the 'Theatre Royal,
Haymarket', and it was not, for that matter, to stay 'little' for very
long either.

On the same day George III made over to the Duke of York,
his 'dearly beloved brother', the wardenship as Keeper of Windsor
Park and Forest, 'with all privileges, immunities, profits and appur-
tenances',[54] and also the deeds of 'Cranburn [sic] Lodge' in
Berkshire, formerly the home of their uncle, the Duke of Cumberland. Ahead of this Samuel Foote had already paid several news-

papers to advertise his new 'Royal' company and theatre. It was a happy day to bask in that sun of York.

From 1766 until the end of his life Foote was obliged to attend Court on the great feast days of the royal calendar, as one of the three Theatre Royal patent holders. 'The first nobility,' one friend remarked, 'were as glad to see him there [at St James's Palace] as any other acquaintance or intimate friend,'[55] as well they might. His cork leg dressed in silk stocking and silver buckle, his wit and bonhomie polished as ever, Foote became one of the minor ornaments of the Court of George III. And this royal favour – indeed, the personal admiration of the King himself – would play a vital role in years to come in protecting Foote and his Haymarket theatre.

The Little Theatre on the Haymarket, so called to distinguish it from John Vanbrugh's grand opera house on the other side of the street, His Majesty's, had been built in 1720 on Crown land immediately to the north of the present Theatre Royal. Foote had paid £222 10s. ground rent a year since 1762. But later, in 1766, after his first summer season as a royal patent holder, he had the confidence to tear down the old theatre and rebuild on the same site a house with capacity of around a thousand.[56] The company later moved into the Nash theatre that stands on the adjacent site to this day – Foote's building was not used as a theatre after 1820 but stood until 1929.[57] This first Haymarket Theatre Royal was riotously successful from its initial season. Foote was back performing by early summer, returning to his much-loved role as Mrs Cole in *The Minor*[58] on 18 June, kicking up his skirts as best he might, a mere five months after the amputation. He endured endless puns about his name and disability, smiled through it, and turned, as ever, tragedy to his own comedic ends. 'Crowded audiences' were there 'in the hottest days of July and August',[59] claimed Tom Davies, and the diarist Sylas Neville noted that he was 'obliged to stand til ye play was over'. Another theatre-goer 'could not get into the Pit, Boxes, or Galleries' at all on 14 August.[60] Foote's depeditation and the inauguration of the new Theatre Royal both made for great box-office.

1766 was so profitable for Foote that he could consider even more than rebuilding and enlarging his own theatre. By the end of the first year after his amputation, he was negotiating for the patent for the theatre in Bath as well, to tour his productions.[61]

§

All might have looked very sunny indeed, but over at Leicester Fields another drama was unfolding. The surgeon Bromfeild, after the gruesome business of embalming Foote's fractured leg for future burial, had consulted with his colleagues. John Hunter, Bromfeild's quondam tutor and main competitor in the higher circles of Georgian surgery, had his doubts about the case of the actor who was treading the boards only a few months after traumatic surgery. There were aspects of the operation and prognosis that troubled him, evidence of which has only recently come to light in the archives of the Hunterian Institute at the Royal College of Surgeons. It has been apparent since the 1820s, when the surgeon's notes were first made public, that Foote consulted John Hunter the year before he died. What has been overlooked is that Bromfeild had also consulted Hunter in the immediate aftermath of the operation. He did so again in the summer of 1766.

'Mr Foote was cured [by Bromfeild] by an amputation of the leg,' recorded Hunter, but then, surprisingly, he added, 'Foote was cured [with a leg amputation] of *a violent pain in the head*.'[62] In other words, Bromfeild related to Hunter that Foote had been suffering terrible head pains at the time of the Methley operation. This is the only known reference to Foote's extreme concussion from his fall, and the distracting pain of cerebral swelling before, during and after his leg amputation. More intriguingly, this conversation informed Hunter's radical further diagnosis, some years later, that Foote's 1766 head injury affected the comedian's psychological state and much-admired lack of inhibition – his free-wheeling and radical impressionistic satire and attacks on establishment figures. It is an arrestingly forward-thinking diagnosis. Hunter's private notes appear to forecast, a full century before the discipline of psychology, that behaviour and brain trauma might be related, in the way that, for instance, it is now widely acknowledged that professional boxers can suffer neurological disorders years after their bouts in the ring. One reading, therefore, of Hunter's notes is that Foote was changed by his accident and amputation in more ways than the obvious disability. He was a different man after February 1766, with a different personal perspective and a different public persona. He had lost a leg and gained a theatre, but he was granted more than royal favour and increased fame. He was also granted the extra years that often embolden trauma survivors to live more bravely, more fully, sometimes more recklessly, than they have before. Moreover, his increasingly erratic, volatile and uninhibited personality – the wildly dangerous rhetoric and flouting of the Lord Chamberlain's censure, the choice through the 1770s of highly dangerous opponents – may well have been, from 1766 onwards, a result of the Methley accident. John Hunter thought so, certainly.

THE DEVIL UPON TWO STICKS

'I have the whole town under my thumb – I can take 'em thus and twirl them about like a top'

Samuel Foote[1]

BROMFEILD ORDERED AN artificial leg for Foote, to be fitted by a Mr Addison of Hanover Street, Long Acre. Its design, which survives, stakes its claim as the first articulated prosthesis used in England. In form and, indeed, articulation, however, it might have been somewhat familiar to Foote from his stage work. Addison made surgical instruments, prosthetics and clay pipes but also puppets – such was the unique economy of Long Acre, Covent Garden, in 1766. Foote is likely to have known him since at least the days of the Panton Street puppet wars with Henry Fielding, and the design and mixed media of the prosthesis – light and heavy woods, leather and metal – owes a great deal to eighteenth-century puppetry. Its articulation at the knee and foot, like a puppet's, was not the only innovative aspect. Bromfeild had limited faith in the mid-thigh stump he had fashioned and its ability to hold Foote's weight, so wrote that 'I ordered Mr Addison to divide that part which embraces the thigh, like splints, to correspond with its shape.'[2] Hence Foote's bodyweight was actually held by two circular straps that took the strain when he leaned on that side of his body, and Addison further adapted the prosthesis to bend at the knee – an innovation of the period of which Foote's seems to

be the first example, though his leg may only have been the most
celebrated. It appears in one medical textbook, with Addison's
name proudly attached, and if it is an exact depiction of Foote's
prosthesis then it is the only evidence that the amputated leg was
the left one.

Whether the articulated knee was just for stage work is unclear.
If it locked at the knee it was truly reformatory, but the leather
strapping attests to a common problem for amputees and to Foote's
ambitions. Stumps change over the first eighteen months and more
as the adumbrated muscles wither and regroup around the bone.
In time Foote would have other versions made. One, seemingly,
stayed permanently backstage at the theatre to be dressed for
different roles and was known as the 'most wooden member of the
[Haymarket] company', against what competition is unknown.
The wings of the Haymarket being a semi-public locale for
metropolitan lovers of actors and actresses in semi-undress, the left
leg of Mr Foote that hung there, somewhat eerily, one supposes,
became a minor celebrity in its own right. This was Foote's regular
number-two leg. It hung near the connective corridor from the
Haymarket wings to the house he bought at this period adjacent
to the theatre's stage-door on Suffolk Street. A wall was knocked
through so that the wings connected directly to Foote's house, the
better for the attention of dressers, but also demolishing the barrier
between his private and public worlds. His other leg travelled with
him.

It is only as a result of images of Foote after his limb loss that
a surmise is possible, and it is only a surmise, that it was the left
leg he lost. The fact that he is several times depicted with a cane
in his left hand is not considered conclusive by modern surgeons
or modern amputees but, 'on balance', a turn of phrase deployed
by Foote in several plays after 1766, it would seem to have been
the left, and the Addison design, assumed to be Foote's, lends
further weight, as it were, to this side of the argument. John
Hunter, so diligent in his notes in every other regard, neglects to
give record.

George Colman the Younger later recalled seeing this famous phantom leg backstage at the Haymarket 'ready dressed in a handsome silk stocking, with a polished shoe and gold buckle'.[3] 'I remember following him after a shower of rain,' Colman went on, 'upon a nicely roll'd terrace [of grass] in which he [made] a deep hole at every other step he took.'

It is an unhappy image. It took Foote a while, perforce, to adjust; modern amputees with much more advanced prostheses and physiotherapy attest to the enormous physical effort of rebalancing an entire body and learning, in effect, to walk again. Foote was unbowed. His lost leg was his new comic muse. A critic in *European Magazine* recorded, 'He often called himself Captain Timbertoe and where a [play] seemed to languish and flag, I have seen him, by a hobbling walk across the stage, accompanied with significant gesture and grimace, set the house in a roar.' For Foote and his audience, the cork leg and stumping gait provided both comedy and pain. The young Irish playwright John O'Keeffe also saw him at this point, backstage:

> With all his high comic humour, one could not help pitying him sometimes. He stood upon one leg, leaning against the wall, while his servant was putting on his stage false leg, with shoe and stocking, and fastening it to the stump: he looked sorrowful, but instantly resuming all his high comic humour and mirth, hobbled forward, entered the scene, and gave the audience what they expected: their plenty of laugh and delight.[4]

To lose a leg is no simple loss, physically or psychologically. The new motion in walking, or just rising from a chair – from now on always two-armed in the Foote households – produces an effect in the middle ear not unlike travel-sickness, though it is referred to by amputees as vertigo. Stairs, of course, are a liability. The good foot has to lead up, but not down. The raked stages of Drury Lane and Covent Garden were a nightmare for Foote and his movements were limited to the flat forestage. There are phantom pains, distressing as well as uncomfortable, that do not always decline as time passes, and these are, I am told, invariably worse in the evening. Yet amputees now, as then, have faced this medical and life crisis and survived, and many, like Foote, have done so in traumatic circumstances. 'I'm more aware of the gain than the loss,' one told me, 'in that I've gained these extra years – I should have died. That changes everything.'[5] And so it did for Foote.

Foote's extension of life warranted him a lifetime's licence for a Theatre Royal at the Haymarket. It was a propitious moment to become the third head of a London patent house. Garrick at the Theatre Royal, Drury Lane, and Colman and Harris at Covent Garden commanded the London theatre-going experience. They had operated a cartel to prevent star names upping their wages, and they rigorously exploited their duopoly, expanding their houses to gigantic proportions – at least three thousand capacity at Drury Lane by the 1760s – to the detriment, it has long been argued, of subtleties in writing or acting. The age of spectacle and of lazily formulaic plays was born of the London Theatres Royal duopoly. But the older Theatres Royal were in a decreasingly fashionable part of town and did not offer a season of plays through the summer, and it was this Foote had sought to exploit since the beginning of his career as a Haymarket theatre producer. Foote had already established himself and a small company there as what might be termed a 'summer stock' group but the patent put him on much safer ground.

During the early 1760s, Foote was already clearing a thousand pounds a year profit on the Haymarket summer venture – usually by the expedient of performing one of his own plays, starring himself.[6] After the patent, his profits ran between three and five thousand pounds each summer. The Haymarket established itself as an institution – a vital part of the theatrical economy of London and one of the best things about a London summer – able to triumph, with comedy, over the many new forms of entertainment that flourished when the weather was good: the pleasure gardens, parks, puppet shows and fairs. And, far from being truly a handicap, the lost leg became emblematic of the third-leg theatre, the Haymarket, and of Foote: something other, different and irreverent. Soon enough Tate Wilkinson, by now renowned all over the country for his impressions, was no longer accepted when he imitated Foote. He couldn't get the limp right and was hissed off the stage.

As both writer and performer, Foote took his impediment as an opportunity to reinvent himself for the London public at his new patent house and he faced the world with the new-found confidence avowed by many amputees. The most famous character created in immediate response to his altered physicality was Sir Luke Limp in *The Lame Lover*, a character and a comic premise that need no explanation. He wrote the play while he was recuperating, though it did not see the flickering light of the stage until the following season. Sir Luke's speech about the manifold benefits of amputation – a classic example of comic irony – was taken at the time as a clear stage rendering of Foote's own bullish defiance.

> SIR LUKE: The worse?! [for having lost a leg] No! much the better my dear. Consider, I can have neither sprain nor gout, have no fear of corns or that another man should kick my shins or tread on my toes . . . no damn it, I am much better. What is there I am not able to do? To be sure, I am little awkward at running, but then, to make amends, I'll hop with any man in town . . . then as to your dancing, I am cut out at Madam Cornellys' [*sic*; the Venetian hostess of Soho Square] I grant because of the crowd, but as far as a private set of six couple, or moving a chair minuet, match me who can.[7]

Sir Luke first appears swathed in lace and with pretentious Macaroni patois dripping from his tongue, but he personifies much more than a satire on urban fashion victims or a joke about Foote's limp. He is also an impressively dangerously comedic invention on a number of levels. When Foote lost his leg, there were plenty of critics ready to see a morality tale unfolding and call his accident reciprocity, a providential rebuttal to his emulation of Faulkner's amputated leg, along with all the other physical and speech abnormalities Foote had mocked. As a physical specimen, Foote lines up all the gags that crowd into the audience's mind, then puts them into his own mouth, rather as he had done, according to Garrick and Cooke, in the immediate aftermath of the accident. To this he added a satire of social climbing: that other aspect of his sorry story, the jester who dared to risk his life over a bet with a prince. For the clearest issue about *The Lame Lover*, beyond the one-leggedness of Mr Foote, was that Sir Luke was a crashing snob. One model for Limp was Foote himself. Another was a notorious social climber whose real name, John Skrimshire Boothby Clopton, might easily have graced a Foote comedy unalloyed and undisguised. Before *The Lame Lover*, Clopton's real-life snobbery had been comic fodder for the small circle who suffered it – the Earls of Carlisle and Derby, the Duke of Rutland and Charles James Fox. Foote made it risible in his eponymous hero. Sir Luke breaks a dinner engagement with an alderman in order to dine with a knight, whom he drops in favour of an earl, then a duke and so on. The British comic obsession with class and with social climbing of course pre-dates Foote, but the new economy of the eighteenth century favoured the ridiculing of the *nouveaux riches* and social pretension, and Sir Luke has had his place as one of the grandfathers of *parvenus* on stage and screen ever since. One constant motif within *The Lame Lover*, specific to Foote's play and to this moment in his life, was the jocund image of a toady climbing the social ladder with only one leg. Another was the close connection between Sir Luke's story and the third butt of the Luke Limp joke: the political radical John Wilkes.

Wilkes's name and story connect first with *The Lame Lover* in the character of Sergeant Whittaker, a verbose lawyer imitated by Sir Luke/Samuel Foote. A real Whittaker had stood against Wilkes in the Middlesex election when Wilkes was elected to his seat in Parliament, which he refused on principle in his quest towards electoral reform. Wilkes was much in the news as *The Lame Lover* was written and then hit the stage, and though Sir Luke is in no sense a direct representation of Wilkes, Foote traded on the libertarian's libertine notoriety to help sell the play.

John Wilkes, political radical, Lothario and wit, Fellow of the Royal Society and MP since 1757, had known Foote at least since the mid-1740s. They shared many mutual acquaintances, as well as closer friends in James Boswell, Benjamin Franklin, Lord Fitzherbert and, unexpectedly, Domenico Angelo, the fencing master. Angelo's stage career had not prospered since he had shared Macklin's classes with Foote, and he had opened instead a fencing school, the *école d'escrime*, in Soho. Frequented by Wilkes, and also the cross-dressing Chevalier d'Éon, the school is the most likely place for Wilkes and Foote to have met, though necessarily Foote was not a regular attendee there after the amputation. Their paths crossed also at the Garricks', with whom Wilkes dined on Half Moon Street on regular occasions, or at the Beefsteak Club, to which Foote was once or twice invited. Wherever they first met, they were well enough acquainted by 1761 to attend together a local-election hustings, along with Garrick, and some have even posited that Foote helped write some of Wilkes's election addresses.[8]

Wilkes, the further allusion in the character of Sir Luke Limp, was cited by many memoirists as the ugliest man in England, and would have been, in his way, an easy stage target, with his Squintum-like squint and prognathous jaw. His boast that it took him only 'half an hour to talk away his face'[9] with women is directly echoed in Sir Luke's *risqué* assertion that his charm can earn him an extra leg. But if Foote had wanted to satirize Wilkes only in Sir Luke, he went off the idea as the play formed in his mind, and the tantalizing allusions in the first act to an unlikely ladies' man and the character of Sergeant Whittaker, which must have made audiences yearn for more on Wilkes, are dropped as the play progresses.

Instead Foote's specific literary endeavour in response to his controversial acquaintance was another work penned between the amputation and the winter season of 1769–70: *Wilkes; An Oratorio.*

As Performed at The Great Room in Bishopsgate-Street. It was published
as being 'written by Mr Foote' with 'Music by Signor Carlos
Francesco Baritini, London'.

Wilkes had been declared an outlaw in January 1764 after
being found guilty of seditious and obscene libel for his publications
North Briton and *An Essay on Women.* He had fled to France but was
in the process of re-establishing himself in London when Foote
wrote *The Lame Lover* and *The Oratorio.* Foote had already alluded in
his play *The Patron* to the case against Wilkes and, popular and
recognized as he was in London, it made sense to make sport with
'Wilkes & Liberty', and the oratorio was scheduled to be premièred, provocatively, on Wilkes's birthday.

Unfortunately it is not entirely certain that the work is Foote's.
Exciting though it would be to link directly the great satirist of the
age and its greatest political radical at a time when both seemed to
be throwing all caution windward, Foote and his first memoirist
neglect to mention the work. It is not really his style, but conversely
it is possible that he had tried to evade accusations of authorship,
only to be outed by the printer. He certainly had every reason to
be wary of involving himself directly with Wilkes, newly appointed
as he was to the court of George III as royal patentee, and given
that it was his predecessor in the Haymarket, Henry Fielding,
who had brought the wrath of the 1737 Licensing Act upon the
theatre community in the first place by taunting the government
on similar themes to Wilkes's. If there is any particular indication
that Foote is indeed the author, as the title page declares, it would
be the playfully lewd and sly recognition that Wilkes is living idly
in debtors' prison, a life Foote remembered well:

> How happy a debtor's life passes
> How free from all care and all strife
> No treasure he ever amasses
> But cheerfully *spends* his whole life.[10]

The most resonant and famous connection between Wilkes and
Foote dates also from this period just after the amputation and

involves one of the more notorious put-downs in the English language. Usually the story is credited to Wilkes, but it has emerged as, almost beyond doubt, a Footeism. Happy to relate, happy for Foote that is, it seems Wilkes's infamous exchange, supposedly with the Earl of Sandwich, is likely to have been, in origin, a quote from Foote. Sandwich, a fellow member with Wilkes of the debauched Monks of Medmenham, or Hellfire Club,[11] is quoted as having said to Wilkes at one of their gatherings: 'Sir, it is unclear to me whether you will die on the gallows or of the pox.'

Wilkes is reported to have replied: 'That depends, my lord, on whether I embrace your lordship's principles or your mistress.'[12]

The first record of the exchange, however, as being a Wilkes quote, is from 1844, and makes no claim that it is an *extempore* remark, but rather Wilkes quoting a French aphorism of the Comte de Mirabeau or Cardinal Maury. An earlier memoirist, in 1809, however, attributes it instead to 1766 and to Foote, which gives him therefore, a very strong claim to being its English-language originator.

'Foote,' says Lord Sandwich, in this earlier record of the exchange, 'I have often wondered what catastrophe would bring you to your end; but I think, that you must either die of the pox, or the halter [be hanged].'

'My lord,' replies Foote, 'that will depend upon one of two contingencies: whether I embrace your lordship's mistress, or your lordship's principles.'[13]

This seems to be one minor example of the deliberate obfuscation of Foote's memory after his scandalous demise and a reattribution instead to a man of heroically heterosexual reputation. It may merely be a mistake, or indeed a relatively well-used insult of the age.

The Lame Lover and *The Oratorio* were the first written works that exercised Foote's time and quill after the accident, but they were not the first post-amputation work to hit the stage. Rather, they were put to one side in favour of a play about surgeons in which

Foote would also use his disability to comic effect: *The Devil Upon Two Sticks*. All appear to have been written, or at least begun, during his convalescence at Cannons Park and then back in London, and in a household that necessarily became more focused around its disabled master. Perhaps it is not so surprising that Foote's work at this period was affected not just by fervour to get things done, and concerns about his image and disability, but also by one figure from his immediate circle.

Ann Edwards first came to work for Foote just before or during his convalescence. She had a position as a scullery-maid. She sang as she worked, and Foote, house- and often bed-bound, fell in love with her voice and considered it perfect for his stage. He arranged for her to be given dancing and singing lessons, then orchestrated her début as 'a young gentlewoman never before on the stage', which was not quite true, in both plays he wrote immediately after the amputation. She played Charlotte in *The Lame Lover* and the *ingénue* in *The Devil Upon Two Sticks*, as well as appearing in some afterpieces with the actor Mr Bannister. She was, however, as quickly out of favour as she had come into it, when she married in early 1768 the Haymarket's treasurer, the occasional actor and close friend of Foote, William Jewell. Foote threw them both out of the company. His pique was uncharacteristic of his management style, and is one reason some have suggested he had feelings for Jewell, which were muddied by this new relationship. Or he may have harboured such feelings for his former maid.[14] In any event, having discharged them both he soon relented and they were both back in the company the following summer. In seasons soon after the accident, Ann also played Maria in *The Citizen* and appeared in *Midas* and later, too, as Polly Peachum – rare occasions of Foote mounting others' work for the furtherance of a company member's reputation. James Boswell was moved to remark that Ann was 'the jewel' of Foote's eye, while *Gentleman's Magazine* wrote that she was 'deservedly a favourite with the public . . . though in private . . . a very respectable character'.[15] Respectable or not, Ann, the maid-turned-singer, and Jewell, the actor-turned-treasurer, set up home in unconventional circumstances: they moved in with Foote to live with him and they looked after him for the rest of his life.

The first season after the accident represented a physical ordeal for Foote, with or without a supportive domestic situation. The summer season of 1766 was the launch of his patent company at the Haymarket and he appeared in fifty-six performances less than six months after the amputation. *The Orators* and *The Commissary* were the two other main pieces of the season along with his return as Mrs Cole in *The Minor*. Acting the Peter Paragraph scene from *The Orators*, with its swift turns of character and intent, was an extraordinary feat physically and emotionally for any actor, all the more so a relatively new manipulator of a prosthesis, playing up to six nights in a row plus matinées, and toiling in a particularly humid summer. Foote's physical stamina was impressive. The playbills for 4 August 1766 promised that 'Mr Foote will perform his usual parts', which involved, as written, one character being taught to ride. Not only was Foote, at the time, the most famous failed horseman in England, but to ride a horse was and is one of the most difficult feats for the limbless. Foote nevertheless insisted on riding a hobby-horse onto the stage to the shock and delight of audiences. His first post-operation season lasted only until 6 August. This was considerably shorter than usual for Foote, yet he was on stage for every single weekday night bar one, and one week for seven nights consecutively. In the final week of the season he appeared twice each evening in different pieces. During all this it was widely held that Foote's Mrs Cole was the best served of his older characters by his new disability as he worked his awkward gait into the characterization of the gouty old brothel-keeper. But there was an expectation, fed by Foote, that he would turn his writing to address his new predicament, and so he did.

The Devil Upon Two Sticks, the first of Foote's post-amputation works to hit the stage, was written at the same time as *The Lame Lover*. The title was taken from a previous translation of Le Sage's *Le Diable boiteux*, a play Foote knew from Paris, and which had

already been on stage at Drury Lane in 1729. Foote's version is a
sentimental romantic comedy – another eloping couple – but took
swipes at the 1760s antiquarian craze and at the 'female historian'
Mrs Macaulay in particular. But it was primarily an attack on
medical quackery. On this subject there was plenty to parody in
Georgian London and Foote was famously better acquainted
than most with the sharp end of the surgeon's knife. Hence a
newsworthy surgical scandal underscored the plot of Foote's first
work as an amputee.

The Devil Upon Two Sticks was the title role and was played by
Foote. It was a quasi-blasphemous personification of Beelzebub
as a doctor. In the 1760s, medicine was both controversial and, in
its way, ridiculous. The Royal College of Physicians restricted its
fellowship to graduates of Oxford and Cambridge, thus barring
equally distinguished Dutch or Scottish graduates, such as the
Hunter brothers, who practised in London. The year of Foote's
amputation by coincidence saw a growing resentment about this
situation, which led eventually to a riot: the storming of the
College's premises by a group of disgruntled 'Licentiates' – doctors
and surgeons who were forbidden full membership and full rights
at the College, including Hunter. They entered the building
accompanied by a blacksmith to remove the locks, to the consternation of the president, Sir William Browne. The event became
familiar to many through a popular engraving, *The March of the
Medical Militants*, published by Robert Sayer, and a subsequent
painting by Zoffany, also rendered as a mezzotint and widely sold.
Bonnell Thornton wrote up the whole dispute in a comic poem,
'Battle of the Wigs', which in turn inspired Foote's play, *The
Devil Upon Two Sticks*, with its third act 'Battle of the Doctors'.
This was Foote's essential addition to Le Sage's play: a parody of
quack surgeons.

President Browne told Foote he thought the notoriety the play
brought the Royal College only improved business. Bromfeild,
however, was unamused. *The Devil Upon Two Sticks* was long adored
by the London public, and the role requiring the 'unipedular charm'

of Mr Foote was played long after this death by actors affecting
a limp. Even the historian Edward Gibbon became sufficient of a
fan to see the play several times in the summer of 1767, with Foote
in it, telling his sister in a letter that he was enjoying writing
through that London summer: 'When I am tired of the Roman
Empire,' he wrote – he was hard at work on *The Decline and Fall* –
'I can laugh away an evening at Foote's theatre.'[16]

§

The 1766 and 1767 performances were impressive enough for a
man only months away from his surgeon's knife and saw, but the
real triumphs came as Foote slowly built a whole new Company of
Comedians with the relaunched Theatre Royal, Haymarket, over
the course of the following year. 1767 marked his first full year as
a royal patentee, on a par with Colman and Harris and his old
friend Garrick. It marked also the twentieth anniversary of his first
steps on the stage of the Little Theatre in *Diversions of the Morning*.
His new regime, however, was not going to be only about him:
indeed, he had been unsure how his health would fare and how
the public would receive him, so he went about building a core of
skilled comedians around him, secure now in a patent theatre
and excited by the prospect of being an actor-manager who pro-
moted comedy. First he approached the Irishman Spranger Barry,
and a Mrs Dancer, who had come with him from Dublin. Foote
offered them a mini-season of afterpieces. As William Cooke
aptly put it, this was a mixture of professional admiration and
'silencing a powerful opposition, forming an alliance both lucrative
and respectable';[17] for otherwise these Smock Alley stars would
have played in competition at the King's Theatre or been hired for
Drury Lane. Ned Shuter joined next, with 'Plausible' Jack Palmer.
Ned was Loader again in *The Minor*, Simon in *The Commissary*,
Scamper in an all-star cast of *The Orators*, Young Wilding, Foote's
role in *The Lyar* but now beyond him, and Pepperpot in *The Patron*.
Shuter also appeared in *The Taylors* and a variety of non-Foote plays.
Garrick took notice of what was going on, and offered better wages

at Drury Lane, but it was too late for many of the biggest comedy names, being drawn to the new Theatre Royal on the Haymarket.

Foote also hired two comediennes, one of whom would work for him, in varying capacities, until his death. Sarah Cheney married William Gardner of the Theatre Royal Covent Garden in 1765. They worked under Foote as Mr and Mrs Gardner in the new Company of Comedians, but Sarah Gardner later moved in with Foote as his housekeeper. In the 1766 and 1767 seasons she was kept busy playing Mrs Mechlin in *The Commissary*, then Kitty in *The Lyar* and Jenny in *The Knights*, but the real star turn in petticoats that season was Mrs Jefferies, who had just returned from Smock Alley where she had received the rarest praise as 'the finest Irish actress since Mrs Woffington'. Foote could begin to count on a useful core of actors with whom he had worked before and whose style and professionalism he trusted: Thomas Davis and Richard Castle, John Quick, fresh from his first season at Covent Garden, and Will Keenall joined him. John Brownsmith ran the company as a prompter, as well as occasional actor. He had been in the same company with Foote in 1758–9 and, as is the way of things, the manager of the new Theatre Royal simply poached someone he had worked with happily before. Brownsmith took an interest in the practical aspects of putting on a play so it is thanks to him, his *Theatrical Alphabet* and *Dramatic Timepiece* that we can, to some extent, understand the working world of Foote's new Haymarket company, the people who worked there and Foote's impressive record as a long-term employer.

In the end, the post-1766 company depended on Foote, his name and presence, as did the royal patent. His energy, far from being dimmed by his disability, seemed unbounded. The patent immediately proved of real value. For one thing, it was golden publicity, appearing in all the leading London papers as news, and then in his advertisements. It also secured a longer summer season. Meanwhile Foote was less at the mercy of the Lord Chamberlain: though he might submit a play that was found to be objectionable, the damage was contained; he was never again at risk of losing his livelihood entirely, of being 'silenced', which secured the goodwill of backers and season bookers. Cooke is clear on Foote's immediate accession into the front ranks of theatre managers: 'This was giving a fortune at one stroke; which our author knew how to avail himself of.'[18] There was even, it would seem, a royal crest to be fitted above a new portico, 'a new front erected, and the inside made as convenient and neat as the building would admit.'[19]

On the minds of the many tens of thousands who flocked to the Haymarket during those summers of 1766 and 1767, there was, doubtless, the exciting prospect of visiting a new Theatre Royal and its vaunted refurbishment, but there was also the more newsworthy issue of its patentee's 'depeditation'. Foote addressed this, immediately and repeatedly, in his original style: a specially written prologue. It was composed to celebrate the new status of the Theatre Royal, Haymarket, and was used and embellished through the 1766 and 1767 seasons.

Two metropolitan wits, Snarl and Laconic, played by Foote, who was accompanied most often by Barry, find themselves alone in the theatre on the forestage before a performance, begin to criticize the newly restored wooden theatre and its half-timber manager. The *London Magazine* commented that 'the improvements Foote has made in his house are prodigious',[20] but even the new chinoiserie proscenium could not detract from the main attraction: Mr Foote's new leg and the two dandies on stage making fun of it, themselves and the lurid fascination the audience had with the proprietor's lost leg. It was accorded its own round of applause, and became known, in reference to the baton in Punch and Judy shows, as Foote's slap-stick. The new prologue was called, redolently enough, *An Occasional Prologue in Prose-Laconic* and became itself celebrated enough to be published and sold as a keepsake.[21]

By the first anniversary of the amputation, Tate Wilkinson was able to write in ebullient form of Foote's utter triumph over adversity. Foote was considering a new production of *The Taylors* in which he hoped to cast Tate either that winter, if a production could be got together for Drury Lane, or the following summer at the Haymarket – a perfect vehicle for his Company of Comedians as the play parodies 'the best passages in [my] most favourite plays . . . conveyed with [comic] gravity in blank verse'. But despite all his well-justified self-assurance and positivity about the upcoming 1767 season, Foote ends an anniversary letter to Tate with an uncharacteristic avowal of his continuing pain: 'I cannot say I am quite so well as I had reason to expect [by now],' he complains. The prosthesis that gripped his upper thigh was insufficient to the task when it came to stage business – notably the ambitious lifting of Mr Barry in one afterpiece. It left Foote sore for days. 'I am now much better', he ends, 'and, except the trifle of a leg, as much yours as ever.'[22]

Despite his triumphant return to the stage, the creation of comedies built around his new physicality, and the evident success of His Majesty's Company of Comedians through 1766 and into 1767, Foote was discovering that which faces many after the loss of a lower limb. Near constant exhaustion can be the reality of return to 'normal' life, and with it, often, and after the euphoria that attends the early months of recovery, the realization that pain is likely to be a constant presence and the strength to face the immediate aftermath of such trauma is only one element of the fortitude demanded to carry on.

SHAKESPEARE'S JUBILEE

'Curse on that Foote – one leg! But ONE to break!
"*A kingdom for a horse*" to break his neck'

David Garrick, in *Love in the Suds*[1]

THE 1766–8 SEASONS turned Foote into a securely wealthy man, netting, it was estimated, at least three thousand pounds per annum. He took a lease on an expensive property, Northend, near Fulham, which functioned as a rural retreat from London and was surrounded by a small park, with a stable and a duckpond. He furnished the villa in the style of a country gentleman with literary and artistic tastes, theatrical tastes, indeed, for anyone who saw his bedroom: it was hung with the same blue and white morine festoons that graced the royal box at the Haymarket.[2] The one surviving painting of the house, which Foote commissioned from the fashionable landscape painter James Canter[3] and had hung in his dining room there, shows an exceptionally elegant neo-classical villa, surrounded by a large garden studded with 'rustic benches' in the Chinese style.[4] Here, Foote could sit between short bouts of walking – he was said to be a great admirer of birdsong – contemplating perhaps his good fortune. If Northend lacked the *élan* of Garrick's grandiose villa in Hampton, it was still a long way from the Fleet Prison.

Foote entertained lavishly. 'Lords Gower and Weymouth yesterday, tomorrow, Mrs Hale and Chetwynds and The Garricks,

Male and Female,'[5] he wrote of his Northend hosting in a 1768 letter to Sarah Mexborough. The eight French armchairs in his saloon were all on castors, the easier to move around for large gatherings when the room was used for dancing. Foote played the new organ there, his dancing days behind him, which had barrels that could be loaded with mechanized musical drums and play 'choice tunes' for cotillions[6] when he became weary. It was worth more than twelve pounds. The room boasted also two specially commissioned telescopes for gazing out of the large bay windows at the stars or, for the myopic, at the lasciviously detailed portrait of Venus with a satyr on the ceiling.[7] In addition to all this, there were six other paintings and a Wilton carpet designed and woven especially for the villa, three tall sash windows overlooking the gardens and lake, all hung with fashionable Venetian blinds. It was a room, and a house, for partying.

The fact that 'The Garricks, Male and Female' were frequently on the guest list at Fulham belies the ongoing frictions between the old rivals and now fellow royal patent-holders. Though Foote played Garrick's *The Lying Valet* as an afterpiece to his *The Devil Upon Two Sticks*, he was quick to put Garrick in his place when his old friend teased him about playing in one of Garrick's farces: 'Why yes, David,' said Foote, 'what could I do better? I must have some *ventilator* for this excessive hot weather.'[8]

Foote had found status, wealth and an unassailable position as leading London satirist by heading up the new Company of Comedians at a royal patent house, and this put him on a new footing, as it were, with Garrick. Their contemporaries Thomas Davies and William Cooke, though admittedly writing much later, both concluded that Garrick had to some extent been in awe of Foote's wit all their lives. 'Garrick lived in fear,' wrote Cooke, 'of Foote's ridicule and timidly tried to soften the blows before they were delivered, by propitiating his tormentor.'[9] It may have been greatly more complex. Garrick eschewed impersonating other actors and their styles in the belief that in the long term it was counterproductive. Mimicry was the mainstay of Foote's stage persona, so this moral condescension may have rankled, abetted by the knowledge that Garrick was an equally skilled impressionist when he chose. Foote, as Garrick later avowed, never put anything before the possibility of a joke, and found Garrick's high-mindedness aggravating at times, pompous at others. Mainly he saw Garrick's foibles as easy targets for public and private jests, many of them recorded in the gossip-hungry papers of the period. Garrick and Foote warred like only actors can, taking each other's failures warmly to heart, dying a little at each other's successes, while maintaining a public face of easy bonhomie and unsure, perhaps, of how much bile was mixed with old affection. Things came to a head after Foote's accession to a patent house, and over the seasons that led up to Garrick's Jubilee in honour of Shakespeare. Their spats became a spectator sport – part media construct, perhaps, part rancour.

For instance, both Foote and Garrick bred dogs at their respective rural retreats, and Foote wrote in 1768 on behalf of one of his to one of Garrick's – dog to dog. Garrick, 'prevailed upon to pimp for a four leg'd favourite', turned down Foote with all the wit and grace of the period, and partly in rhyme. Foote published a vituperative ditty in response, more offended than perhaps he had needed to be over a spurned bitch, for the sake of extra publicity:

> Whenever Garrick dines or sleeps
> He drops a dogg'rel rhyme
> The snail thus marks the road she creeps
> By slobbering sordid slime.[10]

The dogs did have their day, for what it was worth, but the publicized epistolary spat continued the next year, when one of Foote's dogs was sent to stud at Hampton in return: 'Mr Foote presents to Mr Garrick his Compliments and begs with his best thanks to discharge the smaller part of the obligation he was so kind to confer on him last summer. Suffolk Street, Monday.'[11]

Like the lovers in 'The Twelve Days of Christmas', Foote and

Garrick seem to have tried to outdo each other with unwanted gifts, perhaps to amuse their friends and the London public, but clearly to the consternation of their respective servants. Again, some of this even enters the record of the London papers. Later in 1768, Garrick left Fulham forgetting to pack into his coach Foote's gift of several geese: one cannot help but imagine this was a deliberate omission. He wrote his thank-you note, as was his wont, in doggerel:

> Dear Foote I love your wit, I like your wine
> And hope when next with you I dine
> Indeed I do not care how soon
> I hope – nay beg it – as a boon . . .
> Your liquor then each Taste will hit
> Pure clear and sparkling as your wit
> I took my leave in such a hurry
> With drinking too much in a flurry
> With Gibes and Jests so crammed my mind
> I left those b[uggerin]g Geese behind.[12]

With Foote, Garrick knew, no one could really win. As Johnson had warned him, Foote had 'one species of wit in an eminent degree; that of escape. You drive him into a corner with both hands, but he's gone. You think you have got him – like an animal that jumps over your head.'[13]

Their spats turned public not just in published correspondence but as prologues at their respective theatres, spoken by Foote and Garrick to audiences with a very modern taste for star wars. They played up to their antagonistic roles – Aristophanes and Roscius – as the comedy and tragedy muses over their respective proscenium arches. It was, Garrick said, the ordained role of someone with Foote's talents to mock him, but their paths had been so long intertwined that he was solicitous of clear reminders that they were, *au fond*, friends:

> Tho [we the Managers] may war
> Let not, my Friend, our heart-strings jar

You're right to lash me. I confess
The Town Expects it, more or less
In publick wound, in private love me
The polished lancet cannot wound me.[14]

Garrick here enunciates some of his perennial problem in maintaining his long-standing relationship with Foote. For the comedian there was no difference between public and private wounds: all was fair in comedy. It was ironic, therefore, that they most nearly came to proper blows, and to a full capsizing of their friendship, over William Shakespeare when it had been with the works and worship of the Bard that they had first found common ground at the Bedford and under the tutelage of Charles Macklin. It was ironic, too, because Shakespeare was one of the few subjects, along with French classical comedy, on which Foote could be very serious indeed.

§

The first public advertisement for Garrick's 'Shakespeare Jubilee' appeared in the *St James's Chronicle* on 6 May 1769. The jamboree was planned for 5–7 September 1769 in Stratford-upon-Avon, a neglected backwater of Warwickshire without, then, either a theatre or widely recognized connection to its famous theatrical son. This left only the summer of 1769 for Garrick to make manifest what was planned quite simply as the largest public gathering outside the capital since the Civil War. Garrick had visited Stratford in 1767, and begun to form the idea of a pageant or festival riding late upon the bicentenary of the dramatist's birth, but coasting the wave of nationalistic interest in him that Garrick had spearheaded. Like festivals before and since, it was conceived as a synthesis of imperatives: commercial, adulatory and self-promotional. Garrick solicited funds from the public for the venture. Foote greeted it all with wry scepticism: it was, in his opinion, 'Garrick's Folly' (a reference to the Shakespeare shrine Garrick built in Hampton) – an exercise in vaunting ambition for both performer and long-dead writer and an insufficient claim on the good will of the London arts community, obliged to traipse all the way to Warwickshire.

Nevertheless, the summer of 1769 was dominated in the newspapers by Garrick's grandiose plans and, given the scale of his ambition against the backwardness of Stratford, it remains an extraordinary testament to his skills as a producer. There were to be balls, masquerades and a horse race. A rotunda was built, in imitation of the one at Ranelagh Gardens – the first Shakespeare Festival Theatre – designed to accommodate up to two thousand spectators, which amounted to more than the entire population of Stratford. The whole company of both Covent Garden Theatres Royal was involved – Foote's company was not invited – along with the entire orchestra of Drury Lane: 170 actors and singers, in specially made costumes, all illuminated by lights and fireworks. The technicians and scenic artists of Drury Lane were redeployed to plan, build and paint the backdrops, floats and costumes for what was designed as a three-day pageant in Stratford. Franchises were negotiated for printed music and souvenirs, which were mainly, to judge from those that have survived, miniature porcelain figurines of Garrick 'being Shakespearean'.

In August the *London Magazine* dedicated a series of 'paragraphs' – articles – to the glories of Shakespeare, as contrasted with French classicism. It was the regular cultural nationalism of the times – and part of Garrick's argument. The magazine went on, however, to print the first full-length biography of Garrick himself, in instalments. The conflation of Shakespeare's genius with Garrick's was typical of the 1768–9 press – 'the *first* dramatic poet and the *first* dramatic performer' – and the subject of much ribaldry at Garrick's expense, largely from Foote. Garrick was unperturbed by accusations of hubris. If the new icon of Britishness was to be 'the Stratfordian', it was all the better for the theatrical professions that the national poet should turn out also to have been an actor. Foote possibly had sympathy for Garrick's arguments, despite his own lack of success in Shakespearean roles. Nevertheless, he smelt comic potential in the ambitious project plotted for Stratford. He encouraged his friend Thomas Weston, the comic and tumbler, to play as his benefit night that season at the Haymarket *Richard III* as a comedy, mimicking Garrick's hump and sneer. 'You and I are a couple of buckets,' Foote wrote to Garrick, meaning the counter-weights of stage machinery, 'for while you are raising the expectation of Shakespeare, I am endeavouring to sink it.'[15] Weston chickened out at the last minute and Francis Gentleman played the King in the tragic manner.

Next Foote rewrote the end of *The Devil Upon Two Sticks*, and got a huge laugh by having the devil explain theatre finances as a system of having 'the public advance the money, and you in return are to treat them to – *nothing at all*!'

Garrick was offended by this damaging war of rhetoric waged against his Stratford plans. The Jubilee represented a large financial risk on his and Drury Lane's part, and he pitched on as best he might. He wrote a long 'Ode to Shakespeare', to be delivered as the climax of events, and devoted his every waking hour to planning the event, even while the burghers of Stratford appeared to have increasingly mixed feelings about it, and about the impending descent upon them of literary London. In response Foote advertised that he would be attending the Jubilee to sell copies of his own ode, a comedy in verse called *Drugger's Jubilee* (Drugger, the sidekick in Ben Jonson's *The Alchemist*, being a famed Garrick role). Though advertised, the piece was never written, much less rehearsed or played; it was an idle threat, another wind-up of Foote's old friend in a pattern of deliberate comedic harassment. So, as the summer plans progressed, one unnecessary anxiety for Garrick was what Foote would do and say to ridicule things. In consequence he included in his memoranda to staff 'to secure some good lodgings [and] a good bed for Mr Foote'. This was a practical worry but also a professional anxiety about keeping Foote in fine humour. In this, Garrick failed.

Foote travelled to Stratford with their old drama-coach Charles Macklin. It took them several bone-crunching days due to bad weather and rutted roads, and when they eventually made it to the Bear Inn at the hamlet of Bridgetown, near Stratford, they found they were being housed with all the fireworks intended for the festival's finale. Foote affected to be both offended and concerned about safety, accusing Garrick of playing Fawkes in a second Gunpowder Plot and pointing out that he was more flammable than most, but the inn, to the detriment of Foote's back and the fireworks, was damp and cold, and the pyrotechnics, like everything else at Stratford that September, failed to ignite.

Foote had no call to rain on his rival's parade, as the heavens did the damage for him. The rain started on 4 September 1769 and did not let up until the ninth.[16] The downpour ruined the expensively costumed spectacle, dousing the fireworks and forcing the small crowds to run for cover through the mud. The audiences complained about it all: the housing, the prices of drinks, the meagre supplies of food. The horse race was delayed and the rotunda floor flooded before the masked ball, the climatic procession of Shakespearean characters had to be cancelled, and the whole Jubilee was judged a shoddy wash-out. The only successes, according to William Smith, an actor in Garrick's company, were Thomas Arne's music and Garrick's '*Ode*'. His own costume sodden with rain, Smith nevertheless recalled, decades later, feeling rapt that day with the honour and pleasure of 'living in the days of Garrick!'[17]

When they met up later in a Shakespeare tavern, Garrick seemed unshakeable in his positivity. 'Well, Sam, what do you think of all this?' he asked his old friend in the company of Macklin.

'Think of it,' came Foote's reply, 'as a Christian should do: as God's revenge against vanity.'[18]

§

The crowds returned to Warwick and London, pressing into service whatever vehicles would take them, and the newspapers in town had plenty of sport at the Jubilee's expense. Squibs, cartoons and playlets appeared, lampooning the whole affair, yet still Garrick stayed bullish. 'If the Heavens had favoured us,' he allowed, 'Mrs Garrick and I should have returned to town in triumph – but it is over, and I am neither mad nor in a fever, both of which threatened me greatly.'[19] He had made his point about Shakespeare as worthy of national celebration, and he had thought up, he told the artist Benjamin Wilson, who shared his coach back to Hampton, a way to recoup his losses . . .

Back in London, Foote would not let it rest. He again rewrote *The Devil Upon Two Sticks* to include direct criticism of Jubilee celebrations: 'A Jubilee,' the devil explains, 'is a public invitation, urged by puffing, to go post without horses, to an obscure borough . . . to celebrate a great poet whose own works have made him immortal, by an ode without poetry, music without harmony, dinners without victuals, and lodgings without beds; a horserace up to the knees in water, fireworks extinguished as soon as they were lighted, and a gingerbread amphitheatre, which . . . tumbled to pieces as soon as it was finished.'[20]

Garrick's response was spirited – and inspired by Foote: he wrote a comedy about the Stratford festival for Drury Lane and called it, simply, *Jubilee*. He would appear as himself, in an article of singular comic self-deprecation and marketing genius. It was merely a playlet, but it made much comic capital out of the crowding and price-gouging of Stratford, as well as the inclement critics and weather – and even the perceived pomposity of the venture. Garrick's expensively costumed parade of Shakespearean characters became a setpiece in the comedy, ridiculed by an Irish character who mocks the grandiose pageantry of British nationalism. It was a part Foote should have played, but it went to Richard Yates, another skilled mimic, who based his performance on old Thomas Sheridan. His bathetic interruptions, written by Garrick, were the comic counterfoil to the spectacle on stage: a complete restaging of the Stratford pageant as it should have been, which at least made use of the costumes. Nineteen separate tableaux moved across the stage: *Much Ado* bled into *Twelfth Night* and into *Richard*

III, Romeo and Juliet, Hamlet, Henry IV, Antony and Cleopatra and *The Merchant of Venice*[21] – a veritable Greatest Hits of Shakespeare and Garrick and a signal moment, of course, in the transformation of William Shakespeare into cultural artefact: prepackaged, amputated from his written words. Of immediate effect for Garrick and Foote, it turned Garrick's £2,000 personal loss and the danger of bankruptcy for Foote's main business rival, Drury Lane, into a vast commercial juggernaut. Garrick's *Jubilee* ran longer than any play that premièred in the entire eighteenth century – more than ninety consecutive performances before anything else had a look-in at the Theatre Royal.

Foote's attitude to Shakespeare, and to Garrick's colonizing of his name for his own purposes, remains puzzling. He had that grudging regard of the comedian for the apparently purer intent of straight acting, and may have harboured residual jealousy for Garrick's many triumphs in Shakespearean leads, which were in addition, in Garrick's case, to his noted success in comedic roles. Foote was forever 'that Devil dog', the 'buffoon of the Haymarket'. He also saw the Jubilee project as worthy of ridicule, which was how it seemed to many. In this, he attacked Garrick and his supposed vanity, but his main contention was with styles of Shakespearean production – encouraged by the success of the Jubilee pageant, that put spectacle before content and thereby undermined the author and actors' intentions, what he referred to as 'idle pageantry and empty show'. Criticism of selling, with the name of Shakespeare, mere flash and prattle was criticism of much higher order than simply teasing a fellow actor about his vanity.

> Even Roscius [Garrick] blushes at his own success
> And feels some transcient touches for his crime
> To have sunk [Shakespeare's] scenes below a pantomime.[22]

So, it was to be expected, in conclusion, that wags would print eventually Garrick's supposed response to Foote. It was a prologue that was never spoken, and though printed in Garrick's name has little claim to be Garrick's actual hand or even style. Yet its sentiments reflect some of the complexity of emotion he must have felt, faced over and over again with Foote's infuriating whimsy, cruel parody of serious intent, and commercial rivalry:

> O that that too too solid house, which Foote
> Has in the Haymarket, would melt at once
> Thaw and resolve itself into a dew!
> Or that the Royal Pleasure had not fix'd
> A patent for the summer in his hands!
> Fie on it, O Fie – Foote's an unweeded garden
> That grows to seed, things rank and gross in nature
> Possess him merely. That it should come to this!
> But nine months given to me – nay not so much
> Not nine! So excellent an actor! And to him
> Hyperion to a satyr. Heaven and earth!
> Must I remember? Why the town hangs on me
> As if increase of appetite did grow
> By what it fed on . . .
> It is not nor cannot come to good
> But break my heart, for I must hold my tongue.[23]

Foote was right to pay special regard to the festival and what Garrick was doing with Shakespeare's name. The Jubilee planted a seed that grows still. Stratford has been associated ever since with the glover's son, his birthplace and the few sites that attach to his name. Word of the Jubilee spread abroad – to Germany and France especially – where arguments about drama and national culture were also current and where Shakespeare's plays were appearing in new translations. And Garrick successfully married the *texts* to the *business* of performance – not as obvious as it might sound – in Stratford as elsewhere, to the enormous support of the acting profession through succeeding generations, in terms of grafting the respectability of poetry on to the rackety business of theatre. Foote both applauded and denounced aspects of Garrick's Bardolatry, decrying the spectacle that Garrick, as a producer, found commercial, but singing with Garrick the praises of the writer who had first brought them together as students – the actor-playwright of Stratford and a man Foote tellingly described as Britain's pre-eminent 'comedian'.

As heads of the two most successful patent theatres, the Haymarket and Drury Lane, Foote and Garrick were obliged eventually to put personal rancour behind the exigencies of box-office. Although Foote came near to staging his ragamuffin procession, the *Drugger's Jubilee*, back in London, he was dissuaded. A mutual friend, the Marquess of Stafford, arranged a 'chance' meeting between the rival actor-managers and Garrick broke the silence by simply asking Foote: 'So, is it war or peace?'[24]

Foote smiled and shrugged and said, according to his memoirs, 'O Davy! Peace by all means.'[25]

And so their cantankerous friendship rumbled forward, up to and even through a sex scandal that would briefly engulf them both.

WHOLESALE POPULARMONGER

'My work, sirs, is to be a wholesale popularmonger'

Samuel Foote, avoiding being beaten up outside
the Theatre Royal, Haymarket, by nabobs[1]

ISAAC BICKERSTAFFE and Foote had first worked together in 1769, on *The Doctor Last In His Chariot*. The play is mainly credited to the Irishman, Bickerstaffe, but included translation work, done by Foote, from Molière's *La Malade imaginaire*. So Foote was unlikely to be unaware that Isaac Bickerstaffe was homosexual. Nevertheless, it must have come as something of shock to him, as to the rest of London, when in early 1772 a verse satire was published depicting Isaac Bickerstaffe and David Garrick as lovers. It was titled *Love in the Suds*. No one was surprised about the attack on Bickerstaffe, who was discreetly but openly gay, but the traducing of Garrick was another matter, and perforce gave Foote pause for thought. *Love in the Suds* was written by a failed dramatist called William Kenrick, a man who had once published under the wondrous pseudonym 'Whimsey Banter' and who is best remembered in Dr Johnson's epitaph, 'Sir, he is one of those who have made themselves *publick*, without making themselves *known*.' The subtitle of the verse libel he made public and known in 1772, *Love in the Suds*, was *Being the Lamentation of Roscius for the Loss of his Nyky*. Bickerstaffe was the 'Nyky' of the poem, made clear by the reference to his 1772 flight from London after a scandal involving a 'rough cast' guardsman in a London park. Garrick was depicted as 'Roscius', the lead actor of a new Augustan age. Bickerstaffe never risked returning to England after the soldier in question, possibly a professional blackmailer, accused him of having made a homosexual proposition. *Love in the Suds* went through five sell-out editions before the end of 1772.

The libellous piece established two salient facts in Foote's life as he reached fifty. A celebrated actor, like himself or Garrick, was suddenly more open to attack from pamphleteers. Notably, from the late 1760s onwards, actors were exposed in the crossfire of a wider cultural debate over masculinity, which ranged from the epicene Macaroni fashion craze to the marriage problems of George III's brothers. If even a man of exemplary respectability and evident heterosexuality like Garrick could be defamed simply by association with Bickerstaffe, Foote's position as London's most prominent cross-dressing fop looked suddenly somewhat vulnerable. Kenrick was forced to make a public recantation after Garrick threatened to sue, but Garrick was sufficiently shaken by the affair to refuse ever to open Bickerstaffe's desperate letters from France.

The second factor was the other theme of *Love in the Suds*, in which Foote featured too. It pictured Garrick and Foote ever more in competition with each other – over audience figures, critical acclaim and their rival attitudes to Shakespeare's jubilee. As drawn by Kenrick, Garrick is credibly presented as raging still about the Jubilee:

> Curse on that Foote – who in an ill fated hour
> Turned on the heels of my theatric-power
> Who ever ready with some biting joke
> My peace hath long and would my heart have broke![2]

Love in the Suds, embarrassing to both Foote and Garrick, also fuelled an antipathy that had been in abeyance since the Jubilee, and made public the disputatious issue of the patents: in 1772, Garrick was petitioning to extend Drury Lane's season through the summer, and Foote, in retort, appealed to George III to be granted a licence for year-long productions. 'Having received a formal challenge from [Foote] and his merry family,' Kenrick wrote, 'a pitched battle, for which great preparations are now [being made], will be fought between them.'[3] Garrick arranged for Drury Lane technicians to produce firework displays in Marylebone Gardens, as spoilers for Foote's first nights. And while publicly Foote remained undaunted, declaiming centre-stage at the Haymarket, 'Not one malignant aspect can be found/To check the royal hand that raised me from the ground',[4] in private he made wry jokes about Garrick's commercial jealousy: 'I have commissioned a bust of him,' he told friends, 'to sit in my box office. It has, you see, no hands.' By the end of 1772 Garrick was writing to the theatre-loving bluestocking Elizabeth Montagu that he was assured 'Foote hates me,'[5] and had been told that Foote was plotting some further attacks, satirical or practical.

He was, but not in the manner Garrick was expecting. Foote's long and well-argued petition to George III languishes still in the royal archives, unanswered. He never received more than a summer licence, and for his life term only. Foote quipped to Lord Mansfield that the anti-democrat King had given his petition 'no more attention than if all the people of England'[6] had signed it – but the result was that Foote needed to recoup all his costs over the course of a summer season, or subsidize his West End house with jaunts to provincial cities, Dublin and Edinburgh. He hit instead on competition with Drury Lane by a return to puppetry: that which could be performed, indeed, beyond the terms of his Company of Comedians.

Foote's *The Primitive Puppet Show* opened on 15 February 1773 at the Haymarket in direct competition with the Drury Lane season[7] and was publicized as *The Handsome Housemaid* or *Piety in Pattens*. It was another parody of current acting styles, Garrick's in particular. 'The Novelty of it,' wrote the critic of the *Gentleman's Magazine*, 'brought such a crowd . . . that the Haymarket was impassable for over an hour; the doors of the theatre were broke open, and great numbers entered without paying . . . three ladies fainted away and a girl had her arm broke in endeavouring to get into the pit.'[8]

What attracted this excited London crowd, however, was more than the promise of a parody of Garrick: it was Foote's vaunted satire on the vogue for 'hackneyed sentimental Comedies', which 'are become so fashionable of late'.[9]

The new *Primitive Puppet Show* at the Haymarket began with the much-loved Foote curtain piece. This alluded to Garrick's plans for a classical revival in acting by explaining that puppets were a Roman tradition too. But his 'native English wood' – a reference to his puppet company but also to his leg and his supposedly inadequate acting – became a catch-all metaphor for the evening's satire. A wooden company was well set up, he argued, for the 'birching' of his usual foes: 'fraudulent bankrupts, directors, and nabobs . . . incorrigible poets . . . and', moreover, 'for public spirit, we have that lord of the forest the majestic oak . . . of such materials are our performers composed.' It was as fine an argument as he had ever made for the usefulness of satire in social politics.

There is no clear contemporary image of what these puppets looked like, or how they were voiced. Because the Panton Street puppets had been three-quarters life size, these may have been too: that was the Continental model – and though this meant some could be flown out like marionettes, it is as likely that others were manipulated by the actors of the company, perhaps even voiced by them. Clearly Foote did many of the impersonations. As Garrick, the diminutive actor-manager, was the primary object of satire, we have some precise insight into the puppets' scale from this retort by Foote: asked by a lady at the box office if the puppets were to be life-size, Foote replied: 'Oh dear, Madam, no: not much above the size of Garrick.'[10]

Garrick sneaked in to see the puppets, and was spotted by the daughter of his friend Charles Burney. She saw him laughing 'as much as he could have done at the most excellent [play] in the world'.[11] He was mollified, he later recorded, by the realization that the main target of Foote's satire was the vogue for sentimental comedy, which bored both actors. So, in the long, complex and alternating friendship between 'Roscius' and 'Aristophanes', once the Bickerstaffe scandal had died down, there was finally a coming together.

'Foote is a genius,' Garrick wrote enthusiastically to a friend, advising him to see Foote's puppets and have no qualms about loyalty. 'He means me no harm I am sure, and ... I wish him success from my soul.'[12] *The Primitive Puppet Show* was credited with ending the vogue for sentimental comedy, and paving the way for a new robust realism, in particular the following season's *She Stoops to Conquer*, which Foote roundly admired and asked Goldsmith to remount at the Haymarket.

§

Between 1766 and 1771 Foote's plays and puppet shows set the finances of his company at the Theatre Royal, Haymarket, on even firmer ground. He went on a brief but highly profitable tour to Edinburgh, and returned with the funds needed to further enlarge the house. The backstage and wings area had been cramped even when the company was small, but with a comedy troupe regularly numbering more than fifty performers by 1772 – excluding musicians – things were reaching an impasse. Performers had had to enter the stage at the box-door set within the proscenium arch at stage right, squeezing through a tiny corridor behind the front boxes, potentially in hooped skirts. Foote bought the freehold to two properties adjacent to the theatre at the back, on Suffolk Street, and knocked one into extra wings space for the theatre, while the other, his own home, accessible at stage level since 1766, was now securely his. The enlarged company, and enlarged playing area, necessitated and encouraged more ambitious projects – and Foote met this with two hugely successful comedies: *The Maid of Bath* and *The Nabob*.

The Maid of Bath was a true story, more or less, the maid in question being Miss Elizabeth Linley, the sixteen-year-old daughter of the composer Thomas Linley. Thomas Gainsborough and Joshua Reynolds had both painted her famed blue eyes, and of the many who admired them in Bath, she chose the young and not very eligible son of Foote's former employer at Smock Alley. His name was Richard Brinsley Sheridan and their elopement in 1772 caused a brief scandal as they were both legally minors. Elizabeth Linley is Kitty Linnet in *The Maid of Bath*, but her story, and Foote's play, had further life and fame through her young husband, who later used a conflation of truth and Foote's fiction to build *The Rivals*. His wife was known all her life as the Maid of Bath, after Foote's wildly successful comedy. The real story had sufficient fame in the early 1770s to create a buzz of excitement over Foote's rendering of it. Dr Johnson, George Colman, David Garrick and Joshua Reynolds had all heard of it via their Literary Club long before the play opened, and some of them had heard portions of it acted aloud by the author at dinner parties at Northend. But when its opening finally came, with Foote playing an old Jewish suitor, Solomon Flint, the play was stopped several times, mid-flow, for spontaneous applause.[13] It was a commercial and personal triumph for Foote, playing his first comedy geriatric, and typical of the gently subversive politics of his later works. For all *The Maid* is a simple tale of young love's triumph over patriarchy, it also alludes to the libertarian scandals around Foote's exiled fellow wit, John Wilkes, with a running gag about their shared love of clothes and a much applauded line about being, like Wilkes, 'a prodigious patriot and a great politician to boot'.[14] It was near as Foote might dare, at a Theatre Royal, in support of the exiled radical and his controversial Bill of Rights.

§

The triumph of *The Maid of Bath* was tempered for Foote by a personal tragedy: the sudden death of Frank Delaval on 7 August 1771. Cooke wrote that when Foote heard the news at the Haymarket he 'burst into a flood of tears and retired' to his house next door, where he 'saw no company for three days'. On the fourth,

however, he was recovering his *amour propre* in his usual manner –
by making jokes in poor taste. On hearing that Frank's skull
was to be dissected by the Hunter brothers to ascertain the cause
of his death, Foote quipped that they were wasting their time with
his head for 'I have known Frank these five and twenty years and
I could never find anything in it.'[15] He gave more serious concern
to Francis, the small illegitimate son by Miss Roach whom Frank
had left unprovided for in his will (the little girl, Frances, had died).
Foote sold part of his interest in the Haymarket to buy an annuity
for the boy[16] – an act of astonishing munificence.

In the immediate aftermath of his bereavement, Foote spent
rashly and entertained lavishly. The Haymarket profits could
support this at the time, but his extravagance is apparent even
from an account of James Boswell, not in the first rank of Foote's
intimates, of a dinner at Northend 'all served upon plate . . .
sparkling champagne and . . . the best wine in England . . . exquisite'. All through dinner a slightly disapproving Boswell was
regaled by his host with anecdotes and impersonations of Dr
Johnson, of the publisher Faulkner, Lord Mansfield and the famous
grand pauses of David Garrick, 'a man,' Foote opined, 'born never
to finish a sentence'.[17] His increasingly reckless satire continued to
be informed by the trauma of his amputation and perhaps the
more direct physiological distress of his concussion, but this was
compounded it would seem from 1771 by the carelessness that
comes with personal loss, and for that matter the alcohol abuse
that sometimes attends it. Bibulous dinners, like the one Boswell
enjoyed allowed Foote to practise his impersonations, puff his new
works and seek subjects of future satire. His targets were increasingly impolitic. Boswell, so far as we know, was never impersonated
by Foote, but another at that dinner, George Gray, was about to
be held up to very public scrutiny as a subject of Foote's next
comedy.

The Nabob was, in effect, a sequel to *The Maid of Bath* in that it
met the increased expectations upon Foote of a comedy that was
sufficiently topical and tinged with scandal to fill the expanded

Haymarket. This time, however, the nature of the scandal was financial: the East India Company, London's *nouveaux riches* and 'nabobs', or nawabs, who were making fortunes from Indian and Chinese trade. The *London Magazine* immediately identified the models for Foote's anti-hero, Sir Matthew Mite, in *The Nabob*, as George Gray and Lord Clive, citing 'a thousand circumstances'[18] that pointed out the 'heroic' victor of Plassey as the main target of Foote's satire.

The *Nabob* also brought Foote his first brush with the political impact of his comedy house. Early in 1771, Clive of India faced charges against him in Westminster over the governance of Bengal. By the spring, a Bill was before Parliament 'for a better regulation of the affairs of the East India Company, and of their servants in India, and for the due administration of justice', which developed into a full-scale commission on Clive's conduct that dragged on through the whole initial run of Foote's play. It forced the victor of the Battle of Plassey to make defence before the House of Commons that the nabobs were being misrepresented on the London stage; he asserted roundly that not one of them was 'sufficiently flagitious [villainous] for Mr Foote to exhibit on the theatre in the Haymarket'.[19]

The character modelled on Clive and Gray, Sir Matthew Mite, was played by Foote. Though his arrant cupidity was clearly a reference to Clive, who had helped himself in 1764 to £160,000 of Murshidabad's treasury, Foote played the role in a thick Scottish accent, honed in the company of Boswell, as allusion to Boswell's nabob school friend Gray, himself at the centre of a complex sexual and financial scandal involving the Countess of Strathmore.

Friends of Clive, Gray and the countess, and East India Company businessmen more generally, took offence at the play despite or because of its enormous commercial success. Arguments broke out in the Haymarket pit and boxes that spilled into the streets outside. One night two nabobs even accosted Foote, as he left the stage door in Suffolk Street, intent on attacking him with cudgels. Foote defended himself as any comic might, by trying to make them laugh. He told them he was merely a 'wholesale popularmonger' and invited them inside to dinner where, according to Foote's friend Cooke, they were entertained by Foote and 'all sat about laughing'.

Although *The Nabob* makes its attack on Clive and Gray and on the morally dubious acquisitiveness of the East India project, it uses the self-evident venality of early Indian colonialism as an ironic counterpoint to the City of London itself; its targets sat in the audience, laughing at themselves. Foote knew the best comedy hit home, not abroad, and, oddly, *The Nabob* reads now as a recognizably London play about bankers, financial bubbles and the incestuous interconnectedness of international business and government. At the time, however, it was noted also for its firm attack upon racism, not that it was called such: the censure of a nabob for his treatment of his 'Negro' servant. Lord Mansfield's 1772 judgment, that slavery was unsupported in England and Wales, came soon after. Foote, always more satirist than politician, adds his small comedic voice to one of the libertarian agendas of the Enlightenment, nudging towards abolitionism: laughter, as he found, leads an audience in unintended directions.

§

A Georgian Londoner entering his mid-fifties was not considered in the prime of life. Foote, a heavy drinker since his days at Oxford, suffered severe gout from 1772 onwards, to compound the discomfort of his prosthesis and the aches and further malaises that were alleviated, to a minor degree only, by massage from one favoured footman and by opiates and alcohol. But at the height of his success he could not, like Garrick, take on fewer duties or contemplate retirement. The terms of the Haymarket patent obliged him to play for high stakes each summer, recouping all his investments in a four-month season that necessitated hit after hit. His workload, and the pressure to shock as much as amuse, only increased with the expectations of the enlarged Haymarket company and a growing appetite for his style of dangerous satire. The

years from 1770 to 1775 saw Foote at his most productive, and most
satirically reckless. He wrote five plays and a puppet show, and
premièred major restagings of previous hits. He risked censure as
well as the displeasure of his audiences in new works such as *The
Bankrupt*, which satirized corrupt bankers, and *The Cozeners*, which,
though closely following some of the jokes and characters in his
earlier *The Commissary*, risked satirical comment at the same time
on the rebellious American colonists, with whom many Londoners
were broadly sympathetic. He sustained a summer company of up
to fifty actors, in effect producing, acting, directing and writing in
up to a dozen different productions each year, giving sixty or more
personal performances between 15 May and 15 September every
year. Up to forty were in main-piece plays (*The Lyar*, *The Bankrupt*,
The Maid of Bath and *The Nabob* being some of the most successful)
and the rest were comic afterpieces (*Diversions*, *A Dish of Tea*, *An
Auction of Pictures*, endlessly reformed and reworked with topical
reference). And he was obligated further to the social roundelay of
the London Season and the expectations of his aristocratic box-
owners, whom he would entertain before, during and after the
evening performance, limping around the boxes of the Haymarket
and entertaining late into the night at Suffolk Street, such that he
was rarely in bed before the early hours. All of this left him, by
October of each year, a wrecked man. 'I saw Foote one evening,'
a mutual friend wrote to Garrick in November 1774, 'very much
tired . . . that is to say he did not find himself at all *known* or *taken
notice of*.'[20]

'To tell truth,' wrote Foote to Garrick, 'I am [exhausted] with
racking my brains toiling like a horse . . . merely to pay Servant's
wages and tradesmen's bills.'[21] To break the monopoly of the old
patent houses was an astonishing achievement for anyone, to which
Foote had added a punishing writing commitment and the onerous
business of leading a company, before one considers the physical
and mental strain of his infirmity. Financial and artistic imperatives
may have suggested to Foote that he should risk ever more daring
comedy. He might also, as is the now familiar pattern with star

personae, have felt himself beyond censure or the constraints of conventional tastes and mores. His extra, gifted, years after the amputation may also have inspired in him a feeling of inviolability, or boredom even, with the quotidian impositions of 'servant's wages'. But when the Duke of Kingston died in 1773, Foote saw the potential for profitable satire of the most dangerous sort, and set in motion a train of events that would push his triumphant story of comedy into something altogether more tragic, and his personal life into the spotlight of arguably the Western world's first great media storm.

ACT THREE

CASE NO. 409

'Here lies Proof Wit cannot be/Defence against mortality'

Aphra Behn's grave inscription, Westminster Cloisters,
by Samuel Foote[1]

THE LAST SCENES OF FOOTE'S LIFE were darkly dramatic. They
were also unlike anything that had come before in his strange and
chequered story. Three document sources dominate the new
evidence on Foote's final years. One is the manuscript detailing
the trials that ended his career, a manuscript, presumed lost, that
came to light relatively recently in a Scottish castle. Another,
accessed for the first time for this biography, is in the archive of
Mr Christie's Auction House, which trades in St James's just as
it did in Foote's day. The third, again unknown to previous
biographers, is in the collection of London's Royal College of
Surgeons. Quite serendipitously, while I was researching amputation for a previous chapter, notes came to light that related not
to Foote's physiognomy but to his psychological state. Samuel
Foote, famous for surviving an unanaesthetized amputation, was
also one of the 'guinea pigs' in some of the first work ever done
on what would now be termed clinical psychology. What his
aspiring 'psychologist', John Hunter, wrote about him colours
completely what we know separately of his actions, and about his
death.

The first case listed in John Hunter's Case Book under 'N' for

'Nerves' was that of Samuel Foote. The great man of medicine kept the book for study and teaching purposes, and it was used in part towards what became known as his *Posthumous Papers*. Foote was known to Hunter's medical students as 'Case 409'. Hunter was more than the 'Founder of Scientific Surgery', he was a 'giant in the natural sciences and medicine',[2] a pioneering 'scientist' in an era before the coining of the term, before the definition of branches within the sciences or of specialization in professional medicine. He experimented and hypothesized on areas as divergent as palaeontology, placental function, trepanning, and on the origins of species. His inquisitive methods included the dissecting of dead pregnant women of dubious provenance and, more shockingly, the deliberate infection of his own penis with a knife dipped in a syphilitic sore.[3] He found Foote's case, late in the comedian's life, compelling; but his fascination resided not in Foote's lost leg but in his mind. Hunter returned to his notes on Foote over and over again, he wrote, puzzling about the man late into the night until, he said, the very letters on the pages began to float in front of his eyes. He was troubled by Foote's behaviour and symptoms because they seemed to this investigative man of science to hold some wider clue as to the workings of the brain. As a result, Hunter wrote, he began to feel while working on Foote's case that, like Foote, he was suffering some sort of 'cognitive breakdown'.[4] Partly Hunter was distressed by the combination of fame and of erratic behaviour manifest in his celebrated patient, the increasingly eccentric and professionally reckless Mr Foote. Partly he found the case both distressing and intriguing as to him it shone light on shadowy areas in his great study: the inner workings of the mind and the physiognomy of the brain. The case of Samuel Foote stands at the beginning of what has become modern psychology and Hunter, though he never used the term, stands as baptist to these new religions of the mind; he thought Foote's case would help connect behaviour to the physical workings of the brain, and that it might all, somehow, relate to the amputation.

Hunter had known Foote all their adult lives. It is probable that they were familiar with each other from their earliest days in London in the 1740s, and they moved often in the same orbit of Georgian men of the arts and sciences: Joshua Reynolds was 'an intimate of William Hunter' and 'firm friend of John too',[5] as well, of course, of Foote. The artist and the comic doffed hats to the Hunter brothers around London, but they were also their patients. The Hunters' practices in Leicester Fields and Windmill Street saw the comings and goings of the great and celebrated figures of the period, and John Hunter kept detailed notes whether or not he might actually use them in future for teaching purposes. So it is not surprising that Foote turns up there. Along with the comedian, the Hunter brothers' celebrity clients included Charles James Fox, David Hume, Adam Smith, Thomas Gainsborough and the young Lord Byron.[6] Such names add glitter to John Hunter's copious copperplate brown notes, along with the addresses and ailments of hundreds of other less celebrated Londoners, who were referred to them. Regrettably, the notes do not regularly date the symptoms they write about, and the separate appointment books have been lost. John Hunter's reflections on Foote, however, are from the 1770s, and one appears to date to the months before the accusations that destroyed him.[7]

By the mid-1770s, Foote was beginning to trouble his own friends and colleagues. Those close to him, maybe Jewell, perhaps Garrick, suggested he visit again the Hunter brothers, who had overseen his recuperation in the early months after his amputation and had been consulted, in the spring of 1766, by his main surgeon, William Bromfeild. Foote had begun to have fits. He also had wild mood swings, and a series of minor strokes, what would now be termed transient ischaemic attacks, culminating in more serious ones in 1776 and then again in 1777, which saw the end of his stage career. He was in his mid-fifties, but suffered from the usual ailments of what was then considered early old age. He had gout in his remaining foot, and phantom pains in his lost one. On stage, he had begun to experience memory losses. Then he was attacked, as John Hunter wrote, 'with what is commonly called a Fit',[8] of much more severe intensity and medium-term effect.

John Hunter, lover of the theatre[9] and long-time acquaintance of Foote, had also, of course, been aware of the amputation, the serious concussion at the time, and the possibility of long-term effects from the trauma. He wrote at first in terms of 'apoplexy', a catch-all label for strokes, heart attacks, brain lesions and even early onset dementia or brain tumours.[10] He usually treated such symptoms with blood-letting, 'as much as the patient could tolerate . . . from areas close to the head (jugular vein) or on the scalp (temporalis artery).'[11] Foote, however, presented a particularly intriguing case. This is what Hunter records of Foote's first return visit to his Windmill Street practice seemingly in early 1776: 'The first [new 1776 symptom] was the loss of the use of his left arm and hand, and almost immediately he lost in some degree the perfect use of his Tongue. The muscles of his jaw became convulsed, and the muscles of the eye lost their action, by which means the eye became as it were fixed.' These are classic symptoms of a stroke. 'These effects,' Hunter wrote, 'in a little time, became more mild,' and Foote made an almost complete recovery, working intermittently on stage until 1777. But Hunter considered Foote's partial recovery and his changed behaviour, with the clinical background of the amputation, as signals that his 'case was a curious one'.[12]

Though he recognized the clear symptoms of a stroke, he also hypothesized that Foote's condition could be dated to 1766, to the concussion we know, via Hunter, he suffered and that this stroke was within a broader progress of a psychological disorder that linked brain function, behaviour and trauma in an instructive paradigm. His diagnosis was more radical still, for we are now aware that the areas of the brain seemingly damaged in Foote's case have been known to cause aberrant behaviour of various types.[13]

In the margin Hunter has added other or later thoughts, as was his wont. Again, frustratingly, these are undated. 'In [Foote's case],' he wrote, 'there was evidence of a temporary left-sided hemiphlegia [*sic* – partial paralysis] followed by a residual . . . neurological change which indicates a probable cerebrovascular episode . . . one wonders whether this was an early indication of a more serious (and older) neurological condition, such as a space-occupying intercranial lesion.'[14] In other words, Hunter thought he had discovered in Foote an example that illustrated the physiognomy of the brain, and some possible reasons for his behaviour in the short and longer term that related to a tumour or lesion somehow dating back to 1766.[15] It is more than likely that Hunter added some of these notes during or after Foote's trial, for that which had disassociated thought from action in his mind might, he speculated, have disassociated action from conventional morality in the circumstance of violent disinhibition. He wrote:

> I shall endeavour to explain these changes and what they might mean upon the following principles: In a well formed [sound] mind . . . the . . . sensations of Memory are secondary, and a degree weaker. These . . . Memorial Sensations are sooner lost than . . . the power or susceptibility of Sensation, when the disease arises from a <u>fault in the Brain</u>; . . . these principles are immediately applicable to Mr Foote's Case.

There were some very specific signifiers that helped define, for Hunter, what might be going on inside Foote's head.

> To explain [Foote's] dis-ease we must premise that Voluntary Actions arise immediately out of impressions of Sensations . . . [for instance] Mr Foote, when he read, he faltered in the pronunciation, because it was rather an act of habit; but when he talked, he talked perfectly.[16]

Likewise, as Hunter wrote of the immediate aftermath of Foote's first stroke:

> when Foote meant to employ his hand he had perfect command of it; but when he took off his Mind from this Act, and employed it in another, the hand . . . immediately stopt

its action: for instance, when he took a Snuff-Box, he could
do it perfectly, and could hold it as long as the mind was
attentive to this action; but the moment the Mind became
intent upon anything else, the muscles of the hand no longer
acted, and the Box dropped immediately out of his hand.

What puzzled and intrigued Hunter was that Foote was doing
more than dropping snuff boxes and dropping his lines, symptoms
that soon cleared up. Hunter was hypothesizing way ahead of
his time, and with Foote as his example, on what would now be
termed 'reading apraxia',[17] combined with anterograde amnesia,
or short-term memory loss, which is common after any kind of
brain trauma, including strokes, but also previous trauma, such as
an amputation like Foote's, or tumours. Damage in hippocampal
regions deep inside the brain is now known to lead to a permanently reduced ability to encode new explicit memory, also known
as declarative memory, which consists of episodic memory and
semantic memory.

Episodic memory is the memory of actual events in the past,
whereas semantic memory is acquired knowledge – such as an
actor's lines. In Foote's case, there was concern in all areas. This,
Hunter took as evidence of widespread brain damage, either from
the stroke or from concussion at the time of the amputation, a
blood clot from the operation, or a subsequent, or even long-held
tumour. His case books detail dozens of such cases, often with
post-mortem evidence that there had indeed been growths or clots
within the skull.[18]

If, as seems likely, Hunter's notes were written up or added to
during Foote's trial, and the public awareness that came with it of
a radical shift in his usual behaviour and practice, then Hunter
was considering other evidence than the purely clinical. Foote
presented two shifts in character: one, an increasing disinhibition,
a gear-change, as it were, in a character trait that had defined
his career. Another, only hinted at by Hunter, was of darker
consequence: Foote may have exemplified a post-stroke sufferer

who changed to some extent his persona as a result of damage to the brain circuitry, most often in the frontal lobe. The condition is accepted but is rare. According to one recent study, 'Hypersexual behaviour following brain injury is uncommon but when seen is often associated with basal frontal or diencephalic lesions.'[19] A more familiar example of a similar diagnosis would be that offered to Mo Mowlam, former Secretary of State for Northern Ireland, late in the progress of her brain tumour: that her condition, in its earlier form, may have had some impact on her 'disinhibition' through much of her career. In Foote's case, it is worth noting that these frontal-lobe disinhibitions sometimes manifest in specifically sexual terms.

According to another recent study, 'Alterations in sexual behaviour including hypersexuality are important sequelae of acute stroke'; it is now simply considered one of the many changes that may attend the temporary or permanent 're-wiring' of the brain. It is rare, but it is an accepted side effect of some brain traumas. With Foote, things may have been more complex still, in that Hunter described both a stroke and its aftermath, but was also well aware of a decade-long history of disinhibition after a brain trauma. Aberrant sexual behaviour and disinhibition are now understood to be closely linked to frontal-lobe damage, whereas 'mania and psychosis' are more often associated with 'non-circuit lesions associated with the fronto-subcortical circuits'.[20] Another study of a series of post-stroke character mutations suggests that 'a wide range of behavioural alterations' may be linked to 'dysfunction of the frontal subcortical circuits' after a stroke. Yet another specifically found that 'disinhibition of sexual activity and hypersexuality followed medial basal-frontal or diencephalic injury':[21] the sort of injuries Hunter was speculating had happened to Foote. Because this modern study concentrated on 'aberrant sexual behaviour' it allows us to be yet more specific about what Hunter may have observed. 'The [sexual] character of the symptoms is probably associated with the site of the lesion although the nature of the association is more complex; [in other words] the damage

to the circuits ... may be contributory [but is not always] causal
to the changes in behaviour.'[22] In other words, Hunter took Foote's
stroke as symptomatic of a longer-held issue. 'The patient Samuel
Foote,' writes one of Hunter's later medical analysts, '[had] possibly a cerebral tumour or developed a condition in which he
[behaved bizarrely] following a cerebro-vascular accident. Hunter
tried, with considerable success, to interpret the lesion in terms
familiar to the eighteenth-century scientist. This is an early example of the development of the science [now called] psychology.'[23]
It is an astonishing moment in the dawning of modern concepts of
psychology. It is also a thought worth holding in mind when
reviewing the evidence for and against Foote's 'guilt'.

Hunter's inconclusive speculations are based on an inchoate
understanding of neurology and psychological disorders, but they
are more than a historian of the Georgian age has any right to
expect and more than has been addressed before as it translates to
Foote. It was based on Hunter's background knowledge of Foote's
case, and a hypothesis that the radical 1766 surgery, with its huge
dangers of clots and aneurysms, had led to something quite
complex in Foote's case, in what is now understood to be the
circuitry of the frontal lobe and limbic system. Modern medical
opinion is sceptical of Hunter's causality[24] – it is more likely simply
to have been a tumour – but his information and description offer
a new colouring to Foote's tumultuous final years. He was not
himself. He was gripped by fits, by an inability to concentrate and
inexplicable mood swings. He was weakened in the key muscles
needed by an actor or performer – memory and ease with speech.
He seems to have been further 'disinhibited' when he was, frankly,
a stranger to normative inhibition all his adult life. And what is
even more tantalizing as a speculation relative to Foote is that it is
now known that this sort of brain distress often manifests, too,
in extreme or uncharacteristic sexual behaviour and an unleashed
libido. 'This is the age of madness,' wrote Hunter, of the business
of a man like Foote getting old, 'when insanity takes place ... fear
of disappointment and disappointment are not as immediate [as in

youth]; time hardly establishes a security, it rather exposes an uncertainty.'[25] Post-traumatic stress, body dysmorphia, the inappropriate yearnings of one generation towards a younger one: all these are equally conceivable motivations in what Foote did next – or may have done. But Hunter's case book provides the most compelling and specific background to Foote's going off the rails. He compounded, increasingly, a nature that had always been risk-attracted with a troubling disavowal, ultimately, of convention, of normative behaviour, perhaps of morality and possibly even of what had until then been his sexual persona. Or, indeed, as he saw the fast approach of physical incapacity, he just stopped caring what he did or to whom. Which may help explain more effectively than has until now been possible why Samuel Foote, aged fifty-six, found himself at the centre of 1776's greatest *cause célèbre*: not the Declaration of Independence, but his own trial.

A SCHOOL FOR SCANDAL

'Now-a-days a public spectacle is what everybody seems
to be particularly fond of – as this trial will produce'

Earl of Hillsborough, 1776[1]

A LITTLE BEFORE TEN A.M. on Monday, 6 May 1776, a young
coachman-cum-footman called Jack Sangster, usually known as
Sangsty, walked into Bow Street magistrates' and formally accused
his master Samuel Foote of sexual assault.

Sir John Fielding, the blind magistrate who presided at Bow
Street, had carried on a tradition set by his predecessor and half-
brother, the novelist and playwright Henry Fielding, of conducting
such depositions of evidence in a rather public fashion. The
newspapers sent representatives to Bow Street, to the Fieldings'
front room, to attend the 'horrid parade of thieves and cheats',
who were arraigned there, along with aggrieved victims and
'robbers and murderers, rapists and . . . those who battered women
and ravished children'[2] and to report accordingly. A crime victim
– as Sangster necessarily presented himself – was obliged to initiate
an investigation by submitting himself to this media ordeal and by
publicly stating his dispute. The papers that day were not disappointed. The tall young footman had a lurid and exacting tale to
tell about a man whose fame could not easily be overstated. The
story was all the more newsworthy for Foote was already embroiled
in another show trial altogether: that of society hostess Elizabeth

294

Chudleigh, Duchess of Kingston, charged with bigamy before the House of Lords.

Sangster attested that he had twice been assaulted by Foote, with the intention of 'sodomitical acts', once in a room overlooking Suffolk Street at the back of the Haymarket theatre, where Foote had asked to 'have a fuck at' him, and once in the stables of Northend, where Sangster's master had again propositioned him and tried to manhandle his genitals. Such crimes had a unique place in the public consciousness. Sodomy was, in theory, punishable by death. Yet the crime could not be named directly. An allegation could ruin the life of a man in the public eye, with or without a successful proof of 'guilt', and a trade in blackmail and false accusation began to flourish, of which Fielding was watchful, in parallel to unambiguous accusations against those who might or might not be 'gay'. Since late in 1775, Sangster had worked for Foote as a coachman and occasional footman, and later added to his charges a tale of a separate incident the previous winter in Dublin when Foote had asked him about his sexual experiences, asked to see his penis, and shown him his own in a state of arousal. Fielding, who was in the habit of throwing out evidence from blackmailers and aggrieved servants, found the footman to be a strangely compelling witness, even under rigorous cross-examination, and by eleven a.m. he was dictating to the Bow Street clerk, Mr Bond, a bench warrant for the immediate arrest of Samuel Foote.

That same day, the second Continental Congress was forgathering again in colonial Philadelphia and troops were massing in Lower Manhattan and Staten Island in what looked set to be a siege of New York City. But 3,600 miles away, in the capital of America, London, MPs and Londoners alike turned their attention away from brewing revolution and scanned their papers instead for a different tale. The readers of the *Daily Advertiser*, the *Public Ledger*, the *St James's Chronicle* and dozens of other periodicals that covered the two sensational scandals of 1775–6 were slack-jawed with prurient interest instead in Samuel Foote and the Duchess of

Kingston. The notoriety, as a crime reporter, that had launched Foote's name and career, came full circle in the trials that ended his life. As one recent academic has noted, these trials 'occasioned greater popular interest and larger aristocratic crowds in the galleries than any debates on the American war';[3] they literally stopped the House of Commons in its business. These twin trials were some large part of the reason papers had limited print space when it came to the Continental Congress's great work, *A Declaration of American Independence*, signed eventually on 4 July 1776.[4] Why, it was asked, should Londoners care about a very distant Tea Party and a tedious insurgency movement in North America when the Tea Party man himself was on trial at the behest of an infamous duchess, and making fun of his own ridiculous peril, live at the Haymarket, as the world's first celebrity onstage one-legged buggerer? Why indeed?

It's a curious and unedifying scene in the life of a nation when one member of a class – or one celebrity – is singled out to be castigated by those who have got away with similar transgressions themselves. This would certainly be the case for Elizabeth Chudleigh. It is hardly a coincidence that Richard Brinsley Sheridan's 1777 comedy *The School for Scandal* so rocked the Theatre Royal with laughter that neighbours thought the building was collapsing: Britain was in thrall to scandal in the late 1770s and Elizabeth's and Foote's became the twin peaks of this obsession.

In some senses, however, the trial of the Duchess of Kingston in the Great Hall at Westminster, and the subsequent trial of Samuel Foote in the humbler confines of the Court of the King's Bench in the same building, were very much linked to the American war, not just a distraction from it. When a barely understood threat is perceived abroad, and when this is confluent with economic turmoil within a society both self-obsessed and self-doubting, it is a truism that those on the fringes may find themselves attacked. In the *Soldier's Monitor* that year, Josiah Woodward fumed against sexual depravity, linking it directly to the American wars and the premonitions of Proverbs 22:14, warning arrestingly not only that 'The Mouth of Strange Women is a deep Pit'[5] but also suggesting 'the sodomite should . . . have his Genitils [sic] cut off and burnt by the common Hangman'. To some, the Duchess and the Player were clear personifications of a decadent age: a sexually dissolute woman and a sexually ambiguous comedian, the reason the fledgling British Empire appeared, in 1776, to be faltering. Whether or not Samuel Foote was 'gay' – and he may well have been – he was attacked as such; and whether or not Elizabeth Chudleigh was a scheming adventuress – and she was – she was attacked simply as a woman.

How this confluence of scandals and criminal trials came about is the finale of Foote's tragic-comedy. It was risible in its way, but also a game with deadly consequences, as it turned out, and one in which a verdict remains open to doubt. Elizabeth Chudleigh, a.k.a. the Duchess of Kingston a.k.a. the Countess of Bristol a.k.a. Lady Kitty Crocodile, and Samuel Foote had played multiple roles and with danger all their lives. But they played too intimately with fire in 1776 and set themselves and their times ablaze as perhaps only media-circus show-trials can. The law colluded with the press and the public in destroying the reputations of two of the most controversial figures of the previous decades, such that their trials and tribulations become one seamless narrative in a manner that would have appalled them both. For they loathed each other.

§

As so often with Foote, it all started with a reckless joke. But, then, so, too, had Elizabeth Chudleigh's rackety career, which had run parallel to Foote's. His bad joke had been to mock the duchess as she faced the ignominy of being the first peeress to be tried in the House of Lords for nearly two centuries. Her poor taste dated back through two marriages of dubious legality to a first appearance on the London stage, her breasts exposed, as Iphigenia at a masked ball. She had been schooled in scandal ever since she had decided to keep her position as maid of honour to the then Princess of Wales by conducting her first marriage in secret. It was not secret for long, and nor did the love affair that had led to it last beyond a season or two; such that her vaunted honour remained intact, but also publicly doubted. Elizabeth Chudleigh had lived most of her life in the lee of infamy, but had triumphed in her way nevertheless, until the mid-1770s when both she and Foote became caught up in the new moral agenda of a self-doubting London.

Like Foote, Elizabeth Chudleigh was also signal to the age. The fifty-four-year-old widowed duchess represented to many all that was most reprehensible about Georgian high society, that which had proved most newsworthy but that which was also proving most blameworthy as the country faltered militarily. With apparent disregard for both morality and the niceties of the law, she had secretly married one man and then, finding herself likely to be able to marry a man of significantly greater wealth and status, she had denied, on oath, her first marriage and married again. This second husband, the Duke of Kingston, had died, leaving her putatively one of the richest women in the richest city in the world. But her in-laws had challenged her over the will on the basis that this second marriage, to Kingston, was bigamous. It was. But Elizabeth Chudleigh, like Foote, having risen from provincial obscurity to become one of the most talked-about characters of her age – a woman of great wealth and apparent status – was not about to forgo everything she had earned by dint of her beauty, politicking and playing at the law.

Elizabeth was presented in the press at the time as a sort of anti-heroine: Moll Flanders with royal connections. Sexual allure, wilfulness, playfulness and recklessness had brought her to her prominent position in Georgian society, and if she had played her cards a little differently she might never have ended up in the dock at Westminster Great Hall or have been portrayed by the leading comic impressionist of the day, Samuel Foote, as 'Lady Kitty Crocodile', a national laughing stock once her letters to Mr Foote were, ungallantly, published by him.

Her notoriety dated from some years earlier, though its origins were far from forgotten in the public mind as her image was literally fixed by graphic artists, and in the mind's eye of the public, as a result of a famous incident in her youth. By 1749 Elizabeth had successfully parlayed minor connections within the West Country gentry, her sparkling if unconventional beauty and noted vivacity into a court position as maid of honour that paid her a little money but allowed her the prefix 'The Honourable'. Everything changed after her appearance at a masked ball in the spring of 1749, one of many official events that marked the peace of Aix-la-Chapelle and the return of George II to British soil. The press ran stories constantly of London's various celebratory fêtes and of high society bad behaviour. From Mr Handel's new anthem to be sung at the Chapel Royal to the dresses of the maids of honour to the Green Park fireworks, the 'brightest assembly of Ladies and Gentlemen . . . ever met together' found a wider audience for their posturing via a hungry press. Elizabeth Chudleigh, effervescent maid of honour to Augusta, Princess of Wales, took this as her cue to wear very little indeed to a Court event at Ranelagh Rotunda. Just how little is unclear, as the outfit became subject to anecdotes and cartoon representations for decades to come, and a series of prints drawn by artists who were not there and could not have known. She came dressed as Iphigenia, Agamemnon's daughter, possibly in flesh-coloured stays and diaphanous material, possibly with no stays or corset at all, and draped in gauze. Her breasts might have been exposed in the Georgian equivalent of a wardrobe malfunction: that which can be both denied and enjoyed as a media event. Others specifically bore witness to an outfit 'so naked ye High Priest might easily have inspected ye Entrails of ye Victim'.[6] The truth of how daringly lewd her entrance was is uncertain after the many misrepresentations that crowd Elizabeth's later life. The key point behind this minor scandal of public nakedness was that Elizabeth Chudleigh, a maid of honour to the intended queen, whose virginity and respectability formed her essential *résumé*, was widely suspected at the time to be 'secretly' married, which gave particular currency to images of her displaying herself in such a provocative manner.

Maids of honour would lose their place at Court if they married. This was no disincentive to the many who lobbied for such positions. They abased themselves as train-carriers to launch themselves into London high society and towards an advantageous marriage to a courtly young man. However, only five months into her appointment, and while receiving propitious advances from the Dukes of Ancaster and Hamilton among others, Elizabeth fell in love with a twenty-year-old naval officer called Augustus Hervey.

Rashly, unadvisedly, lightly and indeed wantonly, to quote the marriage-service admonition as read at their secret nuptials, Elizabeth and Augustus wed. It was a classic clandestine union of the period such as might have been penned by Foote himself, featuring an elopement, a candle-lit ceremony in a country chapel, a lone serving woman in on the secret, and the families on both sides left in ignorance. After only a few days of heady conjugal felicity the young officer sailed from Portsmouth to the Caribbean, leaving his bride 'in a flood of tears'.[7] Elizabeth would regret her early marriage for much of the rest of her life.

The marriage remained a secret, as did the birth and early death of a baby boy, and their less than amicable separation a few years after that. It is a sorry tale of subterfuge and masquerade. In an age before affordable divorce, and when clandestine marriages frequently trumped imperatives of class and money as they rubbed against the urgencies of sex and love, the situation for Elizabeth and Augustus was far from uncommon. What became unusual, and what led towards confrontation with the law and the satirical pen of Samuel Foote, were the ensuing accidents in both their lives.

Augustus and Elizabeth remained married until his death in 1779. In the meantime, the lowly naval officer, a second son of a grandson of a peer, came unexpectedly to inherit the earldom of Bristol with its vast wealth and titles. If Elizabeth had stayed the course she might have gained her 'advantageous marriage', despite having been sidetracked by youthful infatuation. But her life had taken strange turns.

Her 1749 appearance as Iphigenia was a turning point in her marriage plans. The scandal put a final nail in her relationship with Augustus Hervey, who refused to support her debts. Meanwhile, her Iphigenia had infatuated old King George II sufficient for Horace Walpole to write that the King was 'so in love'[8] with his daughter-in-law's maid of honour that he ordered another masked event in her honour, and appointed her mother, Mrs Chudleigh, housekeeper at Windsor Castle. Thereafter in the highest orbit at Court, neither properly married nor eligible as a bride, Elizabeth decided to accept the advances of the forty-one-year-old Duke of Kingston and become his mistress.

At this point, Samuel Foote came into their lives. 'The Chudleigh', as Elizabeth was widely known, was soon confident enough in the affections and finances of the rich duke to build a grand Palladian mansion at his expense, then to move into Chudleigh House, which stood in Knightsbridge just south of the park, near what is now Prince's Gate. There, in the early 1760s, Elizabeth reigned as society hostess and aristocratic courtesan; notionally a virginal maid of honour, conspicuously a duke's mistress, and so widely known to be married to the heir presumptive to the Earl of Bristol that the deeds to her house even called her 'Elizabeth Hervey'. Into Elizabeth's salon in Knightsbridge stepped Samuel Foote, quite at ease in a house that straddled decorum and scandal, stiff royal protocol and a party-loving mistress; a woman so louche, it was reported, she cooled herself after meals by spreading her legs and 'fanning up her petticoats'. He was first at Chudleigh House at the behest of the Delavals, and came again for the coming-of-age of Prince Edward, a few years before his fateful visit to the Delaval–Mexborough estates.

The back-story to the trials of 1776 was the entwined lives and fortunes of Foote and Elizabeth. This involved her first husband, Augustus, who finally became Earl of Bristol in 1775 and her second husband, the Duke of Kingston, whom she married in 1769. She achieved this only after a complex legal wrangle in which both she and Augustus claimed there was no proof of their marriage. Foote followed it all closely: it was perfect material for a comedy. The background also to their linked trials was the world of Chudleigh House itself. It was a world that allowed a kaleidoscope of refracted moralities to exist in one time and place – rich material for satire, but also for censure, as society shifted in its attitudes.

Foote understood the duality of Elizabeth's world – one in which her delicacy might be attested by her readiness to swoon in public but her audacious sexuality was displayed in prints and satirical poems – because it was a parallel duality that informed the life of every Georgian actress but also the infamous career of Foote himself: satirist, crime writer and friend of royalty. Foote knew well the comedic and dramatic gold mine of irony: of knowledge held but not enunciated. It was part of the masquerade of Georgian public life that seemed sophisticated to some just as it seemed morally bankrupt to others. Chudleigh House, presenting its Palladian and dignified façade to the passing population of Knightsbridge, many of whom were also aware that it held all the 'brilliancy and indulgence' of a decadent age, was the stage-set of the first unwritten scene of Foote v. Kingston. But Foote held back the idea of the duchess for another decade, until after Chudleigh House had been renamed Kingston House upon her elevation to the duchy and he had found the best – or worst – moment at which to satirize the morality of a shifting century and the rackety rakehelly career of Elizabeth herself.

§

In September 1773 the Duke of Kingston died. It had never been Foote's way to forgo a good joke at the beck of good taste, and Elizabeth's newsworthy antics after the death of her duke seem to have made him aware of what a good subject for satire Elizabeth was. A Georgian audience loved nothing more than a story of subterfuge and mistaken identities, and Elizabeth's story presented it all. The duke had died suddenly when he was in Bath with Elizabeth for the summer season. His widow travelled back to

London with her husband's corpse, at 'the pace' wrote Horace Walpole, 'of Queen Eleanor', whose grieving spouse had 'constructed [charring] crosses . . . where she and horses might stop to weep'.[9] Elizabeth's extravagant mourning, which included black outfits for her horses and even her dog, was much ridiculed. It had its dramatic purpose, of course: she needed to present herself as a very far from merry widow. The duke's sister and family – heirs to the fortune before his marriage to Elizabeth – immediately challenged his will on the basis that Elizabeth had never been legally married to him. Their determination and, indeed, the payment of their lawyers were fuelled by the financial stakes, which were notably high: the Kingston estate was valued at £80,000, which became the standard amount for stage fortunes of the period,[10] and the duke's personal wealth at £16,000 per annum.

After months of threats and disputes, in May 1774 Lady Frances Meadows, the duke's sister, finally achieved a bill in the Court of Chancery to have the will invalidated. The grounds were Elizabeth's bigamy. Ironically, Lady Frances was herself the subject of a bigamy case, but proceeded nonetheless on the advice of her lawyers, husband and her sons. Elizabeth fled the country. Her in-laws escalated the challenge in her absence from a civil case to a grand jury indictment on criminal charges of bigamy, which obliged Elizabeth to return.

Then Augustus Hervey's elder brother died and he became Earl of Bristol. Consequently, whether or not Elizabeth was married to Kingston or Hervey, she was a peeress, either duchess or countess, and therefore her case, as was her right, had to be heard in front of her peers: the House of Lords. These things took time to arrange, and the cloud of suspicion and scandal hovered over her until her trial was set for early 1775.

Foote followed it all closely. Press coverage of Elizabeth's case had been muted and respectful at first, through the winter of 1773–4, but it was unclear how much support she had from her former friends and the young King George III. Papers gave space instead to the prospect of Foote's new season at the Haymarket, the news trickling in about the siege of Boston, and a forgery trial of one Mrs Rudd who, daringly, was conducting her own defence. Meanwhile, Elizabeth spent heavily on legal advice, even from the Lord Chief Justice himself, Lord Mansfield. As the newspapers began to round on her through the course of 1774 and it became clear she would be tried in the Court of Public Opinion, she made the ill-advised move to appoint what amounted to a media adviser. It was a very modern take on her position but, as it turned out, a disastrous one, for she employed or, rather, bought the support of, one William Jackson. He was editor of the *Public Ledger*, which had offices just yards from Dr Johnson's house in Gough Square. He also happened to hold a vast animus against the King's policies in North America – and against Samuel Foote.

Gossip about a new Foote comedy at the Haymarket tended to start early in the spring of each year. Foote talked about what he was writing at the Bedford and in the Green Rooms of the West End, at Northend and Suffolk Street, and was known to try out characters and satirical ideas with friends. Whitefield, the preacher, had been well aware of Foote's intention to represent him on stage long before the première of *The Minor*; so, too, had Dr Johnson before the idea was dropped from *The Orators*. Before Foote even submitted his new 1775 play, *A Trip to Calais*, to the Lord Chamberlain's office, word was out that 'Lady Kitty Crocodile', sometimes misnamed also as 'Lady Barbara Blubber', was to be a blatant skit on Elizabeth. Foote, in drag, was to play the duchess: his impersonation of her was said to be uncanny.

Ever since his accident in 1766 he had worked closely with the office of the Lord Chamberlain, Francis Seymour-Conway, Earl of Hertford, who had taken over from the Duke of Devonshire. Plays had been submitted, usually at the last minute, and a few passages might have been altered but, to judge by the records in the Huntington Library to this day, Foote barked at his targets with a fairly long leash. This time, however, Hertford gave Foote's sprawling manuscript to William Chetwynd, his deputy examiner of plays. Chetwynd immediately marked it with crossings-out and scrawls noting that it referred repeatedly to the travails of the duchess.

As was the usual custom, the manuscript play then travelled back from Westminster over Whitehall to Suffolk Street for Foote to amend the passages that were deemed offensive. In the past he had seen fit to accept all edits. This time something stuck in his craw – or he simply brazened for a scrap. The jokes were, perhaps, just too tempting, the prospect of playing the century's most notorious bigamist just too daringly attractive.

Foote invited over to Suffolk Street the one mutual friend he shared with the duchess, the thirty-two-year-old Lord Mountstuart. They read the play aloud together. Son of Lady Mary Wortley Montagu and the Earl of Bute, distant relative of the duchess and friend of James Boswell, Mountstuart, diplomatic but realist, seems to have recognized he was in an impossible position. At first he declared the play he read with Foote 'collected from general nature', and 'applicable to none but those who . . . were compelled to a self-application'.[11] Or so wrote Foote. In other words, he claimed Mountstuart's complicity in attesting that there was no libellous intent. Perhaps Mountstuart was being oblique, for he next asked if he could take the text to Kingston House in Knightsbridge. Foote acquiesced. (It is to be presumed he had at least one other copy, for the duchess might have chosen to burn it.) Then he could tell Hertford that the duchess had seen it and, assuming she would be unwilling to affirm a true likeness in Lady Kitty Crocodile, Foote would be able to proceed.

Elizabeth read it and was appalled. Mountstuart showed her the passages where Kitty Crocodile advises her young ward to marry bigamously, where she entertains guests in a 'Chamber of Tears' draped in widow's weeds, where she pronounces marriage a 'solemn, awful occasion', where she objects to being 'decked out like another Iphigenia'. Elizabeth invited Foote to Knightsbridge for a showdown.

This was a risky strategy on her part for Foote had, as it were, the upper hand. She could neither dispute nor allow the claims of the play, as it was a satire that could only damage her further if she chose to acknowledge the many references to herself as personal libels. At the same time, the bigamy case was at a delicate stage, one where she might still hope to avoid a full trial before the House of Lords. The one thing everybody wanted to avoid, apart from the press, was a full-scale scandal in face of the young King's firm admonition that the governing classes should be setting a better example 'to our peoples and our Empire'.

In a room in Kingston House, doubtless one of the great bow-windowed chambers that overlooked Hyde Park, where the party for the Duke of York had been held, Foote and Elizabeth met once more. Exactly what happened is unclear. 'Her Grace saw the play,' wrote Foote to the Lord Chamberlain, 'and in consequence I saw Her Grace, with the result of that interview I shall not trouble your Lordship. It may perhaps be necessary to observe,' he added, 'that her Grace could not discern . . . a single trait in the character of Lady Kitty Crocodile that resembled herself.'[12]

This was a wile Foote had used before. When he had asked the Archbishop of Canterbury to mark passages in *The Minor* that offended, he had retained the right to publish, citing the Archbishop 'as editor'. In the same way, he attempted to entrap Elizabeth by having her cite that which referred to herself, which he knew she would not and could not do. As he admitted, she was 'too cunning to bite at this.'[13] Publishing and not performing the play remained, however, a second choice for him. The scandal and impending trial of the duchess meant it would sell well, but few authors could expect to net over one season what Foote knew he could take at the Haymarket. Dr Johnson, after all, made more in a season from his only play than 'from anything else he had ever written'.[14]

Hertford, however, banned the play. This was not what Foote was used to. Usually the marking of a text amounted to a tacit acknowledgement that a licence would be granted after some horse-trading on which passages were changed and how. Foote's shock at being censored may explain what he did next. Quite uncharacteristically, he took his spat with the duchess and the

Foote by Gainsborough. Painted in Bath as a study in celebrity, Gainsborough
used it to advertise himself. Foote wears his favoured bottle-green velvet.

THE FRATRICIDE,

OR

THE MURDERER'S GIBBET;

BEING PART THE SECOND OF THE

Right Tragical Hystorie of Sir John D. Goodere, Bart.

Like a mildew'd ear, blasting his wholesome brother.—HAMLET.

Let us pursue the trace
Of light and shade's inconstant pace;
And wild as cloud, or stream, or gale,
Flow on, *flow unconfined* my tale !
W. SCOTT's *Marmion*, CH. III.

Exactly opposite the entrance gate
Of ST. AUGUSTINE'S CHURCH, in low estate,
Being as its ROWLEY neighbour half as high,
As you will see if you cast up your eye,
There stands a dwelling, having, at its top,
The No. 41—below's the shop

Foote's career began and ended in notoriety. His 1741 accounts of his uncle's fratricidal murder made his name and reputation and have claim, with Dick Turpin, to be the first true-crime bestsellers.

The Bristol inn where the murder was plotted became infamous along with Foote's pirate uncle and his litigious family feud that later inspired Dickens' *Bleak House.*

CAPTAIN SAMUEL GOODERE,
Executed at Bristol 15th April, 1741, for the murder of his Brother, Sir John Dinel
Goodere, Bart., on board the Ruby man-of-war, then lying in Kingroad.
The above wooden figure is copied exactly from the original "last words and dying speech," in the possession of Mr. Richard Smith.

SODOM and ONAN,

A SATIRE.

INSCRIB'D to

Esq.r

alias, the DEVIL upon two Sticks.

Sodom and Onan, William Jackson's scurrilous attack on Foote and his supposed sexuality, was written to curry favour with the Duchess of Kingston and destroy the comedian's reputation. The foot may have been one of Thomas Rowlandson's earliest commissions.

Foote's fashionable villa at Northend in rural Fulham. Sangster's stables are clearly visible.

No. 409 in John Hunter's note book. Sam Foote's case was Hunter's opening example under 'Nerves' as it formed a compelling paradigm to illustrate Hunter's psychological theories.

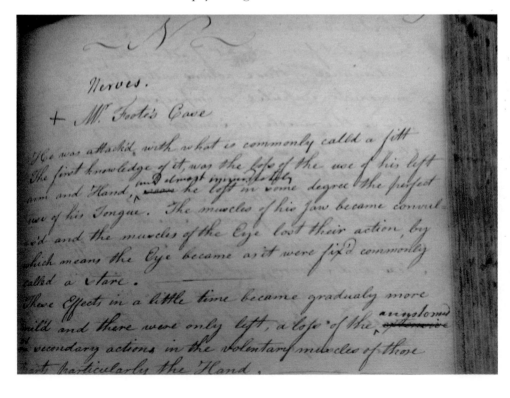

Samuel Foote in late middle age by Jean-François Colson. Post-amputation and during the later trials his weight fluctuated dramatically.

Elizabeth Chudleigh as Iphigenia in 1749 – the 'wardrobe malfunction' that launched her notorious career. Elizabeth, styled Duchess of Kingston, modelled her later trial attire on that worn by Mary, Queen of Scots.

The clandestine marriage of Elizabeth Chudleigh and Augustus Hervey, later Earl of Bristol, rendered her marriage to the Duke of Kingston bigamous – a subject of many satires including Foote's.

Representation of the Trial of the Duchess of Kingston at Westminster Hall

The Duchess of Kingston stood trial in Westminster Great Hall before the House of Lords in a grand state trial that led directly to Foote's trial in the same place.

Foote and Tom Weston in *The Devil Upon Two Sticks*. As he left Suffolk Street for the last time Foote stared at his favourite painting and said, 'Alas, poor Weston: it will very soon be "Poor Foote".'

Sam Foote's Theatre Royal, Haymarket, adjacent to the one designed by John Nash which stands to this day, with Foote's royal licence still attached.

censors straight to the press, writing an open letter to the Lord Chamberlain about Elizabeth. It was published in the *St James's Chronicle* on the evening of 1 August 1775 and began: 'Between the Muse and Magistrate there is a natural Confederacy . . . but when she [the Comic Muse] finds herself deserted by her ancient ally [the Lord Chamberlain] and sees him armed in defence of the foe, she has nothing left but a speedy retreat.'[15]

It was all very Augustan, and somewhat disingenuous. Foote was not retreating, but attacking, and the skirmish between the duchess and the player, with the Lord Chamberlain between them, took over entirely in the news from the skirmishes in New York and the military progress of George Washington. Horace Walpole was typically waspish about the opening salvoes in this paper war: 'Foote has . . . printed his letter to [the Lord Chamberlain] . . . and upon my word if the stage and the press are not checked, we shall have the army on its return from Boston besieged in the Haymarket itself; what are we come to if maids of honour cannot marry two husbands *in quiet*?!'[16]

Foote escalated the petty war. He started reading the play aloud to anyone who would listen – and there were plenty – at the Bedford and at private dinner parties at Northend. One friend said it was beyond doubt 'the most impudent thing that Foote ever wrote'.[17] The thwarted playwright had handbills printed to advertise his new character, Lady Kitty Crocodile, who 'first became an attendant to a great lady at court, afterwards married an admiral . . . and then a . . . duke.'[18] Could anyone guess whom he might be talking about? If anyone had been in any doubt, they no longer were. All this, Foote announced, was a preamble to publishing his new play. With the slogan 'Wilkes & Liberty' in mind, purportedly, he announced that he was morally obliged to subvert censorship by publishing *A Trip to Calais*. The duchess invited him again to Kingston House.

When Foote arrived it was already well into the summer season of 1775, and the Haymarket was in need of a new comic centre-piece. Elizabeth offered him £150 to destroy the play. Although this represented more than he would get for it initially if it was simply published, it was a small fraction of what it would be worth to him performed. Within minutes of alighting from his coach – and with Sangster most likely loitering outside – Foote was explaining to the duchess in no uncertain terms why her offer amounted to an insult. 'Are those earrings composed of diamonds?' he asked her rhetorically, for surely it was doubtful they would be anything lesser. 'Pray put them away lest I should lay my hands on them. No madam, when my necessities reduce me to make use of dishonourable means of supplies, I will sooner go upon the Highway.'

The duchess rejoined, according to Foote's account of their conversation published in all the London papers the next day, that only she and Lord Mountstuart 'need ever know' of their deal. Foote took the moral high ground: 'There is a third person present madam, and with whom I would ever wish to remain on the best of terms, viz, myself.' Head held high and cane in hand, he left the room.

Sangster drove him next to Garrick's apartments at the Adelphi. Garrick exclaimed, when he had heard Foote's version of the exchange, that 'Cato himself, tho' he had one leg more . . . was not more stoically virtuous.'[19]

Virtue and depeditation to one side, Foote had not heard the last of the duchess in the press. She turned to her adviser William Jackson, editor of the *Public Ledger*, who suggested to her that she should go for the jugular. On 10 August the *Ledger* published an allegation that Foote was a sodomite.

§

Risible though all this might appear today, as the latest sod in a public mud-slinging contest, an accusation of buggery had potentially devastating consequences for all parties, and would not have been taken lightly by Jackson either. The editor of the *Ledger* must have felt fairly secure in his evidence, as the crime of a false accusation of sodomy attracted the same penalty as sodomy itself:

it was a hanging offence. This forms some of the surest claim that Foote has indeed some place in the history of gay culture. The attack upon him stopped his career in its tracks, and perhaps the most compelling evidence that there was substance to it was that his accuser had no hesitation in using the slur. Foote, meanwhile, was faced with a dilemma. If he kept silent, he faced being 'outed' in the press as more stories would surely follow, true or false. He could counter-claim libel, but he faced doing so in an atmosphere of increasing paranoia about moral decline, about the degeneracy and effeminacy of those in the performing arts, further inflamed by his powerful, well-funded foes in the *Ledger* – and, meanwhile, he had a season to run at the Haymarket.

Foote was visited by the Duke of Newcastle, a privy councillor. Newcastle was no friend of the duchess, but he had an interest in trying to avoid the scandal of her bigamy escalating in the public mind. Like many in the Lords, Newcastle was unimpressed with the prospect of tying up parliamentary time with a sensational sex-crime trial when the country was going to war. He might have intimated some of this to Foote. He explained to him that the duchess was likely to encourage Jackson to continue his campaign in the *Ledger*. If he did so, Foote was likely to be forced to sue Jackson, or become the subject of a prosecution himself. Foote, again, made public his version of the Newcastle interview in an open letter to the duchess he penned at Northend. Their epistolary spat was becoming one of the main reasons to buy newspapers in London:

Madam

[The Duke of Newcastle] has just left me. He had explained to me . . . that the publication of the Scenes of the Trip to Calais . . . might be of infinite ill consequence to your affairs.

I really, Madam, wish you no ill, and should be sorry to do you an injury.

I therefore give up to that consideration what neither your Grace's offers not the threats of your Agents could obtain: the Scenes shall not be published, nor shall anything appear at my Theatre, or from me, that can hurt you, provided the attacks made on me in the Newspapers do not make it necessary for me to act in defence of myself. Your Grace will therefore see the necessity of giving proper directions.[20]

As well as obliquely suggesting that the attacks had come from the duchess's camp, the letter makes clear that Foote had been effectively silenced by the campaign about his sexuality. This might have been the end of a rather tawdry example of the evolving role of the fourth estate – journalism – in the public and private life of the nation, but Elizabeth was unable to rein in her famously violent temper. Foote's letter arrived when she was at dinner with Jackson at Kingston House in Knightsbridge. They had both, it must be surmised, been drinking, as they penned together a violently abusive letter of rebuke and insult to Foote, which, again, Foote sent immediately to the newspapers:

To Mr Foote

Sir,

I was at dinner when I received your ill judged letter. As there is little consideration required, I shall sacrifice a moment to answer it.

A member of your Privy Council can never hope to be of a Lady's Cabinet.

I know too well what is due to my own dignity, to enter into a compromise with an extortionable assassin of private reputation. If before I abhorred you for your slander I now despise you for your concessions, it is a proof of the illiberality of your satire, when you can publish or suppress it as best suits the needy convenience of your purse. You first had the cowardly baseness to draw the sword, and if I sheath it, until I make you crouch like the subservient vassal as you are, then is there no spirit in an injured woman, nor meanness in a slanderous buffoon.

To a man, my sex alone would have screened me from attack, but I am writing to the descendant of a Merry Andrew [clown or buffoon] and prostitute the name of manhood by applying it to Mr Foote.

Clothed in my innocence as in a coat of mail, I am proof against a host of foes; and conscious of never having intentionally offended a single individual, I doubt not but a brave and generous people will protect me from the malevolence of a theatrical assassin. You shall have cause to remember that though I would have given liberally for the relief of your necessities, I scorn to be bullied into a purchase of your silence.

There is something, however, in your pity at which my nature revolts. To make me an offer of pity, at once betrays your insolence and your vanity. I will keep the pity you send until the morning before you are turned off, when I will return it by a Cupid [kiss] with a box of lip salve, and a choir of Choristers shall chante [*sic*] a stave to your requiem. E. Kingston, Kingston House, Sunday 13th.

P.S. You would have received this sooner, but the servant has been a long time writing it.[21]

The letter was published on 15 August 1775 and was the talk of all London by the next day. Elizabeth was at a vulnerable time to be risking such public exposure of her own bile and her friend Jackson's vituperative pen. They were both known to be drinkers and it was assumed by many that she had made these ill-judged slurs against Foote, his 'manhood' and his parentage, when under the influence. It was neither noble nor ladylike. But it was very funny, as, perforce, was Foote's even more widely read reply. The correspondence was considered so hilarious that it exists not just in the papers and periodicals of London but also in manuscript form in Dublin and in New York, copied out at length and verbatim for those, presumably, who were meant to be kept sheltered from such libels or because eventually the newspapers in which it was printed began to deteriorate through overuse. Foote's reply, according to Horace Walpole, was 'one of the very best things in the English language', a dazzling example of the epistolary put-down, and shared, the next day, with all of London:

To the Duchess of Kingston

Madam

Though I have neither time nor inclination to answer the illiberal attacks of your agents, yet a public correspondence with your Grace is too great an honour for me to decline. I can't help thinking but it would have been prudent in your Grace to have answered my letter before dinner, or at least postponed it to the cool hour of the morning, you would then have found that I voluntarily granted the request which you had endeavoured, by so many different ways, to obtain. Lord Mountstuart, for whose amicable qualities I have the highest respect and whose name your agents first unnecessarily produced to the public, must recollect, when I had the honour to meet him at Kingston House, by your Grace's appointment, that instead of begging relief from your charity, I rejected your splendid offers to suppress the Trip to Calais with the contempt they deserved. Indeed, Madam, the humanity of my royal and benevolent master and the public protection have placed me much above the reach of your bounty.

But why, madam, put on your coat of mail against me? I have no hostile intentions. Folly, not vice, is the game I pursue. In those scenes which you so unaccountably apply to yourself, you must observe that there is not the slightest hint at the little incidents of your life, which have excited the curiosity of the grand inquest for the County of Middlesex. I am happy, madam, however to hear that your Robe of Innocence is in such perfect repair, I was afraid it might have been a little the worse for the wearing; may it hold out to keep you warm for the next winter.

The progenitors your Grace has done me the honour to give me, are, I assume, merely metaphorical persons and to be considered as the Authors of my Muse, and not of my manhood, a Merry Andrew[22] and a prostitute are no bad practical parents, especially for a writer of plays, the first to give the humour and mirth, the last to furnish graces and powers of attraction. Prostitutes and players too must live by pleasing the public; not but your Grace may have heard of ladies, who, by private practices, have accumulated amazing great fortunes. If you mean that I really owe my birth to that pleasant connection, your Grace is grossly deceived. My father was, in truth, a very useful magistrate and respectable country gentleman . . . my mother . . . was upwards of fourscore years when she died, and what will surprise your Grace, was never married but once in her life. I am obliged to Your Grace for your intended present on the day, as you politely express it, when I am to be 'turned off'. But where will your Grace get the Cupid to bring me the lip-salve? That family I am afraid has long quitted your service.

Pray, Madam, is not J[ackso]n the name of the female confidential secretary? and is not she generally clothed in black petticoats made out of your weeds?

'So mourned the dame of Ephesus her love.'

I fancy your Grace took the hint when you last resided in Rome; you heard there I suppose of a certain Joan who was once elected a Pope, and, in humble imitation, have converted a pious parson into a chambermaid. The scheme is new in this country, and has doubtless its particular pleasures. That you may never want the Benefit of the Clergy in every emergency is the sincere wish of

Your Grace's

most devoted and obliged and humble servant

Samuel Foote[23]

One of Elizabeth's lawyers overheard a conversation in a coffee-house about the published letters: 'I believe this duchess is a clever sort of woman,' one Londoner opined, 'but by God she never was so much out in her life as when she ventured to write to Mr Foote!'[24]

§

At the end of August 1775, Foote took to the stage for the first time since the accusations of his homosexuality and the spat with the

duchess in the press. The company had advertised *The Bankrupt* –
already a stock favourite at the Haymarket – as standing in for
of the suppressed *Trip to Calais*. It is a major date in the history of
British comedy, and, whether Foote was gay or not, in the history
of sexuality and its acceptance. Because the Haymarket audience
behaved in an astonishing manner. There was a possibility that
Foote would be hissed off the stage, as had happened to actors
accused of crimes in the past, in particular sodomy. Isaac Bickerstaffe had said in France that he had feared for his life once he was
revealed as homosexual, and had nightmares about theatre-mob
violence. Foote was greeted with silence when he first came on,
but, when he got to 'I have no reason to be ashamed . . .' the
house erupted in supportive applause, and when he continued
'. . . of my family,' the audience applauded again. Everyone had
read his published letter. Everyone rallied to the cause of the
beleaguered comedian whose own life had, since the very beginning, been part of his act on stage.

The duchess, instead of the player, was vilified in the written
and the cartoon press. Prints of her as Iphigenia sold up and down
the Haymarket and along the Strand and Fleet Street through the
rest of 1775. One showed her battling with Foote in the chain-mail
of innocence she had conceitedly advertised in her letter. For those
who had not followed the spat day by day, a useful thirty-page
pamphlet was published, reprinting all the letters and giving the
back-story just as Foote might have done himself in his earliest
incarnation as a crime writer. *The Case of the Duchess of Kingston*
became a bestseller and, as its anonymous author-compiler points
out, without it, 'it is probable the public conversation relative to
her Grace would have subsided till the ultimate issue of the
proceedings were known'. Instead, as a direct result of Foote, the
letters and her allegation against him of homosexuality, they were
shackled together as 'the general topic of conversation'[25] through
late 1775. Her full trial before the Lords in 1776 consequently
became inevitable. Despite her last-ditch resort to her chaplain,
John Forester, who made a deposition on oath that Foote had tried

to blackmail her to the tune of £2,000 (he might have mentioned that this was the real value of the play to him), everyone was siding with the 'slandered sodomite' instead of the 'duplicitous duchess'. As Garrick said, 'notwithstanding Forster's [sic] Oath, Foote had thrown down the Duchess on her back . . . she had made herself very ridiculous in the struggle,' then added, not without a note of professional jealousy, 'Foote's letter is one of his best things, [and] in the best manner [that he has ever written].'[26]

THE DUCHESS AND THE PLAYER

'This day the duchess of Kingston is tried for bigamy and the Whole Town has talked of nothing else!'

Eighteen-year-old Anna Larpent, 15 April 1776[1]

THE TRIAL OF THE DUCHESS OF KINGSTON stands as one of the great courtroom spectacles in British history. It cost more than £10,000 to mount, the whole of the English legal system was suspended while it was in session, it took over all of Westminster Great Hall, and the business of the House of Commons was shut down, along with the livelihoods of many who lived in the area. Yet it was not intended to set any important legal precedent. Neither was it a drama of suspense in terms of its verdict: its decision rendered Elizabeth Chudleigh either a duchess or a countess, hardly the stuff of Greek tragedy, and either way she could claim benefit of clergy, as a peer's wife, to dismiss the sentence that would be handed to a lowlier bigamist. In balance this was rather less important, it might seem, than the fate of New York City, being battled over at the same time. Yet the trial appeared to one foreigner as 'a festival to the whole nation',[2] a forgathering around a media event about a celebrity that 'made a more brilliant Appearance than ... any preceding' trial in history. Without Foote, it would not have happened in the manner it did. Without Foote, the duchess would almost certainly have got away with either a private trial in a back room at Whitehall, or no trial after a quiet dismissal of the case by the embarrassed peers. As it was, all the country now knew of the accusation against her as a result of her own attacks on Foote and his ripostes. It was quite a testament to the evolving power of satire and of celebrity. But because Foote had brought her successfully before the House of Lords, the duchess, and William Jackson, harboured against him the most violent antipathy, and in the public mind the vast spectacle of a state trial was intimately wrapped up in the Merry Andrew image of the laughing one-legged satirist.

Necessarily it took some time to organize. And while Elizabeth's lawyers exhausted the last of her potential avenues of escape, through the summer and autumn of 1775, the *Ledger* mounted occasional attacks upon Foote. He chose to evade publicity and, for the time being, not sue. He remounted *The Cozenors* for nine nights, *The Minor* for eight, *The Maid of Bath* and *The Devil Upon Two Sticks*, and even appeared in a revival of Vanbrugh's *The Relapse*. He kept himself busy and the company afloat, despite the temporary loss of his new comedy, *A Trip to Calais*. All the while, the prospect of Elizabeth's trial hung over Foote's head: if ruin attended her, his safety and a less antipathetic press would be assured; if it revived her fortunes, it would set him up with an indomitably manxome foe intent upon renewed persecution.

Policing London, in the century before the establishment of a metropolitan police force, was a growth industry. Some of the legal system of eighteenth-century London persists to this day – the Old Bailey, for instance – but much that had evolved by the duchess's trial and then Foote's looks as labyrinthine and medieval as the then sprawling Palace of Westminster in which they were housed. The Court of King's Bench, the Courts of Common Pleas and Chancery – the supreme courts in effect – were located within the cavernous Westminster Hall. It was draughty, dirty and very noisy, and the courts were not fully partitioned one from another. The whole was surrounded by a ring of booksellers and tradesmen, rather like hawkers around a giant legal trade conference. 'The openness of the courts,' one observer recalled, 'permitted the judges [on raised daises] to see each other and command a view across the entire hall, the ever moving and incessant throngs of loiterers . . . permitted to laugh aloud and talk.'[3]

About fifteen years before the Kingston and Foote trials in Westminster Hall, the courts had been partitioned off. A principal reason for the expense and delay of the duchess's trial was the removal of the stud panelling and the erection of vast viewing galleries, akin to what had been there for the trial of King Charles I or the infamous Frances Howard centuries before. The whole hung thick with the smoke of incense thuribles, as had the Dineley-Goodere trial, indicative equally of the divine fount of justice as the incorrigible stench of Georgian England.

§

April 15, 1776, dawned for Londoners like the morning of a coronation or a royal wedding. Half the working population seemed to have decided it would mill around Westminster and Whitehall, and four thousand of the leisured élite had tickets for the interior of the Stygian medieval hall. It was a fashion event, as well as a state trial, and when the doors opened at eight a.m., it was said, 'The ladies seemed to outvie each other in the richness of their dresses and the brilliancy of their ornaments.'[4] At least four million pounds' worth of diamonds, one paper estimated, were worn by the ladies who attended – peeresses many of them – such that when the sun finally broke through the windows on the eastern side of the Great Hall the reflection on the internal walls danced 'like firelight'. James Boswell had a ticket, and said he 'had not known there had been so many fine women in the *Universe*', and that 'the mode of dressing, with a deal of hair and feathers and flowers . . . more beautiful than what I had ever seen before'.[5] The towering headdresses of the many women who were interested in the fate of the infamous duchess were one liability of the event. Another was the jerry-built viewing platforms of a makeshift court. The books, files, benches and panelling of the usual Westminster courts had been stored around Whitehall, as was the practice usually only for coronations, to turn Westminster Great Hall into the focal point of the nation. It was both awe-inspiring and preposterous, for here, on the site of the trials of Thomas More and Guy Fawkes, was a lavish state trial of a society hostess, a woman who mattered only to those who might or might not have married her, and to the heirs of two great aristocratic estates. It appeared to matter at the time, however, in part because of an aristocracy increasingly under attack for its supposed degeneracy and its consequent interest in creating a scapegoat for its scape-grace behaviour. It mattered even more to the audience in the hall that day and to newsreaders in coffee-houses beyond as a drama of personalities, and because Samuel Foote had focused such intense interest on the celebrity duchess with his satire.

The hall filled quickly with the ticketed crowd. Many recalled the occasion sixteen years before when Earl Ferrers had been tried for murder, but the lavishness of Elizabeth's trial would surpass his. Though the King would not attend, an empty throne covered with red velvet stood at one end. A bar for the accused was at the other. Raised galleries ten rows deep lined the sides of the hall all the way to high windows by the hammerbeam roof. The coffee-houses that then abutted the medieval hall had all petitioned for the right to stay open and serve refreshments to the crowd through the windows, and the buildings nearby rented out rooms. Privi-leged members of the House of Lords who had apartments connected to the Hall – the Duke of Newcastle was one – found themselves importuned by dozens of friends begging access to the best comedy in London.

The *St James's Chronicle* reported on the glamorous throng. Its correspondent concentrated to begin with on the ladies' attempts to negotiate around each other's elaborate headdresses and hair for the best view. One lady missed her footing towards the top of the highest gallery, and found herself suddenly sitting on the head of a gentleman in the gallery below, 'her bare bum', as the *Chronicle* duly noted, 'squatting' on her new friend. 'She harmed no one but herself,' it continued, while gallantly not naming her, though she and her skirts became entangled in trying to ascend back to her seat above and she trapped herself between the galleries with her lower self exposed, in an era before undergarments, to the audience of London's glitterati. No one claimed to recognize her.

The trial began at ten o'clock, with the procession of the entire House of Lords, in robes of state, into the Hall, with the maces of both Houses of Parliament and the arms of England. Ironically, of the two men who stage-managed the spectacle of Elizabeth's trial and later Foote's, one was Elizabeth's former suitor, the Duke of Ancaster, and the other Lord Hertford, the Lord Chamberlain, who had banned Foote's play. Elizabeth was last to arrive for her trial. In the tradition of sly leading ladies, she chose to make her entrance wearing what no one else was. In a hall packed with London high society in full Georgian bling, Elizabeth had dressed entirely in black, her three attendant ladies in white. Her outfit was modelled on that worn by Mary, Queen of Scots, when she faced trial and execution. Elizabeth had narrowly escaped being confined to the Tower, once the full indictment against her became apparent with Foote's attacks, but she opted nonetheless to play tragic heroine and queenly widow when she arrived from her house-arrest in Knightsbridge. Not since her appearance as Iphigenia had she made quite such an entrance.

Reviews were mixed: to some she looked 'very pale and a deal agitated as well she might', to others a model of 'dignity and deportment'; to Hannah More, the playwright, the diminutive duchess in weeds was 'exactly like a pile of Bombazine'.[6] Two protectors swore to stand bail for many thousands of pounds. Lord Mountstuart, the Duke of Newcastle and Sir James LaRoche accompanied her to the bar. Then Elizabeth prostrated herself on the floor before the Lords and the empty throne, with Queen Charlotte looking on from the shadows of the royal box. So began the first act of one of the most spectacular show-trials and media events of Georgian London.

Elizabeth began elegantly enough, stating her defence. This was entirely the norm in eighteenth-century law. She claimed her first marriage had been invalid, and assessed as such by a Church court in the issue known as jactitation, so no further court could overturn this. This was for many the only interest in the first day of the trial. After all the hype and preparations, it turned out that the Law Lords had a great deal to moot, and they did so mainly out of the hearing of the crowd. By taking her expensive lawyers' advice on the issue of jactitation, she hoped to subvert the show-trial Foote and others had expected for her – with its dirty-laundry testimony of chambermaids and bumbling country vicars – to a debate over court prerogatives. It took three full days of legal argument for the issue to be resolved, and naturally enough, the Queen, the Court, the many ladies in high, powdered hair and diamonds, soon realized that the duchess's trial was not quite the scandalous melodrama they had hoped for.

The Earl of Mansfield presided over Elizabeth's trial – and later Foote's. Tall, patrician, Scottish, of 'extensive and penetrating . . . genius',[7] he had been taught oratory by no less a personage than Alexander Pope and ran a pithily phrased and exacting court. Long on Elizabeth's payroll of lawyers, but also Lord Chief Justice since 1754, Mansfield raised a particular legal argument towards the end of the first day of her trial: he suggested that the whole case would set a precedent in the Constitution, and that the Lords had no jurisdiction over an ecclesiastical court on Church business. The attorney general contested this the next day, arguing that the Church court that had granted Elizabeth her quasi-annulment had been collusive – bought off by Elizabeth – and entered a plea of 'estoppel', the impossibility of trying Elizabeth for a related criminal charge. Eventually, the Lord Chief Justice of the Court of Common Pleas, William de Grey, wrote up a brief for the Lords stating that the ecclesiastical jactitation ruling did *not* bar a criminal trial for bigamy. To this day that ruling is cited as precedent in the rare argument of 'estoppel' or double jeopardy.

On the next day of the trial, the expected drama began. Ann Cradock, the maid who had colluded in the secret marriage in 1744, gave witness against Elizabeth. She had seen the marriage, the couple in bed together, and had heard tell of their baby who had died. Elizabeth swooned in court. Cradock's testimony was somewhat undermined when it became clear she was being paid by the Meadows family – the likely beneficiaries of the duke's original will – but then Lord Barrington and Caesar Hawkins, quondam surgeon to the Princess of Wales, gave evidence that they knew or believed Elizabeth and Augustus to have been married. The tide began to turn decisively against Elizabeth when the parish register, in which the marriage was recorded, was brought in by the widow of the Reverend Mr Amis who had married them.

On the last day of the trial, in front of a packed Westminster Hall, and without real hope of acquittal, Elizabeth rose and faced her critics. She quoted Samuel Foote's famous letter as she did so.

'My words will flow freely from my heart,' she claimed, 'adorned simply with innocence and truth.'[8] She went on with great solemnity for the 'three quarters of an hour'[9] it took her to read her notes: twelve manuscript pages. She had one last major witness to call, she said, her friend and supporter Sir James LaRoche, who had stood bail for her, had witnessed her wedding to the late duke, and who now stands as a lone voice of gentlemanly courtesy in what was devolving into a grand display of state-sponsored misogyny. He tried to explain how the duke had come to believe the jactitation ruling had made his mistress a spinster, and that he might marry her. He was forced to allow, under cross-examination, that there had perhaps been 'a doubt upon the breast'[10] of the duke over the absolute legality of what he was doing. At this Elizabeth fainted again. She recovered sufficient only to wail uncontrollably, in the manner of the stage histrionics favoured by Georgian tragediennes, drowning the last of what Sir James had to say. Her performance, if such it was, was reviewed poorly. It was evident she had lost.

Lord Bathurst instructed the Lords to consider their verdict, which they did elsewhere in the Palace of Westminster. On their return, Bathurst began by addressing the youngest peer, the newly acceded Duke of Argyll: 'What says your lordship? Is the prisoner at the bar guilty or not guilty of the felony whereof she is indicted?'

'Guilty, upon my honour,' he replied.

One by one, the whole House of Lords stood to pronounce the duchess a bigamist. It was an almost unanimous verdict, and as unedifying an example of hypocrisy as could be found in legal history. The jury that found against her included the Duke of Grafton, himself divorced by collusive practice, the Earl of Sandwich, prominent member of the Hellfire Club, the royal Duke of Cumberland, convicted and fined for adultery with Lady Grosvenor, all of whom voted in censure of the 'duchess' now that the duke was not there to protect her. It was not their finest or most gallant hour. Only the Duke of Newcastle demurred. He voted that Elizabeth was 'guilty erroneously, but not intentionally', which was a quibble she had little cause to celebrate.

In the eighteenth century bigamists could be hanged. More regularly they were branded – sometimes on the forehead, more often on the hand or breast – with either a 'B' or a cross. Elizabeth was already prepared. She handed a note to Bathurst, researched by her lawyers, stating that if she was not Duchess of Kingston she was necessarily Countess of Bristol, and wives of peers, like priests, had the benefit in law of being excused sentence on their first offence. It saved her from the pain and ignominy of branding, but it was a Pyrrhic victory. The Meadows family immediately began their legal battle to overturn the will that had left Elizabeth – who obdurately continued to style herself as 'duchess' – in charge of one of the greatest fortunes in the country and she, in consequence, immediately made yet another trip to Calais, to guard it.

§

'Happily in this giant town,' Horace Walpole wrote, 'one is not long troubled with stale events [for] having heard nothing else this fortnight', but after the 'farce' of Elizabeth's trial, attention moved almost directly to Sam Foote.

Sangster, the footman, had chosen suspiciously well his moment to attend the Bow Street magistrates and make his sensational deposition against his master, and the media circus moved directly from the duchess to the player.

William Jackson's *Public Ledger* had continued its occasional swipes at Foote and at his ambiguous sexuality. On the day of the bigamy trial's opening, the *Ledger* had run a satirical poem, almost certainly penned by Jackson, titled 'Asmodeus', one of Foote's characters in *The Devil Upon Two Sticks*. It vilified Foote as the originator of all the duchess's woes, and ends with Asmodeus being hanged and dissected, a clear reference to his murderous uncle, after a trial has convicted him of being a murderer of reputations. 'The brain was much disordered,' it reads, and upon cutting up Asmodeus, 'the surgeons found no heart'.[11] As Elizabeth's trial concluded, 'Asmodeus' was reissued, illustrated, at a shilling. It was sold outside Westminster Hall. Whether or not Elizabeth paid for the publication is not clear – but certainly Jackson thought he would curry her favour by publishing it in the *Ledger* and stirring up feelings anew against the dramatist. Because undoubtedly she blamed Foote for all her woes.

Heading into town in his coach one morning towards the middle of the trial, Foote happened to pick up James Boswell somewhere along Piccadilly. Foote must have been coming in from Fulham, Boswell was going to Westminster. Boswell records Foote's surprise that Mansfield should side so eloquently with the duchess's cause; it is the only evidence that Foote might have attended, incognito, some of the trial. Foote is also recorded by Boswell as mentioning Elizabeth in the same breath as Catherine the Great. The 'Empress of All the Russias' was, of course, one of the most formidable and notorious women of Foote's era, both terrifying and mesmeric. That Foote should link their names tells us a little of his feelings, but there is no record of any further comment. Whatever his thoughts on the trial and its verdict might have been, and whatever further satire or letters to the press he might have been planning, his attitude to the tribulations he helped bring upon the now Countess of Bristol were soon subsumed in tribulations of his own.

§

It was five o'clock on 6 May 1776, the day Sangster first accused Foote of assault. Elizabeth was already on her way to France. It had taken until then – some seven hours after Sangster's initial accusation and the 'hue and cry' for arrest – for Foote to answer the charge. More than an hour of this time had been spent simply pushing Foote's well-recognized sedan chair through the crowds, between the Haymarket and Bow Street, drawn there on the promise of salacious gossip about the man who had kicked off the Chudleigh trial.

Foote was joined at Bow Street by his box-office manager, William Jewell, and his lawyer, William Hickey. He was due to be remanded in custody, such were the seriousness of the charges laid against him and, in Fielding's opinion, the credibility of Jack Sangster. Custody was also recommended for Foote's safety, as the accusation was feared likely to incite riot. Jewell and Foote posted bail, however, and Hickey argued successfully that Foote should remain in Fulham, avoiding the incitement to protest that continuing to perform at the Haymarket presented.

Over the next few days, the *Public Ledger* ran forty pages on the story, which, perforce, was picked up by all the London papers and pamphlets. Foote's supposed offence could not be reported directly or explicitly. Sodomy was, after all, even in legal terms, 'that which Christians could not name'. The papers found other ways to communicate it to the worldly. The Latin epigraph *stans in pedo* (stands on one foot) was misspelled in one reference to Foote as '*stans in pego*' ('pego' being standard slang for 'penis'), begetting a series of jokes and allusions around the business of the one-legged man, named Foote, who was somehow accused of an act that defied, to some, balance as much as naming. But it was no laughing matter for Foote. Boswell, friend and sexual adventurer himself, was shocked by the press reports and their likely impact on Foote's career. To be known around the coffee-houses of the West End as 'Mother Midnight's niece' was one thing, to be 'outed' in the wider press during a connected media storm, and during arguably the first unedifying fit of moral indignation so beloved of the British press, was quite another. Friends were alarmed for Foote, and for his career. Boswell writes that he talked to Dr Johnson about Foote's predicament: 'I mentioned Jackson's shocking stories about Foote [in the *Ledger*].'[12] They discussed what the worst slur against a man in public life might be, and agreed it was to be accused of sodomy.

For the second time in less than a year, Foote was faced with stark choices. Things had intensified. His name and image were everywhere but for all the wrong reasons, and the *Ledger* was printing invective against him several times a week. 'Asmodeus', despite or perhaps because of its vituperative homophobia, was selling well. One choice was to run. In setting him free on bail, Fielding had left this route open to him, and it would have been ironic, dramatic and comic at once if Foote had indeed followed fresh on the heels of Elizabeth to the Continent. But he did not: his second choice was to countersue. To libel someone for sodomy was also a capital crime, so Jackson as writer and one Thomas Brewman as printer of the *Public Ledger* had gambled that Foote's many powerful friends would advise him to run. Perhaps this was what he had done in 1748. Now, though, Foote bravely chose to stay, and fight.

Over the ensuing week, from 7 to 14 May 1776, as reports of his supposed sexual proclivities came out in the *Ledger*, Foote sent a friend, William Hamilton, to Globe Court by Shoe Lane, yards from Dr Johnson's house, where the paper was printed. Hamilton collected copies as evidence for a libel action. Next Foote hired the lawyers James Wallace and Thomas Hawkins. Together on Friday, 17 May, Wallace, Hawkins and Foote presented their evidence and case at the Court of the King's Bench at Westminster. They were seeking to charge Jackson and Brewman at the *Ledger* with libel for the 'slanderous accusation of unnatural practice' that carried the death penalty.

All was in confusion at Westminster. The grand edifice of Elizabeth's state trial – the galleries and daises, the ersatz throne and temporary prisoner's bar – was still being dismantled. The courts that usually sat within Westminster Great Hall were being reassembled, but Wallace and Hawkins presented to Justice John Willes a suit accusing the *Ledger* of libel. Willes issued a warrant for the paper's printer, Thomas Brewman, to appear before him.

On the following Monday, 20 May, Brewman and his lawyer, Mr Morgan, were instructed by Lord Mansfield himself, the Lord Chief Justice, that they would stand trial. Perhaps in an effort to appear even-handed and judicious, Lord Mansfield, who had argued a fortnight before *in favour* of clemency towards the duchess in the trial that Foote had rendered necessary, now argued *against* the intrusion of the press into Foote's life. The *London Chronicle* duly reported that Mansfield raged against 'the licentiousness of the press' and their *sub judice* arrogance in alienating a 'public against a party previous to . . . his trial'.[13]

§

In modern urban life, the reaction of the press and public can be more revelatory than a news story itself. London, the new metropolis with its unbridled press but evolving discomfort around the barracking of individuals, revealed itself in 1776 in all its contradictory complexity. Foote was terrified there would be a riot. Until 1775 he had been basking in a rare new light of metropolitan fame as satirist of an establishment whose favour he seemed to enjoy. His image was strongly fixed in the public mind's eye: he was the one-legged Sam Foote, subject of cartoons and jokes, and relished for his notoriety ever since his crime-writing had reached a far wider public than those many who attended the London and Dublin theatre. Now, added to this, an accusation against him mixed lewdness with ridiculousness and moral outrage and was consequently instantly unforgettable. Many laughed, as they do today, at the image or idea of the arraigned one-legged bugger. Others had him fixed as the other face of moral depravity in metropolitan culture: a devil on a wooden stick who dared to laugh at societal norms and masculine ideals precisely as British manhood was tested at home and abroad. The 'Detestation and Abhorrence of the Publick' the *Ledger* threatened – now regularly selling out its print run of several thousand – would prevent him 'opening the Theatre and representing'[14] himself upon the open stage.

Foote put two strategies into action: one, to defend his name by the libel action, and another, which amounted to a forced retirement from public performance, and the sale of his Haymarket licence. The press, his friends and his own mind seem to have vacillated on what response would be best. Foote had intermediaries approach George Colman the Elder about the potential of taking over the Haymarket, and spoke to Garrick and Jewell, among others, about how best to handle the volatile Haymarket crowd. He had advertised already a season including *The Maid of Bath*, *The Cozeners*, *The Nabob* and *The Bankrupt*, and a new comedy, as yet unannounced. Some of the press was supportive. The *St James's Chronicle* wrote that 'The Treatment [Foote] has lately met with, while his Guilt is problematical . . . is . . . atrociously cruel.'[15] And there were plenty of those in Foote's circle and company at the theatre who counselled him to brazen it out with a public appearance.

On Monday, 20 May 1776, having consulted Jewell, Foote advertised that he would reappear that evening in *The Bankrupt* – his satire on newspaper libels – at the Theatre Royal, Haymarket. It was to be the second great night in the whole débâcle when Foote bravely and publicly tested the temperature of the London audience.

Crowds began to gather on the street and behind the theatre at Suffolk Street from late morning. It was noted, ominously, that no women were buying tickets, only men, which was one traditional harbinger of a theatre riot. 'The crowd,' the *London Chronicle* informed its readers, 'pressed in with eagerness . . . threatening the limbs' of the box-office guards. When the theatre finally opened late in the afternoon, the pit filled in six minutes, though 'not a single woman in it'. A few aristocratic supporters of Foote had booked boxes and arrived around four o'clock with ladies, 'but on their appearance, the galleries made a dreadful noise', and the ladies were met with gestures and dumbshow mimes from the men in the pit – gestures that alluded to Foote's disgrace – 'which obliged them immediately to retire'.[16] Things were turning very ugly.

Backstage, in the corridor that linked the Suffolk Street house with the Haymarket theatre wings, Foote listened to the audience, and struggled to attach his dress prosthetic.

Theatre lore tells variously what happened next. Like the first appearance of Garrick on the London stage – an event so many claimed to have witnessed when they could not have been there – the entrance onto the Haymarket stage of Samuel Foote when all London knew he was about to face a charge of sodomy has about it the stuff of legend. The first time I heard of the unipedular charm of Samuel Foote, from an old actor, it was with the following epilogue. It was said that Foote's last ever appearance on the London stage was to make one speech only and then leave, as bailiffs entered through the Haymarket stalls doors. He declaimed, in this version of events, at the footlights and Wilkes-like, an encomium on Liberty and, indeed, on freedom of sexual expression, before disappearing through a trap-door in the stage as the bailiffs stormed the pit. I was told Foote escaped, and died the next day in Dover waiting for the ferry, thus evading the problematic issue of life's third act by not having one. The structure of what happened on the night of Monday, 20 May 1776, was, perhaps sadly, not quite so perfectly bathetic. It was, however, in its way, Foote's finest hour, and one of the London theatre's.

After the musical prelude that preceded any drama at the Theatre Royal, Haymarket, the house fell silent. The entire Haymarket company watched backstage from the wings as Foote made his lumbering approach across a darkened stage to behind the centre of the fallen curtains. Charles Bannister was there, as were John 'Plausible' Palmer, Ann Jewell, sometime maid to Foote, Robert Baddeley and Martha Weston, with another thirty actors and dancers, all on the payroll and consequently awaiting their fate. The house was packed to the rafters and a crowd had gathered outside, expectant of a riot. All fell silent. The great green curtains of the Haymarket twitched at their centre parting, and Foote made his customary Prologue entrance, his cork leg arching around the valance that Charles Dibdin pulled askance for him, into view of the paying public. According to the *London Chronicle*, he was greeted not with orange peel or the ordure reserved for sexual assailants. He was greeted by 'a roar of applause' – which was followed, immediately, by a chorus of boos that marked the likely opening of a riot.

Foote bowed as best he could to his mercurial and troubled audience, looked around him, and quietly began this speech:

'GENTLEMEN [there were no ladies in the audience] –

'It was not my intention after the charge that has been made against me to appear before the public . . . but as this charge was made at the critical point in time when I usually opened my theatre, and having engaged performers . . . it was the unanimous advice of my friends that I should open my house in confidence that the public were too noble, and too just, to discard an old servant . . . I – I – I can say no more.'[17]

The house erupted again into cheers, this time uninterrupted with boos, and Foote, unable to speak, moved back behind the curtain and, according to witnesses, began to cry. It was relief beyond measure, for that loving response afforded him the knowledge that the accusation on its own was not enough to dent his appeal. He was beloved of the London audience, even those suspicious of his sexuality. He was indomitable, for the time being. 'I have been most cruelly used,' he wrote to Garrick, before bravely quipping, 'but I have, thank God, got to the *bottom* of this infernal contrivance.'[18]

'The candour and humanity of the public,' wrote the Theatrical Intelligencer in the *Gazetteer*, 'deserves to be recorded.'[19] Londoner theatre-goers had chosen wit over censoriousness. Or they had, at least, chosen Foote over the duchess. A story went round that Foote was joking about it all before the evening had even come to an end. Just as had been the case with his amputation, his wit gave wings to an anecdote of courage over misadventure: it was said that, on the day following his victorious return to the stage (though *if* it had been said it had been said earlier), Foote had responded to hearing the accusations against him as only a one-legged comedy superstar could: 'Sodomite?' he had spluttered. 'I'll not stand for it.'[20]

The curtain speech was, of course, only the beginning of the evening. Those who were there that Monday for the tumultuous performance of *The Bankrupt* swore there had been nothing like it in London in living memory. It was a play and a real-life drama that seemed perfectly aligned to each other, uniting in a lead performer who purged the anxieties of the moment and his own celebrated predicament and forged a catharsis of laughter. Most famously, in one scene Foote's character is traduced in a print shop by an unscrupulous newspaper editor, who boasts that he and the fourth estate had and would have more power in the administration of justice than the judiciary itself, stating, '*I* hold the scale.' It is a moment of eye-popping prescience, in terms of what Foote feared might happen – a trial by newspaper slur, and in terms, of course, of what the press has since become. It was a moment, briefly, when the London public sided against an intrusive press and in favour of its 'old servant'. It was, wrote the *Gazetteer*, an 'astonishing' evening – and the scene stopped the play.

The support of his public was not going to be enough, however, to save Foote, though it was a vital rebuttal to Jackson and the machinations of the duchess. He and Jewell began to timetable the summer season at the Haymarket, but the Sangster case hung over him with no trial date set, and little likelihood of gaining information on what the ex-footman would say, why, and with what corroboration. Meanwhile, Foote could not proceed with the libel case against the *Ledger* while an accusation hung against him that might prove the substance of what Jackson had published.

The next volley in the media war belonged to Jackson and the woman who continued to style herself Duchess of Kingston. In late June 1776 Jackson published anonymously a new work he inscribed 'To Foote Esq., alias the Devil upon Two Sticks'. It was almost certainly written by Jackson, though there are other candidates. Its title has confined it to the Special Materials of the British Library Rare Books section ever since, and it has some claim to be the most scurrilous, scabrous and obscene poem held there, from an age famed for such. It was called, pithily enough, *Sodom and Onan*. It's quite a read. Its 540 lines of doggerel narrate initially the rape of Sangster by Foote, but also toss ordure around the whole establishment who might collude to protect such 'Sodomites' and thereby infect the body politic. It attempts to 'out' anyone Jackson thought might be a homosexual and might help Foote's cause. These names ranged from Isaac Bickerstaffe to the Duke of Ancaster, from Lords Tylney and Cowper – who were widely credited as 'gay' – to Lord Sackville, 'the pederastical American Secretary', and even rounded on the monarch:

> King George, inveigled by Scotch Insinuation
> To pardon Sodomites, and Damn the Nation.[21]

All are accused of being either sexual deviants or the protectors of such and, worse still, dangerous blasphemers to the will of the vengeful Old Testament God, who had punished the city of Sodom for the sins that took place there, and Onan for abusing, as the story goes, the gift of his seed.

It ends shockingly and violently, imagining Foote's innards consumed by 'rank corruption' too horrid even for the anatomists to dissect, unable at last to enunciate a single joke as his mouth is clotting with syphilitic sores and pus. Lewd, inhumane, misanthropic though it might seem, *Sodom and Onan* stands as one of the key documents that link the trials of Foote and Elizabeth Chudleigh to the paranoia about the sexual health of the nation as it lost its American colonies. It presages the 1916 Pemberton-Billing trial,[22] when the country was again losing a war, a secondary trial in effect of Oscar Wilde, as much as it does the McCarthyist witch-hunts of the Cold War; it happens, it seems, in beleaguered bellicose nations. In 1766 this convocation of politics worming at one celebrated disfigured body, concentrated on Foote, who was fast becoming the most famous sodomite in Georgian England, without necessarily being one.

Though it smacked of desperation, *Sodom and Onan* cannot have been other than deeply alarming for Foote. It is unclear how many copies were printed or sold, but its survival in multiple editions in several major collections suggest it circulated widely in London and even abroad. It also alarmed Foote's box-office manager, Jewell, left wondering how long the Haymarket crowd could stay supportive, with the Sangster trial proceeding *before* the intended libel action, a long and drawn-out process, and the prospect still of it all proceeding *against* Foote.

Rumours began to circulate that Sangster was in the pay of Jackson, the *Ledger* and the now Countess of Bristol. This in itself would be neither surprising nor without precedent at this period. Criminal conversation trials invariably called upon the witness of servants, and usually they were known to be in the pay of one or other of the parties involved, or even both. Sangster seems to have gone to live with a former employer, and made no further comment or accusation as all parties waited for a trial date to be set. The payments he took, with his lawyer Luke Naylor, from Jackson and the so-called duchess, by now in Rome, were not seen as essential proof of Sangster's mendaciousness but rather of the collusion of Jackson, a likely libeller. In other words, as the summer season continued, Foote's innocence or guilt as a sodomite or someone merely attracted to Sangster was not the subject of debate. Rather, it became the guilt or innocence of Jackson and the duchess in trying to ruin the reputation of a favoured come-dian. Some Georgians were happier with sophisticated façades than with the vilification of an individual. And the King himself, it turned out, was one of them.

§

One thing must be made clear in all of this: the population of London were in utter ignorance of the details of the case. They were aware by hearsay of what was charged against Foote, whose fame and the notoriety of his spat with the then duchess served to amplify the story, as did *Sodom and Onan*. But the only 'details' of the case made public were those misreported in the *Public Ledger*. The other papers referred to an impending trial, and to 'accusations' against Foote, but left the rest to the murmur of the crowd. Even at the trial, the prosecution counsel demurred from describing or repeating Sangster's testimony. It was all utterly unmentionable. The *details* of what Sangster said, and what Sir John Fielding had taken to be a credible accusation, have remained shrouded till recent years.

Scone Palace in Scotland is the ancestral seat of the Earls of Mansfield. When rioters in London burned down the townhouse of the lawyer-earl, it was assumed, by everyone from Horace Walpole to Charles Dickens, that Mansfield's incomparable collection of legal notes and records – his jottings on the trials of Elizabeth Chudleigh and Samuel Foote among many others – had been lost along with his library and art collection. At Scone Palace, however, some of these manuscript records, kept separately, survived. They came to light only recently,[23] so it has been possible to reread the trial evidence brought against Samuel Foote in all its compelling detail, and hear, as if from the mouths of those involved, the totality that was denied Londoners at the time.

On the one hand, Foote was fulsomely supported by the London élite and his audience, increasingly so as his trial approached. How aware they were of the seriousness of the charges against him is less clear. Sir Joshua Reynolds rallied to his side and publicly appeared at the theatre. On another evening at the Haymarket, 'two royal dukes, the Duke of Roxburgh, the Marquis

of Townsend, Mr [Edmund] Burke . . . and Mr [William] Fitzherbert' were spotted. Foote was described by those who were alarmed
to see it that, in the midst of accusations too heinous to print, he
was nevertheless 'caressed by the brightest geniuses, and persons of
the most exalted stations in the kingdom'.[24] These exalted persons
were not to know, and could not know unless they attended the
trial, the testimony of Sangster. Jackson continued to do all he
could in the *Ledger* to make it abundantly clear that what Foote
was accused of amounted to attempted homosexual rape. He even
wrote lewdly that attractive young members of the Haymarket
company had been issued with corks, by none other than the
constantly attendant Mr Jewell, 'for their further safety'[25] against
their master. Yet Foote's friends and public stayed loyal. The more
Jackson fulminated against the decadence of high society and the
theatre, the more the one chose to support the other, and the more
ridiculous he looked – to some. Quite unexpectedly, into these
murky waters stepped the highest arbiter of good behaviour in the
land.

King George III, who had come to the throne with the stated
aim of ridding his kingdom and especially those 'nearest to our
person' of the moral turpitude that had sullied other reigns, may
or may not have thought Foote was a sodomite. He is unlikely to
have had cause to read the trial reports, though he had a right to:
it was his court and Foote was prosecuted in his name. It seems
likely, however, that he simply refused to believe it could be true.
Because, as the trial edged ever nearer, the King began attending
the Haymarket; it was the first time he had done so. George III,
often represented as dour and puritanical, had nevertheless a
profound interest in the theatre. It was not as marked as that of his
brother, Edward Augustus – who had argued for Foote's patent at
the Haymarket – but it was nonetheless sufficient of an interest for
it to be bizarre that, prior to 12 June 1776, he had never visited
his new Theatre Royal. He chose that night to do so, with Queen
Charlotte and other members of the royal family, for a Royal
Command Performance featuring Samuel Foote.

It was the clearest signal in his gift that Foote had his support in the war of words and litigation with Elizabeth Chudleigh. It showed that he either did not believe or possibly, like many sophisticated Georgians, dismissed as irrelevant the rumours about Foote's sexuality. Foote had the royal box re-studded with scarlet velvet, a material he would have cause to use again. He escorted the royal party himself from the Haymarket to their box, not an easy progress, with many stairs and hooped skirts to negotiate, and was sufficiently his old self to josh modestly with the King that the comedy they were about to see was clean enough to have been written by one of the King's bishops. George requested a second Command Performance, and timed this just as Foote's Westminster trial began. This time he commanded *The Orators*, in which Foote lampooned religious hypocrites while dressed in drag in a character he had originated with Christopher Smart. Their Majesties, according to the *Gentleman's Magazine*, 'laughed immoderately'.[26] The support at this critical juncture of the King himself was also a signal of Foote's earlier ties to royalty. Prince Edward Augustus had died unexpectedly in Monaco only a few years before, and the King may have been moved to help Foote in his hour of need out of loyalty to his lost brother. It is in any event not so much the usual image of Farmer George, the scourge of his brothers' debauchery, but an unexpected theatrical tableau instead of a broad-minded and garrulous monarch, using that subtle weapon of kingship, presence, to adjust a public debate as it was happening.

For some recent historians, the Haymarket Royal Command Performances in 1776 and the tacit support of the King and Queen mark out Foote as more establishment darling than 'gay' martyr. But the King was as yet unaware, if indeed he ever became so, of Sangster's testimony against Foote. For the time being, he chose to believe it was all a Kingston-inspired plot to discredit a man he had chosen to grace with a royal patent. The presence of the royal couple was one part of Foote's media war. Another was the presence of a woman thus far hidden from the narrative of his life:

his mistress. Horace Walpole had noticed that Foote 'exhibited [a] whore that he kept . . . in a box at [the Haymarket]'. Lord Townsend, seeing her there said, 'Ah – there's Foote's Alibi.'[27] The inference that she was a beard in the sexual comedy being played on and off stage is countermanded only by the possibility, revealed slightly later, that Foote may have had two illegitimate children with her.[28] The truth about their provenance and histories became clearer as the next year progressed.

The Royal Command Performances emboldened Foote still further. Always one to push a joke to extremes, he resubmitted the Chudleigh satire, *A Trip to Calais*, to the Lord Chamberlain, for a licence. He changed the title to *The Capuchin* and changed also the main subject of his ridicule from the duchess to Jackson. But it was the same play. Jackson was lampooned in the oleaginous form of Dr Viper, editor of the *Scandalous Chronicler*, a libeller and creep. It was stamped for approval by Lord Hertford's office on 6 August 1776. As in *The Minor*, one subject of satire was religious hypocrisy, for Dr Viper, scandal-monger and scourge of aristocratic sexual laxity, is blindly besotted with an aristocratic widowed vamp. The new rendering of Kitty Crocodile is Lady Deborah Dripping, who resides, in exile, in Calais. Both Jackson and the duchess were therefore equally recognizable to a London audience, and with Foote announced as the star player to wear drag as Lady Dripping, it was evident that life, art and comedy would collide once again.

It is perhaps the most telling example of Foote's reckless contempt for propriety and personal safety, an instinct that had won him so many laughs and so much trouble over the years, that *The Capuchin* played out as it did. This was not just because of its satire on viperous newspaper editors or even a fallen duchess. He risked a scene of truly shocking self-reference and sexual innuendo, one that should stand legally as a precursor to the infamous *Romans in Britain* case two centuries later, for in it, and in the face of an impending buggery trial, Foote parodied onstage the very act of sodomy. For evidence of this I am indebted to one academic's close attentions to the only surviving manuscript of the play as it was presented to Lord Hertford. It resides, with much else of this period, in the collection of the Huntington Library in California. Here, the text that was actually performed in 1776 may be examined and contrasted with the one later *published*. They are rather different: in the *performed* version, Foote simulated sex. This ought to be the stuff of theatre legend for, bugger, buggeree or neither, Foote is shown using everything in his unusual armoury of wit and wooden leg to poke fun at his own predicament – and the morality of the age.

The first two acts of *The Capuchin* run almost word for word as *A Trip to Calais*. In the new version, as submitted and performed, though not printed, a new third act takes the plot in a whole new direction. Dr Viper and the Capuchin, Brother O'Flam, to be played also by Foote, plan to lure the *ingénue* lead away from her convent with the pretence of taking her to her true love, Dick. Instead, they will deliver her to the lecherous old Sir Harry Humper, a rich Englishman, who intends to pose as 'Dick' in a darkened bedroom and thus enjoy his debauched fantasy of sex with a nun. So far, so farcical. It is typical of Foote's sardonic satire and his take on Jackson and the press that Viper explains the publicity value of this nun-groping escapade:

> VIPER: I think it will be right, at your time of life Sir Harry
>   to report it a rape, it will do your vigour a good deal of
>   credit . . . a rape, and upon a nun too, for so we must call
>   her, it will show a noble contempt for decency, religion
>   and virtue.[29]

These were daring lines, too, to be spoken in a play by a man charged with attempted homosexual rape.

The plan goes awry, in the way of farces of this period, and the tumescent Sir Harry is left, in the dark, not with 'Sister' Jenny but with Brother O'Flam (Foote) who takes it upon himself to impersonate Jenny in the dark, while being molested by Sir Harry. This is what happened on stage at the Haymarket:

SIR HARRY: Miss Jenny.

BROTHER O'FLAM: Where are you dear Dick?

SIR HARRY: Here – give me your hand . . . Egad, you have a
good thumping fist! [*Aside*: If she is all grown in proportion,
she must be devilishly throve [grown, also, hirsute]. Well,
my dear Jenny, let us make best use of our time.

BROTHER O'FLAM: I hope, dear Dicky, you don't mean to be
rude.

SIR HARRY: [*Aside*] How hoarse her voice is when she speaks
out! – Come my love, come a little this way . . .

BROTHER O'FLAM: [*Aside*] What the Devil will I do? If Doctor
Viper does not speedily come, I shall be ravished here in
spite of my teeth . . . Nay but Dicky –

and at this point Sir Harry kisses his unnervingly large and hirsute
nun . . .

And so on. If this is merely the text, any comic actor would
immediately recognize the potential for comic business of the most
graphic sort – indeed, it is inconceivable that the scene would be
played without misplaced hands, mouths, groins and petticoats
when it involved a sexually frustrated stage-idiot and a comedy
Irishman dressed as a nun. It is all fairly silly stuff on the page, but
such darkened bedroom larks are some of the simplest and most
effective forms of stage irony for all the possibilities they plant in
an audience's mind. The tension of seeing Foote impersonating
O'Flam impersonating Jenny being kissed on stage at the Haymarket by William Parsons as Sir Harry Humper is difficult to re-
imagine. It may have been farcical, but it was also topical and,
sexually, it was at the outer edges of edgy. It would have been
risqué in 1776 without the background of the Foote charges. With
them alive in the imagination of every audience member, it was
supremely reckless comedy.

One might have thought therefore that Foote was in confident
mood by the time he finally faced Sangster at trial, and that he
could only have joked in this manner if he was convinced his
innocence would be evident. Yet, as so often with Foote, the path

anyone else might follow was rarely one he favoured. He was in dire danger and his stage antics can be read also as symptomatic of wanton recklessness, an assault on taste as on tact. If the trial proceeded as Jackson and the duchess desired, and as Foote knew it might, he was in real danger of losing his name, his fortune, his theatre, his liberty and, plausibly beyond those, his life.

§

A date was set for Foote's trial as the theatre season was drawing to its close. It was to begin on 9 December 1776. The duchess followed the news of the impending mirror-trial to her own as closely as she could from the Continent, plotting further revenge against Foote if things went her way. The weeks passed with rising tension for Foote, but he kept to his schedule of appearances. Little of substance was written in the press, partly compliant with the decorum of the age, partly in deference to Mansfield's known concerns on contempt of court. Even after the trial, however, details were kept hidden, in the spirit, as Daniel Defoe wrote, of ensuring that 'sodomitical crimes and the reporting thereof should be a secretive affair, smothering the Crime and the criminal [together] in the dark'.[30] This was effective only in that Foote's reputation was darkened by rumour. What Mansfield tells us and you are about to read was never seen by his contemporaries. Perhaps they would have reacted differently if they had. But the dark cloud that hung over Foote is explained by what must have spread, by word of mouth, once all this was heard in open court.

ROGER THE FOOTMAN

Who is this man? Is he a friend to justice or an enemy
to Mr Foote?[1]

THE COURT OF THE KING'S BENCH in Westminster Great Hall
was not at all as the Hall had appeared for Elizabeth's amphi-
theatrical trial a few months earlier. The King's Bench where
Mansfield now presided was 'a small room in the south-east angle
[corner] of the Hall, and here together [Mansfield], the jury,
the counsel, the attorneys . . . crowded with little accommodation
for the bystanders'.[2] It was difficult to hear – one of the reasons
Mansfield took careful notes. Business was fast. Mansfield told
James Boswell he tried seven hundred cases a year, and claimed
he was once obliged to hear 225 cases 'before Christmas Day'[3]
that were given over to him on 11 December. Foote's case, being
vexatious and well resourced with lawyers and witnesses, would
take longer.

Foote's indictment, for assaulting Sangster 'with an intent to
commit buggery', was problematical for a number of reasons and
Mansfield decided the case should be tried before a 'Special Jury
of gentlemen of the county of Middlesex'. Sangster never claimed
he had had sex with Foote, or had been raped, as was miscon-
strued. It was not a charge therefore carrying the death penalty,
though similar cases had led to transportation. A sexual assault
upon a footman, however, had led the Marquis de Sade to be

sentenced to death *in absentia* only four years before, and quite aside from the fame of the accused, a footman was a privileged but discomforting member of the Georgian domestic realm. He was in a uniquely intimate relationship with his master, and the abuse of his person was tinged with hues of incest – a perversion of the rightful order of things within a hearth and home. The joke that Sangster the footman was called Roger – he was not – forged laughter out of a deeply shocking idea, which was one reason that the story, and the joke, spread. The problem therefore was of the potential spectacular ruin of Foote or, if proved innocent, the impending libel action against Jackson, together with the notoriety and imagery of the case: the one-legged bugger and Roger the Footman. This necessitated the special jury.

The specialness of the jury related to their class, as determined by the attorneys. The four lawyers for the prosecution and the four for the defence doubtless argued lower and higher on the social scale respectively, in the hope of aiding their clients. However, special jury provision, though encouraged by Mansfield, had to be paid for by either the defence or the prosecution. The request and payment in criminal cases almost always came from the prosecution. It was likely therefore that Jackson and the duchess paid.

Sangster had with him four lawyers: Mr Davenport, Mr Cooper, Mr Howarth and William Jackson's brother-in-law, Luke Naylor. Foote had representing him James Wallace and Francis Buller but also his playwright friend and lawyer Arthur Murphy, and the rake and memoirist William Hickey. Foote himself was not obliged to appear and opted not to. He waited anxiously at Suffolk Street for news to be couriered to him.

§

The trial began at nine thirty a.m. on Monday, 9 December 1776. The clerk called John Sangster.

Sangster was relatively young to be a coachman-footman, somewhere in his mid-twenties. Like many coachmen in London at the period he was probably a country lad who had found a position in London through his knowledge of horses. Foote's household, Sangster said, included a Swiss valet, known variously as Louis Valley or Bally, a housekeeper, the former actress Mrs Garner, and an elderly housemaid called Nan, at Suffolk Street. Walter, the hairdresser, was attached to the Haymarket staff. At Northend there was a separate housekeeper, Mrs Baxter, a major-domo, Mr Campbell, and various lodgers more correctly in the employ of the Haymarket theatre who seem also to have been working for Foote privately: Jeffrey Pearce, Thomas Davis, and Mr and Mrs Jewell. Sangster had had a very responsible job. He was in charge not only of Foote's two coaches, one for travelling back and forth to Fulham and around the West End and one for the long journeys to Dublin – valuable items worth more than thirty pounds each[4] – but also responsible for the hayloft, with its valuable store of hay, which was worth more, it turned out, than the all the Zoffany canvases in the household when they were sold together. He also tended a half-dozen horses, and Foote's pets, which included a large mastiff dog.

The Foote household was peripatetic, with the servants obliged to wait on Foote at the Haymarket theatre and his London address in Suffolk Street, but more often at Northend in Fulham. A coach-man like Sangster was very much akin to a modern chauffeur, obliged to hang around at his master's bidding, and when he did so, he drank at local taverns in the West End. He slept in the store-room in Fulham and in the front garret in Suffolk Street, and spent, necessarily, much of his time with the horses in the Fulham stables, grandly set back from the house in the far corner of the gardens.

He performed odd jobs around the house as well and from this came his segued role as footman. Tall, good-looking members of male household staff like Sangster were often tried out by London employers as footmen in an era when, eccentrically, the height and presentability of one's footmen seems to have been some gauge of rank and status. And this seems to have been what happened to Sangster. He had two 'costumes'. At Northend, he was often a footman; at Suffolk Street he was a coachman. By eliding his original role to that of footman, he joined the ranks dubbed by Londoners the *inutiles* (the useless), the primary function of footmen being to look good in livery and hang around. In popular slang they were known as 'fart-catchers', 'from their walking behind their master or mistress'[5] with no discernible job. Despised by many, envied by some, footmen often projected the fashion-consciousness or arrogance of their employer by adopting aristocratic poise and *ennui*. They occupy also a liminal space in the erotic imagination of Londoners of the period to judge by the plays and songs that mention them – mirroring their masters' morals, attending too assiduously their mistresses' calls. Sangster moved his master's heavy lead bath from the back kitchen of the Fulham house, for instance, when Foote wanted to bathe, and helped his one-legged master in and out of the tub – their relationship in that regard was tellingly intimate – and he waited at table, but only at Northend, when there were guests.

He seems also to have been responsible for the songbirds kept in cages in the house at Fulham – and kept a cage of his own in his room. Poetically enough, his master's birds were later sold, still in captivity in their gilded cages, while Sangster had either released his, or perhaps taken it with him when he left. A picture might emerge therefore of a strong but gentle man, or maybe a simple one. Or as we shall never know or as you will also judge, perhaps a conniving young man, who happened to like songbirds but had an eye for detail and a dramatic flair for delivering devastating dialogue, as vicious as it was fictitious. He was a compelling witness. Partly this was because of the wealth of detail – of domestic arrangements, interior decoration and snatches of remembered conversation that jarred shockingly with the pornographic content of what he said – partly because he was exactly the era's idea of a potential victim of aberrant lust: a simple and attractive young man in an impossible domestic dilemma. That he came across as an innocent in the big city helped his cause, but it was not the whole truth. Like many London servants of the period, he also seems to have had a pretty serious drink problem.

In early 1776, on Foote's last trip to Dublin, Sangster fell ill with measles. He made a complete recovery, and credited this to the kindness of his master, who paid his medical expenses. The whole household returned to London in the early spring of 1776. Summer came early that May – the first few days of the month were not spring-like at all, but in London 'very fine, very bright' and hot.[6] The carriage was ordered to the door of Northend on 1 May at ten a.m. for Foote to head to the Haymarket. It took about forty-five minutes. The date, and time, looked dramatic in several ways. The case hinged around what happened within a few days at the beginning of May, before Sangster left his master's employ, arrived in tears at the home of Dr Fordyce, a former employer, then attended Bow Street and made his accusations. But that week was also the start of the theatrical season at the Haymarket, which was due to be dominated by the new satire of the duchess, exactly when his master would most need his services and when Foote was least likely to let him go. And the morning of 1 May was when Foote, traditionally, addressed the Haymarket company about the new season. Either Sangster was unusually skilled at first-person narrative, or Mansfield used his impressive shorthand to fashion a dramatic monologue out of what had been in court a dialogue of question and answer. Either way, the record reads arrestingly and graphically in the voice of Sangster, for which reason it is quoted here at length.

> On the 16th of November 1775 [began Sangster], I went to live with him Mr Foote as Coachman. I had been Coachman to Dr Fordyce for five and half years. I continued in the employ of Mr Foote til 3d May 1776.
>
> We got to town on 1 May a quarter before eleven. Mr Foote went on stage & continued there about an hour & $^1/_2$.[7]

Sangster was then obliged to loiter at the stage door in Suffolk Street, dressed as a coachman. Williams, the senior coachman, sat above the carriage.

A woman enquired for Mrs Garner, the housekeeper at Suffolk

Street, and asked Sangster to find her, which obliged him to go in via the stage wings, which connected to the servants' quarters of the house. Foote saw him, asked what he was up to, and told him to tell the woman to find Mrs Garner at the front of the theatre, where she sometimes took deliveries.

The Suffolk Street house was therefore empty when Foote went back inside. Sangster went on:

> In five minutes he rang the bell. I ran upstairs into the drawing room where he stood, which was going to be fresh-papered. The paper lay in the window.

This room was on the first floor, overlooking Suffolk Street. A coachman would never see it under normal circumstances. The Chinese paper had arrived and been put in the bay of the window.

> "Sangsty, [Foote said], is this the paper?"
>
> "I don't know" I said "I'll ask the maid." I went to the stairs and called out "Nanny". I came back to the drawing room. Mr Foote bid me come into the adjoining room [towards the back of the house] & take down some books. I went in.
>
> He said: "Take these books into the country [to North-end]." He kept looking at the book, and asked: "John are you quite well of the measles?" & turning round and laughing [he] called "John reach me this" – seeming to mean a looking-glass. While I stood up to take down the glass, he shut & as I found afterwards locked the door ... Mr Foote then stood with his back to the door, laughing and grinning in my face. He said "Have not all my servants been good to you, while ill of the measles?"
>
> "They have" [I said].
>
> "Have not I taken a great deal of care of you? Giving you physic & things?" I thanked him.
>
> He said "The best recompense you can make is to let me have a fuck at you."
>
> I said, "What?! What do you mean by that?"

"Don't you know?"

"Yes," says I, "and I had sooner be hanged. I am very much surprised a man like you would offer such a thing to a servant. I did not know you was such a person before I came. Had I known you was such a person I would not have with you for 100 guineas a year."

"Why John, what is your reason?" [says he.]

"Sin and shame worse than a brute beast."

"Damn the sin, it is no sin at all, & the shame, who knows it? Louis [Bally] would let me fuck him every day. I cannot get into him. I have frigged him 500 times & he had buggered me, but his damn little nasty prick gives me no pleasure."

I answered: "Louis Bally and you may do as you please, sir."

I stood in the middle of the room.

The Defendant's back [was] at the door. All the time he had his prick in his hand. I went to get out [&] found the door locked. Defendant got hold of me [&] wriggled against my thigh.

"Damn you, I'll be in you – I'll be in you   I'll be in you – damn you."

[He] got his hand into my breeches, tore the button off [&] got hold of my testicles. I had like to drop down [because of the pain].

"Damn your blood," [said Foote], "if you don't let me fuck you I insist upon frigging you."

I tried to shove him off. He held my testicles fast & began shaking my prick. I took him by the breast [&] gave a shove. "Damn you, you dirty dog," [I said]. "I'll call out of the window."

He held [my] testicles so fast [they] were swelled many days. After I got clear he stood buttoning up [his] breeches. He said "By God John there is no fellow I should like better to have to do with."

Taking the key out of his pocket, I said: "If I do not make you suffer for this, never believe me more."

"What will you do?" [Foote said.] "If you say I wanted
to fuck you, I have not fucked you, and if I had, nobody will
believe you."

I told him "You shall see whether they do or not."[8]

In a society, indeed a courtroom, where sexual acts were most
often referred to obliquely if at all, this had the effect of a depth
charge. There is little of the period in terms of courtroom testimony that matches the Mansfield manuscript record of Sangster's
words for a combination of lucidity and sexual frankness, and it
must have immediately occurred to Foote's lawyers, long kept in
the dark about the precision of the charges, that the clarity of
description would count strongly against them.

Garrick heard tell of it all, and quipped blithely that this was
all 'a Foote too far', but it was no laughing matter for the accused
or his lawyers. For many, it seemed that, irrespective of the verdict,
a pall of scandal would for ever hang over Foote after such
damning testimony and that his mask had slipped in a way the
public would never forgive. Richard Brinsley Sheridan, at work
that year on the play that would define the age of surfaces then as
now, *The School for Scandal*, put it bluntly: 'Foote – I suppose you
have heard – is likely never to show his face again.'[9]

Because there had been so many cases of attempted blackmail
of homosexuals, and of servants who accused employers of sexual
assault instead of accepting a dismissal, one immediate concern of
the court was how Sangster had responded in the immediate
aftermath of the assault, and what precedent there might have
been within the household to this sort of incident.

Sangster answered as clearly as he could. When he went down
to the hallway of Suffolk Street, a maid – possibly Nan – who had
returned from some errand expressed surprise that the coachman
had been up in the drawing room as he was not in livery as a
footman. She said, 'Jack, what have you been doing above stairs?'
This sentence is marked in the margin by Mansfield as one of the
statements he might want to corroborate with further testimony.

He was not able to. More than that, Mansfield may have been aware that Sangster, who acted as footman at Northend, was only ever at Suffolk Street in his capacity as a coachman so, in theory, would never have been upstairs or known what it looked like. This, ultimately, was more telling than Mansfield could know . . .

Sangster said, 'You shall hear what very soon,' and went to take his hat from the coat pegs near the two plaster busts on mahogany brackets that faced each other nearest the door: one was of Garrick, the other Foote.[10] As Sangster was storming out of the house, Foote came to the head of the stairs and shouted after him, 'John, where are you going?'

'You'll see by and by,' said Sangster, already perhaps forming a plan to make a complaint. Foote, he claimed, was instantly afraid for his reputation, and was keen to impress on Sangster the futility of a claim against him.

'"I suppose you are going to tell Sir John Fielding I wanted to fuck you,"' Sangster enunciated clearly in court, '"but by God if you do, it shall be your ruin. You shall never get a place."' Sangster claimed Foote added, '"For I am acquainted with all the nobility and gentry."'

Perhaps most compelling was Sangster's credible description of remorse and embarrassment after a sexual advance has been rejected. He continued:

"I don't care a farthing. I won't stay with you another minute. I'll expose you and all such rascals."

This passed in the hall. Mr Foote walked into the parlour and said, "John come here."

I refused.

He said: "I'll tell you something you don't know."

I walked just to the door.

He said "Damn you, what are you afraid of? I don't want to fuck you now. Damn me if I ever touch you more." I went in [to the parlour]. He shut the door [and] came up to me. "John, you are a lad. I wish you very well, & for your sake, don't say anything about it, for by God it will be your ruin. I have all the nobility on my side. Your character will be gone, you never will get a place. Consider. Stay with me till tomorrow. I'll pay your wages, give you a character & then you may get a place. Sir John Fielding would not take your oath, my oath will be taken before yours."[11]

Sangster then said he consented, reluctantly, to return to Northend, as there was a great deal of company at dinner that evening and his services were needed as footman.

Perhaps Sangster thought it would all blow over. Perhaps he thought he had made his peace or stated his orientation and, like the many sexually harassed servants of Georgian London, more women than men, he had drawn a line. It was not to be. As it turned out, according to Sangster, there had been a previous incident, in Dublin, in the winter of 1775–6, which he went on to detail.

On or about 15 or 16 January 1776, Sangster said, Foote had come in from rehearsals at Smock Alley and rung the servants' bell for Louis Bally, the Swiss valet, who then informed Sangster back in the kitchens that 'Your Master wants you.'

When Sangster went into Foote's bedroom, Foote was sitting on a settee. He asked Sangster for some sort of a massage, which may have been to do with his leg. He seemed to be unsurprised by the request, as was the court. Snuff was drying at the fire, Sangster added, in his typical style of redundant but vivid detail.

'Well, John,' Foote said, 'have you had a whore? Does your prick never stand? I daresay you have a large prick?'

Sangster did not elaborate how, or if, he evaded the questions. 'The next day,' Sangster continued, 'the bell rang. Louis said he was ordered out. The bell rang furiously. I went in. Mr Foote was on the settee. He said 'John, come and undo my leg, it pains me.'

The cotter, or pin that attached the leather straps moving parts of the leg, broke while he was undoing the prosthesis. This would have obliged Sangster to stand very close above his sitting master, possibly facing away from him, re-strapping the prosthesis. While he was doing this, Foote next, Sangster said, 'slipped his hand into my breeches & I asked what he meant. He said he only wanted to see what sort of prick I had got.'

The other servants, Sangster claimed, were all aware of what was going on. Sangster told the cook. Louis Bally 'came down crying' after some encounter with Foote, and Sangster told him about his own experiences with his master and said he 'was convinced [Mr Foote] was a Sodomite & [we] should not choose to live with him,' but this was before Foote had explained to him that he and Bally were regular sex partners.

Nothing more happened on the return to London. Perhaps, Sangster explained, he would have stayed on after the Suffolk Street incident, but for what happened, the next day, back in Fulham.

The morning of 2 May, Sangster was in the stables at North-end, grooming the horses. Foote came out of the villa, via the pond, to the stables, where he found Sangster alone. He shut and bolted the stable door.

Sangster described his last conversation with Foote verbatim:

"Now, John, this is the last day of your service, 10 or 20 guineas shall be yours [and a reference] if you'll let me have a do at you" [said Foote, reaching again for his servant's crotch].

"You damned old buggering rascal" [I said].

He took hold of me as before [by the testicles]. I struck him with my fist and swore if he did not let me out at the door, I would get out of the window. He threw the key down upon the [floor]. I took it and went out and stood in the yard.

"You old sodomitical rascal," I shouted "see how I shall serve you."[12]

Sangster decided to walk out on the Foote household for good, and seek refuge and advice with his former employer. He walked all the way back into the West End, and called at Suffolk Street to collect the trunk he kept there in the top garret.

He realized when he got back to central London that he had left the key in Fulham, and begged the other coachman to get it for him. When another servant at Suffolk Street, possibly Louis, remarked that he had been missed, Sangster stormed out shouting that they were all 'nasty sodomitical rascals' and seems to have wandered the streets through the night, or drunk himself into a stupor. He went next to his former employer, Dr Fordyce, on 3 May at half past ten in the morning – which Fordyce was able to corroborate. 'I was let in by his servants before he came in,' Sangster explained, so that when the doctor returned from his morning round, he found his former coachman, in his front parlour, in tears.

§

Sangster had been a devastating witness, but Hickey and Murphy had a lot up their sleeves. First, under cross-examination, they won from the footman that on 23 May he had been approached by 'a gentleman' who had said 'he would stand my friend and support the prosecution . . . He was a stranger to me,' said Sangster. He also admitted he had 'laid a wager Foote would not play his part at the theatre that night [6 May]' because he 'thought people would not suffer him'. The case was thereby exposed as a prosecution with a third-party interest, and with possible intent to profit on the part of the victim, which counted against Sangster, but not necessarily in a terminal way. None of this was as damning, in Mansfield's eyes, as the seeming errors in Sangster's testimony exposed next by Wallace, Murphy and Hickey for the defence.

They called to the stand the clerk of the Bow Street magistrates, Mr Bond. He affirmed that 'Sangster came in the morning of 6 May. When the Information was taken, he said [the assault took place] "On Monday last." Sir John dictated from the mouth of the man and I wrote. I do not remember a syllable [about] the 1st of May being mentioned that morning.' It became unclear therefore whether the alleged attack had taken place on 1 May, the day the players were supposedly forgathered at the Haymarket, as

Sangster had said, or the 'Monday last' Sangster had also spoken of, which would have been 29 April. Sir John Fielding was called to clear the matter up.

While the court waited for him to arrive, evidence was presented in corroboration of Sangster. Dr Fordyce told the story of Sangster in tears. Campbell, the major-domo at Northend, who had been dismissed, said that 'Sangster a day or two before he left Mr Foote said he was going to leave Mr Foote for reasons he was "too ashamed to express".' And Williams, the coachman who had fetched Sangster's key from Northend for the trunk in Suffolk Street, and had been subpoenaed against his will, swore on oath that 'Sangster asked me if I had heard Mr Foote was a buggerer [*sic*] and I said no. He said he was pretty sure he was [because] Mr Foote had wanted to commit an unnatural crime.' All of which might have proved conclusive in corroboration of Sangster's evidence, had not the blind magistrate Sir John been led at that moment into Westminster Great Hall to give his evidence. He, like his clerk Bond, had little recollection of what Sangster had specifically said about the *date* of the assault but confirmed that Sangster had said it took place just after Foote had addressed the Haymarket company. This proved to be Sangster's undoing.

The defence presented as evidence a newspaper clipping. It was from the *Morning Chronicle* of 3 May 1776 and it reads: 'Foote's Players to meet Monday the 6th May 1776.' By this, Mansfield has scribbled: 'Information: J Sangster "Sangxty" (*vide*)' – for it proved that the moment Sangster had sworn he was being assaulted by his master in Suffolk Street was the same moment at which he had been in fact at Bow Street swearing against his master to Sir John.

Next Jeffrey Pearce of the Haymarket company confirmed to the jurors that though '1st of May was the *usual* day of meeting the players, I and many more went last 1st May on a Wednesday from 12 to 2. Foote never came. At 2, the company went away. No business [was] settled that day.' The meeting had been rearranged and advertised as taking place on the sixth. Other players lined up to confirm this version of events. Sangster's case tottered.

To give a final solution to why he might have so perjured himself, the defence called Mr and Mrs Jewell, Foote's lodgers and fellow actors. For some, Jewell was the least compelling reason to believe Foote's side of things – despite the presence in court of his wife, he was given the telling description in one press report as 'an handsome boy – A Jewel in [Foote's] eye'.[13] But Mansfield credited him with telling the truth, and this is what he said:

> On Friday 3 May, I went early to town. I saw the [senior] Coachman [Williams] and Sangsty & the carriage and horses of Mr Foote at a public house. [They were drunk.] I later went to Northend and Sangsty [said] "You are come to tell my Master you saw me drunk."
> I said "I did not know it, but I see you are drunk now."
> We had words.
> I did not see him till the next day, but I immediately told Mr Foote who went down to discharge him, but he was gone.

Mrs Jewell, Ann Edwards, the maid-cum-actress, confirmed this version of events. So, too, did Mrs Baxter, the Northend house-keeper, and Louis Bally, the Swiss valet, who swore he had lived with Foote for nine years, never suspected him of any impropriety, and that Sangster had 'never complained of any indecent liberties' taken by their master.

As a last-ditch attempt to regain credence in Sangster's testi-mony, the prosecution lawyers called Williams, the other coach-man, back to the stand. Somewhat tarnished in reputation, now that he was suspected also of being a drinker and of having tried to get out of giving evidence at all, or saying anything so long as Foote would give him a good reference, he nonetheless held an important key. If Foote was not addressing the company on 1 May, why wasn't he and where was he? And would it not be reasonable for Sangster to assume that that was what they were doing at the Haymarket whatever day in early May it was?

Williams began to explain that they had driven Foote to Suf-folk Street on 1 May, even though other servants and the Jewells insisted he had stayed in Fulham. He was in the middle of trying to recall whether or not Foote had eaten in town that day when he was interrupted by Hickey, who told the court that, contrary to what Williams had previously sworn, the witness had told him privately that Sangster had never complained about Foote. This was impermissible as evidence, but made its impact on the court: 'Williams told me,' Hickey declaimed, 'that this is a bad accusation.'

At this Mansfield interrupted, and the trial, in effect, was brought to an end. Mansfield felt he and the jury had heard enough.

They were asked to consider their verdict.

§

The press could not report precisely what was said for fear of obscenity prosecution. They could nevertheless ridicule Foote, the one-legged alleged bugger, and they could attack Sangster and his putative motives. For those who championed Foote, and many did, as a maligned enemy of the duchess and much-loved comedian, it was obvious that Sangster must be lying. Jewell had attested to the young man's drink problem, and the joke about 'Roger the Footman' took another turn as Sangster was portrayed as the thwarted blackmailer. The doggerel in the press could even swing both ways, attacking Foote and his 'Roger' in one – the music is lost, but the lyrics exist in various forms for a ditty sung around the West End during the trial, called 'Roger and Sam'.

> 'I love you my Roger, but cannot tell why
> Tis not for your beauty or wit.'
> 'What can it be for sir?' He made his reply:
> 'You love me for what you can get.'[14]

Without the first-hand record from Mansfield and the words he recorded as spoken by John Sangster, the bare bones of the case rang very differently. Foote and the duchess had rowed publicly. Her bigamy trial had ensued; she had lost and been humiliated as roundly as could be imagined. At precisely this moment, a servant came forward with an accusation, a servant who appeared to have been fired for drunkenness, and whose prosecution was funded, it was rightly assumed, by Jackson, the *Ledger* and the duchess. Mansfield may have felt differently after hearing the evidence that was denied a reading public, but he chose to present Foote's innocence to the jury in the most theatrical and tendentious manner possible. The plot was neatly constructed around a third-act accident: the 1 May Haymarket meeting. This did not, unbeknown to Sangster, take place. The hand of Providence, Mansfield intoned, a *deus ex machina* theatrical device, would save Samuel Foote from ignominy, with the aid of the twelve honest men of the Middlesex special jury. Above the hubbub of the other Westminster Great Hall courts, Mansfield addressed them:

> The indictments appear founded on conspiracy, and a prosecution supported by perjury . . . It was expensive, it was cruel . . . The Providence of God interposes . . . to fix on such a day as Mr Foote did *not* go into town, though he had done it for many years back – and in such cases it can only be by Providential means of the Prosecutor's contradicting himself in evidence, that the innocent escape ruin. Gentlemen, I say this more for the sake of the audience than for you; you are in possession of the Evidence, you are masters of the whole matter and will, I do not doubt, do your duty.[15]

The Special Jury of Gentlemen of the Middlesex County did their duty as directed by Mansfield 'without a moment's hesitation' and found the defendant, Mr Samuel Foote, of Suffolk Street and Northend, Fulham, not guilty.

Arthur Murphy left the court immediately. He ran all the way from Westminster Hall up through Whitehall and the royal mews, out of breath, doubtless, by the time he reached the slight incline that is Suffolk Street from the south. Foote was pacing in the very room of the alleged attack, overlooking Suffolk Street at the back of the theatre. When he saw Murphy out of the window, near which the Chinese wallpaper still lay, unused, his friend waved his tricorn hat and smiled. Samuel Foote – who had braved the Haymarket rioters and the prospect of utter ruin and arrest – stumbled on his cork leg and fell to the floor, rasping with tears. The 'wittiest man in London' was unable to speak for more than an hour.

§

Such was the evidence placed in front of the special jury at Westminster Hall, and such was Lord Mansfield's summing up. The jurymen were instructed to acquit on the point that the date, 1 May, of the alleged attack was one on which Foote could prove he was not addressing the Haymarket company, as Sangster had assumed he was. It was a complete alibi. This error in the prosecution case, compounded by the apparent conspiracy against Foote, weighed heavily on Mansfield's mind, which was strange for a number of reasons. Prosecutions were regularly funded by a third party. In cases like Foote's this would very often have been the Society for the Reformation of Manners, founded in 1691 and supporting hundreds of prosecutions, notably against homosexuals, in the mid-eighteenth century. Mansfield had sat on cases so funded in the past and not objected. And it hardly mattered what Foote was doing at the Haymarket on the day of the alleged attack – Sangster had every reason to assume he was at his usual early-May duty of addressing the company.

There was also the clear if tacit support of Foote, in the face of the Jackson and Chudleigh-supported prosecution, of the King himself and influential members of the establishment. Against this was balanced evidence considered so obscene it could not be reported in any London paper or periodical, enunciated by a witness Mansfield chose to disbelieve, largely because he had accepted money to support his legal counsel, and had laid a bet, as many others must have done on the day before that famous Haymarket appearance on 7 May, that Foote would not risk the angry opprobrium of his audience. Dr Fordyce, meanwhile, was assumed to have an animus against Foote, like so many in London, for Foote's cruel impersonation of a family member in a previous satire, which undermined his evidence.

So, Foote was acquitted and, for some, the trial goes down as a malicious prosecution and Foote's place in the history of 'gay martyrdom' as a hinged question over how much his career and health were affected by the ordeal, and how much one counts the insinuation of homosexuality as an attack irrespective of the fact. His health never recovered from the strain, and we now find, in Hunter's notes, documentation of a likely pattern of seizures that gripped him before, during and after the trial. Perhaps he was utterly maligned, a victim only of censure over what it was to be famous in a troubled age. Perhaps he was 'gay' or 'bisexual', and the victim of a malicious prosecution, artfully evaded with the aid, bizarrely, of George III and the Georgian aristocracy, who sided with him against the widowed duchess. Perhaps he was the victim of a paid perjurer and righteously defended by his friends. The establishment seemed at first to rally round him, or against Elizabeth. George Colman the Younger recalled being invited to his father's table around this time and seeing in the dining room with his father Dr Johnson, Edmund Gibbon, Edmund Burke, Garrick, Topham Beauclerk, Joshua Reynolds and an apparently rehabilitated Samuel Foote.[16] And in June, at King George III's thirty-eighth birthday reception, it was noted that there was 'Much nobility, plus Messers Garrick, Colman, Sheridan, Harris . . . and Foote.'[17] He tried to re-establish himself at the centre of the established order. But it was not to be.

§

There was a third possibility – and one that seems more plausible now, given what has come to light only recently of Sangster's evidence, Foote's mental state and, strangely, the records of Christie's auctioneers. This third possibility is hinged on the unexpected evidence from the Sale of Foote's Effects by Mr Christie and the tour it afforded of Mr Foote's private home for a curious

London audience. For that, however, they would have to wait until after his death, but the London public, confused and ambivalent about the guilt or innocence of the English Aristophanes, did not have to wait very long. Within months of the trial's end, Foote had been forced to quit the Haymarket stage. In less than a year he was dead.

CURTAIN CALL

This life is but a tragic comic jest,
And all is farce or mummery at best.

Samuel Foote[1]

FOOTE WENT DOWNHILL RAPIDLY after the momentous events of 1776. His health deteriorated precipitously, he lost weight to the alarm of his friends and audience, and his 'fits', or strokes, continued and worsened. He began to move quickly in the negotiations he had started before the trial to sell his interest in the Haymarket and lease his patent to George Colman the Elder, perhaps aware that he might not be able to perform for much longer. He did all this in tandem with a spirited attack upon William Jackson for libel, which was thwarted only by Jackson's own hasty trip to Calais in the footsteps of his duchess. Foote appeared to be a man in a hurry.

The Jackson case proceeded swiftly. It looked as though it would go easily in Foote's favour. And the Haymarket was known to be a going concern, with or without Foote and his plays, such that Foote could boast to Garrick that 'opponents are numerous' in competition for the lease. It was agreed that Colman would gain control of the Haymarket, with Foote remaining as occasional writer and performer, if his health allowed, but the details were kept secret until after the conclusion of the buggery trial, the outcome of which closely informed Foote's marketability. The

support of some continued. Queen Charlotte invited Foote to one
of her overcrowded drawing rooms in January 1777, and Arthur
Murphy, in his last play, *Know Your Own Mind*, created a heroically
comic character called Dashwood, who was taken to be an affectionate portrait of Foote. But others shunned him. The cloud of
scandal hung heavily and the slow descent of his reputation into
embarrassed obscurity began. Even Foote noted that the younger
male members of his company 'now all come in pairs'.[2]

Early in 1777 Foote wrote to his old friend Sarah Hussey-
Delaval, Lady Mexborough, to thank her for her 'compassionate
kindness' during his trial. He had waited, he wrote, for 'an hour's
relaxation from pain' in order to put quill to paper, and had been
delayed further by headaches and 'an artery having burst yesterday', leading to a great loss of blood. The blood vessels in his leg
were rupturing, but his doctors were less alarmed by this distressing symptom than by the apparent effect of the trauma of his trial
upon his mental state. To judge by Hunter's notes, this might as
easily have been caused by a growing brain tumour. In a plaintive
postscript to his letter to Lady Mexborough, Foote wrote, 'What
a trouble have I been to all your Family!'[3] neatly summarizing
where he stood on the Delaval house-party of 1766 and the ensuing
accident: it was costing him still in mental and physical anguish.
He was a broken man.

His terms with George Colman the Elder over the lease of the
Haymarket stipulated that Foote would perform in some of his
more famous roles. The running of the theatre would be turned
over to Colman, who had previously run Covent Garden, for
£1,600 pounds a year for the term of Foote's life, and £500 as a
buy-out on the rights to all Foote's plays, even though Foote
insisted he could get £1,000 'if to be sold to the Trade'.[4] Foote
would become an annuitant on his own lease as patent-holder,
and, if he owned the freehold, which is unclear but possible, he
made this over to Colman, too. To this day, the legality of all this
is uncertain. The terms of the 1766 licence were categorical: the
Theatre Royal licence was for Foote and Foote alone; 'transfer

or alienation . . . are to be deemed Void and of None Effect',
according to the original Haymarket statutes.⁵ Nevertheless, the
St James's Chronicle of 26 October 1776 reported that 'Mr Colman
had at last purchased Mr Foote's patent.' Perhaps out of respect
for Foote, or a discreet desire not to rake over the business of his
disgrace, the royal household failed to address the terms of the
royal patent, which stayed in place. Consequently the Theatre
Royal tag has stuck ever since, in a sense erroneously.

Foote expressed a keen willingness to appear in the 1777
summer season, to reinforce the message that he was an innocent,
slandered man, but his health was simply not up to the demands
of live comedy and it was unclear also how sympathetic the
London audience really was. He appeared in *The Nabob*, and
The Devil Upon Two Sticks, but audiences were now wary of him,
divided about his once universally appealing sexual ambivalence
and alarmed by his physical deterioration.

Foote's last performances in 1777 were distressing affairs. It was
put out that he was suffering from rheumatism 'which on occasion
prevented his performing'⁶ but his bravado, used to such heroic
effect before the trial and in the months just following the amputation, deserted him. Increasingly shambolic and confused, the
implosion of a star persona became a spectacle in itself, and sold
tickets for Colman and Jewell for all the wrong reasons. There is
one highly unusual, and avowedly partisan, account of Foote on
stage at the very twilight of his career, most probably in May 1777.
It makes for harrowing reading, in its depiction of a man who had
once made the entire Haymarket rock with laughter:

> The Prompters Bell rings. The music stops. From the side-
> wing advances on the top of a grossly ill-made body a large
> inexpressive apology of a face, with a mix'd stare from the
> hazy eyes, its okerhued [*sic*] complexion flaringly illuminated
> with rouge. As soon as the figure hath fidelingly hobbled on
> the middle of the stage a short necked bow ensues with a
> circling leer rather than a smile at the audience. While he
> speaks, his head frequently drops and rises like a duck in a

pond. [From] the up and down jerking, fidgeting and tightened sprawling of his hands . . . the tremulous relaxation lately
observable in his cheeks . . . it is apprehended that he is not
far from a like disaster in the countenance . . . as he hath
already inherited a wooden supplement . . . And from this
unbrac'd state of the fibres we can account for the whissling
[at the] unsteadiness of his . . . speaking . . . which he injudi-
ciously variegates with frequent gratings, shivers, and fritters
of pronunciation . . . His utterance is never melodiously pleasing, but hurried, or husky, or growling and sometimes inar-
ticulate . . . and his forced laughs . . . are like the convulsed
exertion of apes . . . It is to be presumed that a mortal who
has taken such wanton and unpardonable liberties with others,
cannot be offended at our remonstrance . . . wherefore such
idle and unavailing efforts hereafter will make the disapproving public cry out with general indignation.

No more – again be in the bottle ramm'd
Offensive scribbler and actor damn'd.[7]

Then, on 6 June 1777, Foote fell suddenly onto the stage in the
middle of a performance of *The Devil Upon Two Sticks*. He lay there
shaking. When an accident happens on stage, audience and actors
alike tend to freeze. After a few minutes of this *tableau tremblant*
the curtain was brought down. The prompter addressed the audience to say that Mr Foote was 'suddenly affected with a paralytic
stroke'. Colman decided immediately that this would 'compel' his
star performer to take the advice his friends had been proffering.
He was forced to retire.[8]

§

John Hunter advised Foote to quit London instantly for France, or
to head for the coast for a sea cure. The imperative at the time,
as now, has a dual implication: Foote was evidently unfit for performing, but he was also being hushed away out of town. It was
announced publicly that he was finally quitting the stage, and
ceding the Haymarket to Colman permanently. Some old friends

had the decency to mark the occasion with solemnity – notably
Garrick, who was also retiring from live performance and ceding
his theatre patent. But where Foote was ill and disgraced, Garrick
was bowing out in the full face of public adoration. He had the
grace to treat the retirement of his old friend and adversary with
solemn style:

> When Mr Foote retired from the stage Mr Garrick ordered
> the lights [at Drury Lane] to be let down, which consisted of
> six chandeliers hanging over the stage, every one containing
> twelve candles in brass sockets and a heavy iron flourished
> and joined to each bottom, large enough for a street palisade.
> This ceremony being complied with, Mr Garrick said it would,
> with the lamps also lowered, be a convincing proof to the
> audience that *all was over*.[9]

Foote spent the summer in Brighthelmstone – Brighton as it
would become – with Louis Bally, his spirits briefly lifted by the
rakish company of John Wilkes and Lord Lyttelton. In October he
returned to London and held his last dinner at Northend. It was a
sombre affair compared to previous occasions, though it still kept
to the theatrical calendar: it was a Sunday night. Guests included
Caleb Whitefoorde,[10] the Jewells and Archibald Hamilton of Fleet
Street, Foote's publisher. It was the last time they would see the
elegant contents of the villa until the sale at Christie's three months
later. Foote was said to be 'in as good a state of health as at any
time since his illness'[11] had begun. But it was a farewell party
before he quit the country for France. He travelled from Northend
back into Suffolk Street to pack up there, but was advised by
Hunter to spend time first back on the south coast to try to gain
strength before traversing the Channel.

Foote travelled to Brighton and later to Dover with Bally. By
the end of October, he was waiting for the tides and weather at
the Dover harbourside Ship Inn. He was familiar to the staff there
from previous trips to France and soon 'set all the servants in a
roar at his jokes and stories', being, according to another report,

'remarkably cheerful and diverting'.[12] On the morning of 21 October he had Bally strap on his leg, then walked to the quay and back again, about eleven, to check on the tides, but 'complained of being cold, and told [Bally] to warm a cloth and rub him with it as he feared a return of his disorder [the stroke] was approaching'.

Bally persuaded him to go to bed where, in a short time, he was seized with a tremulous fit, which lasted for upwards of three hours, and agitated his body violently, 'particularly the thigh from which his leg had been amputated', but did not at all affect his face. 'As soon as the fit was over he lay composed, and seemed inclined to sleep. Upon his valet offering to leave the room, he bid him stay, and putting his hand in his, lay pretty quiet for a few minutes, then began to breathe in a moaning tune, at length, fixing his eyes hard on the servant, he fetched a deep sigh and expired.'[13]

It was two p.m. on 21 October 1777.

§

Jewell was one of the first to get news of Foote's death, as he was staying at the house at Suffolk Street. Dr Johnson knew by the second day: 'Did you see Foote at Brighthelmstone?' he wrote to a Brighton friend. 'Did you think he would so soon be gone? Life, says Falstaff, is a shuttle. He was a fine fellow in his way; and the world is really impoverished by his sinking glories. Murphy ought to write his life, at least to give the world a *Footeana*. Now will any of his contemporaries bewail him? Will Genius change *his sex* to weep? I would really have his life written with diligence.'[14]

By Sunday, 26 October, Jewell had prepared everything in Dover for the return of Foote's body. The corpse, dressed by Louis Bally, 'arrived in Charing Cross . . . about eight o'clock Monday evening . . . brought to town for the interment,' one paper was moved to note, 'at the particular request of several of his intimate friends'.[15] The funeral was set for 3 November.[16]

Despite the seeming collusion of the King himself in supporting

Foote through the trial, attitudes shifted markedly once he was dead, or after the last shambolic appearances at the Haymarket. For those of an Old Testament cast of mind his sudden demise was read as a judgement. 'Alas poor Sam,' was all Doctor Johnson was heard to remark that day in Gough Square, and he, like everyone else Foote knew, from the Bedford to the theatre to Downing Square, declined to attend the funeral.[17] It became apparent that even the Haymarket company would not be expected there, for fear, perhaps, of public outcry. His Majesty's Company of Comedians watched instead their master's final exit at the stage door of the Haymarket from the top walls of the James Street tennis courts. This parapet adjoined their dressing rooms and gave them, too, their exits and entrances, unseen by their creditors who blocked the stage door.[18] They removed their hats, and some their wigs.

The Hunters, it is presumed, had kept Foote's leg at their anatomy school on Windmill Street, where indeed it might have stayed as a curio of celebrity and surgery, but someone, presumably Jewell, asked for it to be brought to Suffolk Street. John Hunter is almost certain to have asked to examine Foote's skull, but no post-mortem was allowed, or it would appear in the case book with the many others. Foote's other leg was reunited with him within a coffin that was elaborately upholstered, inside and out, with the same studded scarlet Genoese velvet[19] that decorated the royal box at the Haymarket.[20] It took six men to lift the coffin, even before it was occupied. Wrapped in cerecloth, encased in lead, the actor-manager went to meet his Maker, in whom he had held intermittent faith, in theatrical style and, at last, with 'a sufficiency of limbs for the role'. He was carried out through the long hallway of his Suffolk Street house, under Zoffany's portraits of him as his most famous characters, and past busts depicting William Shakespeare, David Garrick, Samuel Johnson and himself, Sam Foote, into the little back-alley by the royal mews.

A few hundred yards away, Benjamin Fidoe, clerk of works to Westminster Abbey, was counting out money: ten shillings extra that evening for four night-time bell-ringers, torches and torch-bearers, and extra pennies, too, for the abbey's undertaker, Mr Galley, to ensure the latter's discretion. 'The pall was supported by intimate acquaintances,' wrote the *Morning Chronicle* the next day, but the reports were in error. The funerary records kept by Fidoe make it clear that pallbearers had to be hired and paid and the reported 'long train of friends'[21] was likewise made up of a few hired Westminster schoolboys. There was 'no choir, no anthem' at Foote's torch-lit funeral, and the lone abbey cantor[22] rushed through the Book of Common Prayer, 'merely what is read over every pauper that is buried by the parish',[23] his graveyard scene illuminated only by the flicker of torches held aloft by Louis Bally, Jewell,[24] Foote's publisher Hamilton, and the other beneficiary of his will, the illegitimate or adopted boy named Frank.[25]

It didn't go unnoticed that the celebrated Mr Foote had the quietest of funerals. Though his friends in high places had helped him weather the trial, in death he was shunned. For many, despite his acquittal and the likely victory in his libel action, Foote had been outed. Mrs Thrale took some pains to inform Dr Johnson that in her opinion Foote was 'in some better place', before she went on to insinuate that he had been heading to France not for better air but to avoid further litigation. A private note written in the margin of her letters observed that 'Doctor Johnson was not aware that Foote broke his heart because of a hideous detection; he was trying to run away from England, and from infamy, but death stopped him.'[26] Many were of the same opinion. The combination of an accusation of homosexuality and a trip to France drew one inevitable conclusion. That became the black joke: that Samuel Foote, the one-legged bugger, was running away to France after the ignominy of the trial or the prospect of another, but died in Dover waiting for the ferry.

The records of Westminster Abbey yield little on the hushed burial of Samuel Foote, but beg one important question: who were his heirs? The little boys who were the beneficiaries of his will are named, but only in his will, as Frank and George Foote.

'He bequeathed his possessions,' the record states, 'in trust for his two illegitimate sons . . . with remainder, if they should die in their minority, partly to William Jewell, treasurer of the Haymarket Theatre.'[27] The will, however, was a decade old, and one of the boys, George, seems to have died. Their mother might have been one of two women who feature in Foote's cruel jokes about a mistress – but even here, the comic verve that introduces an ''er indoors' may or may not refer to a real person. In one, Foote narrates a mistress who left him for a bass-viol player from the orchestra. When she regretted her choice and returned to him, he told her, 'But madam, have you not been basely violated, and do you want to run your gamut on me?'[28] In another supposedly jocund anecdote, Foote described walking with his two little boys and being asked by a French acquaintance '*Sont-ils par la même mère?*' Foote's reply, or punch line, went '*Oui* – by the same mare, but I have strong doubts by the same horse.'[29]

A writer in 1830 named this mistress as one Jane Nuthall 'who lived to an advanced age', and therefore may have been a former acquaintance;[30] and a separate reference sadly supposes George Foote dead by 1777.[31] One George Foote, son of 'Samuel Foote', is recorded as being baptized at St Martin's in the Fields in 1767. The mother is noted simply as 'Mary' though Mary Foote, Sam's wife, had died in 1763, and to perplex slightly further, the birth takes place about nine months after Foote's amputation. There are no records of any children under the name Frank Foote or Nuthall being born or baptized in the relevant period in London or the south of England.[32] Perhaps Frank carried, initially, the name of another mother, some other guardian or possible natural father. Perhaps, given that the boys were called Frank and George, Delaval rather than Dineley-Goodere-Foote names, they were in the tradition of the little Roach children: fruits of Frank Delaval's catholic labours, and godfathered, like other Francises and Franceses, by Foote, and in one case baptized as his son, born to a dead wife. The Regency theatre star Maria Foote, later Countess of Harrington, let it be written that she was a descendant of Samuel Foote, without ever clarifying how, or if, her father was 'Frank Foote'. The boys disappear from record except in terms of the sale their inheritance necessitated, as Colman did not honour his commitment to pay the Foote heir or heirs the annuity on the Haymarket: he simply paid off Frank Foote and found it simpler not to mention that the 'Royal' name of the theatre was tied to Foote alone.

As a result of his hushed-up obsequies and lonely death, the drama of his ending was more firmly imprinted on those who remained, and immediately work began on preserving elements of his fame, his *bons mots* and his unpublished plays. Arthur Murphy, his old friend, encouraged by Dr Johnson, wrote, 'If I have health enough, my intention is to write the life of SAMUEL FOOTE; whose memory I now esteem and value; a man to whose company I owe some of the greatest pleasures of my life.'[33] But he never did, and it was Lord Byron, who grew up with Foote's image firmly in his mind as a ruined jester and a tragic fool, who left him instead his only literary epitaph:

> Farce follow'd Comedy and reach'd her prime
> In ever-laughing Foote's fantastic time.
> Nor church nor state escaped his public sneers,
> Arms, nor the gown, priests, lawyers, volunteers.
> 'Alas poor Yorick!' now for ever mute!
> Whoever loves a laugh must sigh for Foote.[34]

No marker was ever erected, and his exact grave site has since been lost. No application was risked by his friends to the Dean and Chapter of Westminster for the erection 'of monument or even a tablet'.[35] The abbey archives list only the side of the cloister – the West Side – as his resting place, furthest from Poets' Corner and traditionally a side reserved for lowly abbey servants, like Fidoe, who buried him. Schoolchildren run laughing over his resting place, these days, as the abbey has seen fit to install a cafeteria over adjacent graves. In death, as in life, the theatre star Samuel Foote is accompanied by jocund bustle, laughter and, as in his theatre, by the oil-sweet smell of orange peel.

AFTERPIECES

A SINGULAR TALENT

BOSWELL: 'Foote; he had a singular talent.'
DR JOHNSON: 'Sir, Foote's was not a talent, it was
    a vice . . .'[1]

Foote's story properly starts with crime, and ends with it, too, for
to understand him, and for that matter his times, is to try to
understand the violent undercurrents below the elegant terracing
of eighteenth-century London. Like the shape and architecture of
the new London through which Foote limped, the Georgian age
sought to confine behind neo-classical façades the tumultuous and
emerging truths of a new world and the troubling nature of being
human. The elegant canvases of Foote's friends Reynolds and
Zoffany are no less accurate depictions of the times than the
earthiness and violence of Hogarth, whom he also knew. It was all
true. Foote's life and works are vital testaments in understanding
his times, but also, indubitably, our own. Foote also left an
astonishing body of work. One recent historian has written that it
is rare to find, from the well-documented terrain of Georgian
London, a figure like Foote, so 'notorious, significant, brilliant' yet
now so 'completely ignored'.[2]

His significance is various, and is only partly to do with the
plays. Though these are described as 'a surer and more lively guide
to the mid-eighteenth century . . . than [plays] of other dramatists
and actors who have received far more attention',[3] their close

concern with personal parody and impersonation, as well as the centrality in the later plays of an actor with 'one leg too few', has combined to narrate their obscurity. The title his French friends gave Foote of the English Aristophanes was as partial as the subsequent claim that he was an eighteenth-century Oscar Wilde. He resembled the ancient Greek in his broad, sometimes lewd humour, and the ease with which he ridiculed vice and hypocrisy in an age dissipate with new-found freedoms. He especially resembled Aristophanes in his depiction of real people on stage, recognizable characters in a city in thrall to personality – audaciously so because in theory such caricature was illegal. But he was less than an Aristophanes in the themes he chose to address: his satire was biting, but it evaded universal issues in favour of the shallower waters of fashion. Foote wrote that Molière's *Les Femmes savantes* had 'in fifteen days put an entire stop to female pedantry in Paris'. None of his plays could boast such successful satirical impact.

For students of the history of comedy, however, his plays are important genealogy. The ridiculing of vanity and of class pretension has remained a mainstay of British comedy ever since. The antecedents for classic situations recognizable in modern sit-com abound. These would include the clash of cultures and snobberies to be found in *The Englishman in Paris* and *The Englishman Returned from Paris*, as well as the upstairs-downstairs comedy of *The Nabob* and *The Lame Lover*. Recognizable, too, are the mistaken identity, or 'screen', scenes from *The Author*, *The Lame Lover* and *The Patron*. *The Maid of Bath* and *The Knights* both closely informed *The Rivals*. *The Minor* has strong parallels in the character and circumstances of Charles Surface in *The School for Scandal*. This is merely the close cross-pollination of comedy of the era: originality was neither chased nor applauded. Many of the plays, though rarely performed, have their place as signifiers simply of what was funny *then*. Foote frequently spun comic plots out of relatives returning after long absences to make unexpected discoveries about long-lost loves. This was the real human scale of a dawning empire and an industrial revolution, the new world in action, but became stock-in-trade for the new sentimentalist dramas of the later eighteenth and early nineteenth centuries.

One can recognize also Foote's descendants in the comedies of then and now: the stupid son of proud parents: Tim in *The Knights* or Caleb in *Taste*; the wicked stepmother Lady Riscounter in *The Bankrupt*; the apparently naïve young wife who reveals herself an arch manipulator in the war of the sexes, Becky in *The Author*; the vain middle-aged woman who falls for flattery, the clear precursor to Mrs Malaprop, Mrs Pentweazle in *Taste*; the miser, Flint, in *The Maid of Bath* and Penurious Trifle in *The Knights*, the pretentious aesthetes, Lord Dupe in *Taste*, Sir Matthew Mite in *The Nabob*, Cadwallader in *The Author* are all standard 'types' such that Foote's claim to Boswell that he had given the English stage sixteen new comic archetypes[4] suddenly does not seem so preposterous a boast. Intriguing to relate, Foote was able and willing to interpolate new material into nearly all of his plays, and did this with relish in those that dealt with more topical themes. As a result *The Devil Upon Two Sticks* and *The Minor*, for example, exist in multiple forms and had some life beyond Foote's demise – usually with Tate Wilkinson, 'that mere mimic's mimic', playing Foote, even down to his swaying gait.

However, as one critic complained of *The Lame Lover*, 'the drama leaves all parties as it found them, for it contains no plot,' which was true enough but beside the point: it contained sufficient situation and character to amuse and to parody, a framework of relationships, not unlike long-running TV sit-coms, that could be used and reused for differing satirical ends. 'Comedy,' wrote Foote, 'I define to be an exact representation of the peculiar manners of those people among whom it happens to be performed; a faithful imitation' of a recognizable truth. This is at odds with our idea of knock-about eighteenth-century comedy, with its 'slap-sticks' to literally beat home a joke, its 'clap-trap' dialogue to gain applause, and direct appeals in prologue and epilogue to an audience. Foote was trained in naturalism. His skill as a comedian was in depicting that which appeared real, and painfully so, to its live audience.

Little wonder, then, that the texts of his plays are now considered arcane, that, to quote an early-twentieth-century theatre drama-turg, 'His concern was to lose the universal in the particular and for this he paid a heavy price: oblivion.'[5] Tate Wilkinson was aware of this by the end of the 1790s, and in trying to revive Foote's plays wrote: 'Ask any young man of twenty five about these personages [satirized in plays of Foote's from the 1750s] and he will be [unable] to answer.'[6]

It is as a chronicler and satirist of eighteenth-century city life that Foote holds his place as a dramatist: as a social historian, in effect, who is also a comic. In terms of the fashions, foibles and obsessions of Georgians, they are telling documents. Here and there, in his attacks on Methodism, nabobs and the medical establishment, his comedy packed political punch. But his real triumphs were personally more than politically motivated, and his greatest dramas happened offstage. Whatever the odds stacked against him, and there were many even before the amputation and its effect upon his mental health, Foote turned things to his own account and to comedy. His daring, his refusal to bow to conven-tion and to domestic or artistic safety, makes him still commanding of our attention.

Somewhere in the dark of the ill-lit wings lies the truth about Samuel Foote – about his guilt or innocence, the real intention of his flight from the Haymarket and his disappearances to Paris and Dublin, his psychosis that so fascinated John Hunter and the whereabouts of his hugger-mugger-buried corpse. And some of this Samuel Foote intended us never to know. It is the myth-making that is also worthy of our attention. It is not just a prurient interest in the home-lives of the rich and famous that links us to the concerns of the Georgians. A fascination with apparent moral decay, a rabid media, commercial boom and bust, distant wars and economic and fiscal disasters: these are all as familiar to our own age as they became to Foote's, as, suddenly, was celebrity.

Spectators in Georgian London became enchanted with per-formers, Peg Woffington and Kitty Clive, Garrick and Foote, all of them painted by the new celebrity portraitist, Reynolds, and all of them beginning to manipulate anecdotes about their private lives that helped create an aura of availability, not just sexual, allowing audience and readership a fantastical journey into imagined lives, which Lord Byron would go on to do to such great and profitable effect a half-generation later. This marks the beginning of celebrity as a projection of our fantasies onto others. London, with its easy anonymity, its dozens of newspapers and hundreds of print shops, its literate, prurient population, its sociable coffee-houses and theatres, its pleasure gardens and assembly rooms, London was the necessary midwife to the birth of modern urban celebrity, and Foote, as Byron pointed out,[7] its irascible firstborn. Samuel Foote launched himself with a tale of horrific murder from the unique position of a family member. People thought they knew him because they knew *of* him, even before they saw him on stage. He blended this novel form of celebrity, and the novel form of crime-narrative, with a frisson of dynastic intrigue and more than a hint that this vicious family background had tainted his own psyche. Then he parried the expectations of his audience into a unique discourse with them, as prologue speaker and then as interpreter on stage – as Bayes the playwright or Sam Foote the wit – where he stood outside the business of performance to be also himself, a comic, a celebrity.

If modernity is characterized as in part a consciousness of oneself as self-creating, then Foote, perforce, is one major voice at its dawning, and a funny one. If this birth is marked by the launch into commerce of a personal life, then Foote's narrative, from fratricide through amputation to scandalous sex-crime, looks pre-scient as much as tragic. The loss of his leg, and the projection therefore of a despoiled masculinity, as a limping icon of pain and accident – two key ingredients in comedy – made him all the more fascinating as a star, caught, as it were, in the act of falling. Finally there was his Icarus-like descent from the heat of fame when, for whatever reasons, he pushed too hard against the establishment, or picked, in Elizabeth Chudleigh and 'Roger' Sangster, the wrong foes, and then fell both publicly and scandalously and became, for some, 'the opposite of a man'.

That summer of 1776 can seem arrestingly modern in its free-wheeling mixture of celebrity, censure and censoriousness, all in the face of fiscal crashes and revolutions of global consequence: 'Oh madness,' Horace Walpole wrote, 'to have squandered such an empire!'[8] But if anything is instantly recognizable in the story of Sam Foote, it is the creation of the modern trope of the celebrity destroyed, the star trammelled in the mud, who then, ideally, has some comeback either in life, or after death, though Foote, of course, did not. It is this quasi-Christian geometry, the rise and fall and possible resurrection, that signals a more profound need for the projection of celebrity than gossip columns might suggest. For some, the attacks upon a famous actor, with charges of homosexuality and of sexual assault, make Foote a sort of martyr irrespective of the veracity of either 'charge'. For us still, in thrall to the evolving culture of the famous, he is uniquely placed in the tragicomic business of stardom: a body of evidence, in and of himself, that we are as drawn to the pain of celebrity as to its glister.

THE BODY OF EVIDENCE
OR A LAST AUCTION OF EFFECTS

A CATALOGUE
OF THE GENUINE
Neat Household Furniture
Large Wardrobe of Table and Bed Linen
Fine Pictures and Prints, China
CARRIAGES
Farming and Garden Utensils, A Rick of Hay
LIVE and DEAD STOCK
And many other valuable effects
Of Samuel Foote Esq., deceased

. . .

January 29th 1778

. . .

Catalogues may be had at the Pack Horse, Turnham
Green . . . and of Messrs Christie and Ansell[1] . . .

Before Foote left London on the 'journey that would be his last',[2] he walked slowly around the Suffolk Street house. The noise of Colman rehearsing the company at the Haymarket spilled into his home. 'He went into the room where the picture of Weston and Foote together in *The Devil Upon Two Sticks* hung. Foote stopped in front of it, until tears started in [his eyes] and then turning away

379

exclaimed "Poor Weston!" [3] This circulated as an anecdote suffi-ciently widely for *Gentleman's Magazine* to quote it the following month, and again when the house was opened to a curious public before the sale of Foote's effects.[4]

Weston had died in the previous January, to the surprise of no one: he had been drinking himself into an early grave for decades. Foote once caught him in Suffolk Street, sneaking an entire gin bottle into the wings of the Haymarket; Weston claimed it con-tained 'seltzer spa water'.[5] Foote tasted it and flung it to the ground, but Weston refused to go on until his gin was replaced. It was. Perhaps Foote smiled at the memory. He then turned away from the portrait and said, 'Alas, poor Weston: it will very soon be "poor Foote",' and walked out of Suffolk Street for the last time.

On 26, 27 and 28 January 1777 the house was opened to the public. Londoners could take the same tour of the house that Foote had done. It was a theatrical epilogue of sorts: the viewing before the sale of the estate of Samuel Foote, with all the effects – paintings, books and *objets d'art*, still in place.

In the basements under King Street, St James's, is the last piece of the jigsaw, along with Lord Mansfield's Scone Palace manu-scripts and the notes discovered of the doctor, John Hunter, that rebuilds the final acts of Foote: the records of the sale of his estate and the catalogue that details the contents of each room. Mr Christie listed everything as and where it lay, from the Zoffany canvases to the porcelain artichoke plates to Northend livestock and carriages. The sale would yield a total of £1,643 13*s.* 10*d.* – twice the value of the entire library of one nobleman sold later that year. The Haymarket company members bid for costumes and books; others, including Samuel Johnson and Edmund Burke, bought enamel paintings, tortoiseshell boxes and gold snuff boxes.[6] The Zoffanys sold for at least forty pounds each. Suffolk Street had also been Foote's dressing room, so curious Londoners could view his prosthesis, his large collection of theatrical costumes and his many mirrors. There were diamond rings, cluster rings and hand-painted buttons that could be sewn onto different costumes.[7] There were two brass blunderbusses, a neat Woodstock and hilted sword, and an 'air pump with glasses and apparatus',[8] a gift from the Delavals, a memento of wild times at Seaton Delaval and Downing Square, before it had all gone so horribly wrong.

The sale of Foote's books and plays was unprecedented in a bibliophile age. Edmund Burke bought many volumes, but so too did members of the Haymarket company. There were first editions of Dr Johnson's *Dictionary* and the complete works of Ben Jonson, Pope, Congreve, Milton, Marvell, Goldsmith, Smollett, Shakespeare, and the dramas of Molière, Marivaux, Racine, Corneille, Montesquieu and Voltaire. Various of these, along with the 'best known edition' of the 1692 *Collected Ben Jonson*[9] and a rare edition of the memoirs of the transvestite Chevalier d'Éon, were bought by the King himself, via an intermediary; they ended up in the Royal Collection, and form, consequently, a large part of the relevant theatrical sections of the British Library today.

It was also the first ever keyhole view of the private world of a celebrity. As Londoners walked around the house, they could assess the numbered lots, assiduously recorded by Mr Christie, and imagine the celebrated Mr Foote 'at home', a vitrine on a lost life and the one angle on him they had until now been denied. It is also the view we have been denied, as was Lord Mansfield in Westminster. Towards the end of the catalogue are those smaller lots Mr Christie does not accord the courtesy of tallying by buyer. A heavy lead bath. Some songbird cages – one fit only for a servant. A broken bedstead, for an under-footman, along with his uniforms, and the one-legged undergarments of a man who would no longer need them – yet who would? And Chinese wallpaper. Unused. Left in the window bay at the back of the Haymarket, just beyond the sound of laughter, where no coachman's eyes could ever fall.

In every physical point, on the subject of baths and clothes, horses and haylofts, Sangster's evidence stands up two hundred years later with the unexpected corroborative source of an auctioneer's precise cataloguing of what was where. The physical world of Sangster and his master – at Fulham as well as Suffolk Street –

down to the weight of the bath, the buckles on Foote's fake shoe that Sangster polished, the broken bedstead and the crimson curtains in his garret,[10] are all there to be restaged in the mind's eye. Only the protagonists have left the boards: *ob-scena*. And in the upper room at Suffolk Street, where John Sangster could never have been except by invitation, exactly as he had described it, was the valuable Chinese wallpaper due to be put up, still in rolls by the window, and away from the front window, removed from the wall, as if the attack had only just taken place, was the mirror, thirty-seven inches by twenty-three,[11] that Sangster had fetched down for his master.

That Sangster saw wallpaper in a room he should never have entered except at his master's bidding is not, of course, proof. We often lie while being true to specific domestic detail. This would not hold up in a court now or then as guilt beyond reasonable doubt. But it does give the sort of three-dimensionality to tendentious historical testimony that a historian rarely has the opportunity to enjoy.

As does the record of Foote's amateur 'psychoanalyst'. John Hunter attested privately, in a record unavailable to the court, that Foote's behaviour, always erratic, was increasingly reckless and inexplicably self-destructive, and hypothesized that he had brain damage, by whatever cause, in areas now known to disinhibit, and even disinhibit sexually. A malicious prosecution, as it doubtless was, that began the swift final decline of Foote's mind and body was perhaps also a malicious dismissal of a young man utterly out of his depth in the Foote household. Sangster exits the historical record after 1776. Unemployable in London, he left. If Foote was guilty, as now seems entirely possible, he is not 'guilty' of being 'gay' but is implicated in a particularly ugly form of sexual harassment, however vitiated by his troubled psyche. It seems now possible, given the array of evidence unexpectedly extant, that our comic hero, maligned by prejudice and unexpectedly maintained by privilege though he was, was also the domestic villain in his tawdry last scene.

The human touch of the dead brushes softly, indistinguishable often from the breath of invention; those scratch-marks of lives lived and lies loaded that are etched, unexpectedly, on place or paper and are the stuff of crime as well as history. What might or might not have passed between two people, practised both in the Georgian and theatrical arts of surfaces, and in crime, may fall beyond the ken of a historian but the biography of a performer is perforce also the exculpation of myth. 'The past,' E. M. Forster wrote, 'is devoid of all moral dangers and one meets with perfect ease not only kings but people even rarer.'[12] These etchings are the darker hues – the other side of being alive – that Foote was always willing to risk in his work, from his first crime narrative to his last laugh. They are, in a sense, too, the *workings* in a work of art: that which should accompany us from the wings onto the stage when presenting a rounded humanity at the beck of laughter or a more tragic muse. To stand in the ill-lit backstage, slightly to the side of a fully knowable truth, is the business that a biographer and an actor share. Like standing in Suffolk Street by the side of the Haymarket, or in a darkened theatre, trying to recall the sound of laughter.

FINIS

Dramatis Personae

SAMUEL FOOTE, 1720–77 Our hero: a role for which two legs are usually considered the minimum requirement. First celebrity impressionist, original Patentee of the Theatre Royal, Haymarket, crime-writer, playwright, dandy and wit; originator of the 'matinée', and of the term 'Tea Party' to indicate a political satire. On being accused of one-legged sexual assault upon an employee, 'Roger the Footman,' he is said to have quipped, 'Sodomite? I'll not stand for it.'

CAST IN ALPHABETICAL ORDER

ISAAC BICKERSTAFFE, 1733–1812?   Homosexual Anglo-Irish playwright, librettist and former page to Lord Chesterfield, Bickerstaffe collaborated with Thomas Arne and Samuel Foote, among others, for ventures at Drury Lane and Covent Garden, but fled England in 1772, never to return, after a scandal involving a guardsman in a London park.

JAMES BOSWELL, 1740–95   Scottish lawyer, philanderer, exegete to Dr Johnson and the 'greatest biographer in the English language', Boswell ran away to London in 1760, lodging on Downing Square very close to Frank Delaval's and becoming part of the linked orbits of literary and theatrical London that brought him, eventually, the close friendship of Samuel Johnson, the acquaintance of Samuel Foote and, for that matter, the roundelay of actresses from whom he contracted seventeen separate bouts of VD. His three-penny pamphlet on Foote, *Observations, Good, Bad, Stupid or Clever, Serious or Jocular, on Squire Foote's Dramatic Entertainment entitled The Minor*, was published in 1760 under Boswell's pseudonym of *A. Genius*. The *Monthly Review* described it as containing 'all its humour on the title-page'.

WILLIAM BROMFEILD, 1713–92 Son of a Holborn 'druggist', who rose to be Master of the Company of Surgeons, later the Royal College. Concussion specialist, designer of surgical instruments and personal surgeon to the Dowager Princess of Wales, his one play, *The Schemers*, was performed at Drury Lane in 1755 in aid of the Lock Hospital. He amputated Samuel Foote's leg in 1766.

ELIZABETH CHUDLEIGH, DUCHESS OF KINGSTON, COUNTESS OF BRISTOL 1720–88 Vamp, slattern, fortune-hunter, scandal-monger or proto-feminist victim of a misogynist society, depending on your point of view or that of the coffee-house gossips of Hogarth's London, 'The Chudleigh' was the most infamous woman in Georgian England.

KITTY CLIVE, 1711–85 Half-Irish leading lady at Drury Lane, kinswoman by marriage to Clive of India, soprano, comedienne and famed beauty; her impressive dramatic range encompassed Dalila in the première of Handel's *Samson* to bawdy comic maids opposite Foote, and spanned forty years from the foundations of Garrick's first company to retirement in Twickenham; supported by her admirer Horace Walpole.

LORD CLIVE, OF INDIA, 1725–74 Major General Robert Clive, known as Clive of India, established the military and political supremacy of the East India Company in Bengal, which by extension forged eventual British dominion over the subcontinent. His military and mercantile successes were controversial enough by the 1770s for Foote to openly satirize him in *The Nabob*, in the wake of which Parliament reformed the East India Company. Clive committed suicide in 1774 by stabbing himself with his penknife.

WILLIAM COOKE, 1740?–1805? Deputy Treasurer of Covent Garden, 1763–85, friend and acolyte of Foote who later wrote a memoir in Foote's name and collated his '*Bons Mots*'.

SIR FRANCIS BLAKE 'FRANK' DELAVAL, 1727–71 'Consummate puppy and unprincipled jackanape', according to Lord Chesterfield, amateur scientist and student of acting, according to Foote, modelled himself on Tom Rakewell in Hogarth's *Rake's Progress*, by his own confession. Delaval was heir to a great swathe of Northumberland but sought metropolitan celebrity in London, with Foote as his side-kick.

SIR JOHN DELAVAL, LATER LORD DELAVAL, 1728–1808 Stolid second-in-line to the Delaval fortune, succeeded to Doddington Park on the death of his mother, and later to the estate left by his wayward brother. Industrialist and politician, but also unexpectedly gifted actor.

NED DELAVAL, 1729–1814 Polymath, charmer, amateur pioneer of electricity and musician, friend of Benjamin Franklin, youngest and most dazzling of the Delaval brothers; eventually inherited Seaton Delaval.

SARAH HUSSEY DELAVAL, 1738–1821 Later Countess of Mexborough and chatelaine of 102 Piccadilly, Cannons Park and Methley Hall, Yorkshire. Society beauty and Georgian It Girl; she and her sisters, Anne and Rhoda, were known as the Hussey-Delavals.

SIR JOHN DINELEY-GOODERE, 1685–1741 Probable epileptic, violent misanthrope and deeply eccentric uncle to Foote; sent to sea at an early age, involved in an abusive marriage and highly publicized 'crim. con.' trial following his abused wife's adultery.

CAPTAIN SAMUEL DINELEY-GOODERE, 1688–1741   Sam's uncle. Renegade captain of HMS *Ruby* and aspiring pirate, with a string of failed military escapades and affairs; hatched a plot to abduct and have declared insane his older brother in order to reclaim the Dineley-Goodere estates. The botched and ultimately murderous abduction led to the captain's hanging and dissection – and to the launch of his nephew's literary career.

ELEANOR DINELEY-GOODERE-FOOTE, 1694–1774   Sam's headstrong mother met and married Mr Foote of Truro, a lawyer, in Bath in 1711 and bred in her three sons a sense of entitlement based on her illustrious family background and prospects of inheritance. Sadly, her great expectations never materialized and she lived her life in and out of debtors' prison.

'MOTHER' DOUGLAS, C. 1700–61   Known as the Empress of the Bawds, the Scottish Jenny Douglas was a St James's prostitute by the time she was seventeen, a brothel-owner by her mid-thirties, an intimate of Earl Fitzwilliam, the Duke of Cumberland and Rear Admiral Holmes among others and notorious by her fifties as the inspiration for Mrs Cole, the brothel madam in John Cleland's *Fanny Hill; The Memoirs of A Woman of Pleasure*. In Foote's *The Minor*, Mrs Cole was made flesh on stage by Foote himself, who had, in drag, a marked resemblance to the ageing courtesan. Hogarth knew well Douglas's Covent Garden bordello, the former Kings Head in the piazza, as did Foote. She equipped it with fashionably rococo interiors and running water and also sold her own-brand condoms manufactured by Jacobs of the Strand, presented in a silk bag 'with a ribbon round it'.

PRINCE EDWARD AUGUSTUS, DUKE OF YORK, 1739–67   Younger, blonder, duller brother of George III and briefly heir to the British throne, Prince 'Ned' had a lifelong interest in the theatre, even appearing as Lothario in Rowe's *The Fair Penitent*. His connection to the slightly older Mexborough-Delaval set brought Foote into contact first with him and with Elizabeth Chudleigh, at Kingston House, and later with the fateful riding accident in 1766.

Henry Fielding, 1707–54 Author of *Tom Jones*, satirist, novelist, playwright and co-founder of the first police force, the Bow Street Runners. His political satires led directly to the 1737 Theatre Licensing Act that dominated Foote's career and stood in part in statute till 1968. Fielding's rivalry with Foote played itself out oddly in a war of puppetry-satire – 'it is with jealousy as with the gout,' Fielding wrote, 'there is never any security against their breaking out.' He died in Lisbon . . . seeking a cure for gout.

Sir John Fielding, 1721–80 Blind magistrate, brother of the more famous Henry; he took over as magistrate at Bow Street on his brother's death in 1754 and was consequently presiding when John Sangster laid his deposition against Foote in 1776. Called as witness in the trial, Sir John claimed to be able to recognize three thousand criminals by voice alone, and judged character by verbal testimony. He did not hesitate to believe that Sangster's tale was worthy of investigation.

Benjamin Franklin, 1705–90 Polymath, lover of London and its theatre, Founding Father of the United States, but one-time appeaser and London-based diplomat, scientist, oceanographer, writer, political theorist and musician. His inventions, many dating from his years living at Craven Street, Charing Cross, included lightning rods, bifocals and a glass harmonica, played upon by Ned Delaval and Samuel Foote among others.

David Garrick, 1717–79 Actor-manager, playwright, National Treasure; tireless champion of William Shakespeare, of naturalistic acting and of himself. Garrick and Sam Foote trained together under Charles Macklin, and were lifelong rivals and querulous friends. Even Garrick's close friend Samuel Johnson had to admit that, of the two, Foote had 'the greater range of wit'.

Prince George, later King George III, 1738–1820 Princes George and Edward were educated by tutors together at Leicester House (Leicester Square) and maintained a love of the

West End music and theatre scenes all their lives. As King, George III was unexpectedly supportive of Samuel Foote during his 1776 trial, ordering two Royal Command Performances at the Haymarket, which he attended with his wife, Queen Charlotte.

GEORGE GRAY, 1737–98?　Calcutta-born Scottish school-friend of James Boswell, sexual and geographical adventurer, East India Company employee and, by 1771, lover of the heiress Mary Bowes, Countess of Strathmore, who was simultaneously engaged in an affair with James Graham while divorcing her abusive husband. Satirized in *The Stoniad* and, along with Clive of India, as Foote's eponymous *Nabob*.

AUGUSTUS JOHN HERVEY, LATER EARL OF BRISTOL, 1724–79 Lantern-jawed young naval officer who married, clandestinely, Elizabeth Chudleigh in 1744 and later inherited the vast wealth of the earldom of Bristol. The secret marriage had been instantly regretted by both parties and they tried to deny it in a formal act of 'jactitation' but their wedding invalidated Elizabeth's subsequent one to the Duke of Kingston.

WILLIAM HICKEY, 1749–1830　Rake, libertine, memoirist, travel writer and serial philanderer, Hickey was also Samuel Foote's lawyer. Helped represent him in sexual assault trial in 1776.

WILLIAM HOGARTH, 1697–1764　Painter, printmaker, social critic and cartoonist, the subjects of his satire – London life, morality, marriage and politics – often mirrored the comedic concerns of his near neighbour and sometime drinking partner Sam Foote, himself later described as 'The Hogarth of the Stage'.

JOHN HUNTER, 1728–93　Fiery-tempered Scottish surgeon, anatomist, venereologist, zoologist and proto-psychologist who came to London in 1748 to work with his brother and later wrote notes on the strange case of 'Mr Foote's Nerves' and advised William Bromfeild about Foote's surgery. Appointed surgeon to the King in 1776 and surgeon general in 1790. Deliberately infected his own penis with syphilis as a medical experiment.

WILLIAM HUNTER, 1718–83 Glasgow-trained anatomist, obstetrician, bibliophile and physician to Queen Charlotte; his Theatre of Anatomy fed the Georgian appetite for public anatomical and dissection demonstrations. Obsessive compulsive who 'worked til he dropped and died lecturing', he and his brother are credited as the fathers of modern surgery, but may also have been implicated in the procuring of corpses of murdered pregnant women for their greatest illustrated work, *The Anatomy of the Human Gravid Uterus* (1774).

SAMUEL JOHNSON, 1709–84 Critic, Shakespeare scholar, essayist, lexicographer, depressive and possible Tourette's sufferer, he came to London from Lichfield with David Garrick in 1737. Author of *The Dictionary of the English Language* (1755) and friend to many, including Foote, whom he described as 'irresistible'.

EDWARD JONES, c. 1710–64 Ship's carpenter aboard HMS *Ruby*. Key murder witness along with his wife Maggie-Anne.

CHARLES MACKLIN, 1690? 1699?–1797 Born Cathal Mac-Lochlainn in Ulster, Macklin made his acting reputation under his Anglicized name and pioneered a new stage naturalism in London and Dublin. Alexander Pope was moved to write about his Shylock 'This is the Jew that Shakespeare drew.'

MATTHEW MAHONY, c. 1718–41 Ordinary seaman, Irish, illiterate and suggestible, able to 'kill a Spaniard' but also willing to stand as nurse-gaolkeeper to Sir John once incarcerated in a private asylum. In debt by 1740 to a Bristol doctor for treatment of his syphilis with mercury. At first confessed to murder, then withdrew his confession.

LORD MANSFIELD, LORD CHIEF JUSTICE, 1705–93 Scottish aristocrat, schooled and trained in English law. Barrister, rhetorician and abolitionist, Mansfield presided over the trials of both Elizabeth Chudleigh, before the House of Lords, and of Samuel

Foote in the Court of King's Bench, in Westminster Hall. His detailed notes from the trial, discovered at the family home of Scone Castle, are the only record of witness testimony, considered at the time too shocking to publish.

JOHN SAVILE, EARL OF MEXBOROUGH, LORD POLLINGTON, 1719–78   Political host and bluff huntsman, friend of Frank Delaval and Edward, Duke of York; married Sarah Hussey Delaval who was pregnant with their second child when Samuel Foote attended their fateful riding party in 1766, a party to celebrate the creation of the new earldom of Mexborough-of-Lifford.

ARTHUR MURPHY, 1727–1805   Irish actor, writer, friend of Foote, and fellow lawyer and later chronicler of Foote's '*Bons Mots*', he introduced Samuel Johnson to Henry and Hester Thrale and turned his talents increasingly to playwriting rather than performing and thence to biographies of his friends Johnson, Henry Fielding and David Garrick. Johnson suggested he write a biography of Foote but he never did.

JOSHUA REYNOLDS, 1723–92   Friend of Foote and fellow West Country arriviste, he was assistant to the portraitist Thomas Hudson when he and Foote first met in the early 1740s. Reynolds later travelled in Italy and France and was not permanently back in London until 1753, like Foote. He painted the same 'celebrities' Foote parodied, from Elizabeth Chudleigh to David Garrick. First President of the Royal Academy.

JACK SANGSTER, c. 1751–?   Country-born stable boy who rose to become second coachman in the household of Samuel Foote and occasional footman at the villa at Fulham; previously in the employ of Dr Fordyce of Soho. Wrongly named around London and in one ballad as 'Roger' the footman.

RICHARD BRINSLEY SHERIDAN, 1751–1816   Irish playwright, London politician and long-time owner of the Theatre Royal, Drury Lane. A key player in the linked worlds of the Dublin and London theatres, his affair with Elizabeth Linley in Bath in 1771 inspired both Samuel Foote's *The Maid of Bath* and his own later work, *The Rivals*. His reworking of *The Rehearsal* as *The Critic* was suggested by Foote, who had made his professional comedy début in the lead role of Bayes.

THOMAS SHERIDAN, 1719–88 Actor-manager of Smock Alley, Dublin, Ireland's Theatre Royal, father of Richard Brinsley, he later moved to London and to Bath, working mainly as an elocution teacher. Sometime employer of Foote, he liked to remind people that he had once been known as Ireland's Garrick, but his star waned in the light of his son's, and his orotund delivery was parodied by Foote and in his own son's work.

HORACE WALPOLE, 1717–97 Grand Tourist, antiquarian, art historian, first Gothic novelist, son of Prime Minister Robert Walpole and cousin of Nelson, Walpole was an aesthete and man of letters described variously as 'asexual' or 'a hermaphrodite horse' (!) but whose position on romance and indeed on comedy is summed up in his famous remark that 'The world is a comedy to those that think, a tragedy to those that feel.' Defender and admirer of Foote's work, if not his style.

JOHN WESLEY, 1703–91 Anglican evangelist and preacher; with his brother Charles and the preacher George Whitefield, credited as a founding father of Methodism.

THOMAS WESTON, 1737–76 Haymarket comedian, former royal cook and high-functioning alcoholic, Weston made his first appearance in 1759 and was almost constantly in Foote's employ until his death in 1776. Jerry Sneak in *The Mayor of Garrett* was written for him by Foote, and he featured in the role in the Zoffany painting that hung in Foote's Suffolk Street house.

CHARLES WHITE, c. 1705–41 Midshipman from Drogheda in Ireland; fought for the British Crown from 1730. The biggest man on board HMS *Ruby*, 'a stout and lusty fellow', and a heavy drinker, charged with murder.

GEORGE WHITEFIELD, 1714–1770   Charismatic public orator and Wesleyan preacher, transatlantic 'celebrity' and failed actor, Whitefield was blessed with a stentorian voice and arresting presence but cursed with an alarming squint and pronounced hatred of the theatre. Favoured butt of Foote's jokes and impersonations.

JOHN WILKES, 1727–97   MP, libertarian libertine, radical journalist and politician and founder member of the Hellfire Club. He was variously described as the wittiest man in London and the ugliest man in England: he boasted it took him half an hour with a new acquaintance 'to talk away' his face. His writings ranged from the political *North Briton* to the pornographic *Essay on Women*; his name became a rallying call for a rag-bag of causes.

TATE WILKINSON, 1739–1803   Son of a clergyman and Foote's premier acolyte as an impressionist, his ability to imitate Foote himself eventually strained their professional friendship. As actor-manager he ran the profitable Yorkshire circuit of theatres and his *Wandering Patentee* not only provides unique insight into the workings of the Georgian theatre but also the only record of some of Foote's stagework.

PEG WOFFINGTON, 1717?–60   Dublin-born Georgian pin-up, comedienne, former child star, professional muse and leading lady at Drury Lane and Smock Alley, Dublin. Peg and Foote first knew each other when she was sharing her bed and board with David Garrick on Bow Street. Famed for her legs as much as her wit and temper, she starred in a number of 'breeches' roles and even taught one to her young lover, Davy Garrick, but her attack on fellow actress George Anne Bellamy, onstage, with a prop-knife, became the subject of Foote's satire that ended their friendship.

ALL OTHER PARTS – Attendant Lords, Ladies of Good- and Ill-repute, Footmen, Doxies, Blackamoors, Sedan-chairmen, Surgeons' Assistants, Jurors, hangmen & cetera to be played by members of His Majesty's Company of Comedians of the Theatre Royal, Haymarket.

Box Office Figures

In 1750 £1 would be worth over £100 today (2012 figures, Retail Price Index, Bank of England). A guinea was £1 1s.

A Trip to Calais, the play, was estimated by Foote to be worth only £150 to him from a publisher, but £3,000 over the course of a summer season[1] – a potential profit to the Haymarket company of over £300,000 in today's money.

As overview, Boswell's allowance in London in the mid-century was £200 a year. The First Lord of the Treasury was paid £4,000. Boswell lodged opposite him in Downing Street for £40 annual rent. Garrick could command £1,000 a season; his co-star Peg Woffington got by on occasional benefit nights, which brought her £160, and the generosity of her admirers. Foote's footman, Sangster, was paid £20 a year, the stage doorman at the Haymarket £18 a year, but Foote's coach cost at least £40 a year to hire; £40 could instead have bought forty tickets to Ranelagh Rotunda, twenty season tickets to Vauxhall Gardens, or a front box, annual subscription, to Foote's Theatre Royal, Haymarket. Six shillings, meanwhile, could buy a pair of actress's stays, a single shoe for Mr Foote, a dozen skinned rabbits or Dr Rock's Antivenereal Electuary.

All the dates in this book are converted to the new style, which is to say the Gregorian calendar, which was adopted in Great Britain and the American colonies in 1752, skipping forward eleven days and starting the new year on 1 January.

The Georgians were haphazard with spelling as with their

capitalization, but generally littered their typeface and manuscript with many more upper-case letters than is elegant to the modern eye. Some changes have been made. Spellings have also been standardized. Titles and surnames have been simplified, notably where characters have possessed several during the course of the narrative. The name 'Foote' appears with two spellings within Samuel's family, with and without the *e*. He used most often, and always in print, the version favoured here. Apropos, I have struggled to ascertain, as I am asked occasionally, whether the late Labour Party leader Michael Foot, also of West Country descent, was a relative. It seems not. A branch of Samuel Foote's family ended up in Trenwheal, Cornwall, near Godolphin, where some of Michael Foot's family later lived, but the connection seems to be coincidental.

List of Illustrations

Front endpaper. A detail from *A Panorama of the Thames from Westminster Bridge to London Bridge* by Samuel & Nathaniel Buck (London, 1749). © Henry E. Huntington Library, San Marino, CA.

SECTION ONE

1. A detail from *Samuel Foote in the character of Major Sturgeon and Hayes as Sir Jacob Jollup in 'The Mayor of Garrett'*, 1763–4, oil on canvas, by Johann Zoffany. From the Castle Howard Collection. Reproduced with kind permission of the Hon. Simon Howard.

2. *The London Directory or a new and improved plan of London, Westminster & Southwark, with the adjacent country, the new buildings, the new roads and the late alterations by opening of new streets, & widening of others.* [1786–1787] Robert Sayer, 1725–1794. Printed for Robt. Sayer, Map and Printseller, No. 53 Fleet Steet. © Courtesy of the Huntington Art Collections, San Marino, California.

3. *(top)* Portrait of Margaret Woffington (Peg), c. 1735, oil on canvas, by Philippe Mercier. © The Art Archive / Garrick Club.

4. *(bottom) David Garrick as Richard III*, 1745, oil on canvas, by William Hogarth. © Walker Art Gallery, National Museums Liverpool / The Bridgeman Art Library.

5. (*top*) The west or kitchen wing, Seaton Delaval, from *The Country Houses of Sir John Vanbrugh* by Jeremy Musson (2008). © Country Life / The Bridgeman Art Library.

6. (*bottom left*) *The Elder Children of Rhoda and Francis Blake Delaval* by Sir Arthur Pond. From the Doddington Hall Collection. Reproduced with the kind permission of James and Claire Birch.

7. (*bottom right*) Sir Francis Blake Delaval (1727–1771). From the Doddington Hall Collection. Reproduced with the kind permission of James and Claire Birch.

8. (*top*) A case of amputation instruments, by various makers, c. 1750. © Wellcome Library, London.

9. (*middle*) Petit-type tourniquet. © Science Museum, London, Wellcome Images.

10. (*bottom*) Image of Addison's prosthesis for Mr Foote from William Bromfeild, *Chirurgical Observations and Cases*, 2 vols (London, 1773). Prosthesis by Addison – vol. 2, plate 5. From the Archives of the Royal College of Surgeons of England.

11. (*top*) *The Resurrection or an Internal View of the Museum in W—d-m—ll Street, on the last Day* by Thomas Rowlandson, 1782. © The Trustees of the British Museum.

12. (*bottom left*) *Mr Foote in 'The Lame Lover'*, playbill from the Theatre Royal Edinburgh, c. 1770. © The Art Archive / Garrick Club.

13. (*bottom right*) *The Lame Lover.* Courtesy of The Lewis Walpole Library, Yale University.

14. *Henry Angelo as Mrs Cole in 'The Minor' by Samuel Foote*, by Samuel de Wilde © The Art Archive / Garrick Club.

SECTION TWO

1. *A Portrait of Samuel Foote*, c. 1762–3, by Thomas Gainsborough. Copyright: Private Collection, UK.

2. The Fratricide. © Private Collection.

3. Captain Samuel Goodere. © Private Collection.

4. Title page from *Sodom and Onan* by William Jackson (London, 1776). © The British Library Board (2. 11642.g.15.).

5. (*top*) *The Hermitage: A View of Mr. Foote's Villa at North End, London*, 1772. Unknown artist. Image courtesy: the Yale Centre for British Art.

6. (*bottom*) Manuscript page from *The Case Books of John Hunter*, FRS, a.k.a. *Hunterian Manuscript CASES IN SURGERY contained in a large Folio Volume sent by Sir Edward Home to the Board of TRUSTEES of the HUNTERIAN COLLECTION*, 1825, 2 vols, *Case 409 – Nerves – Mr Foote's Case*. From the Archives of the Royal College of Surgeons of England.

7. *Samuel Foote* by Jean-François Colson, oil on canvas, 1769. © National Portrait Gallery, London.

8. (*top left*) Miss Chudleigh in the Character of Iphigenia at the Venetian Ambassador's Masquerade (engraving). © Private Collection / The Bridgeman Art Library.

9. (*top right*) Elizabeth Chudleigh, Countess of Bristol and Duchess of Kingston, 1776 (mezzotint). © Private Collection / The Bridgeman Art Library.

10. A satire upon the Duchess of Kingston, c. 1776. © Private Collection.

11. Engraving of the trial of the Duchess of Kingston at Westminster Hall, 1776. Courtesy: Manuscripts and Special Collections, The University of Nottingham.

12. (*top*) *Samuel Foote as Dr Hellebore and Thomas Weston as Dr Last in 'The Devil Upon Two Sticks'*, 1768, oil on canvas, by Johann Zoffany. From the Castle Howard Collection. Reproduced with kind permission of the Hon. Simon Howard.

13. (*bottom*) View of the New Theatre Royal, Haymarket, Opened July 4th 1821, Showing also the Relative Situation of the Old Theatre Previous to its Demolition, engraved by Dale, 1822 (engraving), Schnebbelie, Robert Blemell (fl. 1803–1849) (after). © City of Westminster Archive Centre, London, UK / The Bridgeman Art Library.

Back endpaper. A detail from *A Panorama of the Thames from Westminster Bridge to London Bridge* by Samuel & Nathaniel Buck (London, 1749). © Henry E. Huntington Library, San Marino, CA.

Acknowledgements

All grateful acknowledgement must go to The Wellcome Foundation and to the Huntington Library Francis Bacon Fellowship for grants towards the research and writing of this book.

First personal thanks, however, must go to Lee Hall. We were working together on Lee's play *The Pitmen Painters* when we first talked about Sam Foote, whose life story I had looked at, laughed, and looked away from. Lee has a finer sense of what's funny – and what makes for a good story – than I. I looked again. He was right. Towards the end of the research it became apparent that the Woodhorn Archives at the colliery in Ashington, where *The Pitmen Painters* is set, had letters to and from Samuel Foote as part of the Delaval Papers, for access to which I must thank Keith Merrin, Liz O'Donnell, Lee Jones and Max Roberts, who also directed me in the play. These things come full circle. But I had heard of Foote long before even my work on Casanova, whose London years overlap with Foote's to some extent. Previous thanks should therefore go, but posthumously, to the wonderful actor TP McKenna, who would not, even were he alive, remember me from a film, *Valmont,* set in eighteenth-century France, on which we both worked. Raconteur and man of the Anglo-Irish theatre, he is responsible for some of the first stories I ever heard about Foote – oral history, if you will, or theatre lore – most of which have turned out, regrettably, to be untrue. I would not have met TP and heard his tall stories, late at night in Fontainebleau, if it had not been for that Milos Forman film and the invitation to be there extended by

Ian McNeice and Kate Nicholls, whose confidence in me as a man of the theatre was inspirational.

Paul Baggaley showed a trust in Sam Foote and in me for which I am forever grateful. Kate Harvey, Sam Humphreys, Camilla Elworthy and, in particular, Kris Doyle, all at Picador, and my friend and literary agent Ivan Mulcahy, likewise expressed early faith while not quite believing I was telling them the truth about Foote. I was. Blessed are those who have not read the sources, but still believe . . .

Of the many academics whose works have directly influenced this one, I am particularly indebted to Nicholas Bromley, Matthew Kinservik, Simon Trefman, Liza Picard, Lloyd Kermode and the late Mary Belden. The work done by many other academics towards the digitalization of the eighteenth-century newspapers and periodicals in the Burney Collection of the British Library has made this sort of overview of a Georgian 'media' event possible for the first time. I would wish to thank the staff of the British Library Rare Books and Manuscripts, the London Library, the Huntington Library, the New York Public Library Performing Arts Collection and Midtown collection, the National Archives in Kew and the Northumberland County Archives at Woodhorn, Ashington, Dublin's Marsh Library and Dublin City Archives, the Theatre Archive of the National Archive of Ireland, Dublin, and of the Manuscripts and Early Printed Materials Collections at Trinity College, Dublin; at Smock Alley itself, the site of the former Dublin Theatre Royal, Patrick Sutton, Lorcan Cranach and Anne Clarke; at the Garrick Club Archive, the kind and helpful Marcus Risdell; at Westminster Abbey Library and Archives, Tony Trowles and Richard Mortimer; at the Huntington Gallery Sydney Moritz-LeVine, at the Morgan Library New York, Declan Kiely, and the introduction via Michael Bundock and Kate Chisholm; and at Christie's Archive, St James's, Marijke Booth. Thanks, too, to the Australian Decorative and Fine Arts Societies, but especially Clive Probyn, Emeritus Professor of Monash University, Victoria, for his guidance on Henry Fielding; Hugh Belsey for guidance on Gainsborough and

Foote, and Ray Cahill for alerting me to the 1779 Jewell case notes. At the Wellcome Foundation, Simon Chaplin, Elizabeth Shaw, David Clayton and Louise Fellingham, and for an introduction to the Huntington Library, John Berendt, Jonathan Bate, Sam Mendes and Nicholas Hytner. At the Hunterian Institute at the Royal College of Surgeons, Louise King and Jane Hughes. For advice on surgery and psychology, then and now, John Kirkup and my brother Andrew Kelly, Henry Marsh, Victoria Kortes-Papp and Larry Dumont, and to those modern-day amputees, who were kind enough to share with me their stories anonymously, thank you, and especially to Gwen Cavaciuti, whose bravery and humour were inspirational. For a fuller understanding of the trials of both Foote and the Duchess of Kingston, which informed the latter stages of this book, I am particularly indebted to the research and writings of Matthew Kinservik, notably at the Huntington Library, California, which both instructed my arguments and pointed me in useful directions very fast when in Pasadena. My site-specific thanks, too, to all those at the Theatre Royal, Haymarket, especially Kara McCulloch, Catherine Penny and Hazel Kerr.

I wish to thank the Provost and Fellows of Worcester College, Oxford, for their permission to quote from the archives held in the college that relate to Samuel Foote, and to the archivist Emma Goodrum for her kind and detailed help. Quite separately I must thank the new Provost, Jonathan Bate, and also Paula Byrne who have been encouraging and supportive friends for many years, in particular with regard to this and my next book.

As a result of my career-juggling as actor and historian I have many thanks due to all those along the road who have been supportive or forgiving, to wit Padraig Cusack, Andrew Speed, Julius Green, Bill Kenwright, my agent here in London Janie Jenkins at PBJ, Lynne Meadows and Barry Grove and the cast and crew of *The Pitmen Painters* at the National Theatre, on Broadway and in the West End but especially on tour in Dublin, where I nearly missed the curtain several times through disappearing into Trinity College archives and Smock Alley. Trevor Fox and Claire

Cartwright, from the cast, even found time to read an early draft: thank you.

A book written by an actor on the hoof, as it were, often in theatre dressing rooms as well as libraries, requires special thanks to those who made this odd adventure possible. I owe thanks beyond measure to Andrew and Blanche Sibbald, Eric Akoto, David Piper, Erica Wagner, Victor Wynd and The Last Tuesday Society, Pippa and Nick Robinson, Vibse and Brian Dunleath, Jane Willacy, Walcot Park and the Castle Hotel, Bishops Castle, Shropshire, Rodney Griffiths, Nicholas Blake, Peter Sabor, Fiona Ritchie, my brother and sister-in-law Andrew and Kate Kelly, my brother David Kelly and, as always, Mum and Dad, for medical pointers, writing retreats, naval and literary advice and childcare variously. In New York, to Martin Gould, Rina Anoussis, Carl Raymond, Ruth Leon, the New York library of the late Sheridan Morley, and to my publicist Susan Schulman and my agent there, Marilynn Scott Murphy, my thanks. In Los Angeles, my thanks and love to Louise and Andy Chater and Olly and Flo, to Lisa Darr and Brian Valente and to Don Krim and David T. Russell. For their thoughts on the British Sense of Humour – a chapter that had to go – Lucy Worsley, Frederick Raphael, Jung Chang, Jon Halliday and Sarah and George Walden. Thanks also to Rachelle Albicy for her technical support, and to the eagle-eyed Hazel Orme for her warm enthusiasm and dedicated copy-editing.

§

In the 'Cupboard' of the British Library Rare Books Room are several thousand unedited and hand-typed tissue-papers from the 1930s, the collection of the Reverend John Wells Wilkinson, whose eccentric interest in Samuel Foote was only matched by his dogged pedantry. Having stated an ambition to write a *Life and Works of Samuel Foote*, he died decades into his task, having completed only the research towards the first few years of Foote's career. I think of him a lot. The Cupboard and Select Materials of the Rare Books Room, as well as the Bristol Records Office, contains several volumes pertinent to the opening chapters that are bound in the skin of some of the protagonists. I think of them often too. And hope I have shown more respect than their original anatomizers.

But thanks, lastly and mainly, to the people who most deserve my respect and gratitude and who make me laugh the most: Claire, Oscar and Celia.

Bibliography

The Works of Samuel Foote

A Genuine Account of the Murder of Sir John Dinely Goodere, Bristol and London, 1741
The Genuine Memoirs of Sir John Dinely Goodere who was murdered on the Contrivance of his own Brother, on Board the Ruby Man of War in King Road Bristol, Jan 19 1740, (1741), London, 1741
Diversions of the Morning, London (not printed), 1747; published in Wilkinson, Tate, *The Wandering Patentee or a History of the Yorkshire Theatre, from 1779 to the present time*, 4 vols, London, 1795
Auction of Pictures (not printed), 1749
The Knights, London, 1754 (premièred 1749)
Taste, London, 1752
The Englishman in Paris, London, 1753
The Englishman Returned from Paris, London, 1756
The Author, London, 1757
The Diversions of the Morning (altered), Dublin, 1758
The Minor, London, 1760
The Lyar, London, 1764 (performed London and Dublin, 1761)
The Captive – A Comic Opera, Dublin, 1762
The Orators, London, 1762
The Mayor of Garrett, London, 1763
The Patron, London, 1764
The Commissary, London, 1765
The Devil Upon Two Sticks, London, 1778 (premièred 1768)
Doctor Last in his Chariot, translated from Molière's *La Malade Imaginaire*, with Isaac Bickerstaffe; Third Act, Foote, London, 1769
The Lame Lover, London, 1770
The Maid of Bath, London, 1778 (premièred 1771)

The Bankrupt, London, 1776

The Nabob, London, 1778 (premièred 1772)

The Cozeners, London, 1778 (premièred 1774)

A Trip to Calais, London, 1778 (never performed; Lord Chamberlain's submitted version in Larpent Collection)

The Capuchin, London, 1778

The Diversions of the Morning, Second Act, in Tate Wilkinson, *The Wandering Patentee*, 1795, and William Cooke, *Memoirs of Samuel Foote*, London, 1805

Tragedy-a-la-Mode. Being the Second Act of Mr Foote's Diversions of the Morning, and substituted in Lieu of the Former Second Act in his Farce called Tea, in Tate Wilkinson, *The Wandering Patentee*, London, 1795

The Tryall of Samuel Foote, Esq. For a Libel on Peter Paragraph, in Tate Wilkinson, *The Wandering Patentee*, 1795, and William Cooke, *Memoirs of Samuel Foote*, London, 1805, performed 1763 as part of *The Orators*

An Occasional Prelude Performed at the Opening of the Theatre Royal in the Haymarket, 1767, extract in *London Magazine*, 1767. First printed entire in *Monthly Mirror*, 1804, and William Cooke, *Memoirs of Samuel Foote*, 1805

The Comic Theatre. Being a Free Translation of the all the Best French Comedies. By Samuel Foote, Esq., and Others, 5 vols, London, 1762

The Dramatic Works of Samuel Foote, Esq.; to which is prefaced A Life of the Author, London, 1809

A Letter from Mr Foote to the Reverend Author of the Remarks Critical and Christian on The Minor, London, 1760

A Treatise on the Passions, so far as they regard the Stage, London, 1747

Apology for The Minor, in a Letter to the Rev. Mr Baine, Edinburgh, 1771

Bee, Jon (ed.), *The Works of Samuel Foote with Remarks on Each Play and an Essay on the Life, Genius and Writings of the Author*, 3 vols, London, 1830

Cooke, William, *Memoirs of Samuel Foote, Esq., With a collection of his genuine bon-mots, anecdotes, opinions, &c mostly original*, 3 vols, London, 1805

Cooke, William (ed.), *The Table Talk and Bons Mots of Samuel Foote*, London, 1902

Cooke, William, with Willingham, Robert, *Wit for the Ton! The Convivial Jester or Sam Foote's Last Budget Opened*, London, 1777

Avis au Public du Sieur Diderot (traduit de l'anglois [sic]), Paris, 1777

Wilkes; An Oratorio (music by Signor Carlos Bartini), London, 1769

Piety in Pattens, 1773, not printed

Prelude on the Opening [Night] at the Haymarket Theatre (Occasional Prologue), London, 1767

The Roman and English Comedy Considered and Compared. With remarks on the Suspicious Husband And an Examen into the Merit of the Present Comic Actors, London, 1747

The Trial or Trial for a Libel on Peter Paragraph, 1763, in Wilkinson, Tate, *The Wandering Patentee or a History of the Yorkshire Theatre, from 1779 to the present time*, 4 vols, London, 1795

OTHER WORKS: PRIMARY MATERIAL

Abbreviations

Add MSS: British Library Additional Manuscripts
BL Cup: British Library Rare Books Cupboard
GCA: Garrick Club, London
HIRCS: Hunterian Institute Library, Royal College of Surgeons, London
NRODel: National Records, Northumberland, Delaval Papers
NYPL: New York Public Library
PRO: Public Record Office, Kew
TCD: Trinity College, Dublin
HLC: Huntington Library, California

MANUSCRIPTS AND ARCHIVES

British Library Manuscripts

Add MSS 5726 C William Bromfeild to Lord Bute, 1761
Add MSS 12116
Add MSS 27826 Place Papers, vol. xxxviii, *Manners and Morals*
Add MSS 30094 Benjamin Wilson, 1743–88: correspondence and papers
Add MSS 33056 f. 269 Licence for Performing Plays, 1766
Add MSS 33488 f. 86
Add MSS 33634 MS Journal of John Skinner, 'Sketches at Oxford'
Add MSS 35612 Hardwicke Papers, vol. CCLXIV, ff. 293–4
Add MSS 36133 f. 198 Royal Patent for the Haymarket Theatre, 1766
Add MSS 36593 f. 135 S. Foote to Caleb Whitefoorde, 10 October 1777
Add MSS 36595 f. 399 'The Character of Foote'
Add MSS D 10 12 116 Mus Brit Bibl Butler: Autographs of Actors, Critics, etc., No. 10, Foote to Garrick
Add MSS Fleet Prison, Collection of Newspaper Cuttings and Broadsides &cetera [PM 11633 h2]
BL Cup 502 f. 31 'The Life and Works of Samuel Foote (to age 24)', manuscript, unpublished, the Rev. John Wells Wilkinson MA, 5 vols,

includes facsimile copy *The Last Will and Testament of Samuel Foote*, prov'd 22 October 1777

RB 23 a.26056 *The Authentick Tryal of Samuel Goodere Esq., Matthew Mahony and Charles White at the City of Bristol on Thursday the 26th and Friday 27th March 1741 for the MURDER of Sir John Dinely Goodere Bart., on board the RUBY Man of War in Kings-Road Bristol*, London, 1741

Richard Smith, FRCS, Bristol, Police Watch Committee ephemera, 1836

RB 11642.g.15, Jackson, William, *Sodom and Onan, A Satire inscribed to Foote Esq., alias the Devil upon Two Sticks*; also contains cuttings from unnamed London papers, 1776

Burney Collection; eighteenth-century newspapers and periodicals. Electronic resource BNB GBA8D7879; system number 014848748

Christie's Archive, St James's

Christie and Ansell Sales Catalogues, Estate of Samuel Foote: Northend and Suffolk Street, contents, January 1778

Folger Library, Washington DC

Macklin, Charles, Memoranda and Anecdotes, Y.d. 515 (1–11) 8–9

Murphy, Arthur, Common Place Book 525, manuscript pages of descriptions of his contemporaries

Garrick Club Archive, London

The Red Album, *Theatrical Scrap Book*, 1800–1845

Theatrical Portraits, vol. II: *Garrick and his Contemporaries*

Original Letters of Dramatic Performers Collected and Arranged by Charles Britiffe Smith (for Sir William Augustus Fraser, Baronet), 1841, vol. 1, no. 60, Samuel Foote to David Garrick; vol. 2, nos 55 and 56, from Maria Foote and Maria Harrington

Dramatic Annals, vol. 1, 1741–1785, collected by John Nixon. Manuscripts presented to the Garrick Club, 1885

Owen's Chronicle, 1773

David Garrick; A Memorial Illustrative of his Life, in Four Volumes, Consisting of original playbills, Bills of contemporary performances by the most famous players of Garrick's period (Henry Irving Collection)

The Morning Conversation, A new song by Samuel Foot [sic], 1753

Guildhall Library, London

K.B. Misc. C 33–339, 518. C 11–603–9: Debtors' Papers *Habeas Corpus* Debts of Samuel Foote

Hunterian Institute Library, London

The Case Books of John Hunter, FRS, a.k.a. *Hunterian Manuscript CASES IN SURGERY contained in a large Folio Volume sent by Sir Edward Home to the Board of TRUSTEES of the HUNTERIAN COLLECTION,* 1825, 2 vols, *Case 409 – Nerves – Mr Foote's Case*
Peachey, G. C., 'William Bromfeild, 1713–1792', in *Section on the History of Medicine* (lectures), 15 May 1915

Huntington Library, San Marino, California

The Larpent Papers, John Larpent Plays (plays submitted to the Examiner from 1737, in possession of J. Larpent, Examiner from 1778, until his death in 1824). Manuscript plays, prologues, diversions submitted by S Foote, some with application for license. No. 93 *The Virtuoso,* application 28 Dec 1751, produced (as *Taste*) 13 Jan 1752. No. 105 *The Knights,* application 16 Jan 1754, MS endorsed 'X' some corrections, added lines, and prologue in hand of author. No. 149 *Diversions of the Morning,* no application, MS consists of the Lady Pentweazle scene from Act I of *Taste* and second act of burlesque rehearsal. No. 177 *The Minor,* application 20 Nov 1760. No. 194 *Taste,* application Mar 1761 (unprinted alteration of the version of 1751). No. 200 *The Lyar,* application 16 Sep 1761, MS prologue and epilogue, separate application 9 Jan 1762. No. 224 *The Mayor of Garratt (sic),* application 20 Jun 1763, MS in Act II lacks passages found in printed text. No. 282 *The Devil Upon Two Sticks,* no application, produced 30 May 1768 – a few corrections in hand of author. No. 310 *The Lame Lover,* application 1 Jun 1770. No. 324 *The Maid of Bath,* application 12 Jun 1771. No. 335 *The Nabob,* application 17 Jun 1772. No. 346 *Piety in Pattens,* no application (puppet show), produced Haymarket 15 Feb 1773. No. 355 *The Bankrupt,* application 8 Jul 1773. No. 375 *The Cozeners,* application 28 Jun 1774, numerous corrections and one two-page insertion in hand of author. No. 413 *The Capuchin,* application 8 Aug 1776, produced 19 Aug. MS Prologue. Slight differences, notably pp. 50–52, Harry Humper and Brother O'Flam, appears differently in published text and 1778, Devonshire Collection of Plays (also in HLC). Elizabeth Montagu, MO 2999 *Essay on the . . . Genius of*

Shakespeare, MS 3 leaves, quarto, 1769. Anna Margaretta Larpent, manuscript diaries, MSS 17 Volumes HM31201. Maps of London: Rocque, 1741, RB 315661. Panorama of London, 1749, Buck, 400576.

Northumberland Record Office, Woodhorn, Ashington

The Delaval Papers

2/DE/44/1 Letters concerning authors John Cleland, *Fanny Hill*, and Samuel Foote

2/DE/44/2 A list of various letters and papers, three pages: notes on Edward Delaval, John Hussey Delaval and Francis Blake Delaval

2/DE/44/3 MSS copy of Shylock, *The Merchant of Venice*, in hand of Frank or John Delaval, Papers of John Delaval, Francis Blake Delaval, Rhoda Delaval, house accounts, Seaton Delaval

2/DE/44/4 Miscellaneous verses and literary notes

NRO 650/K/11 Epilogue to *The Fair Penitent*, by Sir John (later Lord) Delaval, spoken by the Earl of Strathmore

NRO 650/E/11 1752–1801 Miscellaneous accounts, bills and other papers relating to Seaton Delaval Hall

NRO 650/K/13, NRO 650/M/1 nd Miscellaneous papers

NRO 650/D/7 Personal and business letters from Francis Blake-Delaval (1727–1771); personal letters and letters to Lady Delaval relating to the administration of Doddington and Seaton

NRO 650/D/12 1751–1755, NRO 650/D/14 1706–1795 Delaval Halls

Robinson, John, *The Delaval Papers*, four instalments, Newcastle, 1890–1

New York Public Library

TMSS 2001–065, Series 1 Box 2 folder 21 Henry W. and Albert A. Berg Collection, William Appleton Collection, Letter and servant's reference, Samuel Foote, Northend, 2 July 1776

TMSS 2001–065, Series 1 Box 2 folder 21 Henry W. and Albert A. Berg Collection, William Appleton Collection, Burney, Frances, Letter to Esther Burney, 1812

Public Record Office, Kew

PRO IND 6826 (original) Foote, Samuel, Royal Patent for the Haymarket Theatre, 1766

PRO KB10/40 34 and 35 Mr Sangster's deposition against Mr Foote, 8 July 1776

The Trial of Samuel Goodere and Matthew Mahony and The Trial of Charles White,
    Bristol, 1741 (Geo II), with Records Relating to Trials and Proceedings,
    London, 1742

Aylett v. Jewel, Executor, 1 January 1779. (1779) 2 Blackstone W. 1299, 96 E.R.
    761 1779

Howell, T. B. (ed.), State Trials 1726–1743, vol. XVII (*The Trials of Samuel
    Goodere, Matthew Mahony and Charles White, A.D. 1741*), London, 1813

Court of King's Bench, Records

Court of Common Pleas, Records

The Fleet Prison Books

Prerogative Court of Canterbury, Prob 11/1006. Image ref. 218, Probate 2
    March 1775

Trinity College, Dublin

TCD 873–204 (1–20) (written on back of black mourning paper), *An account of
    the part taken in the dispute and epistolary controversy by the Revd William Jackson
    between the Duchess of Kingston and Samuel Foote in 1776*

TCD MSS 10532 Miscellaneous Lives – Literary

TCD MSS 10066/289/226

Westminster Abbey Library and Archives

Chester, Joseph L. (ed.), *The Marriage, Baptismal and Burial Registers of the Collegiate
    Church or Abbey of St Peter, Westminster*, London, 1876

Funeral Fee Book, 1760–83

Westminster Abbey Chapter Minutes, 1768–77

Westminster Abbey Registers, 1777

Worcester College Archives, Oxford

LTB 3, 1737 College Entrance Book

(Genealogical chart annexed to Henry Brooke's letter in LTB 3, 1737 College
    Entrance Book)

LTB 13, 1740/41 College Account Book, with College Register, signed by
    William Gower, Provost; Roger Bourchier, Vice-Provost; John Tottie,
    Fellow; and Samuel Wanley, Fellow

College Bursar's Books (Battels and Scholarship Payments), 1737–40

*Primary Source Periodicals, Pamphlets, Cartoons
and Newspapers*

Annual Register
Complete Newgate Calendar or Malefactors Universal Register
Critical Review
Critical Reviewer
Daily Advertiser
Daily Courant
Daily Gazetteer
Daily Journal
Dublin Journal
Dublin University Magazine
Gazetteer and New Daily Advertiser
General Advertiser
Gentleman's Magazine
Gray's Inn Journal
Grub-Street Journal
Historical Register
*Lady's Magazine or Entertaining Companion for the Fair Sex appropriated solely to their Use
    and Amusement*
Literary Magazine
Lloyd's Evening Post and British Chronicle
London Chronicle
London Chronicle (Dublin reprint)
London Daily Post and General Advertiser
London Evening Post
London Literary Gazette
London Magazine
Monthly Magazine
Monthly Mirror
Monthly Review
Morning Chronicle and London Advertiser
Morning Post
Oracle
*Prompter – A Theatrical Paper, London 1734–1736 by Aaron Hill and William
    Popple*
Public Advertiser
Public Ledger
The Public Record or Freeman's Journal, Dublin

St James's Chronicle
St James's Evening Post
Spectator
Tatler
Theatrical Repertory or Weekly Rosciad
Thespian Magazine and Literary Repository
The Times
Theatrical Biography
Theatrical Bouquet
Theatrical Review
Town and Country Magazine
Universal Magazine (including the 1776 summary of the Trial of Duchess of
    Kingston)
Universal Spectator
Westminster Magazine; or, The Pantheon of Taste

Primary Material: General

Adlard, W., *Wit for The Ton, or Sam Foote's Last Budget Opened*, London, 1777
Ambross, Miss, *The Life and Memoirs of the Late Miss Ann Catley, the Celebrated
    Actress*, London, 1790
Anon., *Advice to the Universities of Oxford and Cambridge*, London, 1783
Anon., *The Authentick [sic] Tryal of Samuel Goodere, Esq., Matthew Mahony and Charles
    White at the City of Bristol on Thursday the 26th and Friday 27th March 1741 for the
    Murder of Sir John Dinely Goodere*, London, 1741
Anon., *The Bristol Fratricide, Being an Exact and Impartial Narrative of the Horrid and
    Dreadful Catastrophe of Sir John Dineley Goodere, Bart.*, London, 1741
Anon., *Characters, Containing an Impartial Review of the Public Conduct and Abilities of
    the Most Eminent Personages in the Parliament of Great Britain*, London, 1777
Anon., *Exhortatory Address to the Brethren in the Faith of Christ Occasioned by a
    Remarkable Letter from Mr Foote to the Rev. Author of Christian and Critical Remarks
    on The Minor*, London, 1760
Anon., *Foote's Prologues*, London, 1770
Anon., *The Genuine Dying Speeches of Captain Goodere, Matthew Mahony and Charles
    White*, London, 1741
Anon. (Portal, Abraham?), *A Letter to David Garrick Occasioned by the intended
    Representation of The Minor at Drury Lane*, London, 1760
Anon., *Memoirs of the life and writings of Samuel Foote, Esq the English Aristophanes:
    to which are added the bon mots, repartees, and good things said by that great wit and
    excentrical genius*, London, 1778

Anon., *Nocturnal Revels, Being the history of King's-Place and other modern nunneries, written by a Monk of the Order of St Francis [Hellfire Club]*, 2 vols, London, 1779

Anon., *The Theatrical Review, for the year 1757 and beginning of 1758*, London, 1758

Anon., *The Trial of the Duchess of Kingston*, London, 1775

Anon., *The Trial of Samuel Goodere*, London, 1741

Bathurst, Charles (ed.), *The Trial of Elizabeth, Duchess Dowager of Kingston for Bigamy Before the House of Peers in Westminster Hall in Full Parliament*, London, 1776

Bellamy, George Anne, *An Apology for the Life of George Anne Bellamy*, 2 vols, Dublin, 1785

Boaden, James, *The private Correspondence of David Garrick, with the most celebrated persons of his times, now first published from the originals with notes*, 2 vols, London, 1832

Boswell, James (ed. M. Waingrow), *Boswell's Life of Johnson: an edition of the original manuscript*, 4 vols, Edinburgh University Press, Edinburgh, and Yale University Press, New Haven, 1994

Boswell, James, *Observations Good, Bad, Stupid or Clever, Serious or Jocular on Squire Foote's The Minor*, London, 1760

Boswell, James, *Private Papers of James Boswell from Malahide Castle*, 18 vols, W. E. Rudge, New York, 1934

Brinley Johnson, R. (ed.), *Letters of Hannah More*, London, 1925

Bromfeild, William, *Chirurgical Observations and Cases*, 2 vols, London, 1773

Bromfeild, William, *A Narrative of Certain Particular Facts . . . Relative to the Conduct of Mr Bromfeild*, London, 1756

Burke, Edmund (ed.), *The Annual Register; or, A view of the history, politiks, and literature of the year 1758 etc.*, London, 1761–95

Burney, Frances (Fanny), *A Busy Day or A Return from India* (a play *c*. 1799), Oberon Books, 2001

Bush, John, *Hibernia Curiosa A letter from a gentleman in Dublin, to his friend at Dover in Kent, giving a general view of the manners, customs, dispositions, &c of the inhabitants of Ireland, etc.*, London, 1769

Byron, George (Lord), *Hints from Horace*, London, 1831

Chesterfield, Philip Dormer Stanhope, Earl of, *Letters* (with introduction, notes and index by John Bradshaw), 3 vols, London, 1913

Coke, Lady Mary (ed. J. A. Home), *The Letters and Journals of Lady Mary Coke*, 4 vols, Edinburgh, 1889

Colman, George, *Random Records*, London, 1830

Colquhoun, A., *A Treatise on the Police of the Metropolis*, London, 1797

Cumberland, Richard, *The British Drama, A Collection of the Most Esteemed Productions, with Biography of the Authors*, 7 vols, London, 1817

Cumberland, Richard, *Memoirs*, London, 1806

Davies, Thomas, *Memoirs of the Life of David Garrick, Esq. interspersed with characters and anecdotes of his theatrical contemporaries, the whole forming a history of the stage, which includes a period of thirty-six years*, 3 vols, London, 1780

Davies, Thomas, *Dramatic Miscellanies. Consisting of Critical Observations on Several Plays of Shakespeare: with a Review of his Principal Characters, and those of Various Eminent Writers. As Represented by Mr. Garrick, and Other Celebrated Comedians. With Anecdotes of Dramatic Poets, Actors &c.*, London, 1785

D'Archenholz, M., *A Picture of England*, 2 vols, London, 1789

Defoe, Daniel, *Augusta Triumphans*, London, 1728

Dibdin, Thomas, *Reminiscences*, 2 vols, London, 1827

Edgeworth, Richard Lovell, *Memoirs*, 3 vols, London, 1820

Ellis, Annie R. (ed.), *The Early Diary of Frances Burney*, 2 vols, London, 1913

Foot, Jesse, *The Life of Arthur Murphy*, London, 1811

Foss, E., *Memories of Westminster Hall*, 2 vols, London, 1874

Garrick, D., *New and Occasional Prologue to The Englishman in Paris*, London, 1753

Heister, L., *A General System of Surgery*, London, 1753

Howard, John, *The Report on the Fleet Prisons*, London, 1777

Humphrey, H., *Revival Sketches*, New York, 1859

Hunter, John, *Essays and Observations, His Posthumous Papers*, 2 vols, London, 1861

Hunter, John, *A Treatise on the Blood*, London, 1780

Ireland, Samuel, *Picturesque Views of the Upper Avon*, London, 1795

Jackson, William (?), *Asmodeus*, London, 1776

Jackson, William (?), *Sodom and Onan*, London, 1776

Johnson, Samuel, *The Works of Samuel Johnson in Two Volumes with an Essay on His Life by Arthur Murphy*, Dearborn, New York, 1837

Kenrick, William, *Love in the Suds, & A Letter to David Garrick Esq.*, London, 1772

Kirkman, James Thomas, *Memoirs of the Life of Charles Macklin*, 2 vols, London, 1799

Kyll, Thomas, *Trial of the Notorious Richard Turpin*, York and London, 1739

Langley, Gilbert, *Life and Adventures . . . written . . . when under Condemnation for a Robbery Committed on the Highway*, London, 1740

Lewis, Wyndham (ed.), *Miscellaneous Antiquities or a Collection of Curious Papers*, nos 3–16, London, 1927

Little, David M. and Kahrl, George M. (eds), *The Letters of David Garrick*, 3 vols, London, 1963

Lynch Piozzi, Hester (ed. A. Hayward), *Autobiography, Letters and Literary Remains, of Mrs Piozzi (Thrale)*, 2 vols, London, 1861

Norton, J. E. (ed.), *The Letters of Edward Gibbon*, London, 1956

O'Keeffe, John, *Personal Reminiscences and Recollections of the Life of John O'Keeffe, written by himself*, 3 vols, London, 1826

Pope, Alexander, *The Dunciad, From the text of Dr. Warburton. With advertisements, prefaces, letters, index of persons, index of matters, parallels, &c.*, London, 1788

Postlethwaite, M., *Universal Dictionary of Trade and Commerce*, London, 1766

Price, Cecil (ed.), *The Letters of Richard Brinsley Sheridan*, 6 vols, Oxford and London, 1966

Robinson, Henry Crabb, *Diary and Reminiscences*, Boston, 1869

Saunders, H. (ed.) *Theatrical Biography, or Memoirs of the Principal Performers at the Three Theatres Royal, Drury Lane, Covent Garden and Hay Market together with Remarks*, 2 vols, London, 1772

Schütz, Freidrich Wilhelm von, *Briefe über London* (*Letters from London*), Hamburg, 1792

Smith, D. A., MD, Professor of Surgery, *Notes on Mr William Bromfeild's Two Volumes of Chirurgical Observations and Cases*, London, 1773

Smith, Richard, *The Fratricide or The Murderer's Gibbet (a dramatic poem)*, (*Bristol Mirror*, 7, 14 and 21 September 1839), Bristol, 1840

Smollett, Tobias, *Peregrine Pickle, a Novel*, London, 1751

Speckman, Charles, *The Life, Travels, Exploits, . . . and Robberies, of C. Speckman, alias Brown, who was executed 23rd November, 1763, . . . written by himself*, London, 1763

Stockdale, P., *Memoirs of the Life and Writing of Percival Stockdale written by Himself*, London, 1809

Summerton, C. R.(?), *Recollections of the Fleet Prison*, London, 1847

Walpole, Horace (ed. W. S. Lewis), *Correspondence*, 47 vols, Yale University Press, New Haven, 1937–83

Walpole, Horace (ed.), *Miscellaneous Antiquities or a Collection of Curious Papers*, nos 1 and 2, Strawberry Hill, London, 1772

Welch, Saunders, *A Proposal to Render Effectual a Plan to Remove the Nuisance of Common Prostitutes from the Streets of the Metropolis*, London, 1758

Weston, Thomas, *Memoirs*, London, 1776

Wheler, Robert Bell, *History and Antiquities of Stratford upon Avon*, London, 1806

Wilkinson, Tate, *Memoirs*, 3 vols, London, 1790

Wilkinson, Tate, *The Wandering Patentee or a History of the Yorkshire Theatre, from 1779 to the present time*, 4 vols, London, 1795

Williams, J., *An Additional Scene to the Comedy of The Minor by Samuel Foote*, London, 1761

Wimsatt, W. K. and Pottle, F. A. (eds), *Boswell for the Defence, 1769–1774*, New York, 1959

Woffington, 'Mrs' Peg, *Memoirs of the Celebrated Mrs Woffington*, London, 1760

Secondary Material

General

Allan, Robert, J., *The Clubs of Augustan London*, Hamden Press, Hamden, Connecticut, 1967

Allen, E., Turk, J. L., Murley, R. (eds), *The Case Books of John Hunter*, Royal Society of Medicine, London, 1993

Appleton, William W., *Charles Macklin, An Actor's Life*, Oxford University Press, London, 1961

Askham, Francis, *The Gay Delavals*, Jonathan Cape, London, 1955

Baker, G. P. (ed.), *Some Unpublished Correspondence of David Garrick*, Boston, 1907

Battestin, Martin C., with Battestin, Ruthe R., *Henry Fielding, A Life*, Routledge, London, 1989

Belden, Mary, *The Dramatic Work of Samuel Foote, A dissertation*, Yale Studies in English, New Haven, 1929

Bevis, Richard, *The Laughing Tradition, Stage Comedy in Garrick's Day*, George Prior, London, 1980

Blake, Nicholas, *Steering to Glory, A Day in the Life of a Ship of the Line*, Chatham, London, 2005

Brown, Roger Lee, *A History of the Fleet Prison*, Edwin Mellen Press, New York, 1996

Burke, Helen, *Riotous Performances, The Struggle for Hegemony in the Irish Theatre, 1712–1784*, University of Notre Dame Press, Indiana, 2003

Burling, William, J., *Summer Theatre in London, 1661–1820, and the Rise of the Haymarket Theatre*, Fairleigh Dickinson University Press, Vancouver, 2000

Carpenter, Edwards, *A House of Kings, The History of Westminster Abbey*, Westminster Abbey Bookstore, London, 1966

Cash, Arthur H., *John Wilkes: the scandalous father of civil liberty*, Yale University Press, New Haven and London, 2006

Chaplin, Joyce E. (ed.), *Benjamin Franklin's autobiography: an authoritative text*, Norton, New York, 2012

Chapman, Robert William (ed.), *The Letters of Samuel Johnson with Mrs Thrale's genuine letters to him*, 3 vols, Clarendon Press, Oxford, 1952

Cordner, Michael, and Holland, Peter (eds), *Players, Playwrights, Playhouses, Investigating Performance 1660–1800*, Palgrave Macmillan, Basingstoke, 2007

Cruickshank, Dan, *The Secret History of Georgian London, How the Wages of Sin Shaped the Capital*, Random House, London, 2009

Dabhoiwala, Faramerz, *The Origins of Sex, A History of the First Sexual Revolution*, Allen Lane, London, 2012

Daneski, Katherine, *A Sociohistory of Cerebrovascular Disease and the Development of Modern Stroke Medicine, A Foucauldian Analysis*, Edwin Mellen Press, New York, 2010

Daniel, C. Henry and Barker, W. R., *Worcester College, Oxford*, Oxford, 1900

Davison, Peter, 'Samuel Foote', in Pickering, David (ed.), *International Dictionary of Theatre*, vol. 3, St James Press, New York, 1996

Donohue, Joseph (ed.), *The Cambridge History of the British Theatre*, vol. 2, *1660–1895*, Cambridge University Press, Cambridge, 2004

Doran, D., *Annals of the English Stage from Thomas Betterton to Edmund Kean*, vol. 2, John C. Nimmo, London, 1888, reprinted AMS Press, New York, 1968

Douglas, Howard, 'Samuel Foote', in Backscheider, Paula (ed.), *Dictionary of Literary Biography*, vol. 89: *Restoration and Eighteenth Century Dramatists*, 3rd Series, Gale Research, Detroit, 1989

Faller, Lincoln B., *Turned to Account, The Forms and Functions of Criminal Biography in Late Seventeenth- and Early Eighteenth-century England*, Cambridge University Press, Cambridge, 1987

Fields, William S. and Lemak, Noreen A. (eds.), *A History of Stroke, Its Recognition and Treatment*, Oxford University Press, Oxford, 1989

Findlay, Robert, 'Charles Macklin', in Pickering, David (ed.), *International Dictionary of Theatre*, vol. 3, St James Press, New York, 1996

Fitzgerald, Percy, *Samuel Foote*, London, 1910

Forster, E. M., *Consolations of History*, London, 1920, essay republished in *Abinger Harvest*, E. Arnold, London, 1936

Forster, John, *Biographical Essays*, London, 1860

Fox, Levi, *A Splendid Occasion: the Stratford Jubilee of 1769*, Oxford University Press, Oxford, 1973

Genest, John (ed.), *Some Account of the English Stage, from the Restoration in 1660 to 1830*, 10 vols, Bath, 1832

Gervat, Claire, *Elizabeth; The Scandalous Life of the Duchess of Kingston*, Century, London, 2003

Gladfelder, Hal, *Criminality and Narrative in Eighteenth Century England*, Johns Hopkins University Press, Baltimore and London, 2001

Goldsmith, Netta M., *The Worst of Crimes*, Ashgate, Aldershot, 1998

Green, Martin, *The Delavals, a Family History*, Powdene, Newcastle-upon-Tyne, 2007

Greene, John C. and Clark, Gladys L. H., *The Dublin Stage, 1720–1745*, Lehigh University Press, Bethlehem, Pennsylvania, 1993

Hartnoll, Phyllis (ed.), *The Oxford Companion to the Theatre*, Oxford University Press, Oxford, 1983

Hawkins, Frederick, *The French Stage in the Eighteenth Century in Two Volumes*, vol. 2, *1750–1799*, London, 1888

Hitchcock, T. and Shoemaker, R., *Tales from the Hanging Court*, Hodder Arnold, London, 2006

Hoare, Philip, *Wilde's Last Stand*, Arcade Books, London, 1998

Holland, Peter, 'Samuel Foote', in Banham, Martin (ed.), *The Cambridge Guide to Theatre*, Cambridge University Press, Cambridge, 1995

Hostettler, J., *Fighting for Justice, The History and Origins of the Adversarial Trial*, Waterside Press, London, 2006

Hunt, A., Mandlebrote, G. and Shell, A. (eds), *The Book Trade and Its Customers, 1450–1900*, Oak Knoll Press, Delaware, 1997

Jerrold, Walter, *Bons Mots of Samuel Foote and Theodore Hook, with grotesques by Aubrey Beardsley*, London, 1894

Kinservik, M. J., *The Production of the Female Pen: Anna Larpent's Account of the Duchess of Kingston's Bigamy Trial of 1776*, facsimile edition, Lewis Walpole Library, *Yale University Miscellaneous Antiquities*, no. 17, University Press of New England, Yale, 2004

Kinservik, M. J., *Sex, Scandal and Celebrity in Late Eighteenth Century England*, Palgrave Macmillan, New York, 2007

Kirkup, John, *A History of Limb Amputation*, Springer, London, 2007

Lavery, Brian, *The Ship of the Line; The development of the Battlefleet 1650–1850*, Conway Maritime Press, London, 2003

Lawrence, W. J., *Old Theatre Days and Ways*, Harrap, London, 1935

Lillywhite, Bryant, *London Coffee Houses*, Allen & Unwin, London, 1963

Lindebaugh, Peter, *The London Hanged, Crime and Civil Society in the Eighteenth Century*, Allen Lane, London, 1992

Litten, Julian, *The English Way of Death, The Common Funeral Since 1450*, Robert Hale, London, 1991

Luckhurst, M. and Moody, J. (eds), *Theatre and Celebrity in Britain 1660–2000*, Palgrave Macmillan, Basingstoke, 2005

McIntyre, Ian, *Garrick*, Allen Lane, London, 1999

McLynn, Frank, *Crime and Punishment in Eighteenth Century England*, Routledge, London, 1989

Mason Vaughan, Virginia, *Othello, A Contextual History*, Cambridge University Press, Cambridge, 1994

Melville, Lewis (ed.), *The Trial of the Duchess of Kingston*, John Day, New York, 1928

Midgley, Graham, *University Life in Eighteenth Century Oxford*, Yale University Press, New Haven and London, 1996

Moody, Jane and O'Quinn, Daniel (eds), *The Cambridge Companion to British Theatre, 1730–1830*, Cambridge University Press, Cambridge, 2007

Moore, Lucy (ed.), *Con Men and Cutpurses, Scenes from the Hogarthian Underworld*, Allen Lane, London, 2000

Moore, Wendy, *The Knife Man*, Bantam, London, 2005

Moore, Wendy, *Wedlock*, Weidenfeld & Nicolson, London, 2009

Mounsey, Christopher, *Christopher Smart, Clown of God*, Bucknell University Press, Lewisburg, Pennsylvania, 2001

Murphy, Mary C., updated by Argetsinger, Gerald S., 'Samuel Foote', in Rollyson, Carl and Magill, Frank N. (ed.), *Critical Survey of Drama*, 2nd revised edn, vol. 2, Salem Press, Pasadena, California, 2003

Myers, R. and Harris, M., *A Genius for Letters, Booksellers and Bookselling from the 16th to the 20th Century*, Oak Knoll Press, Delaware, 1995

Nicholson, Watson, *Struggle for a Free Stage*, London, 1906

Nicoll, Allardyce, *The Garrick Stage, Theatres and Audience in the Eighteenth Century*, Manchester University Press, Manchester, 1980

Nokes, David, *Samuel Johnson, A Life*, Faber & Faber, 2009

Norton, R. (ed.), *Homosexuality in Eighteenth-Century England: A Sourcebook*, updated 4 March 2011, http://rictornorton.co.u./eighteen

Norton, R., *Mother Clap's Molly House*, GMP Books, London, 1992

Nussbaum, Felicity, *Rival Queens; Actresses, Performance, and the Eighteenth Century British Theatre*, University of Pennsylvania Press, Philadelphia, 2010

Oldham, James, *English Common Law in the Age of Mansfield*, University of North Carolina Press, Chapel Hill and London, 2004

Oldham, James, *The Mansfield Manuscripts and the Growth of English Law in the Eighteenth Century*, 2 vols (includes transcripts of Rex v. Foote 1776, Court of King's Bench), University of North Carolina Press, in Association with the American Society for Legal History, Chapel Hill, 1992

Palmer, James F. (ed.), *The Surgical Works of John Hunter FRS with Notes*, 4 vols, London, 1835

Parry, Edward Abbott, *Vagabonds All*, Cassell, New York, 1926

Parsons, Clement, *Garrick and His Circle*, Methuen, London, 1906

Peake, R. B., *Memoirs of the Colman Family Including Correspondence with The Most Distinguished Personages of Their Time*, 2 vols, London, 1841

Pettit, A. and Spedding, P. (eds), *Eighteenth Century British Erotica II*, 5 vols, Pickering and Chatto, London, 2004

Picard, Liza, *Dr Johnson's London: Life in London 1740–1770*, Weidenfeld & Nicolson, London, 2000

Pickford, Stephanie (ed.), *Behind the Scenes; The Hidden Life of Georgian Theatre 1737–1784*, Dr Johnson's House Trust, London, 2007

Pottle, A. and Bennett, Charles H. (eds), *Journal of a Tour to the Hebrides*, Heinemann, London, 1963

Quist, George, *John Hunter 1728–1793*, Heinemann Medical Books, London, 1981

Rawlings, Philip, *Drunks, Whores and Idle Apprentices, Criminal Biographies in the Eighteenth Century*, Routledge, London, 1992

Redford, Bruce, (ed.), *The Letters of Samuel Johnson*, 5 vols, Princeton University Press, Clarendon Press, Princeton and London, 1992

Richardson, Ruth, *Death, Dissection and the Destitute*, Routledge, London, 1988

Ritchie, Fiona and Sabor, Peter (eds), *Shakespeare in the Eighteenth Century*, Cambridge University Press, Cambridge, 2012

Russell, Gillian, *Women, Sociability and Theatre in Georgian London*, Cambridge University Press, Cambridge, 2007

Ryskamp, Charles Andrew, *William Cowper of the Inner Temple, Esq., A study of his life and works to the year 1768*, Cambridge University Press, Cambridge, 1959.

Sainsbury, John, *John Wilkes, The Lives of a Libertine*, Ashgate, London, 2006

Scott, W. S., *The Georgian Theatre*, Heinemann, London, 1946

Seymour, Aaron Crossley Hobart, *The Life and Times of Selina, Countess of Huntingdon*, 2 vols, Tentmaker Publications, Stoke-on-Trent, 2000

Shapiro, Fred R. (ed.), *The Yale Book of Quotations*, Yale University Press, New Haven, 2006

Sheldon, Esther K., *Thomas Sheridan of Smock Alley, including a Smock Alley Calendar for the Years of His Management*, Princeton University Press, Princeton, 1967

Stein, Elizabeth (ed.), *Three Plays by David Garrick*, William Edwin Rudge, New York, 1926

Stephen, Leslie and Lee, Sydney (eds), *Dictionary of National Biography*, London, 1890

Stern, Tiffany, *Rehearsal from Shakespeare to Sheridan*, Clarendon Press, Oxford, 2000

Stone, E., *God's Acre or Historical Notices Relating to Churchyards*, London, 1858

Stone, George W. and Kahrl, George M., *David Garrick: a critical biography*, Southern Illinois University Press, Carbondale, 1979

Straub, Kristina, *Sexual Suspects, Eighteenth Century Players and Sexual Ideology*, Princeton University Press, Princeton, 1992

Suarez, M. and Turner, M., *The Cambridge History of the Book in Britain*, vol. 5, *1695–1830*, Cambridge University Press, Cambridge, 2009

Taylor, G., *Plays by Samuel Foote and Arthur Murphy*, Cambridge University Press, Cambridge, 1984

Thomas, Peter D. G., *John Wilkes: a friend to liberty*, Clarendon Press, Oxford, 1996

Thomson, Peter, 'Haymarket, Theatre Royal', in Banham, Martin (ed.),
    The Cambridge Guide to Theatre, Cambridge University Press, Cambridge,
    1995
Tillyard, Stella, *A Royal Affair, George III and His Troublesome Siblings*, Chatto &
    Windus, London, 2006
Timbs, John, *Clubs and Club Life in London*, Chatto & Windus, London, 1872
Tomalin, C., *Mrs Jordan's Profession*, Penguin, London, 1994
Trefman, Simon, *Sam Foote, Comedian, 1720–1777*, New York University Press,
    New York, 1971
Tyson, John R. (ed.), *In the Midst of Early Methodism: Lady Huntingdon and her*
    correspondence, Scarecrow Press, New York and London, 2006
Valentine, Alan, *The British Establishment 1760–1784*, University of Oklahoma
    Press, Norman, 1970
Watson, B. A., *A Treatise on Amputations of the Extremities and Their Complications*,
    Philadelphia, 1885
Webster, Mary, *Johan Zoffany, 1733–1810 Catalogue*, National Portrait Gallery,
    London, 1976
West, Shearer, *The Image of the Actor, Verbal and Visual Representation in the Age of*
    Garrick and Kemble, Pinter, London, 1991
Whitaker, H., Smith, C. U. M. and Finger, S. (eds), *Brain, Mind and Medicine:*
    Essays in Eighteenth-Century Neuroscience, Springer, New York, 2007

Periodicals and Pamphlets

Benson, C. J., 'A note on the Printer of a Dublin Edition of *The Orators* by
    Samuel Foote', in *Longroom, Bulletin of Friends of the Library of Trinity College*,
    no. 38, Dublin, 1973
Bogorod, Samuel N. and Noyes, Ernest C., 'Samuel Foote's Primitive Puppet-
    Shew', in *Theatre Survey, American Journal of Theatre History*, Pittsburgh, Fall
    1973
Ditchfield, G. M. and Thomas, Peter D. G., 'John Wilkes. A friend to liberty',
    in *British Journal for Eighteenth-century Studies*, vol. 20, Voltaire Foundation,
    London, 1997
Kinservik, M. J., 'The Politics and Poetics of Sodomy in the Age of George III',
    British Society for Eighteenth-Century Studies, vol. 29, London, 2006
Kinservik, M. J., 'Satire, Censorship, and Sodomy in Samuel Foote's *The*
    Capuchin (1776)', in *Review of English Studies*, vol. 54, London, 2003
Kinservik. M. J. (ed.), 'The Production of the Female Pen; Anna Larpent's
    Account of the Duchess of Kingston's Bigamy Trial of 1776', in
    Miscellaneous Antiquities, no. 17, New Haven, 2004

Lawson, P. and Phillips, J., *Albion, A Quarterly Journal Concerned with British Studies*, vol. 16, no. 3 (Fall 1984), Boone, 1984

Maslen, Keith, 'George Faulkner and William Bowyer; the London Connection', in *Longroom, Bulletin of Friends of the Library of Trinity College*, no. 38, Dublin, 1973

Miller, B., Jeffrey, L. C., McIntyre, H., Ebers, G. and Grodes, J. M., 'Hypersexuality or altered sexual preference following brain injury', in *Journal of Neurology, Neurosurgery, and Psychiatry*, no. 49, 1986

Nagaratnam, N., Tse, A., Lim, R, and Chowdhury, M., 'Aberrant sexual behaviour following stroke', in *European Journal of Internal Medicine*, vol. 9, no. 3, July–September 1998

Sayles, George O., 'The Court of the King's Bench in Law and History', Selden Society Lecture, Inner Temple, Spottiswoode, Ballantyne, London, 1959

Senelick, Laurence, 'Mollies or Men of Mode? Sodomy and the Eighteenth Century London Stage', *Journal of the History of Sexuality*, no. 1, 1990

Sutherland, Dame Lucy, 'The University of Oxford in the Eighteenth Century', James Bryce Memorial Lecture, Somerville College, Oxford, 1972; Oxford, 1973

Tillyard, Stella, 'Celebrity in the Eighteenth Century', in *History Today*, vol. 55, no. 6, June 2005

Notes

Epigraph

1 Chapman, *Letters of Samuel Johnson*, vol. 2, p. 561.

A SHORT CURTAIN SPEECH FROM THE AUTHOR
AT THE FOOTLIGHTS

1 McIntyre, *Garrick*, 1999, p. 589.
2 The collection of Richard Smith of the Bristol Royal Infirmary, the *Genuine Memoir* of Samuel Foote and all else that he had bound in skin of anatomized criminals is now held by Bristol Records Office. Anthropodermic bibliopegy is known to have been practised since the seventeenth century, and it was common to use murderers' skin in this manner during the seventeenth and eighteenth centuries, though Richard Smith's collection is one of the few surviving examples.

COFFEE-HOUSE COMEDIAN

1 *Spectator*, 26 September 1712.
2 Fitzgerald, *Samuel Foote*, London, 1910, p. 26.
3 'Rule, Britannia' by Thomas Arne, setting to music the poem of James Thomson, first performed 1 August 1740 for a masque at Cliveden House. The lyrics were published three weeks after this event and the music a few months after that.
4 Christie's Sale Catalogue, 26 January 1778, pp. 11–12.
5 Fitzgerald, p. 29.

6 Cooke, *Memoirs*, vol. 2, p. 158.

7 Boswell, *Life of Johnson*, vol. 3, p. 76.

8 Cooke, *Memoirs*, vol. 2, pp. 160 ff.

9 Chester, vol. 10, pp. 394 n.

10 Boswell, *Life of Johnson*, vol. 3, p. 125.

11 *London Chronicle*, October 1763.

12 Fitzgerald, p. 26.

13 Cooke, *Memoirs*, vol. 1, p. 23.

14 Fitzgerald, p. 28.

15 *Historical Register*, 1722; and Timbs, p. 136.

16 Timbs, quoting *Journey Through England*, p. 137

17 Ibid., pp. 138–9.

18 Lillywhite, p. 23.

19 Cruickshank, p. 204.

20 Quoted in Lillywhite, p. 114.

21 Lillywhite, p. 114.

22 Timbs, p. 333.

23 Quoted in Lillywhite, p. 114.

24 Allan, p. 73.

25 Edgeworth, vol. 1, p. 123.

26 Fitzgerald, pp. 29–30.

27 Cooke, *Table Talk*, pp. 91 ff.

28 GCA, Red Album, p. 71.

29 Postlethwaite, p. 197.

30 Suarez and Turner, vol. 5, p. 483.

31 Rawlings, pp. 1–2.

STRIP OR PAY: OR SHYLOCK'S ARGUMENT

1 Foote, *The Englishman in Paris*.

2 BL Cup 502 f. 31, vol. 1, p. 10.

3 BL Add MSS 36595 f. 399.

4 BL Cup 502 f. 31, vol. 1, p. 11.

5 Ibid., pp. 130 ff.

6 Sometimes cited as 1721, see *Dictionary of National Biography*, but because he married in 1741, under some duress of circumstance and seemingly without parental consent, it seems most likely that he was born in 1720, on 9 or 10 January, and the correction from 1720 to 1721 in some sources was unnecessary, based on an assumption that the Truro records had said

1719 (Old Style). The Truro records are inconclusive on this point: see ibid., pp. 179–81.

7 Johnson Vivian's House, formerly on the south side of Boscawen Street. St Mary's church, of which only the south aisle survives, now forms the south aisle of the choir of the cathedral. Foote grew up in the town residence of the Footes, a house on the north side of Boscawen Street, later a pub which survived into the twentieth century.

8 In 1742 Captain Barrington of the Royal Navy made a voyage to Brittany with a Truro sailor who could make himself understood in Breton.

9 Guildhall Records, S. Foote, facsimile in BL Cup 502 f. 31, Appendix 1, p. 972.

10 Daniel and Barker, p. 186.

11 Cooke, *Memoirs*, vol. 1, pp. 35–6.

12 WCA, Entrance Book LTB 3, 1737.

13 Midgley, p. 19.

14 Ibid., pp. 2–3.

15 Ibid., p. 19.

16 *London Evening Post*, 30 December 1747.

17 Midgley, p. 28.

18 Picard, p. 226.

19 Anon., *Advice to the Universities of Oxford and Cambridge*, pp. 55–6.

20 Fitzgerald, pp. 15–16.

21 Add MSS 36595 f. 399.

22 WCA, College Bursars' Books, Second Quarter 1738/9 (ending 22 March); Third Quarter 1739 (ending 21 June); Fourth Quarter 1739 (ending 20 September); First Quarter 1739 (ending 20 December); Second Quarter 1739/40 (ending 20 March); Third Quarter 1740 (ending 26 June).

23 WCA, College Account Book, LTB 13, 1740.

24 Fitzgerald, p. 17.

25 WCA, Account Book, LTB 13, 1740, with College Register.

26 WCA, College Bursars' Books, week ending 22 February 1740 (41?), S. Foote.

27 BL Cup 502 f. 31, vol. 1, p. 161.

28 Ibid.

29 Fitzgerald, p. 20: 'only a week or two after this flight [from Oxford] ... was the murder of Foote's uncle [1741]'. Other sources put the Oxford rustication in the January 1739, i.e. 1740 (new calendar), but this creates a lost year in Foote's life. See also WCA Account Book, LTB 13.

30 Picard, p. 73.

31 Brown, pp. 141 ff.
32 Ibid., p. 142.
33 Summerton, p. 334.
34 February and March 1742, according to BL Cup 502 f. 31, Appendix 1, p. 970.
35 Ibid., pp. 976 ff.
36 Guildhall Records facsimile in BL Cup 502 f. 31, Appendix 1, p. 973.
37 Summerton, pp. 4–5.
38 Brown, p. 183.
39 Ibid., p. 184.
40 Ibid., p. 298.
41 Ibid., p. 190.
42 Ibid., p. 154.
43 Ibid., p. 159.
44 Ibid., p. 155.
45 Fitzgerald, p. 26.
46 I am indebted to the unpublished research of Nicholas Bromley: 'Deaths; Friday, Mrs Foote, Wife of Mr Foote, the Comedian', *St James's Chronicle*, 16 April 1763.
47 Fitzgerald, p. 102.
48 Ibid., pp. 102 ff.
49 *Gentleman's Magazine*, November 1777, p. 534.
50 BL Cup 502 f. 31, vol. 1, p. 184.
51 Kyll, p. 62.

THE FATAL TREE

1 Anon., *Charles Speckman*, p. i.
2 Lavery, p. 168.
3 BL Cup 502 f. 31, vol. 1, p. 301.
4 *Genuine Memoirs*, p. 17.
5 Blake, p. 61.
6 BL Cup 502 f. 31, vol. 1, p. 280.
7 Smith, pp. 7–8.
8 Ibid., pp. 13–14.
9 Ibid., p. 9.
10 Ibid., p. 8.
11 Anon., *Trial of Samuel Goodere*, pp. 14–15; and Howell, vol. 17, p. 17.
12 Anon., *Bristol Fratricide*, p. 19.

13 Shakespeare, *Hamlet*, Act 1 sc. v, as quoted in the trial.

14 BL Cup 502 f. 31, vol. 1, p. 187.

15 Ibid., p. 236 ff.

16 Ibid., p. 206.

17 Ibid., p. 6.

18 Smith, p. 27.

19 *London Magazine*, December 1732.

20 *London Evening Post*, 31 March 1739.

21 BL Cup 502 f. 31, vol. 1, pp. 263–4.

22 Ibid., pp. 265–6.

23 Ibid., p. 13.

24 Anon, *Bristol Fratricide*, 1741 p. 13

25 *London Gazetteer*, later advertisement in contradiction of Foote, 20 April 1741.

26 *London Daily Post* (classifieds), 13 April 1741.

27 *Gentleman's Magazine*, January 1741.

28 Classified advertisement, *Daily Gazetteer*, 16 February 1741.

29 Pope, *Dunciad*.

30 BL, Burney Collection, 1740.

31 Writing as Captain Charles Johnson. Faller, pp. 286 ff.

32 Lindebaugh, p. 7.

33 Burney Collection, BL.

34 *Universal Spectator*, 7 February 1741.

35 Anon., *Tryal of Samuel Goodere*, p. 2.

36 Lindebaugh, p. 77.

37 Hostettler, p. 22.

38 Sir Leslie Stephen, in Hostettler, p. 25.

39 Lindebaugh, p. 75.

40 Foote, *Genuine Memoirs*; quoted in Dublin version, in BL Cup 502 f. 31, vol. 1, p. 507.

41 Ibid., p. 524.

42 Ibid., p. 526.

43 Howell, vol. 17, p. 17.

44 Ibid., p. 18.

45 Ibid.

46 Foote, *Genuine Memoirs*, p. 17.

47 Hitchcock and Shoemaker, p. xi.

48 Foote, *Genuine Memoirs*, p. 18.

49 Tockington Manor, near Bristol, is now a preparatory school; much of the building known by the Dineley-Gooderes is intact. It is said to be haunted, naturally enough, by the mad, strangled baronet.

50 *Tryal*, pp. 32–3.

51 *Trial*, pp. 33 ff.

52 Ibid., p. 40.

53 Foote, *Genuine Memoirs*, p. 20.

54 Howell, vol. 1, pp. 1087 ff.

55 BL Cup 502 f. 31, vol. 1, p. 834.

56 Howell, vol. 1, p. 1094.

57 Foote, *Genuine Memoirs*, p. 34.

58 Gladfelder, p. 48.

59 Samuel Goodere was married first to Jane Nichols, of Deal, 3 February 1713, mother of Eleanor, 'their only child'. She died in August 1721. Then he married Elizabeth Watts, a widow of Monmouthshire; his wife at his death is stated as 'Elizabeth', by whom he had twin boys. BL Cup 502 f. 31, vol. 1, pp. 248 and 258.

60 Foote, *Genuine Memoirs*, p. 33.

61 Edward Goodere died 1761, insane, aged thirty-two. Born *c.* 1729. *DNB*, vol. 15, p. 93.

62 Langley, p. 103.

63 BL Add MSS 27826, *Manners and Morals*, ii, fol. 97.

64 Smith, p. 28.

65 Foote, *Genuine Memoirs*, p. 64.

66 *London Daily Post*, 22 April 1740.

67 In the private collection of Victor Wynd and the Last Tuesday Society Museum, Mare Street, London, 2012.

68 Hitchcock and Shoemaker, p. 205.

69 Foote, *Genuine Memoirs*, p. 36.

70 Smith, p. 31.

71 Ibid., p. 32.

72 Richard Smith, author of *Fratricide* (1839), collected items related to murders and murderers.

73 His collection is now with the Bristol City Archives.

74 Smith, p. 33.

75 Foote, *Genuine Memoirs*, p. 36.

76 Her brother, Samuel's son, and therefore Samuel Foote's cousin, was the last baronet. PRO Kew, Prerogative Court of Canterbury, Prob 11/1006. Image ref. 218, Probate 2 March 1775.

77　*DNB*, vol. 15, p. 93.

78　PRO, Prerogative Court of Canterbury, Prob 11/1006, Image ref 218, Probate 2 March 1775.

79　Anon., *Bristol Fratricide*, p. 42.

80　Belden, p. 3.

81　BL Cup 502 f. 31, Appendix 1, p. 978 ff.

OTHELLO, THE COMEDY

1　*Theatrical Review*, 1758, p. 46.

2　Baker, p. 4.

3　McIntyre, p. 29.

4　Belden, quoting Arthur Murphy, p. 71.

5　Anon., *Foote's Prologues*, p. 32.

6　Davies, *Garrick*, vol. 2, p. 221.

7　Belden, p. 27.

8　Boswell, *Life of Johnson*, p. 622.

9　Parsons, p. 32.

10　Davies, *Life of Garrick*, vol. 1, p. 43.

11　Kirkman, vol. 1, p. 292.

12　Ibid., vol. 1, p. 202.

13　*London Daily Post*, 5 and 6 January, 3 and 7 February 1744.

14　Kirkham, vol. 1, p. 264.

15　McIntyre, p. 37.

16　Kirkham, vol. 1, p. 257 ff.

17　Askham, p. 33.

18　Kirkman, vol. 1, pp. 293–4.

19　McIntyre, p. 39.

20　Kirkman, vol. 1, pp. 293–4.

21　Quoted in McIntyre, p. 210 ff.

22　Cumberland, *Memoirs*, pp. 59–60.

23　McIntyre, p. 39.

24　Little and Kahrl, vol. 1. p. 31.

25　Parsons, p. 35.

26　HLC RB315661 Rocque, Map of London, 1746

27　Nicholson, p. 73.

28　Genest, vol. 4, p. 76.

29　*Daily Advertiser*, 18 February 1744.

30　Fitzgerald, pp. 38–9.

31 Ibid., p. 39.
32 Cooke, *Memoirs*, vol. 1, p. 43.
33 *London Daily Post*, 17 February 1744.
34 Cooke, *Memoirs*, vol. 1, p. 43.
35 Fitzgerald, p. 40.
36 Cooke, *Memoirs*, vol. 1, p. 43.
37 *Daily Advertiser*, 18 February 1744.
38 *London Daily Post*, 8 March 1744.
39 *Daily Advertiser*, 31 March 1744.
40 Cooke, *Memoirs*, vol. 1, pp. 44–5.
41 McIntyre, p. 212.
42 Ibid., pp. 213–14.
43 Fitzgerald, p. 42.
44 Cooke, *Memoirs*, vol. 1, p. 47.

THE TEA PARTY MAN

1 McIntyre, p. 137
2 Fitzgerald, p. 57.
3 Nicoll, p. 25.
4 *Gentleman's Magazine*, September 1765.
5 Nicoll, p. 36.
6 *London Daily Post*, 23 February 1743.
7 Fitzgerald, p. 56.
8 Belden, p. 7.
9 Cooke, *Memoirs*, vol. 2, p. 28. There is no indication at what stage Foote began to flesh out his Bayes with topical allusions. It must be likely that he did so from the beginning: Garrick had already done this.
10 Hitchcock and Shoemaker, p. 197.
11 Belden, pp. 5–6.
12 Actually a description of Tom Weston, from Weston, *Memoirs*, p. 310.
13 Adlard, p. 7.
14 Dibdin, *Reminiscences*, vol. 2, p. 11.
15 Stern, p. 275.
16 Lawrence, p. 131.
17 Stern, p. 281.
18 Ibid., p. 198.
19 Lawrence, p. 76.
20 Scott, p. 16.

21 *Daily Advertiser*, 16 April 1744.

22 Wilkinson, *Wandering Patentee*, vol. 1, p. 286.

23 Cooke, *Memoirs*, vol. 1, p. 48.

24 Wilkinson, *Wandering Patentee*, vol. 4, p. 246.

25 Cooke, *Memoirs*, vol. 1, p. 49.

26 Belden, p. 7.

27 *General Advertiser*, 22 April 1747.

28 Cooke, *Memoirs*, vol. 1, p. 52 ff.

29 Wilkinson, *Wandering Patentee*, vol. 1, p. 286.

30 Foot, p. 172.

31 Wilkinson, *Memoirs*, vol. 1, p. 20.

32 Ibid., pp. 20–1.

33 Cooke, *Memoirs*, vol. 1, pp. 51–2.

34 *General Advertiser*, 6 November 1747.

35 Add MSS 33488 f. 86.

36 Wilkinson, *Memoirs*, vol. 1, p. 242.

37 Cooke, *Memoirs*, vol. 2, p. 64.

38 Ibid., p. 67.

39 Ibid, p. 70 ff.

40 Founded as Baker's in 1744, its name was changed by Baker's nephew, John Sotheby.

41 *General Advertiser*, 19 June 1748.

42 Cooke, *Memoirs*, vol. 2, p. 65.

43 Christie's Sale Catalogue, 26 January 1778, pp. 10–11.

44 Battestin, with Battestin, pp. 434 ff.

45 Ibid., p. 435.

46 Ibid., p. 436.

47 *Daily Advertiser*, 23 April 1748.

48 Battestin, p. 439.

49 Ibid.

AN ENGLISHMAN ABROAD

1 Cooke, *Memoirs*, vol. 1, p. 67.

2 Ibid., p. 60.

3 Fitzgerald, p. 75.

4 Garrick, *New and Occasional Prologue*, 1753.

5 *Public Ledger*, 13 July 1776.

6 Lynch Piozzi, vol. 1, pp. 310–11.

7   Foote, *Englishman in Paris*, Act II sc i.
8   Cooke, *Memoirs*, vol. 2, pp. 6–10.
9   See Kinservik, *British Society for Eighteenth-Century Studies*, vol. 29, pp. 219–36.
10 Foote, *Englishman in Paris*, Prologue.
11 Kinservik, in *Review of English Studies*, pp. 639 ff.
12 Dabhoiwala, pp. 79 ff.
13 Quoted in Cruickshank, p. 27.
14 Defoe, p. 78.
15 Welch, p. 9.
16 Quoted in Mounsey, p. 125, my italics.
17 Ibid., p. 125.
18 Ibid., p. 70; for fuller argument on Smart and transvestism, see Chapter 6.
19 Ibid., pp. 125–6.
20 Ibid., p. 191.
21 Ibid., pp. 125–6.
22 Anon., *Nocturnal Revels*, vol. 1, Chapters 12 and 13, p. 152 ff.
23 'George Selwyn, a necrophiliac, gay transvestite, sat mute, loved, and undisturbed in the House of Commons for 44 years.' *BBC History Magazine*, February 2011, vol. 12, no. 2, pp. 53–4.
24 Ryskamp, pp. 83–4, 147 and 179.
25 Thomas, p. 201.
26 Cooke, *Table Talk*, p. 1.
27 Senelick, *Journal of the History of Sexuality*, vol. 1, pp. 66–7; Straub, p. 64; Goldsmith, p. 104; and Norton, p. 180.
28 Kinservik, in *Review of English Studies*, vol. 54, p. 658.
29 McIntyre, p. 55.
30 Belden, p. 75.
31 Foote, *Roman and English*, p. 42.
32 Wilkinson, *Memoirs*, vol. 1, p. 30.
33 Lawrence, p. 159.
34 Belden, p. 72.
35 Ibid., p. 73.
36 Fitzgerald, p. 42.
37 Wilkinson, *Memoirs*, vol. 1, p. 233.
38 Christie's Sale Catalogue, 26 January 1778, p. 11.
39 Cooke, vol. 1, p. 86.
40 Ibid., vol. 2, p. 80.
41 McIntyre, p. 57.

42 Bellamy, vol. 1, p. 111; and Sheldon, p. 125 and n.

43 Bush, *Hibernia Curiosa*, p. 10.

44 Ibid., pp. 10–11.

45 Ibid.

46 Greene and Clark, p. 30.

47 Ibid., p. 30 ff.

48 Greene and Clark, p. 35.

49 H. Burke, p. 183.

50 Ibid.

51 Ibid., pp. 183 ff.

52 Greene and Clark, p. 36.

53 Sheldon, pp. 126 ff.

54 *Dublin Journal*, 14 March 1748.

55 TCD MSS 10532, p. 42.

56 *Monthly Review*, no. 76, p. 374.

57 Greene and Clark, pp. 39 ff.

58 Cumberland, *Memoirs*, p. 76.

59 Ibid., pp. 76 ff.

60 Acted at the Haymarket in 1763; not published till Tate Wilkinson printed it from Foote's MS, in *Wandering Patentee*, vol. 4, pp. 12 ff.

61 *Critical Review*, no. 14, p. 161.

62 Belden, p. 111.

63 Cumberland, *Memoirs*, p. 117.

64 Chesterfield, *Letters*, vol. 3, pp. 1277–8.

65 *Gentleman's Magazine*, vol. 33, p. 45.

66 *Public Advertiser*, 1 March 1763.

67 H. C. Robinson, vol. 1, Chapter 14.

68 TCD MSS 10532, p. 75.

69 Ibid.

70 The foot drawn by Rowlandson, aged twenty, is on the frontispiece of *Sodom and Onan*, such that Faulkner's reproduction of it, doubtless without credit or payment, was a joke about Foote but also a reference, for some, to the scurrilous 1776 Jackson poem.

71 Wilkinson, *Memoirs*, vol. 2, p. 61.

72 *Rosciad*, vol. 1, p. 414.

73 *DNB*, vol. 61; Wilkinson, *Memoirs*, vol. 1, p. 276.

74 Belden, pp. 18–19.

75 Cooke, *Memoirs*, vol. 1, p. 84.

76 Wilkinson, *Memoirs*, vol. 2, p. 63 ff.

77 Ibid., p. 64.

78 Cooke, *Memoirs*, vol. 1, p. 84.
79 McIntyre, p. 57.
80 Chesterfield, *Letters*, vol. 3, pp. 1287–8.
81 Belden, p. 67.
82 Davies, *Dramatic Miscellanies*, vol. 1, pp. 212–13.
83 Belden, p. 12.
84 Hawkins, vol. 2, pp. 28 ff.
85 Ibid., vol. 1, p. 413.
86 Fitzgerald, p. 97.
87 Belden, p. 27.
88 Hawkins, vol. 1, p. 405.
89 Ibid., pp. 431 ff.
90 Foote, *Comic Theatre*, vol. 1, p. xv.
91 Ibid.
92 Ibid., pp. i ff.
93 Boswell, *Life of Johnson*, p. 190.
94 Cooke, *Memoirs*, vol. 1, p. 66.
95 Belden, p. 67.
96 Kirkman, p. 345.
97 Belden, p. 68.
98 Ibid., p. 70.
99 Foote, *Avis au Public*, p. 5.
100 Nokes, p. 293.
101 Ibid.
102 BL Cup 502 f. 31, vol. 1, p. 501.
103 Cooke, *Memoirs*, vol. 1, pp. 12–14.

METHODISM IN HIS MADNESS

1 Chaplin, p. 211.
2 Ibid., p. 213.
3 Rev. Thomas Prince, Jr, in Humphrey, p. 67.
4 John Wesley: reply to 'Philodemus', *St James's Evening Post*, 17–19 November 1760.
5 Boswell, *Observations*, pp. 7–8.
6 Taylor, pp. 50–1.
7 Ibid., p. 55.
8 Cruickshank, p. 48.
9 Belden, p. 85.

10 Weston, p. 49.

11 Ibid., p. 25.

12 Ibid., p. 32.

13 Ibid., p. 53.

14 Anon., *Exhortatory Address to the Brethren*, pp. 3 ff.

15 Seymour, vol. 1, p. 209.

16 Anon. (Portal, Abraham?), *A Letter to David Garrick*, p. 1.

17 Belden, p. 103.

18 Genest, vol. 2, p. 162.

19 Boswell, *Observations*, p. 11.

20 Foot, *Murphy*, p. 173.

21 Boswell, *Life of Johnson*, vol. 2, p. 342.

22 Ibid., p. 109.

23 Ibid., p. 113.

24 Anon., *Theatrical Review*, pp. 45–6.

THE RAKES' PROGRESS

1 Coke, vol. 3, p. 74.

2 Laurence Whistler, quoted in Askham, p. 13.

3 Askham, p. 15.

4 *Newcastle Courant*, 23 January 1822.

5 NRO, Robinson, instalment 1, p. 8.

6 Cooke, *Memoirs*, vol. 2, p. 65.

7 Ibid., p. 69

8 Askham, p. 119.

9 Trefman, p. 52.

9 Ibid.

10 Robinson, instalment 1, p. 83.

11 Cooke, *Memoirs*, vol. 2, pp. 77–9.

12 *St James's Chronicle*, 5 July 1748.

13 Mason Vaughan, p. 123.

14 NRO, Robinson, instalment 1, p. 85.

15 Ibid., p. 83.

16 Cooke, *Memoirs*, vol. 2, p. 70.

17 Askham, p. 30.

18 The marriage of Tom Quane and Deodata Roach had been the subject
   of previous Chancery proceedings, as it took place, if legal, during her
   minority. She continued to be granted the title 'Miss Roach' despite the

widespread knowledge that she was married, and indeed had been
pregnant the first time when she was fourteen.

19 Ambross, p. 20.
20 Askham, pp. 35–6.
21 Ibid., p. 40.
22 Ibid., p. 50.
23 Ibid., p. 51.
24 Edgeworth, pp. 143.
25 Ambross, pp. 13 ff.
26 Ibid., p. 8.
27 Askham, p. 51.
28 Cooke, *Memoirs*, vol. 2, p. 66.
29 Askham, p. 53.
30 NRO, Robinson, instalment 1, pp. 89 ff.
31 Askham, p. 50.
32 Ambross, pp. 20 ff.
33 Askham, p. 70.
34 Ibid., p. 72.
35 Ibid., Appendix E, p. 245.
36 Cooke, *Memoirs*, vol. 2, p. 71.
37 NRO Miscellaneous verses & literary notes: 2/DE/44/4: Foote's
   dedication to Delaval, *Taste*, London, 1752.
38 Cooke, *Memoirs*, vol. 2, p. 71.
39 Mason Vaughan, p. 114.
40 Ibid., p. 114 and note.
41 Wilkinson, *Memoirs*, vol. 2, p. 105.
42 It is evident from the Delaval *Othello* that Foote was in London, though
   not performing, through much of spring of 1751. *Lloyd's Evening Post,
   Morning Chronicle and London Advertiser, St James's Chronicle*, February 1751.
43 Askham, p. 55.
44 NRO, Robinson, instalment 1, p. 8.
45 Wilkinson, *Memoirs*, vol. 2, p. 105.
46 Mason Vaughan, p. 126.
47 *Dublin University Gazette*, December 1866.
48 Cooke, *Memoirs*, vol. 2, p. 71.
49 Mason Vaughan, p. 128.
50 NRO, Robinson, instalment 1, p. 9.
51 Wilkinson, *Memoirs*, vol. 1, p. 203.
52 Edgeworth, vol. 1, pp. 124–5.
53 Burke, E., *Annual Register*, vol. 62, p. 1204.

54 NRO, Robinson, instalment 1, p. 91.

55 Edgeworth, vol. 1, p. 125.

56 Ibid., pp. 124–5.

57 Trefman, Appendix, pp. 275 ff.

58 Cooke, *Memoirs*, vol. 2, p. 70.

On Losing a Leg and Gaining a Theatre

1 Hunter, *A Treatise*, p. 397.

2 Methley was demolished in 1963. The amputation is sited not at Methley but at Cannons or Canons Park by various sources and even margin scribblers in the London Library (Belden, p. 28); and quite erroneously the accident is often sited to Cannons Park in Edgware, formerly the site of the Duke of Chandos's palace. Cannons (Edgware) itself was largely demolished in 1747. The rebuilt house, owned by one Mr Hallet, has no record of leasing to the Mexboroughs, see *Country Life*, 18 May 1907. However, Foote's memoirist, Cooke, places him at Methley, as do the records of the movements of the Duke of York, *The Journals of Mary Coke*, and the Cannons connection appears to be as a result of Garrick's letter to Foote, Little and Kahrl, Letter 394, 21 March 1766, which places it at *a completely different* Cannons Park, at Kingsclere, near Newbury, 'a small hunting-box briefly used by the first Earl of Mexborough', and *Gentleman's Magazine* places the accident in 'Hants', 3 February 1766. It has proved impossible to verify the rival claims. However, because of the intimately small size of Cannons Park (Newbury) and the other references to Methley (Cooke's *Memoirs*, Mary Coke, Tate Wilkinson, Fitzgerald, *DNB*) I have favoured the accident as happening there, though some element of the recovery clearly did take place in Hampshire. It did *not* happen, assuredly, at the former Chandos residence.

3 More correctly, Pollington, in early 1766 – Viscount and Viscountess in the Peerage of Ireland since 1753 and created Earl (and Countess) of Mexborough, family name Savile. *Burke's Peerage*, 1828, p. 416.

4 ALS in Victoria and Albert Museum, Enthoven Collection; quoted in Trefman, p. 172, as 1768.

5 *Burke's Peerage*, 1828, p. 414.

6 Fitzgerald, p. 245.

7 11 February 1766; *Burke's Peerage*, 1828, p. 416.

8 Askham, p. 108.

9 *DNB*, 1888, vol. 14, pp. 316–17.

10 Fitzgerald, pp. 245–6.

11 Wilkinson, *Memoirs*, vol. 2, p. 99.

12 Noted, however, as 'Mr Foote being on a visit to a nobleman's house in Hants', *Gentleman's Magazine*, 3 February 1766, vol. 36, p. 100.

13 S—, *Bromfeild's Chirurgical Observations*, p. 72.

14 'which he afterwards sold to John Hunter for £200': Peachey, p. 110.

15 Ibid., p. 111.

16 *Gentleman's Magazine*, November 1792; quoted in Peachey, p. 104.

17 Allen, Turk and Murley, p. 668.

18 Peachey, p. 111.

19 Born 1713, not 1712, according to Peachey, p. 110.

20 *London Evening Post*, 4 November 1777.

21 S—, pp. 4–5.

22 Ibid., pp. 12–13.

23 Bromfeild, *Chirurgical Observations*, vol. 2, p. 99.

24 Kirkup, p. 26.

25 Ibid., p. 27.

26 Wilkinson, *Memoirs*, vol. 2, p. 104.

27 Bromfeild, *Chirurgical Observations*, vol. 1, pp. 13 ff.

28 Bromfeild, *Certain Particular Facts*, p. 8.

29 Bromfeild, *Chirurgical Observations*, vol. 1, p. 10.

30 Ibid., pp. 15–16.

31 Heister, p. 113.

32 Ibid., p. 345.

33 Ibid., p. 335.

34 Ibid., pp. 335–7.

35 Ibid., p. 336.

36 Bromfeild, *Certain Particular Facts*, p. 12.

37 Ibid., p. 12.

38 Heister, p. 345.

39 Ibid., p. 345.

40 Bromfeild, *Chirurgical Observations*, vol. 1, p. 321.

41 NYPL Berg Collection, Burney, Frances.

42 Paolo Assalini observing John Hunter in 1785; quoted in Moore, *The Knife Man*, p. 15.

43 Heister, p. 339.

44 Quoted in Kirkup, p. 1.

45 NRO 650/K/13; NRO 650/M/1 nd; 2/DE/44/4; NRO 650/D/7.
46 Tillyard, p. 67.
47 Ibid., p. 68.
48 Little and Kahrl, vol. 2, p. 493.
49 Boaden, vol. 1, pp. 221–2.
50 Little and Kahrl, vol. 2, Letter 394.
51 BL Add MSS 36133 f.198 (copy, with seal – owned by Foote?).
52 Tillyard, p. 68.
53 *Gentleman's Magazine*, March 1766, referring to 25 February.
54 Add MSS 33056 f. 267.
55 Wilkinson, *Memoirs*, vol. 2, p. 33.
56 Burling, p. 80.
57 Ibid.
58 Askham, Appendix, p. 277.
59 Davies, *Life of Garrick*, vol. 2, p. 239.
60 Burling, p. 121.
61 Ibid.
62 Palmer, vol. 1, p. 401.

The Devil Upon Two Sticks

1 Williams, *Additional Scene*, p. 10.
2 Bromfeild, *Chirurgical Observations*, vol. 1, p. 315.
3 Colman, *Random Records*, vol. 1, p. 14.
4 O'Keeffe, vol. 1, p. 328.
5 Gwen Cavaciuti lost her lower leg in a road accident in 2011.
6 Burling, p. 117.
7 Foote, *Lame Lover*, Act 1 sc ii.
8 Belden, p. 115.
9 Cash, *Wilkes*, p. 1.
10 Foote (attrib.), *Wilkes; An Oratorio* (music by Signor Carlos Bartini).
11 The Monks were not called the 'Hellfire Club' until 1776; see Sainsbury, pp. 102 ff.
12 First reference appears to be *Edinburgh Review*, October 1839–January 1840, from a witness who claims he was 'present when the dialogue took place.' See Cash, p. 2 and also n. p. 398.
13 Stockdale, quoted in Shapiro.
14 *Theatrical Biography*, vol. 1, pp. 102–5.
15 *Gentleman's Magazine*, October 1798.

16 Norton, vol. 2, pp. 78–9.
17 Cooke, *Memoirs*, vol. 1, p. 151.
18 Ibid., p. 144.
19 *English Aristophanes*, p. 21.
20 An extract was printed in the *London Magazine* in July 1767, and in its entirety in the *Monthly Mirror* (as *The Occasional Prologue*) in March 1804 and by Cooke, *Memoirs*, vol. 3, p. 142.
21 Ibid.
22 Wilkinson, *Memoirs*, vol. 3, p. 291.

SHAKESPEARE'S JUBILEE

1 Kenrick, p. 56.
2 Christie's Sale Catalogue, 2 January 1778, p. 4.
3 *Burlington Magazine*, April 1984.
4 Ibid., p. 500.
5 Trefman, p. 172.
6 Christie's Sale Catalogue, 2 January 1778, p. 6.
7 Ibid., p. 12.
8 Cooke, *Table Talk*, p. 37.
9 Fitzgerald, p. 82.
10 Askham, p. 112.
11 Add MSS D 10 12 116 Mus Brit Bibl Butler.
12 Little and Kahrl, vol. 2, pp. 623–4.
13 Boswell, *Life of Johnson*, vol. 3, p. 76.
14 25 April 1770; Stone and Kahrl, p. 588.
15 MSS in Harvard Theatre Collection see also Boaden, p. 221.
16 *Gentleman's Magazine*, October 1769.
17 William Smith of Covent Garden, quoted in Stone and Kahrl, p. 581.
18 Cooke, *Memoirs*, vol. 2, pp. 85–6.
19 Stone and Kahrl, p. 583.
20 *Town and Country Magazine*, September 1769, p. 477.
21 Stone and Kahrl, p. 583.
22 *Town and Country Magazine*, May 1770, pp. 229–30.
23 Trefman, pp. 209–10.
24 Stone and Kahrl, p. 588.
25 Cooke, *Memoirs*, vol. 1, pp 166–9.

Wholesale Popularmonger

1 Cooke, *Memoirs*, vol. 1, p. 93.
2 Kenrick, p. 23.
3 Trefman, p. 209, and n., p. 227.
4 Cooke, *Memoirs*, vol. 3, p. 159.
5 Garrick, *Letters*, vol. 2, pp. 835–6.
6 Trefman, p. 209.
7 This discussion largely follows Bogorod and Noyes, *American Journal of Theatre History*, Fall 1973.
8 *Gentleman's Magazine*, February 1773.
9 *St James's Chronicle*, 13 February 1773.
10 Cooke, *Memoirs*, vol. 2, p. 58.
11 (In fact June 1777.) Ellis, vol. 2, pp. 279–80.
12 Little and Kahrl, vol. 2, p. 855.
13 *Lloyd's Evening Post*, 26–28 June 1771.
14 Foote, *Dramatic Works*, vol. 3, pp. 165–6.
15 Cooke, *Memoirs*, vol. 2, pp. 75–6.
16 Askham, p. 170.
17 Boswell, *Boswell for the Defence*, p. 80.
18 *London Magazine*, July 1772.
19 Boswell, *Boswell for the Defence*, p. 90.
20 Trefman, p. 223.
21 Boaden, vol. 2, pp. 5–6.

Case no. 409

1 Aphra Behn's grave inscription, 1689, only yards from Samuel Foote's grave in the cloisters of Westminster Abbey.
2 Whitaker, Smith and Finger, p. 67.
3 See Moore, *The Knife Man*, for a full argument on both issues.
4 Palmer, vol. 1, p. 336.
5 Moore, *The Knife Man*, p. 224.
6 Palmer, vol. 1, pp. 168–73.
7 HIRCS, Case Book, Hunter, J., ref. MS0189/1, vol. 1, Court of Assistants' minutes, 1745–1798; also Adlard, p. 86.
8 HIRCS, ref. MS0189/1, vol. 1, pp. 409–11.
9 Moore, *The Knife Man*, p. 65.
10 Daneski, p. 40.

11 Whitaker, Smith and Finger, p. 79.
12 HIRCS, ref. MS0189/1, vol. 1, pp. 409–11.
13 Nagaratnam, Tse, Lim and Chowdhury, pp. 207 ff.
14 Palmer, vol. 1, p. 336.
15 For fuller discussion of Hunter and contemporaries on strokes, see Fields and Lemak, pp. 12 ff.
16 HIRCS, ref. MS0189/1, pp. 409–11.
17 Whitaker, Smith and Finger, p. 81.
18 Ibid., p. 72 ff.
19 Miller, Jeffrey, McIntyre, Ebers and Grodes, pp. 867–73.
20 Nagaratnam, Tse, Lim and Chowdhury, p. 209.
21 Miller, Jeffrey, McIntyre, Ebers and Grodes, pp. 867–73.
22 Nagaratnam, Tse, Lim and Chowdhury, pp. 207 ff.
23 Allen, Turk and Murley, p. 193.
24 Nagaratnam, Tse, Lim and Chowdhury, p. 209.
25 Hunter, vol. 1, p. 274.

A School for Scandal

1 University of Nottingham, Department of Special Collections, PW F 2810, London, 14 December 1775.
2 Battestin, with Battestin, p. 459.
3 Trefman, p. 224.
4 Valentine, p. 177.
5 Cruickshank, p. 59.
6 Gervat, p. 44.
7 Melville, p. 232.
8 Kinservik, *Sex, Scandal*, p. 70.
9 Walpole, *Correspondence*, vol. 32, p. 146.
10 '*Eighty thousand pounds! Eighty thousand pounds!*': the worth of heiress Eliza Watts, Burney, Act 1 sc 1.
11 Foote, *St James's Chronicle*, 1–3 August 1775.
12 Ibid.
13 Walpole, *Correspondence*, vol. 28, p. 218.
14 Tomalin, p. 49.
15 *St James's Chronicle*, 1?3 August 1775.
16 My italics. Walpole, *Correspondence*, vol. 28, pp. 218–19.
17 BL Add MSS 35612, Hardwicke Papers v. CCLXIV, ff 293–4, 15 August 1775, M. Jeffreys to unknown.

18 Cooke, *Memoirs*, vol. 1, p. 210.

19 Little and Kahrl, vol. 3, pp. 1020–21.

20 *St James's Chronicle*, 1–3 August 1775.

21 TCD 873–204 (1–20).

22 The word has had varied connotations, and is related also to the origins of 'dandy'. It has been related to transvestism and effeminacy, as well as straightforward circus clowning.

23 TCD 873–204 (1–20).

24 Walpole, *Correspondence*, vol. 28, pp. 224–5.

24 Anon., *Duchess of Kingston*, London, 1775 pp. 12–13.

26 Little and Kahrl, vol. 3, p. 1031.

THE DUCHESS AND THE PLAYER

1 Kinservik, *Production of the Female Pen*, p. 83.

2 D'Archenholz, vol. 2, p. 8.

3 Foss, vol. 1, p. 84.

4 *London Gazetteer and Advertiser*, 16 April 1776.

5 Boswell, *Papers, 1775–1776*, vol. 11, pp. 252–3.

6 Brinley Johnson, p. 43.

7 Anon., *Characters*, p. 4.

8 Melville, p. 271.

9 Brinley Johnson, p. 45.

10 Kinservik, *Sex, Scandal*, p. 155.

11 Jackson(?), *Asmodeus*, London, 1776.

12 Boswell, *Papers, 1775–1776*, vol. 11, p. 253.

13 PRO, King's Bench 1 20, part 4.

14 NA Kew, King's Bench 1 20 part 4

15 *St James's Chronicle*, 18–21 May 1776.

16 Cooke, *Memoirs*, vol. 1, p. 221.

17 Ibid., pp. 221–2; also *London Chronicle*, 1–21 May 1776.

18 Foote to Garrick, quoted in Fitzgerald, p. 366.

19 *London Gazetteer*, 23 May 1776.

20 It has proved impossible to date or confirm this quotation, first told to me by TP McKenna, and often attributed to the Foote case, but very possibly of much later provenance.

21 BL, RB 11642.g.15, p. 17.

22 See Hoare, p. 98.

23 In 1979.

24 Cooke, *Memoirs*, vol. 1, pp. 224–6; and Kinservik, *Sex, Scandal*, p. 177.
25 *Public Ledger*, 12 July 1776.
26 *Gentleman's Magazine*, July 1776.
27 Quoted in Kinservik, *Sex, Scandal*, p. 179.
28 BL Cup 502 f. 31. George and Frank 'Foote' noted in Will. George died in 1770?
29 Foote, *The Capuchin*, p. 122. See also for following scene: HLC Larpent Plays No 413 *The Capuchin*, pp. 50–52.
30 Pettit and Spedding, vol. 5, p. x.

Roger the Footman

1 Oldham, vol. 2, p. 1009.
2 Foss, vol. 1, p. 84.
3 Oldham, vol. 1, p. 47.
4 Christie's Sale Catalogue, 2 January 1778, p. 13.
5 Picard, p. 119.
6 *Gentleman's Magazine*, May 1776.
7 All courtroom testimony taken from Oldham, vol. 2, pp. 1004 ff.
8 Ibid.
9 Price, vol. 1, p. 98.
10 Christie's Sale Catalogue, 26 January 1778, p. 8.
11 Oldham, vol. 2, p. 1006.
12 Ibid., p. 1007; underlinings, Mansfield's own.
13 Trefman, p. 258.
14 *Daily Advertiser*, 13 December 1776; Adlard, p. 42.
15 Oldham, vol. 2, p. 1009.
16 Peake, vol. I, p. 314.
17 *St James's Chronicle*, 3–5 June 1777.

Curtain Call

1 Quoted in Askham, p. 46.
2 Cooke, *Table Talk and Bons Mots*, p. 89.
3 NYPL TMSS 2001–065.
4 Colman, *Random Records*, vol. 1, p. 233.
5 BL Add MSS 36133 f.198 (copy, with seal – owned by Foote?).
6 Add MSS 33488 f. 86.

7　Anon., *Foote's Prologues*, p. 35.

8　*Gentleman's Magazine*, November 1777.

9　On the dismissal of an earlier audience, but in keeping with the witness of Garrick's reaction. Wilkinson, *Memoirs*, vol. 1, p. 233.

10　Add MSS 36593 f. 135.

11　Adlard, p. 185.

12　*Gentleman's Magazine*, October 1777.

13　*London Evening Post*, 25 October 1777.

14　Chapman, *Letters of Samuel Johnson*, vol. 2, p. 561.

15　*London Evening Post*, 27 October 1777.

16　'Nov 3 Samuel Foot [*sic*] Esq., aged 55: in the West Cloister': Westminster Abbey Register, 1777, vol. 10.

17　Cooke, *Memoirs*, vol. 2, p. 162.

18　Weston, p. 31.

19　Litten, p. 100.

20　Ibid.

21　*Morning Chronicle*, 4 November 1777.

22　Westminster Abbey Chapter Minutes 1768–1777 – April 1778.

23　Dr Charles Burney, on the 1784 burial of Dr Johnson in Poets' Corner. Carpenter, p. 250.

24　Jewell was also Foote's executor: Aylett v. Jewel [*sic*] Executor, 1 January 1779 (1779) 2 Blackstone W. Prefix PRO 1299, 96 E.R. 761 1779.

25　George and Frank 'Foote' noted in Will. George died in 1770? BL Cup 502 f. 31 *The Last Will and Testament of Samuel Foote*, prov'd 22nd Oct 1777.

26　Norton (ed.), *Homosexuality in Eighteenth-Century England: A Sourcebook*; and Jackson (?), *Sodom and Onan*, 1776.

27　Chester, vol. 10, p. 424.

28　Cooke, *Memoirs*, vol. 2, p. 104.

29　Ibid., p. 103.

30　Bee, vol. 1, p. clxiii.

31　Belden, p. 89.

32　Baptismal records www.familysearch.org/pal:/MM9.1.1/NP92–6FH and death of Mary Foote, *St James's Chronicle*, 16 April 1763.

33　Foot, *Life of Murphy*, p. 18.

34　Lord Byron, *Hints from Horace*, lines 329–36.

35　Westminster Abbey Chapter Minutes, 1768–1777.

A Singular Talent

1 Boswell, *Life of Johnson*, vol. 2, p. 109.
2 Trefman, p. vii.
3 Ibid.
4 Boswell, *Life of Johnson*, vol. 2, p. 110.
5 Belden, p. 174.
6 Ibid.
7 Byron, *Hints from Horace*, lines 329–36.
8 Walpole, *Correspondence*, vol. 8, p. 213.

The Body of Evidence or A Last Auction of Effects

1 Christie's Sale Catalogue, January 1778, p. 4.
2 Cooke, *Memoirs*, vol. 2, p. 97.
3 GCA, Red Album, p. 76.
4 *Gentleman's Magazine*, November 1777.
5 Weston, p. 45.
6 £10 each; Christie's Sale Catalogue, January 1778, pp. 10–11.
7 Ibid.
8 Ibid., p. 11.
9 Ibid., pp. 18–20.
10 Ibid., p. 4.
11 Ibid., p. 8.
12 Forster, E. M., *Consolations*, p. 264.

Box Office Figures

1 See Trefman, p. 239.

Index